The Detection of Deception in Forensic Contexts

One of the most fascinating subdivisions within the rapidly growing field of psychology and law is the area of deception detection. Traditionally this area has been characterised by a number of approaches which have analysed different aspects of deception such as verbal content, non-verbal behaviour, and polygraph testing. Intensive research over recent years has resulted in an impressive corpus of new knowledge about issues such as cross-cultural deception, the detection of simulated amnesia and false confessions, lie-catching expertise and how best to train professionals in detecting deception. This book provides a state-of-the-art account of current research and practice, written by an international team of experts, and will be a valuable resource for academics, students, practitioners, and all professionals within the legal domain who need to tackle questions of credibility and reliability.

PÄR ANDERS GRANHAG is Associate Professor in the Department of Psychology at Göteborg University. He has published extensively in the field of legal and criminological psychology, particularly on deception and eyewitness testimony, and conducts training of law-enforcement personnel.

LEIF A. STRÖMWALL is a researcher at the Department of Psychology at Göteborg University and has published several studies mainly on deception detection.

The Detection of Deception in Forensic Contexts

edited by

Pär Anders Granhag and Leif A. Strömwall

CAMBRIDGE
UNIVERSITY PRESS

PUBLISHED BY THE PRESS SYNDICATE OF THE UNIVERSITY OF CAMBRIDGE
The Pitt Building, Trumpington Street, Cambridge, United Kingdom

CAMBRIDGE UNIVERSITY PRESS
The Edinburgh Building, Cambridge, CB2 2RU, UK
40 West 20th Street, New York, NY 10011–4211, USA
477 Williamstown Road, Port Melbourne, VIC 3207, Australia
Ruiz de Alarcón 13, 28014 Madrid, Spain
Dock House, The Waterfront, Cape Town 8001, South Africa

http://www.cambridge.org

First published 2004

Printed in the United Kingdom at the University Press, Cambridge

Typeface Plantin 10/12 pt.   *System* LaTeX 2_ε [TB]

A catalogue record for this book is available from the British Library

Library of Congress Cataloguing in Publication Data
The detection of deception in forensic contexts / edited by Pär Anders Granhag
and Leif A. Strömwall.
   p. cm.
Includes bibliographical references and index.
ISBN 0 521 83375 2 – ISBN 0 521 54157 3 (pbk.)
1. Lie detectors and detection. I. Granhag, Pär Anders. II. Strömwall, Leif A.
HV8078.D47 2004
363.25′4 – dc22   2004049734

ISBN 0 521 83375 2 hardback
ISBN 0 521 54157 3 paperback

Contents

Figures

Tables

Contributors

CHARLES F. BOND, JR, Texas Christian University, USA

RAY BULL, Leicester University, UK

SVEN Å. CHRISTIANSON, Stockholm University, Sweden

GRAHAM DAVIES, Leicester University, UK

BELLA M. DEPAULO, University of Virginia, USA

PAUL EKMAN, University of California, San Francisco, USA

PÄR ANDERS GRANHAG, Göteborg University, Sweden

MARIA HARTWIG, Göteborg University, Sweden

CHARLES R. HONTS, Boise State University, USA

SAUL KASSIN, Williams College, USA

GÜNTER KÖHNKEN, University of Kiel, Germany

HARALD MERCKELBACH, University of Maastricht, The Netherlands

WENDY L. MORRIS, University of Virginia, USA

MAUREEN O'SULLIVAN, University of San Francisco, USA

SANDHYA R. RAO, Texas Christian University, USA

SIEGFRIED L. SPORER, Univerity of Giessen, Germany

LEIF A. STRÖMWALL, Göteborg University, Sweden

ALDERT VRIJ, University of Portsmouth, UK

Part 1

Introduction

1 Research on deception detection: past and present

Pär Anders Granhag and Leif A. Strömwall

Deception – a central characteristic of human life

To perceive, feel, and remember are all examples of central characteristics of life. Provocative as it may seem, it is possible to argue that the act of lying constitutes another such example. It takes little effort to show that lying has played, and still plays, an important role in man's coping and survival in society (Serban, 2001), and many great thinkers have put forward strong arguments that lying is necessary for life (Kerr, 1990). The truth is often perceived as something rare and unattainable, caught only by the hands of gods, whereas the lie is human, all too human. Hence, it is fully understandable that people are fascinated by lies and how to detect them.

Most people not only lie on a regular basis, but are also frequently forced to reflect upon and make decisions about questions of truth and deception. The outcome of these reflections and decisions may or may not be important. To spend time trying to find out whether a compliment of a close friend was really true may seem nonsensical. In contrast, decisions to set aside resources in order to find out whether the information received on the planning of future terrorist activities is valid, or whether a suspected murderer is telling the truth about his alibi, are seldom questioned. It is easy to make a long list of instances where the work of separating truths from lies is of great importance. Hence, it is essential to deepen our understanding about deception and its detection, and we believe that the current volume has the potential to make an important contribution to this endeavour.

Aims of the present volume

The present volume focuses on the different types of deception that take place in forensic contexts, and the different methods suggested to detect such deceit. We will use the word 'forensic' in a broad sense and view a 'forensic context' as any context in which legal questions are raised. In short, our use of the word 'forensic context' encapsulates all stages in the judicial process.

It is hard (perhaps impossible) to think of a context in which no lies occur. However, we believe that it is of particular relevance to study deception and its detection from a forensic point of view. First, many of those working within the field of law enforcement have to assess veracity on a daily basis. Second, professionals know that deception is quite frequent in forensic contexts. Third, to make mistakes when assessing veracity in forensic contexts can have very severe consequences. Fourth, there are several methods of assessing veracity, and it is of utmost importance to gain more knowledge on the validity of these methods.

In March 2003, several world-leading experts on deception came together in Gothenburg, Sweden. During a two-day symposium entitled 'Deception detection in forensic contexts', these experts delivered twelve state-of-the-field lectures. Each contributor was asked to give a lecture about a topic that was in the very centre of his or her area of expertise. More specifically, the organisers of the symposium had asked the experts to summarise and evaluate the existing scientific knowledge on their topic. In addition, they were asked to present the most established and important research findings in a style suitable for practitioners. An audience of more than two hundred professionals, mostly law-enforcement personnel, attended the symposium.

All chapters in the present volume are based upon lectures given at the symposium; when writing, each expert was asked to expand on the topic that he or she had addressed at the symposium. In short, we asked those who know most about deception to write for those who need the knowledge the most (i.e., people who work in forensic contexts). Many of the chapters address questions pertaining to the application of research, but the volume also covers more basic research. Taken together, this state-of-the-field volume explores what scientific psychology tells us about deception detection. As will be discussed in more detail below, the intense research efforts of the last ten to fifteen years have resulted in an impressive corpus of new knowledge on deception detection, and this volume will summarise where we are today and suggest where we might go next.

Definition and types of lies

To define deception is a difficult task. Whole books have been devoted to the issue, and many scholars have made more or less successful attempts to conceptualise the phenomenon (e.g., Bok, 1978; Galasinski, 2000). The sixteenth-century French philosopher and essayist Montaigne claimed that deception has 'a hundred thousand faces and an infinite field'. Accepting Montaigne's view, it is easy to understand why defining deception is such a taxing task.

However, for the present context we think that the definition offered by Vrij (2000) will suffice. Vrij describes deception as 'a successful or unsuccessful deliberate attempt, without forewarning, to create in another a belief which the communicator considers to be untrue' (p. 6). Note that a person who unintentionally misremembers is not lying, and that lying requires intention. Moreover, someone should be called a liar only if he or she lies without prior warning about his or her intention, and that even an unsuccessful attempt to deceive is a lie.

We will focus on serious lies, and not the 'social lies' (white lies) that most people tell on a daily basis in order to cast others ('Ah, new haircut – nice!') or themselves ('I never fantasise about others') in a more positive light. For a fascinating series of studies on the frequency and type of everyday lying, see the work by DePaulo and her colleagues (e.g., DePaulo and Bell, 1996; DePaulo, Kashy, Kirkendol, Wyer, and Epstein, 1996).

It is possible to make distinctions between falsifications, distortions, and concealments. Falsifications are total falsehoods, where everything that is being told is contradictory to the truth or made up (sometimes called 'outright lies'). Distortions depart from the truth but are more or less altered in order to fit the liar's goal, and in this category one also finds exaggerations. Finally, a liar can claim that he doesn't know (even if he does) or that he doesn't remember (even if he does), that is, he can conceal the truth. The present volume will address all these different types of lies.

The scientific study of deception

The topic of deception is studied within many different scientific disciplines, such as philosophy (Nyberg, 1993), psychiatry (Ford, 1996), psychology (Ekman, 1985), human communication (McCornack, 1992) and linguistics (Galasinski, 2000). In the current volume we will approach the topic from a forensic point of view and stay close to the research methods and research questions characterising the field of 'psychology and law'.

The field of psychology and law is developing rapidly (Carson and Bull, 2003), and over the last ten years the topic of deception detection has received increased attention. At major international conferences, such as those organised by the European Association of Psychology and Law (EAPL) and the American Psychology–Law Society (APLS), 'deception detection' is frequently found among the many different themes. The scientific journals within the field, such as *Law and Human Behavior*, *Legal and Criminological Psychology*, and *Psychology, Crime and Law*, now publish papers on deception on a more or less regular basis.

By tradition, the topic deception detection – as it has been studied within the field of psychology and law – is characterised by three different approaches: the analysis of verbal content, the analysis of non-verbal cues (including micro-expressions), and the psychophysiological detection of deception. In the current volume, all three approaches will be thoroughly examined.

Researchers who study deception from a forensic point of view have mainly concentrated their efforts on the following four lines of research: (1) mapping people's ability to detect deception (i.e., the question of detection accuracy), (2) capturing the beliefs people hold regarding deceptive behaviour, as well as the cues people use in order to assess veracity (subjective cues to deception), (3) tracing systematic behavioural differences between liars and truth-tellers, in terms of both non-verbal behaviour and verbal content (objective cues to deception), and (4) trying to improve people's ability to detect deception (e.g., by testing the effectiveness of different techniques and training programmes). In the present volume, each of these different lines of research will be addressed.

Deception research contains elements from many of psychology's different sub-disciplines. For example, to understand why truthful and false statements might differ systematically in terms of verbal content one must study *memory*; in order to explain why a suspect who is videotaped from one angle is judged to be less credible than when taped from another angle, one must study *social psychology*; and to understand why a liar's internal states might translate into certain non-verbal behaviours, it is useful to study *emotions* and *physiological psychology*. Obviously, the full list is much longer, but the point to be emphasised is that to understand human deception one needs to study different domains within psychology.

A brief historical note

It is worthwhile placing the current volume in a historical context. The topic of deception was acknowledged already at the dawn of legal and forensic psychology. In 1908 Hugo Münsterberg, one of the pioneers of forensic psychology, published the book *On the witness stand*. This book is a collection of chapters on how applied psychology can be used to detect and solve crimes and includes chapters on, for example, witness memory, false confessions, and suggestibility in court. In 1909 Clara and William Stern published *Erinnerung, Aussage, und Lüge in der ersten Kindheit* (translated into English in 1999, *Recollection, testimony, and lying in early childhood*). This book contains chapters on the development of children's memory and testimonial ability, false testimony, falsification through fantasy, pseudo-lies and lies. Both these early volumes addressed the issue of deception in legal contexts.

Modern research on deception can be traced back to the end of the 1960s, when Paul Ekman and Wallace Friesen published their first paper on deception (Ekman and Friesen, 1969). In the 1970s the research and literature on forensic psychology exploded, and it is beyond the scope of the current chapter to systematise how the area of deception detection has developed over the last thirty-five years. Instead, we would like to highlight two previous international conferences on deception detection and relate the content of the current volume to these landmarks.

In September 1981, one of the first international conferences on witness psychology and credibility assessment took place. The meeting was held in Sweden under the name 'The Stockholm Symposium on Witness Psychology', and its subtitle explains the meeting's overall purpose: *An international meeting for the promotion of scientific analysis of human statements in the reconstruction of suspected crimes*. The man behind the symposium was Professor Arne Trankell, one of the pioneers of modern Swedish witness psychology. Trankell was able to attract a team of outstanding researchers; some of whom were already authorities within the field (among them L. R. C. Haward, Friedrich Arntzen, and Udo Undeutsch), and others who were in an earlier stage of, what turned out to be, brilliant research careers (among them Elizabeth Loftus, Ray Bull, Graham Davies and Gisli Gudjonsson). The papers presented at the meeting were published in a volume edited by Trankell, *Reconstructing the past: The role of psychologist in criminal trials* (1982). A majority of the chapters in the volume dealt with different aspects of the analysis of witness statements (analysis of the verbal content), and one section was reserved for chapters on the polygraph.

In June 1988, a conference was held on the theme 'Credibility assessment: A unified theoretical and research perspective'. The conference was held in Maratea in Italy and was organised by John Yuille, with assistance from David Raskin and Max Steller. Also these organisers were able to present a very impressive list of experts. A selection of the papers presented at the conference was published in a book entitled *Credibility assessment* (1989), edited by Yuille. Many of the experts that came together in Stockholm also contributed to the book proceedings of the Maratea conference. In addition, *Credibility assessment* contains contributions from authorities like Paul Ekman and Bella DePaulo.

Contrasting the Stockholm and Maratea volumes against the current, in terms of content and contributors, some interesting observations can be made. First, in terms of content, two themes are found in all three volumes: (a) the analysis of verbal content and (b) questions pertaining to the reliability of the polygraph. Second, both the Stockholm and Maratea volumes contain chapters on eyewitness testimony, chapters that acknowledge factors that may cause witnesses to unintentionally misremember. In contrast, the current volume does not include chapters on mistaken eyewitnesses. This is consistent with the definition of deception presented above, which stresses that lying requires an intentional act. Obviously, issues concerning the reliability of eye-witness testimony are crucial in legal contexts and have been addressed in several ground-breaking volumes over the years (Cutler and Penrod, 1995; Loftus, 1979). Third, the three major themes characterising the Maratea volume, that is, research on verbal content, behavioural cues, and psychophysiological measures, are all expanded upon in the current volume.

Importantly, lie-catchers working within forensic contexts are faced with a multitude of different problems. Hence, beside the main issues of the analysis of verbal content and the reliability of the polygraph, the current volume covers several additional topics not included in any of the above-mentioned international volumes. For example, the detection of feigned amnesia and false confessions, practitioners' beliefs about deception, guidelines on how to detect deception, features characterising lie-catching experts, as well as international and cross-cultural aspects of deception.

In terms of contributors, about half of the chapters in the current volume are written by researchers who contributed to both (Bull and Davies) or one (DePaulo, Ekman and Honts) of the previous two international volumes. We are grateful that these experienced researchers were also willing to contribute to the present volume. It would be far from fair to characterise the remaining contributors as new to the game; most of them have successfully conducted research on deception for more than twenty years. In all, we were very fortunate that such an outstanding team of experts agreed to contribute to the current volume.

Yuille, in his preface to the volume following the meeting in Italy, noted that most of the psychophysiological work on deception has originated in the United States, whereas most of the research on verbal content has originated in Europe. The current volume reflects this division; the researcher who writes about the polygraph (Honts) is from the United States, and the two researchers who write about the analysis of verbal content (Köhnken and Sporer) are both from Europe. Although geography still matters, research on the reliability of the polygraph is not only to be found in the United States (see, e.g, Ben-Shakhar and Elaad, 2003), and research on verbal content is not limited to Europe (see e.g. Porter and Yuille, 1996).

Structure, content and contributors

Apart from the introduction and conclusion, we have organised the chapters in three major parts. The first, 'Lie-detection techniques', covers the traditional areas of scientific lie detection: non-verbal behaviour, verbal content, and physiological indicators of deception. In Chapter 2, *Bella DePaulo* and *Wendy Morris* provide a very up-to-date account of non-verbal (and verbal) cues to deception. In this chapter, the result of more than thirty years of research on reliable cues to deception is found. In addition, this chapter contains some interesting findings about implicit lie detection, that is the human capacity to spot lies and liars without explicitly detecting 'deception'. In Chapter 3, *Günter Köhnken* presents the latest research on Statement Validity Analysis (SVA). He describes the full technique – not just the Criteria-Based Content Analysis (CBCA) part – and discusses relevant issues of training, interrater reliability, and limitations of the SVA. Köhnken has included research previously available in German only. *Siegfried Sporer* offers in Chapter 4 a very thorough quantitative review of the studies that have used reality monitoring (RM) as a lie-detecting technique. He reviews studies on both adults and children, and compares the RM approach with SVA. In Chapter 5, the final chapter of this part, *Charles Honts* presents a state-of-the-art account of psychophysiological detection of deception. He describes how the technique is used and what research has shown about its reliability. The issues of attitudes towards the polygraph and countermeasures employed by those examined are discussed, as well as the use of the polygraph in non-forensic settings.

The second major part, 'Special issues facing a lie-catcher', consists of four chapters. Each focuses on issues or problems that arise quite often in forensic settings but have not traditionally been part of the deception detection research programme. In Chapter 6, *Charles Bond* and *Sandhya Rao* review cross-cultural aspects of deception. Most research has been conducted in Western cultures, and Bond and Rao examine whether beliefs about deception, and non-verbal indicators of deception, are worldwide phenomena or culture-specific. One question this thought-provoking chapter examines is: can we correctly detect deception in someone from another culture? Most deception research has examined adults' lies, and how these can be detected. However, children's deception must also be studied. In Chapter 7, *Graham Davies* provides an eloquent narrative about the reasons why children may lie, and the consequences thereof. In addition, suggestive questioning techniques, and experimental studies of adults' ability to detect children's lies are reviewed. The chapter is centred on the English and Welsh example, where a memorandum of good practice on interviewing children was introduced in the early 1990s. In Chapter 8, *Saul Kassin* provides insights into a phenomenon previously ignored in the deception field, but of high practical relevance for police, prosecutors and judges. He discusses how false confessions can arise, and the difficulty of separating them from truthful confessions. *Sven Christianson* and *Harald Merckelbach* examine another, sometimes neglected, issue that is nevertheless of practical significance in Chapter 9. Quite frequently, suspects claim to have amnesia for the crucial period, and the question then arises: Is this amnesia genuine or simulated? Included are both research on how common feigned amnesia is and techniques that can be used to separate genuine amnesia from simulated. This chapter will be of interest to both police officers and clinicians.

In the third major part of this volume, 'Enhancing lie-detection accuracy', the focus is turned to those trying to detect deception. In Chapter 10, *Leif Strömwall, Pär Anders Granhag*, and *Maria Hartwig* review the research on practitioners' beliefs about deception. Three of the questions the authors try to answer are: Where do beliefs come from? What are the consequences of wrongful beliefs? and How do we come to terms with wrongful beliefs? *Ray Bull* reviews and evaluates the scientific attempts that have been made at training people to be better at detecting deception in Chapter 11. Are there any training programmes that have been successful in enhancing lay people's and professionals' deception detection ability? Perhaps some people do not need to be trained to be successful at lie detection. In Chapter 12, *Maureen O'Sullivan* and *Paul Ekman* describe how they came to identify people who are very good at detecting deception, and what characterises these 'wizards'. This chapter is based on interesting and fresh data from their on-going 'Diogenes' project. Finally, in Chapter 13, *Aldert Vrij* provides the lie-catcher with no less than fifteen scientifically based guidelines. This comprehensive and up-to-date chapter brings together most of what is known in the field of interviewing to detect deception, and thus should be especially useful for those working in the field.

Readership

We hope that this state-of-the-field volume will be of interest to the many different groups of practitioners found within the legal domain, such as judges, lawyers, prosecutors, police officers, customs officers and migration board personnel. We also believe that the book will be a valuable source of information for those groups of professionals who have to tackle questions of credibility and reliability, such as journalists, professionals who conduct job interviews, security personnel, insurance personnel, negotiators, and the military. Furthermore, as the contributors themselves are experienced and very well-known researchers, we hope the book will attract both students (at different levels) and researchers within the field of psychology and law.

REFERENCES

Ben-Shakhar, and Elaad, E. (2003). The validity of psychophysiological detection of information with the guilty knowledge test: A meta-analytic review. *Journal of Applied Psychology*, 88, 131–51.

Bok, S. (1978). *Lying: Moral choice in public and private life*. New York: Pantheon Books.

Carson, D., and Bull, R. (2003). *Handbook of psychology in legal contexts*. Chichester: John Wiley.

Cutler, B. R., and Penrod, S. D. (1995). *Mistaken identification: The eyewitness, psychology, and the law*. New York: Cambridge University Press.

DePaulo, B. M., and Bell, K. L. (1996). Truth and investment: Lies are told to those who care. *Journal of Personality and Social Psychology*, 71, 703–16.

DePaulo, B. M., Kashy, D. A., Kirkendol, S. E., Wyer, M. M., and Epstein, J. A. (1996). Lying in everyday life. *Journal of Personality and Social Psychology*, 70, 979–95.

Ekman, P. (1985). *Telling lies. Clues to deceit in the marketplace, politics, and marriage*. New York: Norton.

Ekman, P., and Friesen, W. V. (1969). Nonverbal leakage and clues to deception. *Psychiatry*, 32, 88–105.

Ford, C. V. (1996). *Lies! Lies!! Lies!!! The psychology of deceit*. Washington, DC: American Psychiatric Press.

Galasinski, D. (2000). *The language of deception: A discourse analytical study*. Thousand Oaks, CA: Sage.

Kerr, P. (1990). *The Penguin book of lies*. London: Penguin Books.

Loftus, E. F. (1979). *Eyewitness testimony*. Cambridge, MA: Harvard University Press.

McCornack, S. A. (1992). Information manipulation theory. *Communication Monographs*, 59, 1–16.

Münsterberg, H. (1976/1908). *On the witness stand*. New York: Doubleday.

Nyberg, D. (1993). *The varnished truth: Truth telling and deceiving in ordinary life*. Chicago, IL: University of Chicago Press.

Porter, S., and Yuille, J. C. (1996). The language of deceit: An investigation of the verbal clues to deception in the interrogation context. *Law and Human Behavior*, 20, 975–86.

Serban, G. (2001). *Lying – Man's second nature*. Westport, CT: Praeger.

Stern, C., and Stern, W. (1999/1909). *Recollection, testimony, and lying in early childhood*. Washington, DC: American Psychological Association.

Trankell, A. (1982). *Reconstructing the past: The role of psychologists in criminal trials*. Stockholm: Norstedts.

Vrij, A. (2000). *Detecting lies and deceit*. Chichester: John Wiley.

Yuille, J. C. (1989). *Credibility Assessment*. Dordrecht: Kluwer Academic.

Part 2

Lie-detection techniques

2 Discerning lies from truths: behavioural cues to deception and the indirect pathway of intuition

Bella M. DePaulo and Wendy L. Morris

Can you tell whether suspects are lying based on what they say, how they say it, how they sound when they say it, or how they look? Can you do so even without any special equipment, such as a polygraph to monitor physiological responses (Honts, this volume) or a camera to record interviews, which can then be studied in microscopic detail (O'Sullivan and Ekman, this volume)? These are the questions we will address in this chapter.

Reading this chapter will not give anyone grounds for feeling smug about his or her deception detection prowess in forensic contexts (nor in any other contexts, for that matter). The study of verbal and non-verbal behavioural cues to deception is an inexact science, and probably always will be. We will offer hints, based on the current state of the science, about the kinds of behaviours that are more or less likely to intimate that a suspect may be lying. Our suggestions may be of some value in cases in which more definitive evidence, such as DNA, is not available or has not yet been uncovered. We hope our review will also prove useful in demonstrating why sweeping statements about perfect cues to deception are deserving of deep scepticism.

There are two fundamental questions in the study of verbal and non-verbal cues to deception. First, are there any such cues? That is, are there any behaviours that indicate whether a person may be lying? And second, if deception does leave a behavioural mark, how, and how well, can we detect that mark?

We will begin with an example of a case in which a victim has been shot to death. Initially, various potential suspects might be questioned. Investigative life would be simple and sweet if all potential suspects could be asked directly whether they shot the victim, and could also be counted on to tell the truth. In that fanciful world (in which all of the potential suspects we rounded up would in fact include the real shooter), we would find that all of the innocent people would say no, they did not do the shooting, and the one murderer would confess. This idealistic outcome is shown in the first row of Table 2.1. Of course, the more likely outcome

Table 2.1 *Suspects' possible answers to the question of whether they committed the crime*

	Innocent suspect	Guilty suspect
Answers desired by detectives	No	Yes
Most likely answers	No	No
Possible answers in response to aggressive interrogation techniques	Yes	Yes
Other possible answers	No	Don't remember

is that all suspects, innocent and guilty alike, would deny the shooting and claim their innocence. This outcome is illustrated in the second row of the table.

At this point, if you were a detective on the case, it might be tempting to become aggressive and accusing, insisting to all of the suspects, in each individual interview, that you know they are lying. In fact, such techniques are sometimes recommended (e.g., Inbau, Reid, Buckley, and Jayne, 2001). The hope is that the guilty will succumb to the pressure while the blameless will stand by their protestations of innocence. However, the risk is that as the pressure becomes ever more aversive with no apparent end in sight, both the guilty and the innocent will confess to put an end to it (Kassin, this volume). That possibility is shown in the third row of Table 2.1.

People who are guilty, regardless of the particular interrogation technique that is used, may sometimes reply neither with a 'yes' nor a 'no' to the question of whether they did in fact commit a crime. Instead, they may claim not to remember, pointing to drunkenness or other memory disabling conditions. (This possibility is shown in the fourth row of Table 2.1.) As Christianson and Merckelbach explain (this volume), insistence on an inability to remember is worthy of suspicion. Still, it is an answer that falls short of an unqualified admission of guilt.

A quick review of Table 2.1 suggests that the fantasised outcome, whereby guilty people immediately confess to the crime and innocent people maintain their innocence, is unlikely to occur. What is more likely is that both types of suspects will give the same type of answer – either both denying any wrongdoing (or at least any memory of it), or both confessing to the crime. That is why we must look to other verbal and non-verbal cues as possible hints to deceptiveness.

In the arena of verbal and non-verbal clues to deception, there is another dreamer's delight: the reverie of a behaviour that always occurs when people are lying and never occurs at any other time. This possibility was immortalised in the story of Pinocchio, the little boy whose nose grew every time he lied, but not at any other time. (Unluckily for Pinocchio, he had no access to telephones or to email. There was nothing he could do to hide the tell-tale sign of his deceit.)

The appeal of poor Pinocchio's nose as a cue to deceit is not only that it is perfectly valid, but also that it requires no other knowledge or points of comparison. Pinocchio lies, his nose grows – right in front of our eyes. We do not need to know how Pinocchio typically behaves when he is telling the truth. It does not matter what Pinocchio is lying about, why he is lying, or how he feels about his lies. If he lies, his nose simply grows.

The real world of behavioural cues is not like this. Lying is not a distinct psychological process with its own unique behavioural indicators. It does matter how liars feel and how they think (e.g., Ekman, 1985/1992). Good human lie detectors, if there are such persons, are likely to be good intuitive psychologists. They would figure out how a person might think or feel if lying in a particular situation, compared to telling the truth, then look for behavioural indications of those thoughts or feelings. They would also try to anticipate the strategies that liars might use to try to appear credible, then look for evidence of those strategies.

Both professionals and laypersons have formal or informal theories about lying. Our own begins with the premise that ordinarily, liars and truth-tellers both have the same goal: to seem honest. Both will want to convey an impression of honesty. The most important difference between the attempts to appear honest authored by liars, compared to truth-tellers, is that the liars' claims to honesty are illegitimate. Liars are therefore vulnerable to pangs of guilt from which truth-tellers are often exempt. Feelings of guilt could be evident in a sense of discomfort and negativity shown by liars. For example, liars could seem nervous, project an unpleasant demeanour, and seem uncooperative. Feelings of guilt could also create the impression that the liars are not fully embracing the stories they are telling. That is, compared to truth-tellers, liars may seem less forthcoming, and may tell their stories in less compelling ways.

Of course, not all liars feel guilty about their lies or about the wrongdoing they are attempting to hide with their lies. Even so, liars may convey an impression of tension or negativity if they are concerned about the possibility of getting caught in their lies. They may be especially afraid if they are covering up a transgression – something that will get them in trouble. But even when people are lying about something trivial – for example, whether they like a mutual acquaintance – they may still feel nervous about getting caught. That is because whenever you are caught, other people then know that you are a liar.

A sense of being less than forthright, combined with the telling of tales that do not seem totally compelling, can be explained by aspects of the lie-telling process other than feelings of guilt. Guilty suspects who make up a story about what they were doing on the night of the shooting, for example, may not have the same command of pertinent facts as would innocent suspects who can straightforwardly describe what they really did that night. It has often been suggested that liars will be tripped up by their lies because they have to work harder at concocting them. For instance, liars may need to make up stories, try to keep all of the details consistent, and then keep track of what they told to whom. However, this is not a necessary burden of all who might deceive. Clever liars could simply describe what they really were doing on a different evening, thereby drawing from as accessible a set of facts and memories as those of any truth-teller. Also, to the extent that suspects can anticipate some of the questions they may be asked, they can prepare their answers in advance. The issue then becomes whether the liars know how to communicate their planned answers in a way that sounds both sincere and spontaneous.

There is another important psychological difference between liars and truth-tellers that could result in the two creating different impressions. Whereas both liars and truth-tellers want to appear sincere, liars are more likely to make a deliberate effort to ensure their success. Truth-tellers ordinarily expect to be believed, and so their behaviour is more natural and less self-conscious. An important exception is when truth-tellers fear that they may not be believed (e.g., Bond and Fahey, 1987). Then they may exert just as much effort as liars in trying to assure that their stories seem honest. As a result, they could seem just as self-conscious as liars, and their stories could seem less compelling than they otherwise would.

To summarise so far, valid cues to deception are differences in the ways that liars behave, compared to truth-tellers. The behavioural differences are created by differences in feelings (such as nervousness about the possibility of being caught), psychological processes (such as the effort involved in deliberately trying to appear honest), and beliefs and strategies (such as ideas about the kinds of behaviours that create impressions of honesty). (See also Bond and Rao, this volume, and Vrij, this volume.) Cues to deception will be more blatant the more liars and truth-tellers differ in their feelings, the deliberateness of their behaviour, and their beliefs and strategies.

Cues to deception: results from 120 samples

The first author and her colleagues (DePaulo, Lindsay, Malone, Muhlenbruck, Charlton, and Cooper, 2003) recently published a comprehensive quantitative review of research on cues to deception. The review covered 120 samples of participants (all adults), 158 verbal or non-verbal cues, and 1,338 estimates of the link between the occurrence of a cue and the telling of a lie. The people who told the truths and lies in the 120 samples included some actual suspects in criminal investigations, as well as salespersons, shoppers, travellers, drug addicts, and high-profile liars who were publicly exposed. In most of the samples, however (101 of the 120), the participants were college students. The liars and truth-tellers hailed from a variety of countries, including Canada, Germany, England, Spain, Japan, Jordan, Italy, Romania, the Netherlands, and Surinam. Most often, though, they were from the United States (in 88 of the 120 samples).

Most of the studies were conducted in university laboratories. Participants told truths and lies about many different topics. For example, in 44 of the samples, participants lied about facts or personal opinions. In another 16 samples, they watched films or slides and lied or told the truth about what they were seeing. In other studies, some of the participants were induced to cheat, or to commit a mock crime, and then lie about it. Card tests or guilty knowledge tests were used in a number of studies. There were also a few studies of actual suspects in criminal investigations (e.g., Hall, 1986; Horvath, 1973; Horvath, Jayne, and Buckley, 1994).

For each cue reported in each study in the review, the authors computed an effect size summarising the extent to which the behaviour was shown more or less often by liars compared to truth-tellers. The effect size was d, which is computed as the mean of the behaviour in the deception condition minus the mean in the truthful condition, divided by the mean of the standard deviations for the lies and the truths (Cohen, 1988). Positive ds indicate that the behaviour was shown more often by liars than by truth-tellers, whereas negative ds indicate that the behaviour was shown less often by liars than by truth-tellers.

We will first present the results that summarise across all relevant studies. For example, to determine whether liars seem more nervous than truth-tellers, we combine the ds for all sixteen studies for which impressions of nervousness were reported. (The effect sizes are weighted by the size of the studies.) Later, we separate the studies in theoretically important ways (e.g., by whether the participants had special incentives for getting away with their lies), to see whether cues to deception are more or less obvious in the different kinds of studies.

Our descriptions of the individual cues will be brief. More complete definitions can be found in the original report (DePaulo et al., 2003). Also, we include here only a subset of the 158 cues summarised in the

Table 2.2 *Are liars more tense than truth-tellers?*

Cue	d	N	k	CI
Pupil dilation	.39*	328	4	0.21, 0.56
Nervous, tense (overall)	.27*	571	16	0.16, 0.38
Vocal tension	.26*	328	10	0.13, 0.39
Pitch	.21*	294	12	0.08, 0.34
Fidgeting				
Object fidgeting	−.12	420	5	−0.26, 0.03
Self fidgeting	−.01	991	18	−0.09, 0.08
Facial fidgeting	.08	444	7	−0.09, 0.25
Fidgeting (no distinctions)	.16*	495	14	0.03, 0.28
Blinking	.07	850	17	−0.01, 0.14
Relaxed posture	−.02	488	13	−0.14, 0.10

Note: N = total number of participants in studies; k = total number of independent effect sizes; CI = 95% confidence interval. From 'Cues to deception', by B. M. DePaulo, J. J. Lindsay, B. E. Malone, L. Muhlenbruck, K. Charlton, and H. Cooper, 2003, *Psychological Bulletin*, *129*, p. 93. Copyright 2003 by the American Psychological Association. Adapted with permission of the author.
* $p < .05$.

original report. Our focus is on those cues that proved to be valid cues to deception, as well as those which were reported in more than just a few studies.

Are liars more tense than truth-tellers?

Behaviours suggesting that liars may be more tense than truth-tellers are shown in Table 2.2. In Tables 2.2 through 2.8, d is the effect size, N is the total number of participants across all of the relevant studies, k signifies the total number of relevant studies or independent effect sizes, and CI represents the 95 per cent confidence interval. The first row of Table 2.2 shows that pupil size (dilation) is markedly greater when people are lying than when they are telling the truth. This could suggest that liars are more tense than truth-tellers, or that they are thinking harder, or both. When observers watch people who are lying or telling the truth (without knowing who is doing the lying), they think that the liars seem more nervous overall, compared to the truth-tellers. If observers can only hear the liars and truth-tellers but not see them, they still rate the liars as sounding more tense than the truth-tellers. Perhaps observers can hear the tension in the pitch of the voices, which is higher when people are lying than when they are telling the truth.

Fidgeting has sometimes been hypothesised to be an indication of anxiety. Different kinds of fidgeting have been reported by different investigators. Some measure fidgeting with objects (such as pencils, paper clips, or anything that happens to be nearby) separately from self-fidgeting (such as touching your own clothes, hair, or face). Still others measure facial fidgeting separately from all other fidgeting, and others make no distinctions at all. In those studies in which all types of fidgeting were combined, liars did fidget more than truth-tellers. However, no meaningful patterns emerged from the studies in which different kinds of fidgeting were measured separately. It is probably best to conclude, at this point, that there is no clear relationship between fidgeting and lying.

Across the seventeen studies in which blinking was reported, liars did not blink significantly more often than did truth-tellers. Liars were also no less likely to be relaxed in their posture than were truth-tellers.

In summary, a number of important cues suggest that liars are more tense than truth-tellers. However, not all behaviours that might indicate tension are more evident among liars than among truth-tellers.

Are liars less positive and pleasant than truth-tellers?

In Table 2.3 are the results for cues to negativity. One of the strongest results in the review of cues to deception was for cooperativeness. Liars are noticeably less cooperative than truth-tellers. However, that result is based on only three studies. Liars also make more negative statements and complaints than truth-tellers do, and they appear somewhat less friendly and pleasant. If you look just at their faces, liars again seem less pleasant than truth-tellers.

The studies of how pleasant people's faces seemed were usually based on other people's impressions. There were twenty-seven studies that reported one particular behaviour: smiling. Across those studies, there were no differences in the frequency of smiling between liars and truth-tellers. However, the investigators who reported those findings did not try to distinguish among different kinds of smiles. Precise coding of different kinds of smiles is more promising (e.g., Ekman, Friesen, and O'Sullivan, 1988). For example, liars who are feigning pleasure may smile in different ways from truth-tellers who are experiencing joy that they are not trying to hide.

So are liars more negative and unpleasant than truth-tellers? In some ways, they are. They are less cooperative, do more complaining, and their faces look less pleasant. Most of the other cues to negativity, however, did not separate the liars from the truth-tellers.

Table 2.3 *Are liars less positive and pleasant than truth-tellers?*

Cue	d	N	k	CI
Cooperative	−.66*	222	3	−0.93, −0.38
Negative statements, complaints	.21*	397	9	0.09, 0.32
Friendly, pleasant (overall)	−.16	216	6	−0.36, 0.05
Facial pleasantness	−.12*	635	13	−0.22, −0.02
Vocal pleasantness	−.11	325	4	−0.28, 0.05
Attractive (overall)	−.06	84	6	−0.27, 0.16
Brow lowering	.04	303	5	−0.08, 0.16
Head nods	.01	752	16	−0.09, 0.11
Eye muscles (AU 6), not during positive emotions	−.01	284	4	−0.13, 0.11
Smiling (no distinctions)	.00	1313	27	−0.07, 0.07
Lip corner pull (AU 12)	.00	284	4	−0.12, 0.12

Note: N = total number of participants in studies; k = total number of independent effect sizes; CI = 95% confidence interval. From 'Cues to deception', by B. M. DePaulo, J. J. Lindsay, B. E. Malone, L. Muhlenbruck, K. Charlton, and H. Cooper, 2003, *Psychological Bulletin, 129*, p. 93. Copyright 2003 by the American Psychological Association. Adapted with permission of the author.
* $p < .05$.

Are liars less forthcoming than truth-tellers?

To see whether liars were less forthcoming than truth-tellers, we looked at three kinds of behaviours. First, how much did they have to say? Second, how detailed or complex were their answers? And third, did they seem to be holding back? The results for those cues are shown in Table 2.4.

One of the measures of amount of responding is talking time, defined as the percentage of time during the entire interaction that one person spends talking. A person who is lying talks for a smaller percentage of the total time than does a person who is telling the truth. The other measures are in the same direction, but they are not statistically reliable. So, for example, if one person is lying, the entire interaction takes a little less time than if both people are telling the truth. Most investigators simply count the number of words people say when lying or telling the truth; by that measure, there is very little difference between liars and truth-tellers.

Do liars provide fewer details than truth-tellers do? The answer to that question is yes. The stories told by liars include fewer details; they seem less complete.

Table 2.4 *Are liars less forthcoming than truth-tellers?*

Cue	*d*	N	*k*	CI
Amount of responding				
Talking time	**−.35***	207	4	−0.54, −0.16
Length of interaction	−.20	134	3	−0.41, 0.02
Response length	−.03	1812	49	−0.09, 0.03
Detailed, complex responses				
Details	**−.30***	883	24	−0.38, −0.21
Cognitive complexity	−.07	294	6	−0.23, 0.10
Holding back				
Presses lips	**.16***	199	4	0.01, 0.30
Rate of speaking	.07	806	23	−0.03, 0.16
Response latency	.02	1330	32	−0.06, 0.10

Note: N = total number of participants in studies; k = total number of independent effect sizes; CI = 95% confidence interval. From 'Cues to deception', by B. M. DePaulo, J. J. Lindsay, B. E. Malone, L. Muhlenbruck, K. Charlton, and H. Cooper, 2003, *Psychological Bulletin*, *129*, p. 91. Copyright 2003 by the American Psychological Association. Adapted with permission of the author.
* $p < .05$.

With regard to the measures of holding back, there was only one behaviour that suggested that the liars seemed to be holding back. Compared to truth-tellers, liars were more likely to press their lips together.

When you look at all of the results in Table 2.4, can you say that liars are less forthcoming than truth-tellers? Almost all of the answers are pointing in that direction. However, only a few of the results are statistically significant.

Do liars tell less compelling tales than truth-tellers?

We examined six qualities of truths and lies that might make them seem compelling. First, do the stories seem to make sense? Second, are the stories told in an engaging way? Third, are the stories told in an immediate (direct and personal) way or are they told in a more distant way? Fourth, how certain do the liars and truth-tellers seem as they tell their tales? Fifth, how fluently do they speak? Finally, how much activity do they show in shifting their posture, or moving their head, hands, or feet?

Table 2.5 *Do liars tell less compelling tales than truth-tellers?*

Cue	*d*	N	*k*	CI
Makes sense				
Discrepant, ambivalent	.34*	243	7	0.20, 0.48
Logical structure	−.25*	223	6	−0.46, −0.04
Plausibility	−.23*	395	9	−0.36, −0.11
Engaging				
Verbal and vocal involvement	−.21*	384	7	−0.34, −0.08
Illustrators	−.14*	839	16	−0.24, −0.04
Facial expressiveness	.12	251	3	−0.05, 0.29
Involved, expressive (overall)	.08	214	6	−0.06, 0.22
Immediate				
Verbal and vocal immediacy (impressions)	− .55*	373	7	−0.70, −0.41
Verbal immediacy (all categories)	−.31*	117	3	−0.50, −0.13
Verbal immediacy, temporal	.15	109	4	−0.04, 0.34
Generalising terms	.10	275	5	−0.08, 0.28
Non-verbal immediacy	− .07	414	11	−0.21, 0.07
Eye contact	.01	1491	32	−0.06, 0.08
Uncertain				
Verbal and vocal uncertainty (impressions)	.30*	329	10	0.17, 0.43
Chin raise	.25*	286	4	0.12, 0.37
Shrugs	.04	321	6	−0.13, 0.21
Fluent				
Word and phrase repetitions	.21*	100	4	0.02, 0.41
Ritualised speech	.20	181	4	−0.06, 0.47
Pauses (silent + filled)	.03	280	7	−0.11, 0.17
Silent pauses	.01	655	15	−0.09, 0.11
Filled pauses	.00	805	16	−0.08, 0.08
Active				
Foot or leg movements	−.09	857	28	−0.18, 0.00
Posture shifts	.05	1214	29	−0.03, 0.12
Head movements	−.02	536	14	−0.12, 0.08
Hand movements	.00	951	29	−0.08, 0.08

Note: N = total number of participants in studies; k = total number of independent effect sizes; CI = 95% confidence interval. From 'Cues to deception', by B. M. DePaulo, J. J. Lindsay, B. E. Malone, L. Muhlenbruck, K. Charlton, and H. Cooper, 2003, *Psychological Bulletin, 129*, p. 92. Copyright 2003 by the American Psychological Association. Adapted with permission of the author.
* $p < .05$.

Were the stories told by liars as logical, plausible, and sensible as the ones told by truth-tellers? The answer to this question is quite clear. Stories told by liars do not make as much sense as do true stories. As shown in Table 2.5, liars' answers sound more discrepant and ambivalent, the structure of their stories is less logical, and their stories sound less plausible. (As Granhag and Strömwall (2000) have shown, however, over the course of repeated interrogations, deceptive statements will not necessarily be any less consistent than truthful ones.)

In some ways, liars are also less engaging. They sound less involved in what they are saying. They also use fewer illustrators, which are hand movements that illustrate what people are saying.

Liars also sound less immediate than truth-tellers do. The way liars talk seems more distant, impersonal, evasive, and unclear. That is the impression people get when they listen to liars (as indicated by the cue, 'verbal and vocal immediacy (impressions)'). That is also the result that emerges when specific linguistic behaviours (verbal immediacy) are coded that suggest distancing (e.g., passive vs. active voice). However, the non-verbal immediacy cues are not as powerful as the verbal immediacy cues. For example, there are thirty-two studies of eye contact, and when the results are combined across those studies, there is no difference what-soever in the amount of eye contact that liars make, compared to the amount that truth-tellers make.

In the impressions they convey with words and with tone of voice, liars seem significantly more uncertain than truth-tellers do. In another way, though, liars seem more certain than truth-tellers. They raise their chins as they speak, in a gesture that can almost seem cocky. That result was unanticipated and is based on only four studies.

Fluency has been measured in many ways. In some studies, silent pauses are distinguished from pauses that are filled with sounds such as um, er, uh, and ah. In other studies, the two are combined. A different kind of disfluency is the cluttering of speech with ritualised expressions such as 'you know', 'I mean', and 'well'. Speakers can also seem inartic-ulate when they say a word or phrase, then repeat it before continuing the thought. Of the several varieties of disfluency that we found in studies of lying, only one reliably separated liars from truth-tellers. Liars are more likely to repeat words and phrases.

Head movements, shifts in posture, and other gross movements of the hands and legs were of little use in distinguishing liars from truth-tellers. However, more specific hand and arm movements are less often made by liars than by truth-tellers, as Vrij has predicted (e.g., Vrij, Akehurst, and Morris, 1997). (Those results are not shown in the table as they are based on only two studies.)

In summary, there are some indications that liars tell less compelling tales than truth-tellers do. The stories they tell are less plausible, and they tell them in a way that sounds less involved and more distancing and uncertain. Liars do not seem to make any more or fewer gross body movements, such as postural shifts, than do truth-tellers. Also, liars are not markedly inarticulate, except perhaps in their tendency to repeat the same word or phrase within the same sentence, without doing so deliberately for emphasis.

Do lies include fewer ordinary imperfections and unusual contents than truths?

A system of coding verbal protocols for signs of credibility has been developed, called Criteria-Based Content Analysis (CBCA). The system is described in more detail elsewhere (e.g., Köhnken, this volume; Yuille and Cutshall, 1989). What is especially intriguing about it as it has been applied to deception is that it gets inside the heads of people who are trying to sound credible, asks what they are likely to believe about cues to deception and how they might strategise, and suggests that liars may tell stories that are too good to be true. In ordinary conversations, when people tell true stories, they tell them in a way that is not perfect. They might start to tell a story, then realise they forgot some of the details, and admit that. They might also realise that something they said was not quite right, and go back and correct that. These are signs of credibility. People who have nothing to hide do not mind admitting that they may have forgotten some of the details or said something that was not quite right. They make those kinds of minor corrections unself-consciously. But people who are worried that someone might catch them in a lie are reluctant to admit to such ordinary imperfections. They tell stories that are too good to be true.

We found some hints that liars are more reluctant than truth-tellers to admit to ordinary imperfections. The relevant results are shown in Table 2.6. For example, compared to truth-tellers, liars were less likely to admit they did not remember some things, and they were less likely to correct something they said before. Other behaviours suggested by this method of assessing credibility were less successful in separating liars from truth-tellers. The system, however, was originally developed to assess the credibility of children, especially in cases of alleged sexual abuse. Its application to other kinds of credibility issues, especially those involving adults, is somewhat controversial (Vrij, 2000).

So far, we have selectively pointed out the cues to deception which show some promise of distinguishing liars from truth-tellers. However, in these analyses in which we combined results over all relevant studies, most behaviours were not shown any more or less often by liars than by truth-tellers. For the eighty-eight cues for which at least three independent effect sizes were available, the median effect size was only a d of $|.10|$.

Table 2.6 *Do lies include fewer ordinary imperfections and unusual contents than truths?*

Cue	d	N	k	CI
Admitted lack of memory	−.42*	183	5	−0.70, −0.15
Spontaneous corrections	−.29*	183	5	−0.56, −0.02
Contextual embedding	−.21	159	6	−0.41, 0.00
Unusual details	−.16	223	6	−0.36, 0.05
Unstructured production	−.06	211	5	−0.27, 0.15
Verbal and non-verbal interactions	−.03	163	5	−0.25, 0.19
Superfluous details	−.01	223	6	−0.21, 0.19
Unexpected complications	.04	223	6	−0.16, 0.24
Subjective mental state	.02	237	6	−0.18, 0.22
Another's mental state	.22	151	4	−0.02, 0.46
Related external associations	.35*	112	3	0.02, 0.67

Note: N = total number of participants in studies; k = total number of independent effect sizes; CI = 95% confidence interval. From 'Cues to deception,' by B. M. DePaulo, J. J. Lindsay, B. E. Malone, L. Muhlenbruck, K. Charlton, and H. Cooper, 2003, *Psychological Bulletin, 129*, p. 94. Copyright 2003 by the American Psychological Association. Adapted with permission of the author.
* $p < .05$.

Moderators of cues to deception

Do lies become more obvious when the liar is highly motivated? In many of the studies included in our review, the liars may not have had any special motivation to tell a successful lie. Many simply participated as part of an experiment and anticipated no special rewards for succeeding or punishments for failing. Perhaps, then, it did not matter to them whether or not they got away with their lies. We thought it would be important to look separately at those studies in which participants had some special motivation to do well, and those in which they did not. The question is this: If people are motivated to get away with their lies, does that mean that there will be fewer cues to deception because they are trying harder to tell a good lie, or will their lies become even more obvious as the stakes go up (cf. DePaulo and Kirkendol, 1989)?

Table 2.7 shows the cues to deception for studies in which participants had no special motivation to get away with their lies, and for studies in which they did have some incentive. The first thing to notice is that when participants had no special incentives, there were no obvious cues to deception. There were thirteen cues for which we had sufficient data to test differences in cues between low and high motivation (nine are shown in Table 2.7). Not one of them revealed any consistent differences

Table 2.7 *Cues to deception under low and high motivation*

	Motivation		
Cues	Low	High	Q_B
Pitch			
d (CI)	−.02 (−0.23, 0.20)	.59* (0.31, 0.88)	18.6*
k	6	6	
Nervous, tense			
d (CI)	.15 (−0.15, 0.44)	.35* (0.11, 0.58)	3.0
k	8	8	
Eye contact			
d (CI)	.09 (−0.01, 0.19)	−.15* (−0.29, −0.01)	9.0*
k	20	12	
Foot or leg movements			
d (CI)	−.02 (−0.15, 0.11)	−.13* (−0.22. −0.03)	1.4
k	9	19	
Fidgeting (no distinctions)			
d (CI)	.09 (−0.33, 0.53)	.18 (−0.08,.043)	.3
k	3	11	
Self-fidgeting			
d (CI)	.08 (−0.03, 0.18)	−.12 (−0.25, 0.01)	5.5*
k	11	7	
Filled pauses			
d (CI)	.09 (−0.03, 0.22)	−.13 (−0.28, 0.02)	6.5*
k	8	8	
Non-ah disturbances			
d (CI)	.13 (−0.15,.041)	−.10 (−0.34, 0.14)	6.3*
k	7	10	
Silent pauses			
d (CI)	−.02 (−0.18, 0.15)	.06 (−0.16, 0.29)	.5
k	8	7	

Note: Q_B = homogeneity between the two levels of the moderator being compared; significance indicates rejection of the hypothesis of homogeneity of effect sizes (ds). The CI = 95% confidence interval; k = total number of independent effect sizes. From 'Cues to deception', by B. M. DePaulo, J. J. Lindsay, B. E. Malone, L. Muhlenbruck, K. Charlton, and H. Cooper, 2003, *Psychological Bulletin*, *129*, p. 98. Copyright 2003 by the American Psychological Association. Adapted with permission of the author.
* $p < .05$.

between lies and truths when participants had little motivation to be believed. When people do not care very much about getting away with their lies, others will have a hard time knowing when they are lying. However, when liars do care about getting away with their lies, then several behaviours betray them. As shown in the first row of the table, it is only when participants are motivated to do well that they speak in a higher pitch when lying than when telling the truth. Although liars also seem somewhat more tense than truth-tellers regardless of motivation, the difference is significant only for those who are highly motivated to get away with their lies.

The results for eye contact are also important. In the previous section in which results were summarised over all thirty-two studies that reported eye contact, there were no differences whatsoever in how often liars looked at the other person and how often truth-tellers did. But when participants are motivated to do well, then one stereotype about liars becomes a reality: they make less eye contact than truth-tellers do. There was also some evidence, under high motivational conditions, that liars are more inhibited than truth-tellers: they made fewer foot and leg movements (Vrij, 2000).

Are lies told to conceal transgressions more obvious than other lies? Across the 120 studies included in the review of cues to deception, there were important differences in the kinds of lies that participants told. Most relevant to the forensic context is the distinction between lies that were or were not told to cover up transgressions. Lies about transgressions were told to hide and deny misdeeds such as cheating, stealing, and committing other small and large crimes. The other lies were not told to cover up bad behaviours. For example, in some studies, people pretended to like people they really did not like, or they lied about their age or their opinions. Is there a different profile of cues to deception for lies that are or are not about transgressions? There were twelve cues for which we had sufficient data to address that question. The results for nine of them are shown in Table 2.8. The first column of the table shows the results for lies that were not about transgressions, and the second, for lies that were about transgressions. The results for the lies that were not about transgressions show that there is only one behaviour that separates the liars from the truth-tellers, and that cue is fidgeting. When participants were talking about their likes or dislikes, their opinions, personal facts, or anything else that did not involve a bad behaviour, they fidgeted more (overall) when lying than when telling the truth. However, there were no significant differences between liars and truth-tellers for any of the other eleven cues when lies were not about transgressions. The cues to lies about transgressions are more telling. People lying about transgressions look more nervous than do truth-tellers. They also blink more and speak more quickly. In addition, they are more inhibited than truth-tellers: they move their feet and legs less often.

Do liars give themselves away by saying too much? In some of the studies we reviewed, liars and truth-tellers spoke very briefly – sometimes all they said was just one word. In other studies, liars and truth-tellers talked

Table 2.8 *Cues to deception when senders did and did not commit a transgression*

Cues	No transgression	Transgression	Q_B
Nervous, tense			
d (CI)	.09 (−0.11, 0.29)	.51* (0.28, 0.75)	13.9*
k	12	4	
Blinking			
d (CI)	.01 (−0.14, 0.16)	**.38*** (0.03, 0.73)	12.2*
k	13	4	
Rate of speaking			
d (CI)	.01 (−0.08, 0.10)	**.32*** (0.13, 0.52)	6.6*
k	18	5	
Foot or leg movements			
d (CI)	−.04 (−0.12, 0.04)	**−.24*** (−0.38, −0.09)	3.8*
k	21	7	
Fidgeting (no distinctions)			
d (CI)	**.24*** (0.02, 0.46)	−.16 (−0.58, 0.27)	6.1*
k	10	4	
Self-fidgeting			
d (CI)	.07 (−0.03, 0.17)	−.14 (−0.28, −0.00)	5.7*
k	12	6	
Non-ah disturbances			
d (CI)	.17 (−0.04, 0.38)	−.24 (−0.49, 0.01)	19.7*
k	11	6	
Response latency			
d (CI)	−.07 (−0.24, 0.11)	.27 (−0.02, 0.55)	13.7*
k	24	8	
Eye contact			
d (CI)	.04 (−0.05, 0.14)	−.13 (−0.33, 0.07)	3.3
k	26	6	

Note: Q_B = homogeneity between the two levels of the moderator being compared; significance indicates rejection of the hypothesis of homogeneity of effect sizes (ds). The CI = 95% confidence interval; k = total number of independent effect sizes. From 'Cues to deception', by B. M. DePaulo, J. J. Lindsay, B. E. Malone, L. Muhlenbruck, K. Charlton, and H. Cooper, 2003, *Psychological Bulletin*, *129*, p. 101. Copyright 2003 by the American Psychological Association. Adapted with permission of the author.
* $p < .05$.

for a longer amount of time. Therefore, we could look at the question of whether liars are more likely to give away their lies the longer they talk. The way we addressed this question was to look at whether cues to deception were any stronger when liars and truth-tellers talked for a longer amount of time. We had enough data to test this hypothesis for three of the cues: pitch, response latency, and response length. For all three, we found that the more time the liars had to talk, the more obvious these cues became. Among people who talked longer, those who were lying had a significantly higher pitch than those who were telling the truth. There was also a bigger difference in how long it took liars to begin to respond to a question, compared to how long it took truth-tellers to do so, when the answers they were about to give were longer. Finally, in the studies in which participants generally talked longer, liars were markedly less talkative than truth-tellers.

Are lies more convincing when prepared in advance? Sometimes suspects know in advance that they are going to be asked certain questions. That gives them a chance to prepare their answers. Do liars sound more like truth-tellers when they can plan their answers in advance than when they cannot? We had enough data to answer this question for eight cues, and we found the clearest results for response latency. In the earlier analyses, in which we made no distinction between people who did or did not have an opportunity to prepare their responses, we found little difference in how long it took liars to start to answer a question, compared to how long it took truth-tellers. But when we looked separately at studies in which people had no chance to plan their answers in advance, we found that liars took longer to start answering than truth-tellers did. However, when they did have time to plan, the liars actually started their answers more quickly than did truth-tellers.

Direct and indirect deception detection

The review of cues to deception showed that behavioural differences between liars and truth-tellers are generally few in number and unimpressive in size. Does this mean that people are not very good at detecting deception (i.e., recognising lies as lies and truths as truths)? Yes. Generally, accuracy at detecting deception is little better than chance. Bond and DePaulo (2004) have summarised the results of 253 samples in which participants were shown equal numbers of truths and lies, and asked to indicate whether they thought each message was a truth or a lie. Overall accuracy was only about 53 per cent.

The vast majority of studies of skill at detecting deception use measures such as the labelling of a message as either a truth or a lie, or rating scales assessing perceived degrees of deceptiveness. These are direct or explicit measures of deception detection and they suggest that people are not very good at discriminating lies from truths.

For many years, we have included in our studies of deception detection other measures in addition to the direct measures of deception

Table 2.9 *Direct and indirect deception detection: age changes in discriminating truths from lies*

Age group	Direct[a]	Indirect[b]
6th-graders	−.24	.05
8th-graders	.10	.06
10th-graders	.04	.57*
12th-graders	.23*	.36*
College students	.25*	.52*

Notes: From 'Age changes in the detection of deception', by B. M. DePaulo, A. Jordan, A Irvine, and P. S. Laser, 1982, *Child Development*, *53*, p. 706. Copyright 1982 by Blackwell Publishers. Adapted with permission of the author.
[a] Ratings of deceptiveness of the lies minus ratings of deceptiveness of the truths.
[b] Ratings of mixed feelings of the lies minus ratings of mixed feelings of the truths.
* Ratings of truths and lies differed significantly.

detection. In one of the first such studies, participants talked about other people they liked and disliked, either honestly or deceptively (DePaulo and Rosenthal, 1979). The perceivers who rated the videotapes of those person descriptions were asked to report not just their impressions of deceptiveness, but also their impressions of ambivalence. The perceivers rated the lies as more deceptive than the truths. So, they were accurate in the usual way. More interestingly, the perceivers' ratings of ambivalence distinguished the truths from the lies even more clearly than did the more direct ratings of deceptiveness. The lies seemed especially more ambivalent than did the truths (DePaulo, Rosenthal, Green, and Rosenkrantz, 1982).

In a subsequent study (DePaulo, Jordan, Irvine, and Laser, 1982), the same videotape of person descriptions was shown to perceivers ranging in age from sixth-graders to college students. They were asked to make the same judgements. The results are shown in Table 2.9. The scores in the first column show the degree to which the perceivers rated the lies as more deceptive than the truths – a standard, direct measure of accuracy at detecting deceit. Those accuracy scores increased with age. The second column shows the degree to which the perceivers rated the speakers who were lying as seeming to have more mixed feelings than the speakers who were telling the truth. Those numbers also generally increased with age. With this indirect measure, accuracy occurs at an earlier developmental point. In tenth grade, when perceivers still cannot discriminate truths from lies with their direct ratings of deceptiveness, they can distinguish truths from lies with their ratings of ambivalence.

A similar finding was reported without much comment a few years later. Hurd and Noller (1988) asked participants to talk aloud as they tried to figure out whether a message they had just heard was a truth or a lie. Participants' accuracy at separating the truths from the lies by their direct judgements of truthfulness or deceptiveness were, as is customary, not all that impressive. However, something very interesting emerged from the verbal protocols. When participants had just heard a lie, they were more likely to entertain the possibility that the message was a lie than when they had just heard a truth. So they had the right answer – they even said it out loud! – but when it was time to commit to an explicit guess, truth, or lie, they did not always listen to their own correct intuitions.

In a longitudinal study of deception detection between same-sex friends, Anderson and his colleagues (Anderson, DePaulo, Ansfield, Tickle, and Green, 1999) added several similar findings to the growing set. In that study, one of the friends in each pair told true and fabricated life stories, and the other friend tried to figure out which of the stories were true and which were made up. The results of the dichotomous measure showed that accuracy was about the same as is typically found in studies in which judgements are made by strangers. The friends' accuracy of just under 55 per cent did not quite differ from chance.

The perceivers in the study of friends were also asked to write down whatever it was that made them think that the story was truthful or deceptive. The cues that were mentioned in these open-ended responses were sorted into a number of categories. The two that proved most important were verbal cues (e.g., references to the content of the story and whether it seemed internally consistent and plausible) and visual cues (e.g., direct eye contact, general demeanour such as nervousness). When the friends mentioned verbal cues, they were more likely to have just heard a truthful story than a deceptive one. When the cues they mentioned were visual or demeanour cues, they were more likely to have just heard a fabricated story than a true one. So the cues the perceivers wrote down to justify their explicit guesses as to whether the stories were truthful or not *did* significantly distinguish the truths from the lies.

In addition to making explicit judgements of whether the stories were truths or lies, and describing the cues they used to decide, the perceivers answered a series of other questions about how they felt while listening to each of the stories. For example, they indicated how comfortable they felt, how suspicious they were, the extent to which their friend (the storyteller) seemed to sense their suspicion, and so forth. Videotapes of the interactions between the pairs of friends were also shown to new perceivers who answered many of the same questions (Anderson, DePaulo, and Ansfield, 2002).

The results are shown in Table 2.10. At the top of the table are the results of the direct measure of deception detection accuracy for the two groups of judges. As usual, both scores were just a shade above chance. Beneath, the table shows the results of many other indirect measures. On those measures, the perceivers did respond differently when they were reporting their impressions of deceptive interactions, relative to truthful ones. The original perceivers, the friends, felt more comfortable while listening to the true stories than the lies and thought their friend who was telling the stories seemed more comfortable. They also felt more confident when listening to the true stories, and they felt that they had got enough information, which was less likely when they had heard a lie. The original perceivers, sitting face to face with a friend who was lying to them, felt more suspicious, tried to hide their suspicions more, and thought their friend sensed their suspiciousness more, compared to when their friend was telling the truth.

The raters of the videotapes also made many of the same discriminations. They thought the storyteller seemed more comfortable when telling the truth than when lying, they felt more confident themselves when they had just heard a truthful story compared to when they had just heard a lie, and they felt that they had obtained enough information from the truthful stories. They also felt more suspicious when hearing the lies, and they thought that the original judges interacting with the sender friends also seemed more suspicious when the story was a lie than when it was true.

In all of the studies of explicit and implicit deception detection conducted in our lab, the same people made both the explicit and the implicit judgements, and the participants were college students. Vrij and his colleagues (Vrij, Edward, and Bull, 2001) extended the study of indirect deception detection in two important ways: they recruited police officers to make direct and indirect judgements, and they randomly assigned the officers to make either direct or indirect judgements. The indirect judgements in this study were impressions of whether the people on the tape needed to think hard.

The police officers showed at least a hint of accuracy on both measures. They rated the liars, compared to the truth-tellers, as somewhat more likely to be lying. They also rated them as significantly more likely to be thinking hard. Although the difference between the implicit and the explicit measure was not statistically significant (because of the fairly small sample size of thirty-nine officers), the effect size for implicit deception detection was more than twice as large as the effect size for the explicit deception detection.

Table 2.10 *Direct and indirect deception detection: judgements of original judges (friends) and raters of videotapes*

Direct deception detection	% accuracy		
Original judges	54.6 n.s.		
Raters of videotapes	50.6 n.s.		

Indirect deception detection

	Type of story		
Indirect cues	True	Lie	Indirect accuracy
	Original judges (friends)		
Own comfort	7.56	7.13	.43***
Perceptions of sender comfort	6.83	6.36	.47**
Confidence	6.38	5.75	.63**
Got enough information	6.52	5.82	.72***
Own suspiciousness	4.88	5.51	.63**
Thinks sender senses suspicion	4.60	5.01	.41*
Tried to hide suspicion	3.62	3.97	.35#
	Raters of videotapes		
Perceptions of sender comfort	5.90	5.78	.12***
Confidence	5.30	5.21	.09***
Got enough information	5.10	5.03	.07**
Own suspiciousness	4.26	4.81	.55***
Perceptions of judge suspicion	4.48	5.05	.57***

Note: Direct deception detection: Chance accuracy = 50%.
$p = .06$. * $p < .05$. ** $p < .01$. *** $p < .001$.
Indirect deception detection: Ratings were made on 9-point scales.
From 'The development of deception detection skill: A longitudinal study of same-sex friends', by D. E. Anderson, B. M. DePaulo, and M. E. Ansfield, 2002, *Personality and Social Psychology Bulletin*, 28.

Enough relevant studies have now accumulated that meta-analytic summaries of measures of indirect deception detection are beginning to be reported. The first was a review of confidence at detecting deceit. DePaulo and her colleagues (DePaulo, Charlton, Cooper, Lindsay, and Muhlenbruck, 1997) found that perceivers reliably report that they are more confident when the message they just rated was truthful than when it was deceptive. Perceivers' feelings of confidence can sometimes distinguish the lies from the truths even when their direct judgements of deceptiveness are not so discriminating.

In the meta-analysis of cues to deception described in detail earlier in this chapter (DePaulo et al., 2003), most of the cues were measured objectively. For example, to assess verbal immediacy, specific linguistic features (such as the use of an active vs. a passive voice) could be coded and counted. To measure eye contact, the number of seconds that the liar or truth-teller looked at the listener could be recorded. However, these cues and others could also be measured subjectively, and were in some studies. For example, perceivers could be asked to record their subjective impressions of how immediate (personal, direct) the liars and truth-tellers seemed, or to what extent the communicators seemed to make direct eye contact. These subjective impressions are indirect measures of deception detection. When objective and subjective measures of cues to deception differed significantly in strength, it was always the subjective measures that were stronger. Subjective impressions of immediacy separated truths from lies more powerfully than did objective linguistic measures. Subjective impressions of eye contact showed liars to be more gaze aversive than did objective measures. Furthermore, subjective impressions of facial pleasantness showed liars to be more negative than truth-tellers, even though objective measures of facial pleasantness did not.

We have one last study of indirect deception detection to report. In this study, Anderson (1999) modelled the situation of asking your romantic partner the impossible question, 'Do you think that person is attractive?' One member of a heterosexual romantic couple watched a series of slides of very attractive and very unattractive people. Only that one member of the couple could see the slides. The person who could see the slides lied half the time and told the truth half the time about his or her actual feelings about the attractiveness of the people in the slides. The other member of the couple tried to tell when the first member was lying or telling the truth. On this direct measure of lie detection accuracy, partners were correct 52 per cent of the time. However, Anderson also included complete strangers in the design. The strangers were accurate at detecting the exact same truths and lies 58 per cent of the time. So the strangers were better than the romantic partners at knowing whether the person really did find the various people in the slides to be attractive. (See Table 2.11.) The strangers were also more accurate than the romantic partners when their direct ratings of deceptiveness were made on rating scales rather than on dichotomous measures.

Anderson also included a series of indirect measures. He asked the judges to indicate, for example, how confident they felt about each of their judgements of deceptiveness, whether they felt that they had got enough information, and how suspicious they felt. On almost all of these indirect measures, both the strangers and the romantic partners were

Table 2.11 *Direct and indirect deception detection: strangers and heterosexual romantic partners*

	Direct deception detection (% accuracy)	
	Strangers	*Partners*
	58	52
	Indirect deception detection[a]	
Indirect Cue	*Strangers*	*Partners*
Confidence	.35	.58
Got enough information	.15	.41
Suspiciousness	.11	.60
Other judge seems suspicious	.12	.41
Judge thinks sender senses suspiciousness	−.19	.04

[a] Scores are difference scores, e.g., confidence ratings when judging truths minus confidence ratings when judging lies. Positive values indicate accurate discriminations. Ratings were made on 9-point scales.
From 'Cognitive and motivational processes underlying truth bias', D. E. Anderson, 1999, unpublished dissertation.

accurate. They could both distinguish the truths from the lies with these indirect ratings. For example, they felt more confident when they had just heard a truth than when they had just heard a lie. They also felt that they had obtained more information when they had heard a truth, and they felt more suspicious when they had just heard a lie. Interestingly, on all of these indirect measures, the degree to which the perceivers could separate the truths from the lies was greater for the romantic partners than for the strangers! (See Table 2.11.) So, even though the partners did worse than the strangers on the most direct and explicit measure, which involved calling their partners liars some of the time, they did reliably better than the strangers on the more indirect measures. In some ways, the partners were picking up on some important behaviours that the strangers were missing.

What we do not yet understand but would very much like to explore, is this disconnection between partners' direct ratings of deceptiveness and their gut intuitions. Are the partners not aware that their feelings of confidence and suspiciousness and perceptions of other people's suspiciousness are varying in ways that could be meaningful? Do they have any clue at all that there could be a link between these kinds of feelings and whether or not their partner is lying? And if they were clued in on this clue, would it even matter? Could they use that information effectively, or would their attempts to use it undermine the process whereby they form these meaningful impressions and intuitions? And finally, the more sinister question: If they could use this information to find out who their partners really did find attractive, would they really want to know this? Maybe they should just let sleeping frauds lie.

Conclusions

As we noted at the beginning of this chapter, the existing research on deception detection should instil little faith that people are particularly good at this elusive skill. Although there are some ways in which liars behave differently from truth-tellers, there are no perfectly reliable cues to deception. Moreover, cues to deception differ according to factors such as the type of lie and the motivation for getting away with it. Practitioners working in a forensic context (or any other context) may be best served by using the results of our review as a source of suggestions, each of which needs to be validated within that context. For example, if detectives had a set of videotapes of actual interrogations in which suspects had been confirmed to be lying or telling the truth, those tapes could be useful in several ways. First, the tapes could be analysed to determine whether the same behaviours that generally separate liars from truth-tellers also do so in the context of the interrogations. Second, the tapes might be useful in training detectives to detect deception more successfully. Perhaps the detectives could be trained to attend preferentially to the cues that really are valid and to ignore the ones that are misleading. Our research also raises the question of whether deception detection would be improved if detectives were trained to monitor and use indirect cues such as their own comfort level. This remains to be seen. It is not clear whether people can successfully introspect on how they are feeling once they are aware of the relationship between indirect cues and deception. We hope that future research will shed some light on the many important questions that still need to be addressed.

REFERENCES

Anderson, D. E. (1999). Cognitive and motivational processes underlying truth bias. Unpublished doctoral dissertation, University of Virginia.
Anderson, D. E., DePaulo, B. M., and Ansfield, M. E. (2002). The development of deception detection skill: A longitudinal study of samesex friends. *Personality and Social Psychology Bulletin*, *28*, 536–45.

Anderson, D. E., DePaulo, B. M., Ansfield, M. E., Tickle, J. J., and Green, E. (1999). Beliefs about cues to deception: Mindless stereotypes or untapped wisdom? *Journal of Nonverbal Behavior*, *23*, 67–89.

Bond, C. F., Jr, and DePaulo, B. M. (2004). Accuracy and truth bias in the detection of deception. Manuscript in preparation.

Bond, C. F., Jr, and Fahey, W. E. (1987). False suspicion and the misperception of deceit. *British Journal of Social Psychology*, *26*, 41–6.

Cohen, J. (1988). *Statistical power analysis for the behavioral sciences* (rev. edn). Hillsdale, NJ: Lawrence Erlbaum.

DePaulo, B. M., Charlton, K., Cooper, H., Lindsay, J. J., and Muhlenbruck, L. (1997). The accuracy–confidence correlation in the detection of deception. *Personality and Social Psychology Review*, *1*, 346–57.

DePaulo, B. M., Jordan, A., Irvine, A., and Laser, P. S. (1982). Age changes in the detection of deception. *Child Development*, *53*, 701–9.

DePaulo, B. M., and Kirkendol, S. E. (1989). The motivational impairment effect in the communication of deception. In J. C. Yuille (ed.), *Credibility assessment* (pp. 51–70). Dordrecht, the Netherlands: Kluwer Academic.

DePaulo, B. M., Lindsay, J. J., Malone, B. E., Muhlenbruck, L., Charlton, K., and Cooper, H. (2003). Cues to deception. *Psychological Bulletin*, *129*, 74–118.

DePaulo, B. M., and Rosenthal, R. (1979). Telling lies. *Journal of Personality and Social Psychology*, *37*, 1713–22.

DePaulo, B. M., Rosenthal, R., Green, C. R., and Rosenkrantz, J. (1982). Diagnosing deceptive and mixed messages from verbal and non-verbal cues. *Journal of Experimental Social Psychology*, *18*, 433–46.

Ekman, P. (1985). *Telling lies*. New York: Norton. (Reprinted, 1992.)

Ekman, P., Friesen, W. V., and O'Sullivan, M. (1988). Smiles while lying. *Journal of Personality and Social Psychology*, *54*, 414–20.

Granhag, P. A., and Strömwall, L. A. (2000). Deception detection: Examining the consistency heuristic. In C. M. Breur, M. M. Kommer, J. F. Nijboer, and J. M. Reintjes, (eds.), *New trends in criminal investigation and evidence II* (pp. 309–21). Antwerpen: Intersentia.

Hall, M. E. (1986). Detecting deception in the voice: An analysis of fundamental frequency, syllabic duration, and amplitude of the human voice. Unpublished doctoral dissertation, Michigan State University.

Horvath, F. S. (1973). Verbal and non-verbal clues to truth and deception during polygraph examinations. *Journal of Police Science and Administration*, *1*, 138–52.

Horvath, F., Jayne, B. C., and Buckley, J. (1994). Differentiation of truthful and deceptive criminal suspects in behaviour analysis interviews. *Journal of Forensic Sciences*, *39*, 793–807.

Hurd, K., and Noller, P. (1988). Decoding deception: A look at the process. *Journal of Nonverbal Behavior*, *12*, 217–33.

Inbau, F. E., Reid, J. E., Buckley, J. P., and Jayne, B. C. (2001). *Criminal interrogation and confessions* (4th edn). Gaithersburg, MD: Aspen.

Vrij, A. (2000). *Detecting lies and deceit*. Chichester, England: John Wiley.

Vrij, A., Akehurst, L., and Morris, P. (1997). Individual differences in hand movements during deception. *Journal of Nonverbal Behavior*, *21*, 87–101.

Vrij, A., Edward, K., and Bull, R. (2001). Police officers' ability to detect deceit: The benefit of indirect deception detection measures. *Legal and Criminological Psychology*, *6*, 185–96.

Yuille, J. C., and Cutshall, J. (1989). Analysis of statements of victims, witnesses, and suspects. In J. C. Yuille (ed.), *Credibility assessment* (pp. 175–91). Dordrecht, the Netherlands: Kluwer Academic.

3 Statement Validity Analysis and the 'detection of the truth'

Günter Köhnken

The success of a criminal investigation often depends on witness statements, particularly if no other evidence is available. This is typically – although not exclusively – the case in sexual-abuse cases.

The fundamental question to be answered in evaluating a witness statement is whether or not (and to what extent) the statement is a correct and complete description of the event in question. Answering this question first requires the identification of potential sources of incorrect accounts. Based on this information appropriate diagnostic procedures and techniques can be applied in order to assess the probability of the correctness of the statement. An account may differ from the facts for two possible reasons (see Figure 3.1):

1) A witness, who is motivated to give a correct account of the events in question may be subject to unintentional errors, or
2) The witness deliberately and intentionally tells a lie.

The crucial difference between these alternatives is in the witnesses' motivation. Furthermore, in both cases one can think of stable personal or of transient situational factors as the major cause for incorrect accounts. For example, sensory or intellectual deficiencies may prevent a witness from perceiving or reporting certain events. On the other hand, darkness or lack of attention may result in incomplete perceptions in a certain situation. Similarly, intentional distortions or complete lies can be conceived as being caused by stable personality factors like antisociality (which affect what has been called 'general credibility of the witness') or by a situation-specific motivation to tell a lie (which impacts on the 'specific credibility of the statement'). Although stable personality factors may influence a witness's readiness to tell a lie (e.g., different people may have more or less fear that their lie is discovered), it would be impossible to assess the credibility of a particular statement on the basis of general personality factors alone. Of course, even people who are in general very honest may, under certain circumstances, be motivated to give an incorrect account and vice versa.

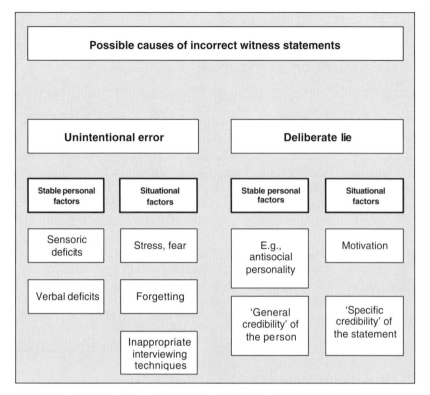

Figure 3.1 Possible causes of incorrect witness statements

Several approaches to assess the truthfulness of a communication (like a witness statement) have been reported in the literature, for example, non-verbal and paraverbal behaviour (see Bond and Rao, DePaulo and Morris, Vrij, all in this volume), and physiological phenomena such as skin conductance or blood pressure (Honts, this volume). All these approaches have in common the focus on indicators of deception. A different approach to judging the truthfulness of an account, the 'Statement Validity Analysis' (SVA) has emerged in forensic psychology in Sweden (Trankell, 1963) and in Germany (Undeutsch, 1967; Arntzen, 1970). Rather than attempting to detect deception by looking for behavioural or physiological correlates of deception this approach focuses on variables which are associated with the truthfulness of an account. Although SVA has primarily been applied to assess the credibility of child witness statements in sexual-abuse cases (when no other evidence than the child's statement is available), it is by no means restricted to this particular constellation. The underlying idea or theoretical framework applies as well to adults as it does to children. Furthermore, this method is not limited to the assessment of accounts on sexual abuse. There is now a substantial body of empirical research that has evaluated the validity of SVA with children of different ages as well as with adolescents and adults and with accounts on a large variety of topics (Vrij, 2003).

This chapter will describe the basic ideas underlying SVA, the diagnostic procedure and the techniques to assess the truthfulness of a statement, empirical research on SVA and the limits of this technique.

What is Statement Validity Analysis?

SVA is a comprehensive procedure for generating and testing hypotheses about the source of a given statement. It includes methods of collecting data which are relevant with regard to the hypotheses in question, techniques of analysing these data, and guidelines for drawing conclusions regarding the initial hypotheses. The basic question to be answered is: what is the source of this statement? Does the statement describe personal experiences of the witness or does it have another source?

SVA is not a psychometric test nor is it a kind of mechanistic checklist approach. Like many other forms of medical, psychiatric, or psychological assessment it is a combination of psychometric tests, semi-structured interviews, systematic analysis techniques, and clinical judgement. SVA comprises several components (see Table 3.1).

Case-file analysis

A proper interview of the witness can hardly be done without any background information about the witness (e.g., his or her age, cognitive abilities, relationship to the accused person), the event in question (e.g., type of event, a single event, or repeated occurrences), previous statements (e.g., how often has the witness been interviewed, what has he or she reported and case characteristics, are there any inconsistencies between repeated accounts), and other case characteristics (e.g., time interval between the event in question and the first disclosure, degree of consistency of the statement with other evidence, relevant other events such as a divorce, problems in school, etc.). This information is utilised to generate hypotheses about the source of the statement, possible reasons for false accusations, etc. Thus, the first stage of SVA is not, as it has been pointed out by some authors, a semi-structured interview, but a thorough analysis of the case file. It would indeed be rather naïve to conduct an interview without having any diagnostic strategy and hypotheses to test using the interview data.

Table 3.1 *Components of SVA*

Analysis of the case file
Generation of hypotheses about the source of the statement
Decision on assessment methods which are appropriate to test the hypotheses

Examination of the witness
   ➢ history-taking interview with witness or parents
   ➢ application of personality questionnaires and cognitive abilities tests
   ➢ interview of the witness about the event in question

Content analysis of the statement (or relevant parts of it) using CBCA criteria

Evaluation of the CBCA results taking into account
   ➢ cognitive abilities of the witness (e.g., verbal fluency, creativity, general intelligence)
   ➢ particular knowledge and experiences of the witness (e.g., previous sexual experiences in a case of sexual abuse, access to porno videos, literature, conversation with others about similar events)
   ➢ case characteristics (e.g., time between the event in question and the interview, complexity of the event)

Analysis of consistency of repeated statements

Analysis of the origin of the statement and its further development
   ➢ circumstances of initial disclosure
   ➢ responses of others to first disclosure
   ➢ previous interviews

Evaluation of hypotheses in light of the results of the various assessments methods; hypotheses, which are not compatible with the diagnostic results are rejected; if all hypotheses for other sources than own experience are rejected, the veracity of the statement is assumed.

Generation of hypotheses

One of the most important and indeed crucial components of SVA is a careful generation of hypotheses, that is, assumptions about potential sources or origins of the given statement. Everything else, the whole assessment procedure, the data to be collected, and the particular evaluation strategies depend on these hypotheses.

One hypothesis assumes that the statement is the result of one's own experiences with the accused person, that is, that it is a truthful statement, whereas the alternative overall hypothesis claims that the reported event has never happened, at least not in the form that is described or not with the accused person. This overall hypothesis is then broken down into more specific assumptions about potential sources of a presumed incorrect statement.

Complete fabrication

The event that is described in the statement may be completely fictitious, that is, it never happened to the witness. The witness may have intentionally invented the statement in order to achieve certain personal goals (e.g., jealousy against mother's new partner, excuse for own inappropriate behaviour or bad school achievement). According to this hypothesis the complete statement has been intentionally fabricated.

Partial fabrication

It is possible that large parts of the statement are correct accounts of a certain course of events, whereas some crucial elements are fabricated. This sometimes happens in cases of alleged rape. The accused person may admit contacts with the witness, even a sexual relationship and an encounter at the location mentioned by the witness. It is, however, denied that any sexual activity happened without explicit or at least implicit consent. Obviously, under such circumstances the lying witness would not have to fabricate the complete statement. For example, the location, clothing, physical characteristics, and certain behaviours of the accused person can be described from the witness's original memory. Only those sequences of the statement that describe his or her resistance and any resulting specific forms of interaction would have to be fabricated.

Incorrect transference

Another form of partial fabrication can occur if the witness has indeed experienced the event in question (or at least something similar to it), but with another person than the one who is accused. For example, a child may have had previous experiences of sexual abuse or a woman may have been raped before. In such a case the event itself is reported from memory while the particular relations to the accused person, the time and location would have been fabricated.

Instruction by others

It is possible that a child witness has been instructed by another person, usually an adult, to claim incorrectly that something has happened. This may happen, for example, in custody conflicts after a divorce. The statement would then not be fabricated by the child witness, but by an adult instructor, and communicated to the child.

Suggestion

Research has shown that suggestive procedures in interviews or in psycho-therapy can produce false memories which are subjectively perceived as truthful. It is therefore possible that the witness has experienced suggestive influences and that these have produced a statement which is now perceived as a truthful account by the witness.

Mental illness

A witness may have problems distinguishing fact and fantasy as a symptom of mental illness (e.g., a psychosis). He or she may then take fictitious events as real and subjectively give a truthful account.

These hypotheses are just some examples, not an exhaustive list, of potential sources of incorrect statements. On the other hand, not all of these hypotheses are relevant in any specific certain case. For example, there may not be any indication for a mental illness nor opportunities for any suggestive influences.

Setting up a diagnostic strategy and deciding upon assessment methods

The hypotheses which have been generated based on the results of the case-file analysis are now used to set up a diagnostic strategy, to decide which assessment techniques (e.g., psychometric tests, interviews) are suitable in light of these hypotheses and how certain assessment techniques have to be fine tuned. For example, in the case of a 'partial-fabrication' hypothesis (see the example of alleged rape above) the interview has to focus on those elements of the event/situation which are diagnostically relevant, which are likely to discriminate between a truthful and a (partially) fabricated statement and thus help to decide upon the plausibility of this hypothesis. A detailed description of the location may be of minor diagnostic significance only if it is not disputed that the witness has been there. If the hypothesis of incorrect transference has been proposed, the interview would focus particularly on those elements that relate the described event to the accused person and to the time and location where it presumably happened because these are the elements which would have been fabricated according to this hypothesis. These are, therefore, the diagnostically relevant parts of the statement.

If a hypothesis of mental illness has been proposed, it may be necessary to evaluate hospital files, to ask the court to hear the report of the psychiatrist who has treated the witness, or to apply clinical assessment procedures before interviewing the witness. Similarly, if the case file reveals that a witness has been inappropriately interviewed before, has been in psychotherapy, etc., data would be collected with regard to the hypothesis of false memories before any interview is done. In this case a thorough analysis of the circumstances of the first disclosure, the responses of others to these reports, the type of conversations and questions that have been asked, the types of therapy, etc. has to be performed.

In order to evaluate the hypothesis of a complete or partial fabrication of the statement, a judgement has to be made as to whether or not the witness would have been able to fabricate this statement. This is done using the CBCA criteria. However, since the quality of a statement's content is obviously related to his or her cognitive and verbal abilities, it is usually necessary to assess these variables, too, for example with cognitive abilities tests.

These examples demonstrate that the assessment procedure and techniques largely depend on the hypotheses that have been generated based on the case file analysis. It is therefore obvious that an interview of the witness cannot reasonably be the first stage of SVA. Indeed, in light of some hypotheses it may not even be advisable to interview the witness at all. If, for example, the witness has participated in a highly suggestive therapy over a considerable period of time, it may be impossible to generate an uncontaminated statement. In such a case interviewing the witness may be useless.

Examination of the witness

When the diagnostic strategy has been set up and relevant assessment techniques have been selected, the witness is examined. If it is a child witness the examination usually begins with a history-taking interview with the parents. Such an interview helps to determine whether or not critical life events have happened to the witness (e.g., accidents, divorce of parents, school failure) which may be related to the statement. It also provides additional background information about a witness, his or her developmental stage, diseases, etc.

The exact sequence of the application of further assessment procedures largely depends on the particular circumstances and may vary from case to case. However, the examination almost always includes an interview of the witness. Furthermore, it is necessary to assess the witness's cognitive and verbal abilities. Sometimes psychometric tests (e.g., intelligence tests) are applied. In other cases other sources of information (personal impression during the examination, school reports, and results of previous tests) are available so that no additional testing is required.

The interview is a crucial part of SVA. The details of this special form of investigative interview have been described elsewhere (e.g., Köhnken, 2003) and need not be repeated here (see also Bull, 1998). This interview is *investigative*, not therapeutic. Indeed, therapeutic interviews should, whenever possible, be postponed until after the investigative interview(s) in order to avoid any suggestive contamination of the statement. It is important to stimulate the witness to give a free report of the event in question before asking any questions. The questioning part of the interview should start with open-ended questions. Of course, a witness should not be prompted to produce certain contents which relate to any CBCA criteria. Most of the CBCA criteria depend on proper interviewing. For example, an 'unstructured production' can occur in a statement only if the interviewer does not structure the interview and does not force the witness into a particular schedule. Police interviews, even if they are available as verbatim transcripts, are usually not suitable for a CBCA because they are often highly structured by the interviewer and focused on details which are relevant for the criminal investigation, while other details are more or less neglected (e.g., accounts of own or perpetrator's mental state during the incident). Furthermore, police interviewers have rather different hypotheses in mind from the ones outlined above. Consequently, their interviews will focus on different aspects of an incident. Katofsky (2002) and Eggers (2002) have shown that, although police interview transcripts can be coded reliably, the proportion of correct classifications as truthful or fabricated is considerably lower than the ones reported in other studies (e.g., Vrij, 2003).

Criteria-Based Content Analysis

Before a CBCA is applied the diagnostically relevant parts of the interview transcript have to be selected. As it has been pointed out above, any components of a statement are meaningful only if they are able to distinguish between truthful and (partially) fabricated statements. Applying CBCA criteria without any selective differentiation can lead to completely meaningless results. This again demonstrates the importance of appropriate hypotheses *before* the examination begins.

CBCA is based on the hypothesis that statements based on memory of one's own experiences differ in certain content features from fabricated statements. This hypothesis was originally stated by Undeutsch (1967). He has assumed that fabricated accounts, among other things, contain fewer details, are less vivid and less colourful than statements derived from original memory. Köhnken (1996) has later proposed to differentiate this global hypothesis into a cognitive and a motivational part. The latter can be related to impression management theory (Tedeschi and Norman, 1985). The cognitive part of the hypothesis states that, given a certain level of cognitive and verbal abilities, only a person who has actually experienced an event will be able to produce a statement with the characteristics that are described in the CBCA criteria (see Table 3.2). It is, for example, deemed unlikely that a child who fabricates an account will deliberately invent unexpected complications that allegedly happened during the incident. The impression-management component relates to motivation and social behaviour. It is assumed that lying is a goal-directed behaviour and that a person who deliberately invents a story wants to be perceived as honest in order to achieve his or her goals. Therefore, the person is likely to avoid behaviours which, in his or her view, may be interpreted as clues to deception. For instance, if a liar believes that admitting lack of memory will undermine his or her perceived credibility, he or she will try to avoid such behaviour. This impression-management approach assumes that people have a common stereotype about the typical behaviour accompanying a lie. Provided that a particular behaviour can be sufficiently controlled it is expected that a liar, in order to conceal his or her lie, attempts to avoid such behaviour. Based on these hypotheses a number of content features have been described which are likely to occur in accounts of genuine experiences but less likely to be found in fabricated statements. Thus, these criteria can be used to test the hypothesis of (partial) fabrication of the statement. Undeutsch (1967) was the first to describe a comprehensive list of such features which were initially named 'credibility criteria'. Similar lists of content characteristics have been published by Arntzen (1970) and Littmann and Szewczyk (1983). These lists have been combined and integrated by Steller and Köhnken (1989) into a list of nineteen reality criteria (see Table 3.2).

Logical structure requires that the statement contains no contradictions or logical inconsistencies. It is important to note that neither the account of unusual details (criterion 8) nor the report of unexpected complications (criterion 7) interfere with the logical consistency. Furthermore, logical consistency is not the same as plausibility. A statement may sound implausible but nevertheless be logically consistent.

Unstructured production. Sometimes a witness reports various elements of an incident in an unsystematic, chronologically disorganised manner. They follow their momentary associations rather than a logical and chronological sequence. This is extremely difficult without any genuine memories and, therefore, unlikely to occur in fabricated statements.

Quantity of details. The event, the location and surroundings, and the people involved are described in great detail.

Table 3.2 *CBCA criteria (from Steller and Köhnken, 1989)*

General characteristics
  1. Logical structure
  2. Unstructured production
  3. Quantity of details

Specific contents
  4. Contextual embedding
  5. Descriptions of interactions
  6. Reproduction of conversation
  7. Reporting of unexpected complications during the incident

Peculiarities of content
  8. Unusual details
  9. Superfluous details
  10. Accurately reported details misunderstood
  11. Related external associations
  12. Accounts of subjective mental states
  13. Attribution of perpetrator's mental state

Motivation-related contents
  14. Spontaneous corrections
  15. Admitting lack of memory
  16. Raising doubts about one's own testimony
  17. Self-deprecation
  18. Pardoning the perpetrator

Offence-specific elements
  19. Details characteristic of the offence

Contextual embedding means that the event in question is described as related to particular locations, time schedules, personal relationships to the accused and other persons before and after the incident. Furthermore, a congruence of the witness's own behaviour as it is described in the statement and his or her personality characteristics can be particularly interesting.

Descriptions of interactions. Naturally occurring events are usually characterised by a sequence of actions and reactions. The reactions or responses can be explained psychologically as consequences of previous actions. Particularly for child witnesses, it is difficult to fabricate psychologically comprehensible sequences of interactions.

The *reproduction of conversation* differs from the previous criterion in one important aspect. It means that the witness reproduces conversations between different persons in a kind of role-play, thereby using the particular speech behaviour, vocabulary, etc. of those persons.

Reporting of unexpected complications. Sometimes the course of events is interrupted by unexpected complications and obstacles. The range of these complications can extend from an unforeseen interruption or difficulty to the spontaneous stopping of the event before its logical completion. Fabricating witnesses rarely mention any deviations from the 'normal', simple way.

Unusual details refer to particular elements or details of a statement which are unexpected and surprising, e.g., odd details which are not obviously unrealistic.

Superfluous details. Details are superfluous if their reporting is not strictly necessary for the description of the incident in question.

Accurately reported details misunderstood. This criterion is particularly important for the evaluation of children's testimony. It means that details and actions are reported which are obviously not understood by the child in their particular meaning and function (as sometimes indicated by erroneous interpretations of correctly described observations).

Related external associations. It means that, for example, a witness describes conversations with the perpetrator that refer to earlier events which are in some way related to the incriminated actions. For example, in a report about an incestuous relationship, such associations would be reports of the witness (daughter) about conversations with the perpetrator (father) in which they discussed the sexual experiences of the daughter with other partners.

Accounts of subjective mental states. The accounts of subjective mental states include the description of feelings such as disgust or fear and the reporting of crime-related cognitions like, for example, thinking about how to escape. However, the mere mentioning of a particular emotion like, for instance, fear would not be sufficient to fulfil this criterion. What is important is the description of the development and change of emotions and/or cognitions during the event.

Attribution of the perpetrator's mental state means the description of emotions, cognitions, and motivations which were attributed to the alleged perpetrator.

Spontaneous corrections. A witness corrects or modifies previous descriptions without having been prompted by the interviewer.

Admitting lack of memory. A witness expresses concern that he or she may not remember all relevant details, that the description of particular details may be incorrect, etc.

Raising doubts about one's own testimony. The witness indicates that part of his or her description sounds odd, implausible, unlikely, etc., that he or she can hardly believe that this is a correct account of what had happened.

Self-deprecation. The witness mentions personally unfavourable, self-incriminating details.

Pardoning the perpetrator. The witness excuses the accused person for his or her behaviour.

Details characteristic of the offence. The witness describes elements which are typical for this type of crime but, on the other hand, are counter intuitive for the general public or discrepant to everyday knowledge or stereotypes.

Evaluation of CBCA results

Similar to the evaluation of psychometric tests CBCA is a two-step process. The first stage is the analysis of the statement with regard to the CBCA criteria. The result of this first stage is a 'raw score', a compilation of content characteristics which are related to any of the CBCA criteria. As such, these data are completely meaningless. Remember that the question to be answered with the help of CBCA is whether or not *this* witness would have been able to fabricate *this* statement with the content qualities identified in the account without having personally experienced the event described. Obviously an adult witness with good cognitive and verbal abilities, creativity, general knowledge, etc. will be able to fabricate a much more detailed report with, for example, rich contextual embedding, complications, etc. than we can expect from a young child. As a consequence, the same content-analysis results (i.e., the 'raw score') have to be judged differently for a young child than for an adult, for a less intelligent, less creative child than for a child of the same age but with better cognitive abilities.

Therefore, in a second step, the results of the content analysis (i.e., the compilation of certain content characteristics) have to be related to a reference or a standard. This is the reason why SVA includes the assessment of the witnesses' cognitive abilities: this information is utilised in order to generate a standard to which the content qualities can be compared. A certain criterion is then and only then fulfilled (or more or less pronounced) in a statement, when this particular content feature is unlikely to occur in a statement fabricated by *this* witness. For example, a witness in a sexual-abuse case reports that the accused person has threatened the victim because of the possibility that he or she might tell others about the incident. This detail is *related to* the criterion 'details characteristic of the offence'. 'Related to' does not mean, however, that the criterion is automatically fulfilled. If, for example, the witness knows (from the literature, magazines, TV, teachers, etc.) that perpetrators often threaten their victims in order to prevent them from telling others about the event, then this detail is rather trivial. It does not discriminate between fabricated and truthful accounts and is, therefore, diagnostically meaningless.

There are, of course, no quasi-psychometric or statistical rules which can be applied in order to generate these standards or references. There will probably never be any 'norm tables' like there are for psychometric tests or personality questionnaires, because it is very unlikely that all potentially relevant variables (e.g., type of event, time interval, previous interviews, cognitive abilities) can ever be taken into account. Hence, this is part of the expert's clinical judgement.

If CBCA leads to the conclusion that a fabrication of this statement by this witness is unlikely, then this (fabrication or partial fabrication) hypothesis is rejected. Note that this is only an intermediate result. As long as there are other potential sources of the statement (e.g., suggestion), it does not automatically mean that it is based on own experiences. It only means that it is unlikely to have been fabricated. If, on the other hand, the CBCA results are not sufficient to reject the fabrication hypothesis, no further analyses are necessary. It will then not be possible to conclude reliably that the statement is based on own experiences.

It is, of course, possible that some events which are described in a statement have been experienced whereas others are fabricated. In the case of such a 'partial-fabrication' hypothesis the statement is segmented into individual descriptions of single events or components. CBCA is then applied to each of these elements separately. This procedure may lead to a rejection of the fabrication hypothesis for some of the reported events but not for others (e.g., if certain events are described in great detail, with complications, contextual embedding, etc. whereas the description of other elements remains vague). Thus, there is no general assumption underlying CBCA that a statement is either completely truthful or completely fabricated, as Vrij (2003) has pointed out. Consequently, the proposition that there is no procedure to distinguish between experienced and non-experienced portions within the same account (Vrij, 2003) is not correct.

Analysis of consistency

If the witness has been interviewed repeatedly and if these interviews are well documented in the case file, it is possible to compare the statements in order to identify any discrepancies. Contrary to widespread assumptions it is not required that two or more accounts do not differ in any detail in order to be judged as credible. Indeed it has never been claimed that truthful accounts given at different times have to be identical (e.g., Arntzen, 1970; Köhnken, 2003; Undeutsch, 1967). On the contrary, one would rather become suspicious if two statements given at different times are almost identical (e.g., Littmann and Szewczyk, 1983). In line with this position recent research has shown that truthful accounts given at different times are more or less inconsistent (see, e.g., Granhag and Strömwall, 1999, 2002). If, however, substantial discrepancies are found in the description of the core of an event, then this would at least require an explanation.

Evaluation of additional hypotheses

If the (partial) fabrication hypothesis is rejected, it is still possible that the statement does not describe own experiences. The statement could be the result of previous suggestive interviews or psychotherapeutic interpretations. In this case CBCA may produce results which are similar to the ones obtained for truthful statements (Böhm, 1999; Erdmann, 2001). Therefore, CBCA cannot help to decide upon a suggestion hypothesis. Instead, based on relevant information taken from the case file and on additional statements from other witnesses, the circumstances of the first disclosure, the 'birth of the statement' is analysed. If, for example, the first disclosure was made immediately after an alleged incident and the witness was interviewed shortly thereafter by the police, there may not have been any room for suggestive influences, and this hypothesis can thus be rejected. In other cases many conversations, formal and informal questionings, and perhaps psychotherapeutic sessions may have preceded the first documented interview by the police. It will then be much more difficult, or perhaps even impossible, to rule out the possibility of suggestion as the major source of the statement. Other hypotheses like, for example, the possibility of a mental disease and a related inability to distinguish fact from fantasy are usually evaluated before the witness is interviewed and a CBCA is performed.

Final judgement of statement credibility

The final conclusion on statement credibility is the result of evaluating all relevant hypotheses about potential sources of the statement. Data are collected and evaluated in light of these hypotheses. A hypothesis which is incompatible with the diagnostic findings is considered to be insufficient and thus rejected. This process is continued until either all hypotheses which suggest that the statement is incorrect are rejected (leaving only the hypothesis of own experiences as the source of the statement) or until an alternative hypothesis (i.e., one that assumes another source than own experiences) cannot be rejected based on the available data. In this case, the conclusion would be that SVA cannot positively confirm that the source of the statement is the witness's own experience. Note that this does not automatically mean that the witness is lying. It is quite possible that the statement is a truthful account of own experiences but due to inconclusive, ambiguous data or suggestive questioning alternative hypotheses could not be rejected. SVA is, therefore, a one-dimensional assessment procedure. If all other hypotheses are rejected, the hypothesis of own experiences as the source of the statement remains the only plausible explanation. Thus, SVA can be called a method for 'detection of the truth' rather than a 'lie-detection' technique.

This does not mean, however, as Rassin (2001) has pointed out, that CBCA is 'exclusively directed at the detection of signs supporting credibility' (p. 273). Furthermore, the assumption that CBCA 'seeks to confirm the allegations' made by victims of alleged sexual abuse and 'is directed at proving that the suspect is guilty' (p. 273) is a complete misrepresentation of the basic idea underlying SVA and CBCA. The extended discussion of the importance of generating and testing alternative hypotheses has shown that SVA, just contrary to Rassin's (2001) notion, indeed follows exactly the guidelines of Popper's (1968) falsification theory.

Limitations of SVA

Like any other diagnostic technique or procedure, SVA has a 'focus of convenience', that is, circumstances under which sufficiently reliable and valid classification results can be expected, and situations in which it is only of limited value or may even not be applicable at all.

No statement available

Since the major part of SVA is the content analysis of a statement, it cannot be applied if no statement is available. This can, for example, happen with very young children or with people with learning disabilities.

Insufficient material

In particular circumstances a detailed statement may be available but it may nevertheless not contain enough material that is suitable for a CBCA. This happens sometimes in cases of alleged rape where the accused person admits sexual intercourse at the location in question but denies that it happened without the consent of the witness. The basic assumption underlying CBCA and SVA is whether or not the witness would have been able to fabricate the statement without having personally experienced the event in question. If the witness has indeed been at the location and had sexual intercourse with the accused person, then it would not be necessary to fabricate the description of the location, the clothing, perhaps even physical characteristics of the accused person. Therefore, the diagnostically relevant part of the statement may, for example, be reduced to the description of resistance, violence, and related interactions. This may then not be sufficient to apply CBCA. It is also possible that the event in question was rather short, simple, without any special elements (e.g., a single inappropriate touch). If, in addition, the time interval between the event in question and the interview is rather long, the resulting statement may be too short to allow a thorough content analysis.

Previous suggestive questioning

Research on suggestion has shown that repeated suggestive questioning might produce statements which are very similar to accounts of own experiences (for reviews, see, e.g., Eisen, Quas, and Goodman, 2002; Westcott, Davies and Bull, 2002). CBCA and SVA have been constructed to discriminate truthful from fabricated statements, not to discriminate truthful from suggested accounts. Recent research has shown that it may indeed be impossible to discriminate reliably truthful from suggested statements using CBCA (Böhm, 1999; Erdmann, 2001). Similar problems can arise from previous psychotherapeutic treatment. Some forms of psychotherapy have a considerable suggestive potential (e.g., if the therapist suggests interpretations to the patient or if anatomically correct dolls are used to 'uncover' suspected sexual abuse).

Coaching

There is now increasing empirical evidence which shows that witnesses can be coached to produce statements with CBCA-relevant contents. Coached (fabricated) statements may, therefore, not be distinguishable from truthful statements (Lösel and Raichle, 2001; Volbert and Rutta, 2001; Vrij, Kneller, and Mann, 2000; Vrij, Akehurst, Soukara, and Bull, 2002).

Inappropriate interviewing

It has been emphasised that a proper interview of the witness is required in order to apply CBCA. It is not only important to follow the general guidelines for good practice in interviewing (e.g., Bull, 1998). In addition, the interview has to be focused on those aspects of the event in question that are relevant for evaluating the initial hypotheses. We have found, for example, that although the CBCA criteria could be reliably coded in police interviews, the proportion of correct classifications was rather poor and well below the results of other studies (Eggers, 2002; Katofsky, 2002). In the light of these results it is at least questionable whether CBCA can reliably be applied to statements which have been generated using insufficient interview techniques. Preferably the interview should be conducted by a person who is experienced in CBCA and SVA.

Given these limitations of SVA it appears necessary to evaluate whether the requirements for the application of SVA and CBCA are met. If they are not, SVA will probably not be of much help in evaluating the truthfulness of a statement.

Empirical foundations of SVA

Although SVA has a long tradition at least in Germany, systematic empirical research, and experimental research in particular, has been rare until fairly recently (apart from an early experimental study by Köhnken and Wegener, 1982). Almost all of the more recent studies have evaluated the classification accuracy of CBCA rather than the validity of the outcome of the whole SVA procedure (see Vrij, 2003, for a review). Although interrater reliability of coding of CBCA criteria is an essential prerequisite for valid classifications, systematic research on this issue is even more recent.

Interrater reliability

Since CBCA is a major part of Statement Validity Analysis, a reliable coding of the criteria is essential for valid classifications of statements as fabricated or truthful. Identifying CBCA criteria in transcribed statements, particularly in children's accounts, is a rather complex task which requires a good deal of training and experience. Without any training, little consistency/agreement can be expected in the coding of CBCA criteria between raters (interrater agreement) as well as for the repeated coding of the same statements by one coder (intrarater agreement). This will result in high proportions of error variance in the outcome of content analysis. As a consequence, it will be less likely to find significant differences between truthful and fabricated statements. Vrij (2003) found in a review of thirty-seven studies on CBCA and SVA that in most of these studies the differences in CBCA scores were in the predicted direction but sometimes missed the significance levels. It is quite possible that some of the failures to significantly discriminate truthful from fabricated statements were due to insufficient training of the coders.

Table 3.3 *Components of CBCA coder training*

1. Reading of relevant book chapters, research papers, and detailed descriptions of CBCA criteria
2. Lectures on observation and rating methods and common rating errors
3. Presentation of extended criteria descriptions; discussion of positive and negative examples (i.e., sequences which are likely to be erroneously assigned to a certain criterion) of each criterion, homework assignment
4. Discussion and evaluation of homework, rehearsal of criteria descriptions, identification of criteria in transcribed statements, homework assignment
5. Discussion and evaluation of homework, introduction of rating scale, presentation and discussion of examples, homework assignment
6. Discussion and evaluation of homework, application of rating scale to transcribed statements, discussion of consistencies and discrepancies, comparison with expert ratings, homework assignment
7. Discussion and evaluation of homework, discussion with experts, presentation and discussion of examples of transcribed statements

Table 3.4 *Agenda of day 4 of CBCA coder training*

09:00–10:00	Knowledge test, rehearsal of criteria definitions
10:00–11:30	Evaluation and discussion of homework, comparison of criteria ratings, discussion of discrepant ratings
11:30–12:30	Analysis of example statement, identification of criteria, feedback, and discussion
12:30–13:30	Break
13:30–14:15	Group work: generation of 2–3 examples of a subset of criteria
14:15–15:00	Discussion of examples, participants identify criteria in transcribed statements
Homework assignment	Generation of additional examples

In order to reduce error variance in CBCA coding we have developed a thorough training programme for coders which has been used in all our studies on CBCA since the mid-1990s (e.g., Höfer, 1995; Köhnken and Höfer, 1999). The programme extends over three full weeks with five days a week and 7–8 hours per day during week 2 and 3 and comprises several components (see Table 3.3). The agenda of a typical training day is shown in Table 3.4. Several studies have been conducted to assess the effects of this training package on inter- and intrarater agreement using different indices of reliability (Eggers, 2002; Köhnken and Höfer, 1999; Krause, 1997; Petersen, 1997). In one of these studies (Petersen, 1997) three groups of coders read several articles and book chapters on CBCA, or attended a university seminar on statement credibility and SVA, or participated in the training programme. A control group received no treatment at all. Different selections of several transcribed statements were coded according to the CBCA criteria before and after training. In addition, raters re-coded the same statements again after a delay of three weeks in order to assess the intrarater agreement or stability of the codings.

The CBCA criteria were coded on five-point rating-scales ranging from $0 =$ 'not present' to $4 =$ 'strongly present'. A five-point scale was used (rather than three-point scales which have been applied in a number of other studies) because it proved to be more sensitive for smaller differences between truthful and fabricated statements.[1] Four indices of interrater agreement were used (kappa (Cohen, 1960; Fleiss, 1971), Maxwell's RE (Maxwell, 1977), percent agreement, and correlation) because each of these indices has its particular strengths and weaknesses. Kappa, for example, has the advantage of correcting for random agreement but may give inappropriate results in cases of asymmetric margin distributions (Petersen, 1997; Köhnken and Höfer, 1999). A correlation coefficient, on the other hand, underestimates the actual agreement when the variance is small (e.g., if raters highly agree that a particular criterion is *not* present). Training significantly increased the average interrater agreement across all criteria and all statements from around above 40 per cent in the baseline condition to almost 70 per cent whereas no improvement was achieved in the reading, seminar, and not training control group. The pattern of results was highly similar when agreement was expressed in terms of kappa or Maxwell's RE.

These results show that just reading texts on CBCA and SVA or attending a seminar does not increase interrater agreement substantially compared to a no-treatment control group. A retest shows that these effects appear to be fairly stable over a delay of three weeks with an average intrarater agreement around 75 per cent, as compared to around 50 per cent in all other groups. Six similar studies using different groups of raters and different statements lead to similar results.

When we looked at the interrater reliability for each individual CBCA criterion we found that the majority of discrepancies are not larger than one point on a five-point scale. For sixteen out of the nineteen reality criteria more than 90 per cent of the ratings did not differ more than one point on a five-point rating scale. Agreement between raters never fell below 80 per cent.

Taken together these results show that CBCA criteria can be coded at reliability levels which are comparable to the ones reported for common personality questionnaires. However, sufficient levels of intra- and interrater agreement were achieved only after thorough training. Without such training a high level of error variance may cover differences of small magnitude between fabricated and truthful statement.

Validity of CBCA scores

Vrij (2003) has recently reviewed thirty-seven (English language) studies on CBCA. He discovered that the expected differences were found in CBCA scores between liars and truth-tellers in all experimental research paradigms (actual involvement, watching a video or statements derived from memory). The findings published so far also support the assumption that CBCA is not restricted to statements of children who have been victims of sexual abuse but can also be used with adults and with different types of crime. Furthermore, the hypothesis that truth-tellers will obtain higher total CBCA scores than liars was examined in twelve of the studies reviewed by Vrij (2003), and in eleven out of these studies the hypothesis was supported. The differences were always in the expected direction but they were not always statistically significant. However, this may be due to insufficient training or to insensitive three-point rating scales.

The proportion of correct classifications in the studies reviewed by Vrij (2003) varied from 65 to 90 per cent with an average accuracy rate for truths of 73 per cent and for lies of 72 per cent. A recent experiment with 144 children that was not included in Vrij's review found an accuracy rate for false statements of 95 per cent and for correct statements of 75 per cent (Niehaus, 2001). These results clearly contradict Rassin's (2001) notion that investigations have 'suggested that CBCA primarily yields false positive results' (p. 269) and that 'CBCA suffers from an inherent truth bias, which results in an alarmingly high number of false positive decisions' (p. 276).

Conclusions

SVA has now been widely accepted by many courts in continental Europe (Germany, Switzerland, Austria, the Netherlands, Sweden) as well as in the United Kingdom. Recently the German Supreme Court has ruled that SVA is the method of choice whenever psychological experts submit their opinion regarding the credibility of a statement to a court. Similar rulings exist, for example, in Switzerland. Obviously, this acceptance is the result of strongly increased empirical, mainly experimental, research during the past two decades. Furthermore, attempts to develop a theoretical framework for SVA, to link CBCA to approaches like, for example, Reality Monitoring (Alonso-Quecuty, 1992; Johnson and Raye, 1981;

Sporer and Küpper, 1995; Sporer, this volume) and to apply basic principles of diagnostic procedures and hypothesis testing have substantially helped to advance SVA as a scientific method and increase its acceptance. This does not mean that SVA claims to be the ultimate solution to all legal problems. Like any other diagnostic procedures it has its strengths and weaknesses and its limitations. However, the question is not whether or not SVA is perfect in distinguishing truthful from incorrect accounts. Instead, the crucial question is whether or not SVA is significantly better in identifying the credibility of a statement than other judgement procedures which are also available. Polygraph techniques are not always applicable and in many countries not admissible as evidence. Global judgements of credibility by laypersons almost invariably result in accuracy rates around chance level. Research on non-verbal indicators of deception has in the past primarily focused at group differences and has not yet sufficiently proved to be applicable in the assessment of individual statements.

REFERENCES

Alonso-Quecuty, M. L. (1992). Deception detection and reality monitoring: A new answer to an old question? In F. Lösel, D. Bender, and T. Bliesener (eds.), *Psychology and Law* (pp. 335–44). Berlin: DeGruyter.

Arntzen, F. (1970). *Psychologie der Zeugenaussage*. Göttingen: Hogrefe.

Böhm, C. (1999). Qualitative Unterschiede zwischen erlebnisbegründeten und suggerierten Aussagen von Kindern. Unpublished thesis, Freie Universität Berlin.

Bull, R. (1998). Obtaining information from child witnesses. In A. Memon, A. Vrij, and R. Bull (eds.), *Psychology and Law: Truthfulness, accuracy and credibility* (pp. 188–210). Maidenhead, England: McGraw-Hill.

Cohen, J. (1960). A coefficient of agreement for nominal scales. *Educational and Psychological Measurement, 20*, 37–46.

Eggers, J. (2002). Glaubwürdigkeit von Zeugenaussagen: Eine Evaluation des Kieler Trainingsprogramms zur Beurteilung der Glaubwürdigkeit von Zeugenaussagen. Unpublished thesis, Universität Kiel.

Erdmann, K. (2001). *Induktion von Pseudoerinnerungen bei Kindern*. Regensburg: S. Roderer Verlag.

Fleiss, J. L. (1971). Measuring nominal scale agreement among many raters. *Psychological Bulletin, 76*, 378–82.

Granhag, P. A., and Strömwall, L. A. (1999). Repeated interrogations: Stretching the deception detection paradigm. *Expert Evidence: The International Journal of Behavioural Sciences in Legal Contexts, 7*, 163–74.

(2002). Repeated interrogations: Verbal and non-verbal cues to deception. *Applied Cognitive Psychology, 16*, 243–57.

Höfer, E. (1995). Glaubwürdigkeitsdiagnostik unter differentiellen Beanspruchungsbedingungen. Unpublished doctoral dissertation, Universität Kiel.

Johnson, M. K., and Raye, C. L. (1981). Reality monitoring. *Psychological Review*, *88*, 67–85.

Katofsky, I. (2002). Unterschiede in den Realkennzeichen zwischen High- und Low-Selfmonitorern bezüglich wahrer und falscher Aussagen. Unpublished thesis, Universität Kiel.

Köhnken, G. (1996). Social psychology and the law. In G. R. Semin and K. Fiedler (eds.), *Applied social psychology* (pp. 257–82). London: Sage.

(2003). Glaubwürdigkeit. In R. Lempp, G. Schütze, and G. Köhnken (eds.), *Forensische Psychiatrie und Psychologie des Kindes- und Jugendalters*. Darmstadt: Steinkopff.

Köhnken, G., and Höfer, E. (1999). Assessing the credibility of witness statements. Paper presented at the 24th International Congress of Applied Psychology, San Francisco.

Köhnken, G., and Wegener, H. (1982). Zur Glaubwürdigkeit von Zeugenaussagen. Experimentelle Überprüfung ausgewählter Glaubwürdigkeitskriterien. *Zeitschrift für Experimentelle und Angewandte Psychologie*, *29*, 92–111.

Krause, S. (1997). Konzeption und Evaluation der Validität des Kieler Trainingsprogramms zur Beurteilung der Glaubwürdigkeit von Zeugenaussagen. Unpublished thesis, Universität Kiel.

Littmann, E., and Szewczyk, H. (1983). Zu einigen Kriterien und Ergebnissen forensisch-psychologischer Glaubwürdigkeitsbegutachtung von sexuell missbrauchten Kindern und Jugendlichen. *Forensia*, *4*, 55–72.

Lösel, F., and Raichle, N. (2001). Kann man durch das Wissen über Realkennzeichen glaubhaft lügen? Paper presented at the 9th Arbeitstagung der Fachgruppe Rechtspsychologie der DGPs, Münster.

Maxwell, A. E. (1977). Coefficients of agreement between observers and their interpretation. *British Journal of Psychiatry*, *130*, 79–83.

Niehaus, S. (2001). Zur Anwendbarkeit inhaltlicher Glaubhaftigkeitsmerkmale bei Zeugenaussagen unterschiedlichen Wahrheitsgehaltes. Frankfurt, Main: Lang.

Petersen, R. (1997). Konzeption und Evaluation der Validität des Kieler Trainingsprogramms zur Beurteilung der Glaubwürdigkeit von Zeugenaussagen. Unpublished thesis, Universität Kiel.

Popper, K. R. (1968). *The logic of scientific discovery*. London: Hutchinson.

Rassin, E. (2001). Criteria-Based Content Analysis: The less scientific road to truth. *Expert Evidence*, *7*, 265–78.

Sporer, S. L., and Küpper, B. (1995). Realitätsüberwachung und die Beurteilung des Wahrheitsgehalts von Zeugenaussagen: Eine experimentelle Studie. *Zeitschrift für Sozialpsychologie*, *26*, 173–93.

Steller, M., and Köhnken, G. (1989). Criteria-Based Content Analysis. In D. C. Raskin (ed.), *Psychological methods in criminal investigation and evidence* (pp. 217–45). New York, NJ: Springer.

Tedeschi, J. T., and Norman, N. (1985). Social power, self-presentation, and the self. In B. R. Schlenker (ed.), *The self and social life* (pp. 293–322). New York: McGraw-Hill.

Trankell, A. (1963). *Vittnespsykologins Arbetsmetoder*. Stockholm: Liber.

Undeutsch, U. (1967). Beurteilung der Glaubhaftigkeit von Aussagen. In U. Undeutsch (ed.), *Handbuch der Psychologie Vol. 11: Forensische Psychologie* (pp. 26–181). Göttingen, Germany: Hogrefe.

Volbert, R., and Rutta, Y. (2001). Verbesserung der Inhaltsqualität von Falschaussagen durch Training. Paper presented at the 9th Arbeitstagung der Fachgruppe Rechtspsychologie der DGPs in Münster.

Vrij, A. (2003). Criteria-Based Content Analysis: A qualitative review of the first 37 studies. *Psychology, Public Policy and the Law.*

Vrij, A., Akehurst, L., Soukara, S., and Bull, R. (2002). Will the truth come out? The effect of deception, age, status, coaching, and social skills on CBCA scores. *Law and Human Behavior, 26,* 261–83.

Vrij, A., Kneller, W., and Mann, S. (2000). The effect of informing liars about criteria-based content analysis on their ability to deceive CBCA-raters. *Legal and Criminological Psychology, 5,* 57–70.

NOTE

1. The limited sensitivity of three-point rating scales may be another reason for the failure to find significant differences in some studies although differences in the CBCA scores were in the predicted direction.

4   Reality monitoring and detection of deception

Siegfried L. Sporer

Research on eyewitness testimony has primarily focused on memory errors. In this chapter, the focus is not on eye-witness errors but on the application of Johnson and Raye's (1981) reality monitoring (RM) model to detection of deception. The central question is whether or not it is possible to discriminate truthful from deceptive statements on the basis of content aspects outlined by the RM theory. This approach is akin to Statement Validity Analysis, in particular the Criteria-Based Content Analysis (CBCA) component, which also has focused on qualitative differences between truthful and deceptive accounts (for reviews, see Ruby and Brigham, 1997; Sporer, 1983, 1997a, 1997b; Steller and Köhnken, 1989; Vrij, 2000, in press).

Reality monitoring approach

In a seminal paper, Johnson and Raye (1981) asked how people go about discriminating *memories of* externally derived (perceptual) experiences from *memories of* internally derived experiences. This process has been termed reality monitoring (RM). In a deception situation, a communicator constructs an event either from scratch or on the basis of similar experiences, thus reporting on a *new* current event, not a memory of a past event. According to RM theory, people rely on *qualitative characteristics* of memories to decide whether a memory is based on an actual experience or not. It is assumed that externally derived memories contain more references to sensory information (visual details, colours, sounds, odours, touch, taste), contextual information (about space and time), emotions and feelings, and semantic information. On the other hand, internally derived memories are supposed to contain more references to cognitive operations at the time of encoding ('I must have dreamt this because I know I have never been in Australia.').

Judging respondents' accounts: the meta-meta level

However, the focus of my review is not on phenomenological differences between perceived and imagined/false events, since participants

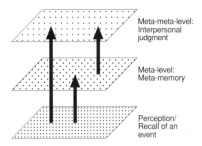

Meta-meta-level:
Interpersonal
judgment

Meta-level:
Meta-memory

Perception/
Recall of an
event

Figure 4.1 Three levels of judging somebody's report

themselves have introspectively rated their *own* memories, that is the *meta-memory* level (e.g., via self-ratings). Instead, I focus on how other observers (memory judges or fact finders) evaluate statements of other people, that is the *meta-meta level* (see Figure 4.1). Johnson, Bush, and Mitchell (1998) have referred to this as 'interpersonal reality monitoring'. At the meta-meta level, memory judges may use both respondents' recall statements as well as their accompanying meta-level statements, for example the confidence with which certain memories are expressed, expressions of vividness of the memories, or evidence that the respondent seems to be 'reliving' his or her autobiographical memory. Memory records to be evaluated may consist of written recall, or of videotapes and audiotapes, or transcripts thereof which are then evaluated by trained judges or raters.

Reality monitoring applied to detection of deception

Using a typical misinformation paradigm where participants were suggested the presence of a traffic sign through misleading post-event questioning, Schooler, Gerhard, and Loftus (1986), and Schooler, Clark, and Loftus (1988) observed that true statements contained more sensory and more geographic details regarding the sign, while suggested statements contained more references to cognitive processes. Schooler, Gerhard, and Loftus (1986), and Johnson and Suengas (1989) have also noted the similarity of some of the memory characteristics described in the RM approach to the content criteria that German forensic psychologists (e.g., Undeutsch, 1982) have used in evaluating claims of (child) sexual abuse. Hence, more pertinent to the question of detection of deception investigated here are studies that have analysed systematic differences between reports of self-experienced, as opposed to reports of (freely) invented or intentionally falsified, events with the intent to convince the recipient (listener) that the storyteller has actually experienced the event as told (lies).

Presumably, the first study to apply the RM approach to the detection of deception was a pilot study ($N = 22$) by Alonso-Quecuty (1992), followed by several other studies, most of which are available only in Spanish (for a detailed review, see Masip, Sporer, Garrido, and Herrero, in press). Some of the findings seem to depend on whether or not participants were children or adults, and whether the event to be reported on was experienced live or via video- or audiotape (Alonso-Quecuty, 1993, 1996; Alonso-Quecuty and Hernández-Fernaud, 1997; Alonso-Quecuty, Hernández-Fernaud, and Campos, 1997). Unfortunately, these studies have been conducted with relatively small sample sizes (particularly regarding the cell sizes for some of the complex interactions obtained). Most of them also lack methodological and statistical details that prevent a thorough examination. For example, none of the studies provided clear operational definitions of Sensory, Contextual, Semantic, and Idiosyncratic information, nor evidence about inter-coder reliability of these constructs. Finally, none of these studies controlled for the number of words in the accounts, thus confounding report length with truth status.

Studies with adults

To provide more precise operational definitions, Sporer and Kuepper (1994, 2004) translated the MCQ by Johnson, Foley, Suengas, and Raye (1988) into German and expanded the definitions of the individual items, along with an answer sheet for participants. I refer to this form of the MCQ which was used for participants' *self-ratings* of their accounts as *Self-ratings of Memory Characteristics Questionnaire (SMCQ)*.[1] A parallel version specifically adapted for *judging other people's* memory reports was constructed which here is referred to as *Judgement of Memory Characteristics Questionnaire (JMCQ*; see Appendix). Based on factor analyses of the SMCQ as well as theoretical considerations, eight RM scales were derived:

(1) Clarity and vividness of the account (items 1, 3, 8, 9, 10, 33);
(2) Sensory information (e.g., taste and smell; items 2, 4, 5, 6, 7);
(3) Spatial information (arrangements of persons and objects; items 13, 14, 15, 16);
(4) Time information (from time of year to time of day; items 17, 18, 19, 20, 21);
(5) Emotions and feelings (items 24, 27, 29, 30, 32);

(6) Reconstructability of the story (despite complexity of the action; presumed and factual consequences and certainty/doubts about the memory; items 11, 25, 26, 36);

(7) Realism (item 12; items 40, 41, 42, 43 were later added to this scale by Sporer and Hamilton, 1996); and

(8) Cognitive operations (including repeated thinking about the event, etc.; items 11, 25, 26, 36).[2]

One hundred participants wrote down both a report of a self-experienced and an invented account (with a one-week interval in between, in counterbalanced order). About 30% were from the last days or months, about 54% from the last several years, and about 16% from teenage or childhood days. All events described were about a personally significant event that had been in some way exciting or otherwise special to them (e.g., an operation or an illness, the loss of an important person or object, a vacation experience). About half of the events were more negative in nature (44%), the others more positive (56%).[3]

The participants rated their own accounts with the SMCQ. As expected, self-experienced accounts received significantly higher ratings on all scales except Emotions and Reconstructability, for which the means were also in the expected direction (see Figure 4.2). Note that for Cognitive operations, self-ratings of self-experienced events were *higher* than for those of invented events.

Next, all 200 reports were assessed with the JMCQ by a trained rater who was blind to the experimental conditions. In a pilot study (Kuepper and Sporer, 1995) with forty similar reports of invented and self-experienced accounts, interrater reliability for three independent raters was established (see Table 4.1). Some of the pairwise interrater reliabilities are small as a function of ceiling (for Clarity/Vividness) and floor effects (Sensory information, Cognitive operations). Pairwise interrater reliabilities are generally higher for scales involving dimensions which can be better operationalised (Spatial information, Time information), while they tend to be lower for scales that involve more global subjective judgements (Realism, Reconstructability, Cognitive operations).

While pairwise interrater reliabilities were satisfactory for some scales but not for others, the Spearman-Brown interrater reliabilities R were between .57 and .95, except for Cognitive operations, which was only .32. To demonstrate that interrater reliability can be elevated to more satisfactory levels after more intensive training, I have also included the interrater reliabilities by Strömwall, Bengtsson, Leander, and Granhag (in press). Here, all interrater reliabilities were above $r = .71$, except for

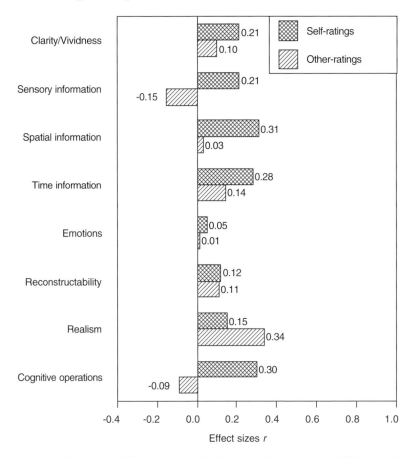

Figure 4.2 Effect sizes r of self- and other-ratings of RM criteria in true and invented accounts (data from Sporer and Kuepper, 1995; 2004)

Realism, for which it was only $r = .52$. Other authors who have used the JMCQ scales (or parts thereof) have also obtained fairly high interrater reliabilities (Santtila, Roppola, and Niemi, 1999; Vrij, Edward, Roberts, and Bull, 2000; Vrij, Edward, and Bull, 2001). Generally, interrater reliabilities obtained with frequency counts are higher than those calculated for rating scales.

Together, the scales discriminated significantly between invented and self-experienced accounts. Generally, the differences in means between self-experienced and invented accounts were small but in the expected direction (see Figure 4.2). Time information and Realism

Table 4.1 *Pairwise interrater reliabilities and Spearman–Brown reliabilities for 3 raters for reality monitoring criteria derived from the JMCQ in the Study by Kuepper and Sporer (1995) and Strömwall et al. (in press)*

RM criteria	Kuepper and Sporer (1995)					Strömwall et al. (2003)
	Pairs of Raters					
	A–B	A–C	B–C	Mean-r	Spearman– Brown R	r
Clarity/Vividness	.29	.23	.39	.30	.57	.71
Sensory information	.67	.79	.86	.77	.91	_a
Spatial information	.79	.80	.68	.76	.90	1.00
Time information	.86	.80	.92	.86	.95	.79
Emotions	.63	.75	.46	.61	.83	_b
Reconstructability	.45	.48	.36	.43	.69	.73
Realism	.19	.48	.34	.34	.60	.52
Cognitive operations	−.14	.34	.20	.13	.32	.90
Visual details	_a	_a	_a	_a	_a	.80
Auditory details	_a	_a	_a	_a	_a	1.00
Smell	_a	_a	_a	_a	_a	_b
Taste	_a	_a	_a	_a	_a	1.0
Physical sensations	_a	_a	_a	_a	_a	1.0

Notes: [a] Sensory information was either reported as a summary score or not reported. [b] Could not be computed.

received significantly higher ratings for the self-experienced compared to the invented accounts. As expected, Cognitive operations were rated lower for invented accounts but this difference was not significant. However, contrary to the original hypothesis, and opposite to the findings with the self-ratings, ratings of Sensory information (which were close to a floor effect) were rated lower for invented reports. Surprisingly, some of the differences observed were *stronger* when participants had one week to prepare their account (e.g., Clarity and Vividness and Spatial information) than when the reports were given immediately after receiving the instructions.

Perhaps one of the reasons why the differences may have been so small is that the events chosen by participants may not have been very involving or invoking strong emotions. Also, providing a report in writing allows *storywriters* more time for planning and editing than oral *storytelling*. None the less, a multiple discriminant analysis with all eight criteria resulted in 69% correct classifications, 68% of the self-experienced, and 70% of the invented accounts.

Sporer and Hamilton (1996) also used the SMCQ and the JMCQ with $N = 240$ adults (160 females, 80 males), manipulating the effects of truthfulness (invented vs. self-experienced) in a between-subjects design by randomly allocating participants to either condition. In addition, the life period (under 15 vs. over 15) in which the events to be reported took place was varied experimentally. All participants wrote either an account of a self-experienced or an invented, personally significant experience. After writing down their account, participants rated their own event with the SMCQ. In addition, using a *yoked design*, each storywriter was randomly assigned the story written by another participant in the experiment, and rated that person's report with the JMCQ.

The differences in SMCQ ratings were similar to the ones reported by Sporer and Kuepper (1994, 2004). For the JMCQ, there was a main effect of truth status but no main effect for age of the story nor their interaction. The results revealed higher ratings for self-experienced accounts than for invented accounts on Clarity/Vividness, Time information, and Realism. Contrary to expectation, invented stories showed a non-significant tendency to be rated to contain more Sensory information and more Feelings/significance in the life of the storytellers. The results did not differ as a function of the lifetime period from which the events originated, or age of memory with which lifetime period is naturally confounded. A multiple discriminant analysis with the seven RM scales rated by the yoked partner reading the storywriter's report resulted in 64% correct classifications, 65% of the self-experienced, and 63% for the invented accounts.

Taking together these two studies with written reports, Clarity/vividness, Time information and Realism seem to be the best indicators of truth status, although the effect sizes are all rather small (but not lower than the ones reported in the recent meta-analysis by DePaulo, Lindsay, Malone, Muhlenbruck, Charlton, and Cooper, 2003). Also, note that in both studies, the differences in Sensory information are opposite to predictions, although this effect may be clouded by floor effects in both studies. In both studies, cases could be classified via multiple discriminant analyses above chance level (see below).

More recently, Vrij, Edward, Roberts, and Bull (2000) had seventy-three nursing students watch a video film (lasting about two mins) and interviewed them twice. Participants either had to report truthfully the content of the film, or had to lie about it, in counterbalanced order. The film took place in a hospital setting and dealt with a theft of a bag from a patient by a visitor. After the film, each participant was asked three questions about the actions of the nurse, the patient, and the visitor, which they were to answer truthfully or to lie about. Truthful accounts were twice as long ($M = 89$ s) as deceptive accounts ($M = 42$ s), a difference which was highly significant (effect size $r = .57$).

From the videotaped responses, a series of non-verbal behaviours were coded. The responses were also transcribed from the audiotapes, and two raters coded the frequencies of the presence of a series of CBCA and RM criteria. Coders were trained with a detailed description of how the RM criteria should be scored, including case examples.[4] Interrater reliabilities for the RM criteria Perceptual information: vision ($r = .96$), Perceptual information: sound ($r = .77$), Spatial information ($r = .72$), Temporal information ($r = .85$), and Cognitive operations ($r = .75$) were excellent. Affective information, which was considered equivalent to the CBCA criterion 'Accounts of subjective mental state' and hence was included as part of the RM construct, was coded with a reliability of $r = .58$. The five RM criteria appeared significantly more frequently in truthful accounts than in deceptive ones, including Cognitive operations (see Figure 4.3). Considering that truthful and deceptive accounts also differed considerably in length, I wonder to what extent the criteria would still discriminate reliably if account length was controlled for.

A multiple discriminant analysis with a summative RM total score (by summing the first four criteria and excluding Cognitive operations) yielded 71% correct classifications of truthful and 64% correct classifications of deceptive accounts (overall: 67%). Taking into consideration also several non-verbal indicators and the CBCA total score, classification accuracy was boosted to 81% overall, 77% for the truth-tellers and 85% for the liars. However, the RM score did not contribute to the discriminant function but only the CBCA score, latency of responding, hand and finger movements, ah-speech disturbances (filled pauses), illustrators, and speech rate. It appears that the CBCA score and the RM score cover common variance leading to an elimination of the RM score as a useful separate predictor. We shall return to this at the end when we discuss the possibility of an integration of the SVA and RM approach.

In a follow-up study (actually, a subset of data not reported in the previous study), Vrij, Edward, and Bull (2001) found that reports by truth-tellers were rated significantly higher with respect to Visual details, Sound details, Spatial and Time details than those of deceptive respondents. Affective information, which was considered equivalent to the CBCA criterion 'Accounts of subjective mental state' and hence was included as part of the RM construct, was also rated higher in truthful than in deceptive accounts.

Since the participants had not experienced the event personally, the Cognitive operations could not refer to their *own* thoughts and

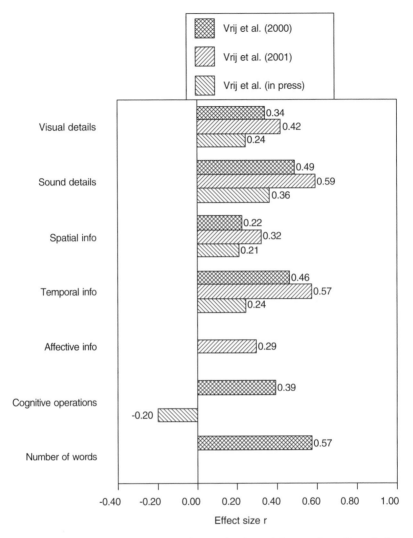

Figure 4.3 Effect sizes *r* of RM criteria and the number of words (computed from data by Vrij et al., 2000, Vrij, Edward, and Bull, 2001; Vrij et al., in press)

emotions but to the protagonists' thoughts and emotions, which are either expressed explicitly in the video, or only inferred or attributed from observing the actors' behaviour. Although it may sound like nit-picking to draw this distinction, it is important considering the inconsistent findings with Cognitive operations and Emotions in previous studies.

Studies with children

One of the questions that is central to application of the RM approach to the detection of deception is whether or not RM criteria differentiate equally well with children as with adults. In a study by Santtila, Roppola, and Niemi (1999) sixty-eight Swedish children aged 7 to 8 ($n = 24$), 10 to 11 ($n = 22$), and 13 to 14 ($n = 22$) reported on an emotionally significant, negative autobiographical event involving a loss of control (e.g., being attacked by an animal, receiving an injection), thus trying to fulfil and replicate Steller, Wellershaus, and Wolf's (1992) criteria for a 'simulation study' of child sexual abuse. Each child also gave a false account of a similar event, in counterbalanced order. Children chose the two topics to be reported on from a list one week prior to being interviewed. All 136 interviews were transcribed and coded by two raters with the JMCQ (see Appendix). Interrater correlations were quite high (with a mean correlation of $r = .79$ for all items), with all but four items having an r greater or equal to .70. Exceptions were items 6 (touch): $r = .03$, 12 (realism): $r = .25$, 25 (seriousness of implications): $r = .61$, and 36 (doubts about accuracy): $r = .51$. Items were summed to the same eight scales as in the study by Sporer and Kuepper (1995) and Sporer (1997a; see above).

Time information and Emotions/Feelings (Affective information) were significantly higher in true than in false events. The effect for Sensory information was marginally significant. It should be noted that some of the effects (although not significant) were opposite to the direction predicted by the RM approach. Most importantly, however, there were clear developmental trends across the three age groups. For seven of the eight RM scales (all but Emotions), the differences between the groups were significant. Figure 4.4 shows the means of the (log transformed) ratings for the three age groups. For most of the scales the increase was linear, except for Realism and Emotions. A logistic regression analysis yielded 64% correct classifications, 62% of the true, and 66% of the false statements.

Most recently, Vrij, Akehurst, Soukara, and Bull (in press) compared children at various age levels (5–6, 10–11, 14–15 years; $ns = 35, 54, 55$) with adults ($n = 52$ undergraduates) who were induced to report either truthfully or deceptively about a small incident in a classroom setting (about who had wiped off important information from the blackboard). This study is remarkable in several respects: The total sample size ($N = 196$) was relatively large compared to many previous studies, all participants were involved in a live event (playing the game, or imagining playing the game 'Connect 4'), providing all participants with a short

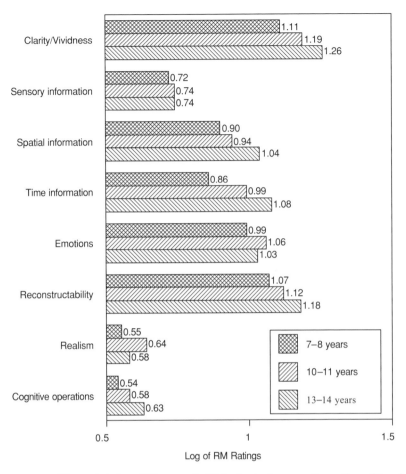

Figure 4.4 Age differences in RM criteria (log transformation of 7-point scales) (from data by Santtila, Roppola, and Niemi, 1999)

opportunity to prepare their accounts before reporting, and offering a motivational incentive (a monetary reward), as well as threatening with a 'punishment' (having to write a report – which was considered within ethical boundaries of experimental research, particularly with children). The study also compared non-verbal and content-oriented approaches to the detection of deception in a single experimental design.

Videotapes and transcripts were analysed with respect to six non-verbal and paraverbal indicators of deception, nine CBCA criteria, and five RM criteria (via frequency counts). I report here only the results for the RM criteria. Inter-coder reliability (Spearman–Brown *r*) was again excellent

(Visual information: .80, Auditory information: .92, Spatial information: .61, Time information: .78, Cognitive operations: .54). Across age groups, truthful accounts contained highly significantly more Visual, Auditory, Spatial, and Time information than deceptive accounts. As predicted, there were also significantly more Cognitive operations in deceptive than in truthful reports. A multiple discriminant analysis with the RM total score (consisting of the first four RM criteria mentioned above) and Cognitive Operations yielded 72% correct classifications of truthful, and 67% of deceptive statements (69% overall).

However, there was also a clear increase (mostly linear) across age groups, which accounted for substantially more variance ($eta^2 = .24$, .22, .18, .27, .20, for these five RM criteria, respectively) than the truth status manipulation ($eta^2 = .06, .13, .04, .06, .04$). The deviation from linearity was due to the fact that the children in the 10–11 and 14–15 year age groups did not differ from each other on any of these variables, while these groups in turn differed reliably from the children aged 5 to 6 and the undergraduates. Most importantly, however, there was also a significant interaction between Truth status and Age of participants for Auditory, Spatial, and Temporal information.

While differences between truthful statements and lies were most pronounced for adults, the differences were minimal with the youngest age group where the criteria were often completely absent in either truthful or deceptive reports. As one would expect from basic research on reality and source monitoring with children (see Johnson, Hashtroudi, and Lindsay, 1993; Lindsay, 2002), with younger children the RM approach does not (yet) prove to be effective.

One should also note that the speech rate for undergraduates was almost double that of children aged 5 to 6 years. The speech rate was also somewhat (but non-significantly: $p = .078$) higher in truthful than in deceptive accounts across age levels (effect size $r = .13$). If one combines this information with the (also non-significant: $p = .158$) difference between truthful and deceptive accounts for the length of the account (in seconds), one can infer that the reports were also likely to differ as a function of both truth status (truthful: 244.8; deceptive: 216.0 number of words) and age. Again, I wonder to what extent the results reported for RM (and CBCA) criteria may have been affected by report length. Just as the frequencies of non-verbal behaviours were standardised for report length, I would also like to see the content criteria *densities* reported in addition to their frequencies.

Exactly this issue has been raised in a study by Granhag, Strömwall, and Olsson (2001) who compared truthful and deceptive statements of forty-four eleven-year-old children about a magician's show. Half of the children watched a female magician's show lasting about fifteen minutes, the other half were given only a brief outline of its content and made drawings of the magician's appearance and utensils. All children were interviewed on the same day, and again a week later. Two coders counted the frequencies of Visual, Auditory, Sensory, Spatial, Temporal, and Affective information, and Cognitive operations. Inter-coder reliabilities (see Table 4.1) were very high, all r's greater or equal .82. Across the two interviews, truthful reports contained significantly more Visual, Auditory, Temporal, and Affective information, but also *more* Cognitive operations (see Figure 4.5). Two discriminant analyses resulted in 85% overall correct classifications for the first interview (91% of the truthful and 81% of the deceptive accounts), and 79% correct classifications for the second interview (73% and 85%, respectively).

However, the authors also found that the truthful accounts (first statement: $M = 399$ words; second statement: $M = 237$ words) were highly significantly longer than the deceptive accounts (173 and 108 words, respectively). In a reanalysis correcting for the number of words, the differences between truthful and deceptive accounts changed somewhat: truthful statements contained significantly more Auditory, Temporal, and Affective information but *less* Visual information (see Figure 4.5). While the effects for Auditory information and Time information were almost identical for the analyses with the raw frequencies and the corrected data, the effects became smaller for Affective information and Cognitive operations. However, it is particularly noteworthy that the effect size for the analysis of visual details corrected for the number of words is as large ($r = -.51$) but *opposite* in direction as for the raw frequencies ($r = .51$). This is an important finding and should caution us in our interpretation of studies that have used raw frequency counts (of RM, CBCA, or any other content criteria) where the account length has not been reported and hence, apparently, also not been corrected for.

In a field study conducted in a school setting with eighty-seven children aged 10–13 years, Strömwall, Bengtsson, Leander, and Granhag (2003) compared those children who had experienced a live event (a health examination) once or four times with a control group who imagined (also once or four times) to have participated in the examination based on a script read to them by the experimenter. Strömwall et al. (2003) also obtained differences in account length as a function of truth status. As truthful accounts were significantly longer ($M = 611.4$ number of words) than the deceptive accounts ($M = 408.2$), the authors did not use the frequency counts but rather the rated RM scales for their analyses. In addition to the eight RM scales based on the JMCQ described above, the authors separately analysed Visual and Auditory details as well

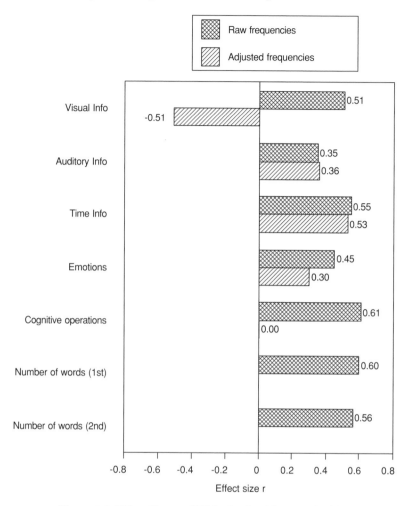

Figure 4.5 Effect Sizes *r* of RM criteria without and with correcting for the number of words (computed from data by Granhag, Strömwall, and Olsson, 2001)

as Physical sensations. Two additional sensory qualities, smell and taste, were excluded due to floor effects. In addition, all transcripts were also rated with Steller and Köhnken's nineteen CBCA criteria, excluding four due to floor effects.

As already noted, the interrater reliabilities were excellent for all of these scales. Truthful accounts were rated significantly higher for Clarity/Vividness, Spatial and Time information, Reconstructability and

Realism. The other differences were not significant but pointed in the same direction. Repeatedly experiencing as well as repeatedly imagining the event also resulted in a significant increase in the ratings of the same scales (except for Realism). However, Truth status and Repetition did not interact with each other. There was a non-significant tendency for Cognitive operations to be rated higher in reports of experienced events. A multiple discriminant analysis with nine RM criteria (excluding Cognitive operations) resulted in 72% correct classifications of the truthful, and 71% of the imagined events (overall 71%). For the analyses with the CBCA criteria, only two criteria supported the underlying hypothesis, viz. Spontaneous corrections and Raising doubts about one's own testimony.

Individual differences

Individual differences in the ability to deceive others, as well as individual differences regarding non-verbal indicators have often been noticed in the deception literature although few studies have examined personality correlates in detail (e.g., Machiavellianism or self-monitoring; e.g., Knapp et al., 1974; Riggio and Friedman, 1983; Vrij, Akehurst, and Morris, 1997; Vrij and Holland, 1999). With respect to RM criteria which are derived from the content of a message (i.e., verbal aspects) I would expect that their presence may be affected by the general verbal ability as well as by the self-presentational skills of communicators. Few studies so far have considered individual differences in relation to the presence of RM criteria.

In the study by Vrij, Edward, and Bull (2001) described above the authors also examined the relation of public self-consciousness and acting ability with non-verbal behaviour, CBCA and RM criteria of seventy-three participants reporting both truthfully and deceptively about the content of a film. There were significant negative correlations between public self-consciousness with the RM ($-.33$) and the CBCA score ($-.36$). Acting ability also correlated significantly negatively with these two scores ($-.36$ and $-.31$, respectively). Unfortunately, the authors did not report correlations separately with the individual RM and CBCA criteria, nor with the length of the accounts and speech rate, which had also been found to differ as a function of truth status (see also Vrij et al., 2000). It may be possible that different criteria are affected more by some of these personality correlates than others, and both groups of variables in turn may be related to verbal skills. In a study by Sporer, Stucke, and Samweber (2000) systematic differences between participants with high and low self-monitoring scores on several RM scales (which are incorporated in Sporer's (1998) Aberdeen Report Judgement Scales (see below)) were found.

Verbal skills have always been considered to play a crucial role by the originators of the content-oriented approach to deception (Arntzen, 1970/1993; Undeutsch, 1967), particularly with children. Empirical studies have also demonstrated that children's verbal abilities, which in turn vary as a function of age, will affect not only the general quality of their statements (see Davies, 1996) but also, probably, the presence of content cues – particularly the ones containing details of some kind or another.

In the study by Santtila, Roppola, and Niemi (1999) described above, RM ratings also varied not only as a function of the age of the children, irrespective of truth status, but also as a function of verbal skill which was assessed with the vocabulary subscale of the WISC-R. Both for true and for false statements, six of the eight correlations between the vocabulary subscale and individual RM criteria were significant (for true and false statements, respectively: Clarity: .37/.49; Sensory: ns/ns; Spatial information: .37/.32; Time information: .53/.36; Emotions: .33/ns; Reconstructability: .30/.41; Realism: ns/.26; Cognitive operations: .33/.26). Together, these studies clearly imply that differences in age, which in turn are likely to covary with verbal ability, need to be taken into consideration when assessing any type of content criteria.

Just as there are differences in verbal ability, there is also a large body of research demonstrating differences in the vividness of visual imagery (e.g., Marks, 1973). To the extent that adults, or children, differ with respect to their imagery vividness, these differences may also be reflected in people's lies, which to some extent will involve a person's fantasy in construing an episode. Although I am not aware of any research linking imagery ability to detection and its deception, individual differences in imagery ability have been linked to differences in judged memory characteristics as assessed with the MCQ (Keogh and Markham, 1998; cf. also McGinnis and Roberts, 1996). Such individual differences may also explain why the Clarity/Vividness dimension has received little support as an indicator of the veracity of a statement (see Sporer and Kuepper, 1995; Sporer, 1997a). At any rate, I encourage future researchers to assess these and other personality variables and relate them systematically to the presence of individual RM criteria.

Accuracy of classification using the RM approach

Accuracy of classifications with multiple discriminant analyses   Several authors have reported the accuracy of classifications using the RM

Table 4.2 *Classification accuracies and SDT discrimination accuracy (A')
and asymmetry in classification accuracy (Response Bias B'') in studies with
the RM approach using multiple discriminant analyses*

Study	N	Hits[a]	CR[b]	Overall accuracy	A'	B''
Sporer and Kuepper (1995)	200	.680	.700	.690	.775	.047
Sporer (1997a)	80	.750	.675	.713	.799	−.182
Sporer (1997b)	200	.740	.640	.690	.777	−.231
Santtila et al. (1999)	136	.617	.662	.640	.718	.097
Vrij et al. (2000)	73	.706	.614	.660	.744	−.203
Vrij et al. (in press)	73	.720	.670	.695	.781	−.118
Granhag et al. (2001)[c]	44	.910	.810	.860	.920	−.407
Granhag et al. (2001)[d]	44	.730	.850	.790	.869	.354
Strömwall et al. (in press)	87	.720	.710	.715	.801	−.025
Hoefer et al. (1996)	66	.610	.700	.655	.738	.197

Notes: [a] Proportion of correctly classified true statements.
[b] Proportion of correctly classified lies (correct rejections = 1 − false alarms).
[c] First interview.
[d] Second interview.

criteria to postdict truth status using multiple discriminant analyses.
When a large set of predictor variables is used, these results have to be
treated with caution, as the results highly depend on the number of cases
to be classified and the number of predictor variables. I have summarised
the classification rates of the studies using either individual RM criteria or
a RM summative score as predictor variables in Table 4.2. Across studies,
the classification rates range from 61% to 91% for truthful accounts, and
from 61% to 85% for deceptive reports (overall, from 64% to 86%).

These classification rates are comparable to those obtained using the
CBCA approach (see also Masip et al., in press; Ruby and Brigham,
1997; Vrij et al., 2000, in press). Some researchers have also combined
CBCA and RM criteria to predict truth status, resulting in somewhat
higher classification rates than when using either CBCA or RM criteria
alone (Sporer, 1997a, 1997b; Strömwall et al., in press; Vrij et al., 2000, in
press). Adding in non-verbal cues may even further increase classification
rates (Vrij et al., 2000, in press).

Although this may be to some extent a statistical artefact due to the
increase in the number of predictor variables (which for purely mathematical reasons increases classification rates), these findings also indicate that
despite considerable overlap of some of the CBCA and RM criteria, the

two criteria sets also seem to cover different ground, which suggests that they are complementary, rather than rival, approaches (Sporer, 1997a, 1997b, 1998).

Discrimination accuracy and response bias in terms of signal detection theory   One of the concerns with the application of RM (or CBCA) criteria – particularly with people who are not sufficiently trained in the complexities of overall statement validity analysis – is that all of the criteria (except for Cognitive operations) are truth criteria, that is they are expected to be higher in reports of self-experienced than of invented events. A potential consequence is that fact-finders who analyse a statement for the presence of these truth criteria may be inclined to classify a statement incorrectly as truthful when encountering a few truth criteria in the account. Exactly how many criteria need to be present (in terms of a cut-off score) before one can ultimately assume that an account is likely to be based on a true experience? This is still an unresolved issue that researchers have yet to start to address. But the premature acceptance of an account as truthful based on the presence of some criteria may invoke a response bias in form of a truth bias, analogous, but contrary to, the lie bias professional lie-catchers, in particular interrogators of suspects, seem to have (Meissner and Kassin, 2002). The danger of employing the RM (or CBCA) approach is that it may invoke a truth bias which may distort assessments.

A possible solution to this issue is the application of signal detection theory (SDT; see McNicol, 1972; MacMillan and Creelman, 1990, 1991). Originally developed in the context of radar technology and perceptual vigilance studies, SDT allows for a separation between performance, viz. detection accuracy, and response bias. SDT researchers have developed separate parametric and non-parametric indices of performance and response bias which are supposed to be largely independent of one another. Adopting the SDT analogy to 'truth detection', I define as a *hit* a correctly classified truthful statement (i.e., the truth is the signal), and as a false alarm (noise) a lie which is incorrectly accepted as a true statement. In doing so, I adopt the perspective of a psychological expert assessing a witness's statement with respect to its truthfulness (like many SVA experts in Germany and Sweden).[5] The advantage of adopting the SDT framework is that it allows me to study the factors that influence performance separately from the factors that affect response bias (e.g., credulity or scepticism as a personality trait; the professional or political background of the evaluator (therapist, social worker, child advocate, civil-liberty advocate); or situational forces like the importance of the case at stake or political pressures to solve a crime).

In Table 4.2 I have also computed the non-parametric signal detection (SDT) parameters A' (Rae, 1976; MacMillan and Creelman, 1990) as an indicator of performance, and B'' as a measure of response bias (Donaldson, 1992). The SDT performance measure A' (with a proportion of .50 indicating chance level, and of 1.0 perfect performance) indicates to what extent discrimination can be achieved independently of response bias. The response bias B'' can range from -1.0 to $+1.0$, with 0 indicating a neutral criterion and positive values a more conservative response criterion in the sense of being rather sceptical about accepting a statement as truthful. Although these indices calculated from the hits and false alarms of multiple discriminant analyses do not reflect individual decision-makers' response criteria, they nevertheless point to an asymmetry in the sense that the criteria are more likely to assess truthful statements correctly than deceptive ones. Given the theoretical premise of the RM approach, this result is not surprising, and would be expected for CBCA studies as well, which can also be labelled better truth detection rather than lie detection.

Classification accuracy by raters with RM criteria

The ultimate validity test for the RM approach to the detection of deception is not whether the individual RM criteria or a summative RM score allow for good discrimination in multiple discriminant or multiple regression analyses. Rather, it needs to be demonstrated whether or not fact-finders can successfully classify reports as truthful or deceptive when using the RM criteria compared to people unaided by these criteria. Of course, other factors (e.g. interview style or suggestive questioning) as outlined by SVA need to be taken into consideration when applying the content-oriented approach to real-life cases.

Unfortunately, there is very little evidence on this question so far. Table 4.3 summarises the accuracy of classifications of the raters in the studies by Sporer (1997a, 1997b) in which the raters had used both CBCA and RM criteria as well as the outcomes from a study by Sporer, Kuepper, and Bursch (1995) which compared a rater using the JMCQ with several control groups of 'naïve' raters (as opposed to trained or expert raters). In the latter study (a follow-up study to Sporer and Kuepper's (1995) study, using the same 200 accounts), Sporer, Kuepper, and Bursch (1995) found that the RM trained rater classified accounts reliably better than two naïve raters who had also evaluated all 200 stories, and also better than two other groups of raters (twenty males, twenty females) each of whom had evaluated different subsets (of ten accounts

Table 4.3 *Classification accuracies, discrimination accuracy (A') and response bias B'' of raters using RM (and CBCA) criteria for assessment*

Study	N	Hits[a]	CR[b]	Overall accuracy	A'	B''
Sporer et al. (1995)						
Rater with RM criteria	200	.740	.630	.685	.772	−.251
Naïve rater A	200	.430	.620	.525	.549	.368
Naïve rater B	200	.580	.480	.530	.557	−.199
40 Naïve raters	20*10	.620	.525	.573	.628	−.192
Sporer (1997b)[c]	200	.740	.640	.690	.777	−.231
Sporer (1997a)[c]	80	.750	.675	.713	.799	−.182

Notes: [a] Proportion of correctly classified true statements.
[b] Proportion of correctly classified lies (correct rejections = 1 − false alarms).
[c] CBCA and RM criteria.

each) of the same 200 reports. Compared to the RM rater, all the control raters were at chance level.

Performance in terms of SDT (see Table 4.3) also indicates that the RM rater ($A' = .77$) was much better in discriminating truthful from invented accounts. Although this rater's response criterion was somewhat less cautious than neutral, it did not differ much from that of the naïve raters (except for naïve rater A who was extremely cautious in accepting a statement as true). Furthermore, an in-depth content analysis of the reasons 'naïve' raters gave when judging the veracity of accounts based on their intuitions revealed that they were relying on commonsense notions about what constitutes a truthful account (Reinhard, Burghardt, Sporer, and Bursch, 2002). As most of the reasons used by these memory judges did not differentiate between truthful and invented accounts, it is not surprising that their veracity judgements were at chance level.

We have also conducted some studies in which raters did not use the RM scales by themselves but in combination with CBCA criteria. Thus, the accuracy rate will be a joint function of CBCA and RM criteria (as well as any other considerations raters may use). In another follow-up study to Sporer and Kuepper's (1995) study, Sporer (1997b) had the same 200 accounts assessed by two raters with the first thirteen of Steller and Köhnken's (1989) CBCA criteria and eight RM scales used by Sporer (1997a; note that not all the 39 JMCQ items but only a summary description of the eight scales were used). Rater A classified 66% of the stories correctly (62% of the true and 70% of the invented accounts; $A' = .74$). Rater B achieved 62% accuracy (80% and 44%, respectively; $A' = .71$).

Note that the two raters employed quite different decision criteria, with Rater B displaying a rather strong truth bias, $B'' = -.67$, while rater A was more sceptical, $B'' = .18$).

The two raters in Sporer's (1997a) study (see above) who had evaluated transcripts of videotaped accounts both with thirteen CBCA criteria and eight RM scales achieved 73% and 65% correct classifications, $A' = .81$ and .74, respectively. As they differed widely in their response criteria, $B'' = .25$ and $-.42$, respectively, they consequently also differed in their classifications of truthful (68% vs. 75%) vs. deceptive accounts (78% vs. 55% for raters A and B, respectively).

While these classification rates per se are not impressive, they do both compare favourably with the many studies that have studied accuracy rates in detection of deception, which show an average correct classification rate of 57% (Vrij, 2000), often ranging between 45% and 60% (where 50% would be expected by chance). Comparisons of raters guided by RM (and CBCA criteria) and naïve raters demonstrate that the content criteria actively contribute to this difference (although these findings have to be replicated with larger numbers of raters). These classification results also compare favourably with training studies in detection of deception, most of which have not led to an improvement in discrimination performance but only to a response bias to classify truthful statements falsely as lies (Meissner and Kassin, 2002).

Still more has to be known about the validity of individual criteria with different types of accounts before raters can be trained about the *relative discriminative value* of individual criteria, and hence the weighting that should be assigned to them in arriving at an optimised decision. The Brunswikian lens model describes a useful framework on how to arrive at optimal weightings as a basis for classification decisions (see Fiedler, 1989a, 1989b; Sporer, 1997a; Sporer and Kuepper, 1995).

Furthermore, an integration of the SVA and RM approaches appears ultimately desirable, which should also consider additional theoretical aspects as well as a variety of moderator variables that may affect the outcomes of the validity of individual criteria, and thus detection accuracy (see Sporer, 1998).

The one-sided emphasis on intrapersonal, cognitive processes by the RM approach has to be complemented by social psychological theorising on interpersonal reality monitoring (Johnson, et al., 1998), on attribution of credibility (e.g., Chaiken's, 1980, heuristic-systematic model), and specific social psychological theorising on deception and its detection (DePaulo and Friedman, 1998; DePaulo et al., 2003; Köhnken, 1990; Sporer, 1997a, 1998; Vrij, 2000). For the last seven years I have attempted to integrate these approaches in an encompassing framework.

In the following, I briefly describe a preliminary study (Study 1) that has led me to the development of the Aberdeen Report Judgement Scales (ARJS), a set of cognitive-social criteria which have been specifically designed to evaluate reports based on theorising from the different domains mentioned. In particular, the ARJS contain a reformulation and operationalisation of all CBCA and RM criteria which are then integrated into scales in order to evaluate an account. Thereafter, I summarise another study (Study 2), which was the first study to test the reliability and validity of the ARJS in a quasi-experiment.

An integration: evaluating reports with the Aberdeen Report Judgement Scales

In several studies Sporer and his colleagues (Sporer, 1997a, 1997b; Sporer and Bursch, 1996) had different raters evaluate accounts of both invented and self-experienced events both with the CBCA criteria by Steller and Köhnken (1989) as well as with the eight RM criteria derived from Sporer and Kuepper's (1995) JMCQ. As these studies involved a large number of accounts (200 and 80 reports, respectively), it was possible to examine the inter-correlations between the CBCA criteria as well as the underlying dimensions via factor analyses.

Study 1

In the present study two female raters who had read several articles on CBCA were subsequently briefly trained with a twelve-page manual describing the nineteen CBCA criteria with examples from the literature. After establishing interrater reliability with various measures, ratings were averaged across both raters. These ratings were then correlated with the ratings on the eight RM criteria from the study by Sporer and Kuepper (1995).

Table 4.4 shows the inter-correlations between the nineteen CBCA criteria and eight RM criteria in this study. Of the 152 correlations, 17 are significant at $p < .01$, and an additional 17 at $p < .05$, far more than one would expect by chance alone. Considering that some of the criteria showed floor effects (Spontaneous corrections, Admitting lack of memory, Doubts about own testimony, Self-deprecation, Exculpation of interaction partner, Event-specific details, Sensory information), or ceiling effects (Logical consistency), the number of significant inter-correlations between the two sets of criteria are probably underestimates.

Similar correlation patterns have been observed by Sporer (1997a, 1997b) and Sporer and Bursch (1996) where also pairs, or three raters,

Table 4.4 Correlations between 19 CBCA criteria and 8 JMCQ scales (N = 200)

CBCA criteria	Clarity/ Vividness	Sensory info	Spatial info	Time info	Emotions/ Feelings	Recon- structability	Realism	Cognitive operations
Logical consistency	.22**	-.13	.12	.10	.16*	-.04	-.05	.11
Unstructured production	-.21**	.00	-.04	-.07	-.06	.06	.09	-.05
Quantity of details	.38**	.10	.19**	.01	.07	.00	-.00	.13
Contextual embedding	.24**	-.16*	.29**	.30**	.02	.09	.12	.07
Interactions	.24**	.02	.28**	.15*	.06	.17*	-.05	.06
Conversations	.19**	-.01	.02	.00	.09	.11	-.12	.15*
Complications	.00	.03	-.10	.05	-.01	.15*	-.08	.15*
Unusual details	.12	.14*	.03	-.06	.03	.09	-.14*	-.07
Superfluous details	.26**	.11	.12	.07	-.06	.11	-.08	.08
Details misunderstood	.11	.10	.12	-.08	.05	.03	-.23**	.16*
External associations	.00	-.10	.09	.07	.06	-.10	.10	.35**
Own psychological processes	.22**	-.13	-.03	-.03	.56**	-.13	.15*	.17*
Partner's psychological processes	.13	.02	-.01	.01	.19**	-.05	.02	-.01
Spontaneous corrections	.03	-.02	.05	.13	.07	.13	-.02	.17*
Admitting lack of memory	.15*	.02	.06	-.00	.06	-.02	-.04	.07
Doubts about own testimony	-.16*	-.10	-.12	-.03	-.02	-.03	-.12	.14*
Self-deprecation	.11	-.07	.02	-.07	.27**	.11	-.04	.17*
Exculpation of interaction partner	.03	-.06	-.02	.08	.12	-.02	-.07	.04
Event-specific details	-.10	.02	-.10	-.13	-.12	.02	-.14	.06

** $p < .01$; * $p < .05$.

Table 4.5 *Common factors of forensic (CBCA) and reality monitoring (RM) criteria in the factor analyses by Sporer (1997a, 1997b) and Sporer and Bursch (1996)*

Sporer (1997a)	Sporer (1997b)	Sporer and Bursch (1996)
(1) Logical consistency/ Realism	(1) Logical consistency/ Realism	(3) Logical consistency/ Realism/Clarity/ Vividness
(4) Clarity/Vividness Unstructured production (−)	(3) Clarity/Vividness Unstructured production (−)	(1) Quantity of details/ Spatial information/ Contextual embedding/ Sensory information/
(2) Quantity of details/ Spatial information/ Contextual embedding/ Time information	(4) Quantity of details/ Spatial information/ (6) Contextual embedding/ Sensory information/ Time information	(6) Time information
(3) Feelings/Thoughts/ Sensory information	(2) Feelings/Thoughts	(2) Feelings/Thoughts
(5) Verbal/Non-verbal interactions	(5) Verbal/Non-verbal interactions	(4) Verbal/Non-verbal interactions
		(5) Surprise effect

Note. The numbers indicate the rank order of the extracted factors in the respective studies. The labels correspond to the factor names or the variable names with the highest loadings ($>.40$): a negative sign in parentheses refers to a negative loading on this factor.

had assessed both the CBCA and the RM criteria. When these inter-correlations were subjected to (varimax-rotated) factor analyses, similar factor structures emerged across several studies. Table 4.5 displays the factor structures that emerged in the factor analyses of these three studies. Despite minor variations between studies, five (or six) dimensions can be distinguished: (1) Logical consistency/Realism, (2) Clarity/Vividness, (3) Quantity of details (and Contextual embedding), (4) Feelings and Thoughts, and (5) Verbal/Non-verbal interactions. These commonalties suggest the integration of these two approaches as well as the integration with other aspects both of the autobiographical memory literature and of the basic social psychological theories, as well as specific work on deception.

Study 2

Based on these factor analyses as well as theorising in autobiographical memory (e.g., Anderson and Conway, 1997; Brewer, 1986, 1996; Conway, 1990; Larsen, 1998) and social psychological considerations, in particular the social psychology of attribution (see Fiske and Taylor, 1991; Gilbert, 1995; Wallbott, 1998) and impression management and deception (see DePaulo et al., 2003; DePaulo and Friedman, 1998; Fiedler, 1989a, 1989b; Pontari and Schlenker, 2000; Schlenker and Weigold, 1992), an integrated set of criteria has been devised, the Aberdeen Report Judgement Scales (ARJS: Sporer, 1998). The ARJS consist of thirteen scales which in turn are made up of a total of 52 individual items. They are grouped into the following five dimensions (1) Global characteristics, (2) Quantity and precision of details, (3) Internal processes, (4) Social aspects, and (5) Autobiographical memory. Each of these subgroups contains several scales which in turn are made up of several items. Table 4.6 summarises these scales and the items belonging to each scale.

Since 1996, we have been conducting a series of experimental and quasi-experimental studies attempting to improve scoring and interrater reliability (see Sporer et al., 2000) as well as demonstrating the validity of these scales in various domains of application. Here I only summarise the results of the first of these studies, a quasi-experiment conducted in Aberdeen, Scotland, which led to the name derivation of these scales (Sporer, 1998).

Participants were seventy-one army officer trainees (36 males, 35 females) who either had already participated in an overnight exercise in early winter in the Scottish Highlands, or were about to engage in this event. They either reported truthfully about the event or were instructed to describe the events as convincingly as possible to a ('blind') interviewer, as if they had actually experienced it. All participants received a short outline with certain key elements of the exercise that were supposed to be contained in their account. Half of the participants were instructed shortly before, the other half received the instructions the evening before, allowing them to prepare their story thoroughly.

All interviews were videotaped and transcribed, and the transcripts were rated by two blind raters. The raters received only a very short training in the use of the scales by the present author, including the rating of five sample accounts from a different study and feedback in the form of discussing these ratings afterwards with the author. Considering the minimal amount of training, interrater reliabilities were satisfactory (except for Realism/Coherence and Extra-ordinary details, which showed an extreme ceiling effect and a floor effect, respectively). Significant differences between ratings of experienced and fabricated accounts were obtained for Time information, Emotions/Feelings, Extra-ordinary details, Lack of social desirability. Thoughts/Reasoning and Personal significance were rated marginally significantly higher for self-experienced events (see also Table 4.6).

Table 4.6 *Grouping of items of Aberdeen Report Judgement Scales and effect sizes r for the difference between invented and experienced events (data from Sporer, 1998)*

Criteria group/Scales	Items	Scale	r
Global characteristics:			
(1) Realism and coherence (cf. logical consistency)	1–4	1	.02
(2) Clarity and vividness	5–8	2	.05
Quantity and precision of details:			
(3) Quantity and precision of details (cf. contextual embedding):			
(3a) Core and peripheral details and precision of details	9–12	3	.17
(3b) Spatial information	13–16	4	−.09
(3c) Time information	17–21	5	.27
(3d) Sensory impressions	22–25	6	.13
Internal processes:			
(4) Emotions and feelings	26–29	7	.25
(5) Cognitive operations:			
(5a) Thoughts and cognitive processes	30–32	8	.23
(5b) Memory processes and rehearsal	34–38	9	.14
(5b′: Internal and external rehearsal: 34, 35)			
(5b″: Embedding and supporting memories: 36–38)			
Social aspects:			
(6) Verbal and non-verbal interactions	39–43	10	.09
(7) Extra-ordinary details	44–45	11	.43
(8) Lack of social desirability	33, 46–48	12	.41
Autobiographical memory:			
(9) Personal significance and implications	49–52	13	.21

A multiple-discriminant analysis resulted in 69% correct classifications, 77.1% of the invented and 62.9% of the self-experienced accounts. The opportunity to prepare an account distracted from the validity of some of the criteria (with more Spatial information in the fabricated accounts) but did not eliminate their utility entirely. This and several other potential moderator variables need to be investigated more closely before these scales would be ready for practical applications.

Since then, I have elaborated the training for the use of these scales and have sought further validation in several follow-up studies with different types of events. By now, for most of the scales, satisfactory inter-coder reliability as well as internal consistency (Sporer, 1998; Sporer et al., 2000) have been demonstrated. In the most recent study (Sporer and Walther, in preparation), nine out of the thirteen scales showed significantly larger means for the self-experienced event than the fabricated one, with effect sizes between $r = .26$ for Clarity/Vividness to $r = .49$ for Memory/Rehearsal. If I compare these findings with many of the results reported above, I believe that the ARJS show both theoretical as well as empirical potential which should be explored in further research with different types of events and different types of participants, including children.

Conclusions

The reality/source monitoring approach provides not only an integrative framework that has been extremely useful in studying errors in reports but also a theoretical framework for studying deception and its detection. On the error side, the SMF has been fruitfully employed to study such diverse topics as the post-hoc assessment of the accuracy of person identifications, the misinformation effect, differences in source monitoring between adults, children, and the elderly, the false/recovered memory syndrome and the role of imagery and vividness in people's reports about experienced events or fantasies. In studying deception, the RM approach has been used by different research groups in Spain, Germany, the United Kingdom, the United States, Canada, Finland, France, and Sweden. Unfortunately, different authors have used different RM criteria, and also have defined and operationalised these differently, which makes it difficult to compare results across studies. Overall, the evidence is mixed. Some studies have shown differences between truthful and deceptive accounts among both adults and children. However, many of the differences are quite small and depend on several other factors that have to be taken into consideration such as scoring method (with frequency counts being confounded with the length of accounts) or opportunity to plan or prepare an account, that have to be taken into consideration.

The presence of RM criteria is also dependent on the age of participants, in particular younger vs. older children, as well as some personality variables like verbal ability, acting ability, self-monitoring, and vividness of visual imagery. While the CBCA approach has traditionally focused on children, the RM approach has not been successful with young children and may hold more promise with adults. Besides cognitive and meta-cognitive differences, at a young age children have not yet learned the narrative conventions of adults (see Fivush and Shukat, 1995, for the development of narrative competencies in preschoolers), including the conversational maxims postulated by Grice (1975), in particular those of quantity and quality.

In summary, there is a need to establish and define in detail a standard set of criteria which should be used by researchers to allow for comparisons across studies. In particular, operational definitions of 'Semantic information', 'Idiosyncratic information', 'Internal information', and 'Cognitive operations' have to become more precise which in turn may improve interrater reliability and resolve some of the contradictory findings observed. I have proposed the JMCQ, a modified version of the MCQ, as an instrument to assess other people's accounts but there is still too little research to draw conclusions about its validity. Also, these instruments need to be tested with ecologically more valid stimulus materials before applications in different fields are possible.

Some of the theoretical considerations when applying the RM approach to the detection of deception, particularly concerning Idiosyncratic information, Internal processes, and Cognitive operations, still have to be ironed out. In particular, which roles do Emotions play? Are they related to Cognitive operations as part of the general category of 'internal processes'? So far, only one study has convincingly demonstrated higher Cognitive processes in deceptive than truthful accounts (Vrij et al., in press). I believe that researchers should differentiate between different types of Cognitive operations. More precisely, supporting memories and rehearsal processes should be considered as cues to memories based on self-experienced events, not of indicators of fantasies or deceptive accounts.

Some of the criteria used are not clearly derived from the RM framework and contradict findings from research in the general detection of deception literature (see DePaulo et al., 2003). For example, in my view, the inclusion of Self-references is not to be considered as a sign of deception. Perhaps, even the opposite may be the case (Biland, Py, and Rimboud, 1999; Knapp, Hart, and Dennis, 1974). Another example is Confidence. While being confident about one's recollection (item 36 on the JMCQ scale) is considered an indicator of a true memory (vs. a suggested or imagined memory) in the RM tradition (Johnson et al., 1988, Exp. 1; Schooler et al., 1986, Exp. 1; for a summary, see Pezdek and Taylor, 2000), in SVA 'Admitting lack of memory' (CBCA criterion 15) is considered an indicator of a truthful (vs. a deceptive) statement. While the two item descriptions may not denote a 1:1 match, such contradictions in constructs need to be addressed when comparing, and integrating these approaches. The two approaches also differ in other aspects but the commonalties are probably stronger than the differences. As both criteria sets entail 'truth criteria', which are supposed to be more prevalent in truthful accounts (with the exception of Idiosyncratic information and Cognitive processes), researchers should extend their search for 'lie criteria' (such as verbal hedges, clichés or repetitions), which should be more frequent in deceptive statements. Deceptive statements may also be characterised by certain linguistic features (like higher levels of abstractness) that can be derived from Semin and Fiedler's linguistic category model (Semin and Fiedler, 1988, 1991).

There is also a need to place more emphasis on the nature of the communication situation in which deception takes place. In particular, the situation when evaluating and scrutinising a person's account with suspicion – as is probably routinely done in legal contexts by police officers or professional judges – is not the same as when a person is asked to imagine an event and report on it. So far, the RM approach has been applied only to the analysis of transcripts or written reports but I don't know whether fact-finders could also use the criteria effectively when judging other people's accounts 'on-line' in on-going interactions.

Although the RM approach has been proposed by some authors as an alternative to statement validity analysis and CBCA, I see the RM approach not as an alternative but rather as a complementary approach which should be integrated with CBCA into an encompassing framework for studying complex lies about factual events. Such an encompassing view also needs to take research on autobiographical and working memory as well as social psychological theorising about the attribution of credibility and impression management into account. I have proposed an integrative framework and presented first data from our on-going research programme that attempts to accomplish this difficult goal. Contrary to previous approaches that have focused on applications in specific domains only, viz. SVA/CBCA on child sexual abuse, or the RM on suggested or induced memories, the ARJS were constructed to allow applications in different domains, both with adults and children. Whether or not validity of this encompassing framework can be demonstrated in these different fields and with different populations is an empirical question.

REFERENCES

Alonso-Quecuty, M. (1992). Deception detection and reality monitoring: A new answer to an old question? In F. Loesel, D. Bender, and T. Bliesener (eds.), *Psychology and law: International perspectives* (pp. 228–332). Berlin: Walter de Gruyter.

(1993). Psicología forense experimental: El efecto de la demora en la toma de declaración y el grado de elaboración de la misma sobre los testimonios verdaderos y falsos [Experimental forensic psychology: The effect of delay and preparation of a statement upon truthful and deceptive testimonies]. In M. García (ed.), *Psicología social aplicada en los procesos jurídicos y políticos* (pp. 81–8). Sevilla: Eudema.

(1996). Detecting fact from fallacy in child and adult witness accounts. In G. Davies, S. Lloyd-Bostock, M. McMurran, and C. Wilson (eds.), *Psychology, law and criminal justice. International developments in research and practice* (pp. 74–80). Berlin: Walter de Gruyter.

Alonso-Quecuty, M. L., and Hernández-Fernaud, E. (1997). Tócala otra vez Sam: Repitiendo las mentiras [Play it again Sam: Retelling a lie]. *Estudios de Psicología, 57,* 29–37.

Alonso-Quecuty, M. L., Hernández-Fernaud, E., and Campos, L. (1997). Child witnesses: Lying about something heard. In S. Redondo, V. Garrio, J. Pérez, and R. Barbaret (eds.), *Advances in psychology and law: International contributions* (pp. 129–35). Berlin: Walter de Gruyter.

Anderson, S. J., and Conway, M. A. (1997). Representation of autobiographical memories. In M. A. Conway, (ed.), *Cognitive models of memory* (pp. 217–46). Hove: Psychology Press.

Arntzen, F. (1970/1993). *Psychologie der Zeugenaussage. Systematik der Glaubwuerdigkeitsmerkmale* [Psychology of eyewitness testimony. System of credibility criteria] (1st/3rd edn). Munich: C. H. Beck.

Biland, C., Py, J., and Rimboud, S. (1999). Evaluer la sincérité d'un témoin grâce à trois techniques d'analyse, verbales et non verbale [Evaluating a witness's sincerity with three verbal and nonverbal techniques]. *Revue Européenne de Psychologie Appliquée, 49,* 115–21.

Brewer, W. F. (1986). What is autobiographical memory? In D. C. Rubin (ed.), *Autobiographical memory* (pp. 25–49). Cambridge: Cambridge University Press.

(1996). What is recollective memory? In D. C. Rubin (ed.), *Remembering our past: Studies in autobiographical memory* (pp. 19–66). New York: Cambridge University Press.

Chaiken, S. (1980). Heuristic versus systematic information processing and the use of source versus message cues in persuasion. *Journal of Personality and Social Psychology, 39,* 752–66.

Conway, M. A. (1990). *Autobiographical memory: An introduction.* Milton Keynes, UK: Open University Press.

DePaulo, B. M., and Friedman, H. S. (1998). Nonverbal communication. In D. Gilbert, S. T. Fiske, and G. Lindzey (eds.), *Handbook of social psychology,* 4th edn, Vol. II (pp. 3–40). New York: Random House.

DePaulo, B. M., Lindsay, J. J., Malone, B. E., Muhlenbruck, L., Charlton, K., and Cooper, H. (2003). Cues to deception. *Psychological Bulletin, 129,* 74–112.

Donaldson, W. (1992). Measuring recognition memory. *Journal of Experimental Psychology: General, 121,* 275–7.

Fiedler, K. (1989a). Luegendetektion aus alltagspsychologischer Sicht [Lie detection based on commonsense]. *Psychologische Rundschau, 40,* 127–40.

(1989b). Suggestion and credibility: Lie detection based on content-related cues. In V. A. Gheorghiu, P. Netter, H. J. Eysenck, and R. Rosenthal (eds.), *Suggestion and suggestibility: Theory and research* (pp. 323–35). Berlin: Springer.

Fisher, R. P., and Geiselman, R. E. (1992). *Memory enhancing techniques for investigative interviewing: The Cognitive Interview.* Springfield, IL: Charles C. Thomas.

Fiske, S. T., and Taylor, S. E. (1991). *Social cognition.* New York: McGraw-Hill.
Fivush, R., and Shukat, J. R. (1995). Content, consistency, and coherence of early autobiographical recall. In M. S. Zaragoza, J. R. Graham, G. C. N. Hall, R. Hirschman, and Y. S. BenPorath (eds.), *Memory and testimony in the child witness* (pp. 5–23). London: Sage.
Gilbert, D. T. (1995). Attribution and interpersonal perception. In A. Tesser (ed.), *Advanced social psychology* (pp. 99–147). Boston: McGraw-Hill.
Granhag, P. A., Stroemwall, L., and Olsson, C. (2001, June). Fact or fiction? Adults' ability to assess children's veracity. Paper presented at the 11th European Conference on Psychology and Law in Lisbon, Portugal.
Grice, H. P. (1975). Logic and conversation. In P. Cole and J. L. Morgan (eds.), *Syntax and semantics, Vol. III: Speech acts* (pp. 41–58). New York: Seminar Press.
Johnson, M. K., and Raye, C. L. (1981). Reality monitoring. *Psychological Review, 88,* 67–85.
Johnson, M. K., and Suengas, A. (1989). Reality monitoring judgments of other people's memories. *Bulletin of the Psychonomic Society, 27,* 2, 107–10.
Johnson, M. K., Bush, J. G., and Mitchell, K. J. (1998). Interpersonal reality monitoring: Judging the sources of other people's memories. *Social Cognition, 16,* 199–224.
Johnson, M. K., Foley, M. A., Suengas, A. G., and Raye, C. L. (1988). Phenomenal characteristics of memories for perceived and imagined autobiographical events. *Journal of Experimental Psychology: General, 117,* 371–6.
Johnson, M. K., Hashtroudi, S., and Lindsay, D. S. (1993). Source monitoring. *Psychological Bulletin, 114,* 3–28.
Keogh, L., and Markham, R. (1998). Judgements of other people's memory reports: Differences in reports as a function of imagery vividness. *Applied Cognitive Psychology, 12,* 159–71.
Knapp, M. L., Hart, R. P., and Dennis, H. S. (1974). An exploration of deception as a communication construct. *Human Communication Research, 1,* 15–29.
Köhnken, G. (1990). *Glaubwuerdigkeit* [Credibility]. Munich: Psychologie Verlags Union.
Kuepper, B., and Sporer, S. L. (1995). Beurteileruebereinstimmung bei Glaubwuerdigkeitsmerkmalen: Eine empirische Studie [Interrater agreement for credibility criteria: An empirical study]. In G. Bierbrauer, W. Gottwald, and B. Birnbreier-Stahlberger (eds.), *Verfahrensgerechtigkeit – Rechtspsychologische Forschungsbeitraege für die Justizpraxis* (pp. 187–213). Cologne: Otto Schmidt Verlag.
Landry, K., and Brigham, J. C. (1992). The effect of training in Criteria-Based Content Analysis on the ability to detect deception in adults. *Law and Human Behavior, 16,* 663–75.
Larsen, S. F. (1998). What is it like to remember? On phenomenal qualities of memory. In C. P. Thompson, D. J. Herrmann, D. Bruce, J. D. Read, D. G. Payne, and M. P. Toglia (eds.), *Autobiographical memory: Theoretical and applied perspectives* (pp. 163–90). Mahwah, NJ: Lawrence Erlbaum.
Lindsay, D. S. (2002). Children's source monitoring. In H. L. Westcott, G. M. Davies, and R. H. C. Bull (eds), *Children's testimony* (pp. 83–98). Chichester, England: Wiley.

MacMillan, N. A., and Creelman, C. D. (1990). Response bias: Characteristics of detection theory, threshold theory, and 'nonparametric' indexes. *Psychological Bulletin*, *107*, 401–13.

(1991). *Detection theory: A user's guide*. New York: Cambridge University Press.

Marks, D. F. (1973). Visual imagery differences in the recall of pictures. *British Journal of Psychology*, *64*, 17–24.

Masip, J., Sporer, S. L., Garrido, E., and Herrero, C. (in press). The detection of deception with the reality monitoring approach: A review of the empirical evidence. *Psychology, Crime, and Law*.

McGinnis, D., and Roberts, P. (1996). Qualitative characteristics of vivid memories attributed to real and imagined experiences. *American Journal of Psychology*, *109*, 59–77.

McNicol, D. (1972). *A primer of signal detection theory*. London: George Allen, and Unwin.

Meissner, C. A., and Kassin, S. (2002). 'He's guilty!'. Investigator bias in judgments of truth and deception. *Law and Human Behavior*, *26*, 469–80.

Pezdek, K. (1994). The illusion of memory. *Applied Cognitive Psychology*, *8*, 339–50.

Pezdek, K., and Taylor, J. (2000). In D. F. Bjorklund (ed.), *False-memory creation in children and adults. Theory, research, and implication* (pp. 69–91). Mahwah, NJ: Lawrence Erlbaum.

Pontari, B. A., and Schlenker, B. R. (2000). The influence of cognitive load on self-presentation: Can cognitive busyness help as well as harm social performance? *Journal of Personality and Social Psychology*, *78*, 1092–108.

Reinhard, M.-A., Burghardt, K., Sporer, S. L., and Bursch, S. E. (2002). Luegst Du? Glaubwuerdigkeitsbeurteilung im Alltag [Are you lying to me? Credibility assessment in everyday life]. *Zeitschrift für Sozialpsychologie*, *33*, 169–80.

Riggio, R. E., and Friedman, H. (1983). Individual differences and cues to deception. *Journal of Personality and Social Psychology*, *45*, 899–915.

Ruby, C. L., and Brigham, J. C. (1997). The usefulness of the Criteria-Based Content Analysis technique in distinguishing between truthful and fabricated allegations. A critical review. *Psychology, Public Policy, and Law*, *3*, 705–37.

Santtila, P., Roppola, H., and Niemi, P. (1999). Assessing the truthfulness of witness statements made by children (aged 7–8, 10–11, and 13–14) employing scales derived from Johnson and Raye's model of Reality Monitoring. *Expert Evidence*, *6*, 273–89.

Schlenker, B. R., and Weigold, M. F. (1992). Interpersonal processes involving impression regulation and management. *Annual Review of Psychology*, *43*, 133–68.

Schooler, J. W., Clark, C., and Loftus, E. F. (1988). Knowing when memory is real. In M. M. Gruneberg, P. E. Morris, and R. N. Sykes (eds.), *Practical aspects of memory: Current research and issues*, Vol. I, S. (pp. 83–8). Chichester: Wiley.

Schooler, J. W., Gerhard, D., and Loftus, E. F. (1986). Qualities of the unreal. *Journal of Experimental Psychology: Learning, Memory, & Cognition*, *12*, 171–81.

Semin, G. R., and Fiedler, K. (1991). The linguistic category model, its bases, applications and range. *European Review of Social Psychology*, *2*, 1–30.

(1988). The cognitive functions of linguistic categories in describing persons: Social cognition and language. *Journal of Personality and Social Psychology*, *54*, 558–68.

Sporer, S. L. (1983, August). Content criteria of credibility: The German approach to eyewitness testimony. Paper presented in G. S. Goodman (Chair), *The child witness: Psychological and legal issues*. Symposium presented at the 91st Annual Convention of the American Psychological Association in Anaheim, California.

(1997a). The less traveled road to truth: Verbal cues in deception detection in accounts of fabricated and self-experienced events. *Applied Cognitive Psychology*, *11*, 373–97.

(1997b). Realitaetsueberwachungskriterien und forensische Glaubwuerdigkeitskriterien im Vergleich: Validitaetueberpruefung anhand selbst erlebter und erfundener Geschichten [Comparing reality monitoring criteria and forensic credibility criteria: Validity experiments with self-experienced and invented accounts]. In L. Greuel, T. Fabian, and M. Stadler (eds.), *Psychologie der Zeugenaussage* (pp. 71–85). Munich: Psychologie Verlags Union.

(1998, March). *Detecting deception with the Aberdeen Report Judgement Scales (ARJS): Theoretical development, reliability and validity*. Paper presented at the Biennial Meeting of the American Psychology–Law Society in Redondo Beach, CA.

Sporer, S. L., and Bursch, S. E. (1996, April). Detection of deception by verbal means: Before and after training. Paper presented at the 38. Tagung experimentell arbeitender Psychologen in Eichstaett, Germany.

Sporer, S. L., and Hamilton, S. C. (1996, June). Should I believe this? Reality monitoring of invented and self-experienced events from early and late teenage years. Poster presented at the NATO Advanced Study Institute in Port de Bourgenay, France.

Sporer, S. L., and Kuepper, B. (1994, September). Fantasie und Wirklichkeit – Erinnerungsqualitaeten von wahren und erfundenen Geschichten [Fantasy and reality – memory qualities of true and invented stories]. Paper presented at the 39th Congress of the German Psychological Association in Hamburg.

Sporer, S. L., and Kuepper, B. (1995). Realitaetsueberwachung und die Beurteilung des Wahrheitsgehaltes von Erzaehlungen: Eine experimentelle Studie [Reality monitoring and the judgment of credibility of stories: An experimental investigation]. *Zeitschrift für Sozialpsychologie*, *26*, 173–93.

Sporer, S. L., and Kuepper, B. (2004). Fantasie und Wirklichkeit – Erinnerungsqualitaeten von wahren und erfundenen Geschichten. [Fantasy and reality – memory qualities of true and invented stories]. *Zeitschrift für Psychologie* 1, 212, 135–51.

Sporer, S. L., Bursch, S. E., Schreiber, N., Weiss, P. E., Hoefer, E., Sievers, K., and Köhnken, G. (2000). Detecting deception with the Aberdeen Report Judgement Scales (ARJS): Inter-rater reliability. In A. Czerederecka, T. Jaskiewicz-Obydzinska, and J. Wojcikiewicz (eds.), *Forensic psychology and law. Traditional questions and new ideas* (pp. 197–204). Krakow: Institute of Forensic Research Publishers.

Sporer, S. L., Kuepper, B., and Bursch, S. E. (1995, April). Hilft Wissen ueber Realitaetsueberwachung, um zwischen wahren und erfundenen Geschichten zu unterscheiden? [Does knowledge about reality monitoring help to discriminate between true and invented stories?] Paper presented at the 37th Meeting of Experimental Psychologists in Bochum, Germany.

Sporer, S. L., Stucke, T. S., and Semweber, M. C. (2000). Individual differences in self-monitoring and content-oriented detection of deception. Paper presented at the 10th European Conference of Psychology and Law in Limassol, Cyprus.

Steller, M., and Köhnken, G. (1989). Criteria-based statement analysis. Credibility assessment of children's statements in sexual abuse cases. In D. C. Raskin (ed.), *Psychological methods for investigation and evidence* (pp. 217–45). New York: Springer.

Steller, M., Wellershaus, P., and Wolf, T. (1992). Realkennzeichen in Kinderaussagen: Empirische Grundlage der Kriterienorientierten Aussageanalyse [Reality criteria in children's statements: The empirical basis of criteria-oriented statement analysis]. *Zeitschrift für Experimentelle und Angewandte Psychologie, 39,* 151–70.

Strömwall, L. A., Bengtsson, L., Leander, L., and Granhag, P. A. (in press). Assessing children's statements: The impact of a repeated experience on CBCA and RM ratings. *Applied Cognitive Psychology.*

Undeutsch, U. (1967). Beurteilung der Glaubhaftigkeit von Aussagen [Evaluation of the credibility of statements]. In U. Undeutsch (ed.), *Handbuch der Psychologie: Vol. 11. Forensische Psychologie* (pp. 26–181). Goettingen: Hogrefe.

   (1982). Statement reality analysis. In A. Trankell (ed.), *Reconstructing the past: The role of psychologists in criminal trials* (pp. 27–56). Deventer, the Netherlands: Kluwer Academic.

Vrij, A. (2000). *Detecting lies and deceit. The psychology of lying and the implications for professional practice.* Chichester: John Wiley.

Vrij, A., and Holland, M. (1999). Individual differences in persistence in lying and experiences while deceiving. *Communication Research Reports, 3,* 299–308.

Vrij, A., Akehurst, L., and Morris, P. (1997). Individual differences in hand movements during deception. *Journal of Nonverbal Behavior, 21,* 87–102.

Vrij, A., Akehurst, L., Soukara, S., and Bull, R. (in press). Detecting deceit via analyses of verbal and nonverbal behavior in children and adults. *Human Communication Research.*

Vrij, A., Edward, K., and Bull, R. (2001). Stereotypical verbal and nonverbal responses while deceiving others. *Personality and Social Psychology Bulletin, 27,* 899–909.

Vrij, A., Edward, K., Roberts, K. P., and Bull, R. (2000). Detecting deceit via analysis of verbal and nonverbal behavior. *Journal of Nonverbal Behavior, 24,* 239–63.

Wallbott, H. G. (1998). Die 'Leakage'-Hypothese – Zum aktuellen Forschungsstand [The 'leakage' hypothesis – its current research status]. In A. Spitznagel (ed.), *Geheimnis und Geheimhaltung* (pp. 197–216). Göttingen: Hogrefe.

NOTES

1. Both copies of the German version as well as an English version of the SMCQ are available from the author on request. I am indebted to Marcia K. Johnson for permission to adopt the MCQ.

2. Note that by including items in this scale that refer to memorial processes, including overt and covert rehearsal and supporting memories, the scale may not represent a uni-dimensional construct of 'Cognitive operations at the time of encoding'. It also assesses memory attributes which can be expected to be higher in self-experienced accounts. With hindsight, it might explain why Cognitive operations were rated *higher* in self-experienced accounts. In subsequent work we have separated these aspects (Sporer and Hamilton, 1996).

3. As we were interested in theory testing rather than applications of these scales to (child) sexual abuse, we wanted to know whether these scales differentiate between invented and self-experienced accounts, irrespective of their emotional valence. In contrast, most research on CBCA has explicitly focused on paradigms involving *negative emotional* events (Landry and Brigham, 1992).

4. Although the authors point out that RM criteria are perhaps easier to code than CBCA criteria (citing also Sporer, 1997a) we believe that an intensive training is likely to increase interrater reliability and consequently increase the chances to demonstrate the validity of these criteria.

5. Note that this definition of hits and false alarms is different from that of Meissner and Kassin (2002) who take the interrogator's perspective of 'lie detection': in lie detection, a hit is a correctly classified lie while a false alarm is a truthful statement incorrectly classified as a lie. The definition of hits and false alarms used here is, however, similar to the one suggested by Pezdek (1994) for studying illusory memories in the context of the recovered/false memory debate.

APPENDIX

Judgement of Memory Characteristics Questionnaire (JMCQ; transl. from Sporer and Kuepper, 1995; items 40 to 43 added by Sporer and Hamilton, 1996)

Please enter all answers on the response sheet (not here)!

(1) **Clarity:**
In your opinion, the event remains how clear in the memory of the person telling the story?

(2) **Colours:**
Are objects, persons, or the environment described without colour or are colours described?

(3) **Quantity of visual details:**
How many visual details are described?

(4) **Sounds:**
How many or how intensely are sounds and tones mentioned?

(5) **Smells:**
How many or how intensely are smells mentioned?

(6) **Touch:**
How often or how intensely is something described when it is being touched?

(7) **Taste:**
How often or how intensely are tastes described?

(8) **Vividness:**
How vividly is the event described?

(9) **Precision of details:**
Are details described only superficially or very precisely?

(10) **Order of events:**
How comprehensible is the order of events described?

(11) **Complexity of storyline:**
How simple or complex is the story line?

(12) **Realism of storyline:**
How realistic is the storyline? Does it appear bizarre or realistic?

(13) **Location:**
How clearly is the location of the event described?

(14) **Setting:**
How familiar does the environment and the setting of the event appear to be to the person?

(15) **Spatial arrangement of objects:**
How clearly is the spatial arrangement of objects described?

(16) **Spatial arrangement of persons:**
How clearly is the spatial arrangement of persons described?

(17) **Time:**
How clearly is the time of the event described?

(18) **Year:**
How clearly is the year of the event described?

(19) **Season:**
How clearly is the season of the event described?

(20) **Day:**
How clearly is the day of the event described?

(21) **Hour:**
How clearly is the hour of the event described?

(22) **Duration:**
How long did the event last?

(23) **Evaluation of event (tone of the event):**
Which overall tone did the event have for the person? Did the person experience it rather negatively or rather positively?

(24) **Role played in the event:**
Which role did the person play in this event?
Was it more that of a spectator or participant?

(25) **Presumed consequences:**
At the time the event occurred, did it seem to have serious implications?

(26) **Factual consequences:**
According to the account, did the event have serious consequences or implications that became clear afterwards?

(27) **Remembered feelings:**
How well does the person remember feelings at the time of the event?

(28) **Type of feelings:**
At the time of the event, were the feelings negative or positive?

(29) **Intensity of feelings at the time:**
At the time of the event, were the feelings weak or intense?

(30) **Intensity of feelings now:**
At the time of telling the story, were the feelings weak or intense?

(31) **Thoughts:**
How precisely are the thoughts which the person had at the time of the event described?

(32) **Implications regarding personality:**
How much does the story reveal about the personality of the person?

(33) **Quality of remembering:**
How well does the person seem to remember the event?

(34) **Description of previous events:**
Is the event embedded into a broader context by describing events which took place before the event described?

(35) **Description of subsequent events:**
Is the event embedded into a broader context by describing events which took place after the event described?

(36) **Doubts about the accuracy of remembering:**
Does the storyteller have any doubts about the accuracy of the memory for the event or is he/she rather sure?

(37) **Repeated thinking about the event:**
How often has the storyteller thought about the event?

(38) **Repeated talking about the event:**
How often has the storyteller talked about the event?

(39) **Age of the storyteller:**
How old was the person at the time of the event?

(40) **Likelihood of event:**
Could an event story like this have happened to you in a comparable way?

(41) **Extraordinariness of event:**
To what extent is the story surprising, unpredictable or extra-ordinary?

(42) Incredible details:
To what extent does the story contain incredible details?

(43) Believability:
If someone else told you the story as the storyteller did, is it likely that you would believe it?

Story Nr.:. . . . . .   Code:. . . . . .   Gender: M___   F___   Age:. . . . .

Rater Nr.:. . . . . . .

Response sheet for the Judgement of Memory Characteristics Questionnaire (JMCQ; transl. from Sporer and Kuepper, 1995)

Please enter the story number and code as well as your gender, age, and subject number above!

Please consider to what extent the following criteria can be located in or attributed to the accounts of the event. For all questions use the following 7-point rating scale:

barely/little, etc. 1-2-3-4-5-6-7 much/strongly, etc.

Enter the number which corresponds best to your judgement into the box on the right. Even though you may have difficulty answering some of the questions, please, make an attempt to answer all of them. Only if you cannot answer a question at all and if even the lowest point on the scale is inappropriate, mark the box with an 'X'.

Question		*What is more correct?*	*Response*	
(1)	Clarity:	dim	sharp/clear	[__]
(2)	Colours:	black and white	entirely colour	[__]
(3)	Visual details:	little/none	a lot	[__]
(4)	Sound:	little/none	a lot	[__]
(5)	Smell:	little/none	a lot	[__]
(6)	Touch:	little/none	a lot	[__]
(7)	Taste:	little/none	a lot	[__]
(8)	Vividness:	vague	very vivid	[__]
(9)	Precision of details:	sketchy	very detailed	[__]
(10)	Order of events:	confusing	comprehensible	[__]
(11)	Complexity:	simple	complex	[__]
(12)	Realism:	bizarre	realistic	[__]
(13)	Location:	vague	clear/distinct	[__]
(14)	Setting:	unfamiliar	familiar	[__]

(15)	Spatial arrangement of objects:	vague	clear/distinct	[__]
(16)	Spatial arrangement of people:	vague	clear/distinct	[__]
(17)	Time:	vague	clear/distinct	[__]
(18)	Year:	vague	clear/distinct	[__]
(19)	Season:	vague	clear/distinct	[__]
(20)	Day:	vague	clear/distinct	[__]
(21)	Hour:	vague	clear/distinct	[__]
(22)	Duration:	short	long	[__]
(23)	Evaluation of event:	negative	positive	[__]
(24)	Role:	spectator	participant	[__]
(25)	Presumed consequences:	not at all	definitely	[__]
(26)	Factual consequences:	not at all	definitely	[__]
(27)	Remembered feelings:	not at all	definitely	[__]
(28)	Type of feelings:	negative	positive	[__]
(29)	Feelings at the time:	not intense	very intense	[__]
(30)	Feelings now:	not intense	very intense	[__]
(31)	Thoughts:	not at all	clearly	[__]
(32)	Implications regarding personality:	not much	a lot	[__]
(33)	Quality of remembering:	hardly	very well	[__]
(34)	Description of previous events:	not at all	yes, clearly	[__]
(35)	Description of subsequent events:	not at all	yes, clearly	[__]
(36)	Doubts about accuracy:	a great deal of doubt	no doubt whatsoever	[__]
(37)	Repeated thinking:	not at all	many times	[__]
(38)	Repeated talking:	not at all	many times	[__]
(39)	Age of storyteller at the time of the event:		[__years/__months]	
(40)	Likelihood of event:	not at all	quite likely	[__]
(41)	Extraordinariness:	common	extraordinary	[__]
(42)	Incredible details:	not at all	quite a few	[__]
(43)	Believability:	not at all	quite likely	[__]

5 The psychophysiological detection of deception

Charles R. Honts

The psychophysiological detection of deception: an applied psychology with a long history and wide application

The use of physiological measures to detect deception, known variously as the psychophysiological detection of deception (PDD), lie detection and the polygraph, has a history in psychological science that goes back to the end of the nineteenth century (Lombroso, 1895). Although applied interest in PDD was primarily an American phenomenon during most of the twentieth century, international application, research and interest has expanded rapidly in recent years (for reviews see Barland, 1988; Honts, Raskin and Kircher, 2002).

PDD is applied in a variety of settings for a variety of purposes. In some jurisdictions in the United States the results of PDD tests are admissible as evidence in legal proceedings. In many countries law enforcement uses PDD as an investigative tool to check the veracity of suspects and informants. PDD can also be used as a pre-employment screening tool to verify a person's credibility as part of the vetting process. In the United States, PDD use in the national security system to screen for persons engaged in hostile actions against the government is ubiquitous. Finally, a recent phenomenon in the United States is to use the polygraph as part of the release programme for convicted sex offenders. As a condition of release, convicted sex offenders are required to take and pass periodic polygraph tests concerning new sex offences or other prohibited behaviour. In that setting, the polygraph is described as both a treatment tool and a prophylactic measure. The use of the polygraph with convicted sex offenders is increasing rapidly and has nearly universal acceptance by the courts in the United States.

It is difficult to know the exact extent of the use of the polygraph worldwide. However, polygraph examinations clearly play an important role in law enforcement in Canada, Israel, Japan, and Korea (Barland, 1988; also see the recent testimony of David Raskin, in *Kevin Lee, et al., v. Honorable*

Lourdes Martinez, et al., 2003). The results of polygraph tests are generally accepted in court in Japan (Hira and Furumitsu, 2002). Polygraph tests are at least occasionally used by law enforcement in the following countries; Belgium, China, Taiwan, Mexico, Russia, Romania, Turkey, and Poland (Raskin, 2003 in *Kevin Lee, et al.,* v. *Honorable Lourdes Martinez* et al., 2003). The use of the polygraph for national security worldwide is not known. However, all uses of the polygraph worldwide appear to be growing. New polygraph research programmes recently started in Belgium (Verschuere, 2003) and the Netherlands (Merckelbach, Smulders, Jelicic, and Meijer, 2003).

Although there is currently a considerable body of scientific research on PDD, that research has focused primarily on the forensic/investigative applications. A much smaller body of research exists on the employment screening / national security applications, and virtually no research has yet been reported on the use of the polygraph in the treatment and monitoring of sex offenders (Honts, Thurber, Cvencek, and Allowey, 2002). This chapter presents a selective review of the scientific literature. No effort was made to make this an exhaustive review, the existing literature is too large and this venue too small for that task. Rather, the current approach was to identify generally accepted methods for high-quality research and then report those studies that satisfy the criteria for high quality. Thus the goal was to show the potential of the technique, not the currently achieved level of performance in the field. Generally, the criteria for study selection assure strong internal validity and a good potential generalisation (external validity, Cook and Campbell, 1979). I first address the science concerning the forensic applications of PDD. Research concerning the attitudes of the American scientific community towards PDD is also presented in the context of the continuing controversy about PDD in the scientific literature. I then consider the use of PDD in screening and national security. Since almost nothing is known about the validity of the use of the polygraph in treatment and monitoring, I do not revisit that issue here.

Current PDD methods and techniques

In practice, all modern polygraph instruments used for PDD record measures from at least three physiological systems that are controlled by the autonomic nervous system. State-of-the-science-field polygraph instruments are digital and use computer software for calibration, data storage, and data analysis. Recordings are made of sweating from the palm side of the hand (commonly known as the galvanic skin response, or the electrodermal response), relative blood pressure (obtained from an inflated cuff on the upper arm), and respiration (obtained from volumetric sensors placed around the chest and/or abdomen). State-of-the-science-field polygraph instruments also make measurements of peripheral vasomotor activity, usually from the palmar surface of the thumb, and monitor the subject's gross body movements with a piezoelectric sensor attached to the subject's chair.

PDD techniques are easily divided into one of two families of techniques. The first family, the Concealed Knowledge Tests (CKT), assesses credibility by presenting a subject with a series of multiple-choice alternatives containing the correct answer (key) and several foils. For example, in a burglary case involving the theft of a diamond ring, a suspect might be presented with the following item: If you were the burglar you would know what item was stolen. Was the stolen item: a ruby ring; an emerald ring; a diamond ring; an amethyst ring; a gold ring. The rationale of the CKT predicts that individuals lacking the critical knowledge will produce a pattern of random responding. Thus, the probability of a false positive error (an innocent person failing the test) on the CKT can be estimated by a probability model. The more key items tested, the lower the probability of a false positive error. Knowledgeable individuals are expected to respond selectively to the key items in each series.

Proponents of the CKT claim that it is scientifically sound and based on generally accepted scientific principles (Iacono and Lykken, 2002). However, the CKT is plagued by three serious difficulties. First, the CKT assumes that the key item is indistinguishable from the foil items (transparency). Transparency presents a serious problem of application in countries where the press frequently publishes many details of the various crime scenes. Moreover, CKT could contain items that might produce a biased non-random pattern of responding. While presenting the CKT items to a naïve group of subjects could assess such general bias, one would have to be careful to use a subject sample representative of the suspects. While the procedure of testing for bias is relatively easy in laboratory experiments, it might prove to be a daunting task in a field case. Moreover, testing for a general bias in the items would not uncover idiosyncratic biases in individuals.

The second major problem for the CKT is one of applicability. Many criminal cases are simply not amenable to the application of the CKT because the suspect is not claiming a lack of knowledge. For example, a person was present and witnessed a murder, and thus has all of the relevant knowledge, but is claiming to authorities that he or she was not involved in the commission of the crime. Podlesny (1993) reviewed the case files at the United States Federal Bureau of Investigation and found that the CKT could be applied in no more than 18 per cent of their cases.

Podlesny (2003) recently replicated this research in a much larger sample ($n = 758$) and estimated that the CKT could now be applied to no more than 8.6 per cent of the FBI's cases.

The third problem for the CKT is the most serious, and that is memorability. Presently there is no scientific way to predict what elements of a crime scene a perpetrator will remember. The literature on eyewitness memory leads one to predict that like bystander eyewitnesses, perpetrators are likely to have problems accurately remembering the details of the crime scene. Laboratory researchers avoid this problem by pilot testing mock crimes to determine memorability for items, or by making sure the key items for the laboratory CKT are over learned. This is simply not possible in real criminal cases. Failure to remember the key items of a CQT should result in increased false negative errors (guilty persons passing the test), and the available research supports the notion that the CKT is prone to false negative errors (see the review by Honts et al., 2002). In field studies as many as 58 per cent of the confirmed guilty individuals pass the CKT (Elaad, 1990). Moreover, as with eyewitness memory, other research has shown that the CKT is prone to distortion from post-event suggestion (Amato-Henderson, Honts, and Plaud, 1996). In the absence of clear guidance as to what items to include in a CKT, the fact that a criminal suspect shows no knowledge on a CKT provides little useful information. Unfortunately, the extensive literature on eyewitness memory suggests that there will be no easy solution to the problem of defining memorability for a specific suspect in a specific case. As the applicability of the CKT is highly limited, and it is plagued by basic theoretical problems, some of which may be intractable, I do not discuss it further in this chapter.

The second family of PDD techniques is the deception tests. These tests directly assess credibility by presenting direct accusatory questions. Unlike the CKT, deception tests are directly applicable in most criminal cases, although they would not be applicable in cases where there are legitimate reasons why the suspect would not remember the event (i.e., high levels of intoxication or subsequent brain trauma). The most commonly applied deception test, and the test with the most scientific research, is the Comparison Question Test (CQT.) The rationale of the CQT is as follows: The CQT assesses a person's credibility by looking for a differential reaction between two types of questions. The first type, the relevant questions, are direct accusatory questions that address the issue under investigation (e.g., Did you shoot John Doe?). The second type, the comparison questions, are ambiguous questions to which the subject is manoeuvered into answering, 'No' (e.g., Before 1994, did you ever do anything that was dishonest, illegal, or immoral?). Some versions of the CQT direct the subject to answer with a lie and establish the salience of the question through the structured interview (Raskin and Honts, 2002). The rationale of the comparison question test predicts that guilty subjects will produce larger physiological responses to the relevant questions to which they know they are deceptive, than to the relatively unimportant comparison questions. Innocent subjects are expected to produce larger physiological responses to the comparison questions, to which they are assumed to be either deceptive, or at least uncertain of the veracity of their answer, than to the truthfully answered relevant questions.

The CQT is administered as a structured and standardised test that moves through the following phases:

- Introduction / Rapport / Biography – basic information is obtained
- Free narrative – the subject is allowed to tell his or her version of the events in a non-accusatory interview
- Test – the examiner explains the procedure, presents the questions, and collects the physiological data
  - Description of the procedure – the subject is informed about the sensors and the test procedures
  - Introduction of questions – all test questions are reviewed with the subject, terms are defined, and subjects' questions and concerns are addressed
  - Data collection – physiological data are collected from at least three presentations of the question series
  - Evaluation – the physiological data are evaluated by the examiner and with computer models
  - Discussion / Interrogation – the subject is informed about the outcome of the test. Test results are discussed and, if appropriate, an interrogation is commenced.

The evaluation of CQT data was the subject of a great deal of scientific research beginning in the late 1970s. Presently two approaches are taken to evaluating the physiological data: human-based numerical scoring and computer based statistical classification analysis (for a general review, see Honts et al., 2002). Over the last twenty-five years numerical scoring has evolved from a subjective and intuitive approach to a highly standardised magnitude-estimation procedure that is highly reliable and valid (Bell, Raskin, Honts, and Kircher, 1999). There presently are several statistical classification models available to practitioners (see Kircher and Raskin, 1988). Generally, statistical classification models have been shown to perform as well as highly trained human evaluators who have access to only the physiological data, but they are outperformed by the original examiners (Honts et al., 2002).

Validity research on the Comparison Question Test (CQT)

As with virtually all applied psychologies, science has approached the problem of assessing the accuracy of the CQT in two venues – laboratory studies and field studies. Laboratory research is an attractive alternative because the scientist can control the environment and manipulate variables. Moreover, with regard to CQT, the scientist can know with certainty who is telling the truth and who is lying by randomly assigning subjects to conditions. Laboratory research on the CQT typically makes subjects deceivers by having them commit a mock crime (e.g., 'steal' a watch from an office) and then instructing them to lie about it during a subsequent test. From a scientific viewpoint, random assignment to conditions is highly desirable because it controls for the influence of extraneous variables that might confound the results of the experiment (Cook and Campbell, 1979). Laboratory research in general, and CQT research in particular, might be criticised for a lack of realism. A lack of realism might, but does not necessarily, limit the ability of scientists to apply the results of the laboratory to real-world settings. However, recent research shows that laboratory research in applied psychology tends to produce valid results in a variety of domains (Anderson, Lindsay, and Bushamn, 1999). If the goal of conducting laboratory research is to make statements about the validity of the CQT, then making the laboratory research as realistic as possible is necessary for generalisability. Kircher, Horowitz, and Raskin (1988) suggest the following as characteristics of high-quality generalisable laboratory studies of the CQT:

- Realistic subject samples – studies should use community samples not college students
- Representative methods and techniques – instrumentation and testing methods should be as similar as possible to those used in the field
- Motivation associated with test outcome – both innocent and guilty subjects should be motivated to produce a truthful outcome

A review of the available laboratory studies of the CQT finds eleven high-quality laboratory studies (Driscoll, Honts, and Jones, 1987; Ginton, Netzer, Elaad, and Ben-Shakhar, 1982; Honts, Raskin, and Kircher, 1994; Honts, Amato, and Gordon, 2004; Horowitz, Kircher, Honts, and Raskin, 1997; Kircher and Raskin, 1988; Patrick and Iacono, 1989; Podlesny and Raskin, 1978; Podlesny and Truslow, 1993; Raskin and Hare, 1978; Rovner, 1986). The results of those laboratory studies are illustrated in Table 5.1. The high-quality laboratory studies indicate that the CQT is a very accurate discriminator of truth-tellers and deceivers. Over all of the studies, the CQT correctly classified about 91 per cent[1] of the subjects and produced approximately equal numbers

Table 5.1 *The results of high-quality laboratory studies of the Comparison Question Test*

Study	Guilty				Innocent			
	n	% Correct	% Inc	% Wrong	n	% Correct	% Inc	% Wrong
Driscoll et al. (1987)[b]	20	90	10	0	20	90	10	0
Ginton et al. (1982)[b]	2	100	0	0	13	85	0	15
Honts et al. (1994)[a]	20	70	10	20	20	75	15	10
Honts et al. (2004)[b]	24	92	8	0	24	92	0	8
Horowitz et al. (1997)[c]	15	53	27	20	15	80	7	13
Kircher & Raskin (1988)	50	88	6	6	50	86	8	6
Patrick & Iacono (1989)	24	92	0	8	24	64	0	36
Podlesny & Raskin (1978)	20	70	15	15	20	90	5	5
Podlesny & Truslow (1993)	72	69	18	13	24	75	21	4
Raskin & Hare (1978)	24	88	12	0	24	88	4	8
Rovner et al. (1986)[a]	24	88	12	0	24	88	4	8
Means	26.8	82		7	23.5	83	7	10
Per cent decisions		91		9		89		11

Notes
[a] Countermeasure subjects excluded.
[b] Conditions representing standard field practice.
[c] Traditional comparison question subjects only.

of false positive and false negative errors. The National Research Council (NRC) of the National Academy of Science recently completed an extensive review of the polygraph. They included a wider variety of studies in their review (n = 52) and came up with an overall accuracy estimate of 86 per cent (NRC, 2003).

The alternative approach to studying the CQT is to conduct field studies. In this approach, polygraph tests conducted in actual cases are examined. Although field studies can be the subject of numerous problems (Cook and Campbell, 1979), the chief problem in detection of deception studies lies in unambiguously determining ground truth. That is, some method that is independent of the outcome of the test is needed for determining who is in fact telling the truth. Although a number of approaches have been taken, it is generally agreed that confessions are the best available criterion for ground truth in these studies. Scientists doing field research in this area (Honts et al., 2002) generally agree that useful field studies of the psychophysiological credibility assessment tests should have all of the following characteristics (Honts et al., 2002):

- Subjects should be sampled from the actual population of subjects in which the researcher is interested. If the researcher wants to make inferences about tests conducted on criminal suspects, then criminal suspects should be the subjects who are studied.
- Subjects should be sampled by some random process. Cases must be accepted into the study without reference to either the accuracy of the original outcome or the quality of the physiological recordings.
- Persons trained and experienced in the field-scoring techniques about which inferential statements are to be made must evaluate the resulting physiological data. Independent evaluations by persons who have access to only the physiological data are useful for evaluating the information content of those data. However, the decisions rendered by the original examiners probably provide a better estimate of the accuracy of polygraph techniques as they are actually employed in the field.
- The credibility of the subject must be determined by information that is independent of the specific test. Confessions substantiated by physical evidence are presently the best criterion available.

A review of the scientific literature reveals four field studies that met the above criteria for meaningful field studies of the CQT (Honts, 1996; Honts and Raskin, 1988; Patrick and Iacono, 1991; Raskin, Kircher, Honts, and Horowitz, 1988). The results of the independent evaluations for those studies are illustrated in Table 5.2. Overall, the independent evaluations of the field studies produce results that are quite similar to the results of the high-quality laboratory studies. The average accuracy of

Table 5.2 *The accuracy of independent evaluations in field studies of the Comparison Question Test*

Study	Guilty				Innocent			
	n	% Correct	% Inc	% Wrong	n	% Correct	% Inc	% Wrong
Honts (1996)[a]	7	100	0	0	6	83	17	0
Honts & Raskin (1988)[b]	12	92	8	0	13	62	23	15
Patrick & Iacono (1991)[c]	52	92	6	2	37	30	46	24
Raskin et al. (1988)[d]	37	73	27	0	26	61	31	8
Unweighted means	108	89	10	1	82	59	29	12
Per cent decisions		98		2		75		

Notes

[a] Subgroup of subjects confirmed by confession and evidence.
[b] Decision based only on comparisons to traditional comparison questions.
[c] Results from the mean blind rescoring of the cases 'verified with maximum certainty' (p. 235).
[d] These results are from an independent evaluation of the 'pure verification' cases.

Table 5.3 *Per cent correct decisions by original examiners in field cases*

Study	Innocent	Guilty
Honts & Raskin (1988)	100	92
Raskin et al. (1988)[a]	96	95
Patrick & Iacono (1991)	90	100
Honts (1996)[b]	100	94
Unweighted means	96.50	95.25

Notes
[a] Cases where all questions were confirmed.
[b] Includes all cases with some confirmation.

field decisions for the CQT was 90.5 per cent. However, with the field studies nearly all of the errors made by the CQT were false positive errors. The NRC (2003) review included a wider range of studies (n = 7) and they came up with an overall validity estimate of 89 per cent.

Although the high quality field studies indicate a high accuracy rate for the CQT, all of the data presented in Table 5.2 were derived from independent evaluations of the physiological data. This is a desirable practice from a scientific viewpoint, because it eliminates possible contamination (e.g., knowledge of the case facts, and the overt behaviours of the subject during the examination) that might be included in the decisions of the original examiners. However, independent evaluators rarely offer testimony in legal proceedings. It is usually the original examiner who gives testimony. Moreover, it is usually the original examiner who makes the decision to interrogate or release a current criminal suspect. Thus, accuracy rates based on the decisions of independent evaluators may not be the true figure of merit for legal proceedings and policy-makers. The results for the original examiners in the studies reported in Table 5.2 are presented in Table 5.3. These data clearly indicate that the original examiners are more accurate than the independent evaluators.

The scientific data concerning the validity of the polygraph can be summarised as follows: High-quality scientific research from the laboratory and the field converge on the conclusion that, when properly conducted, the CQT is a highly accurate discriminator of truth-tellers and deceivers. The research results converge on an accuracy estimate of approximately 90 per cent. Moreover, original examiners, who are most likely to offer testimony, produce even higher estimates of accuracy. There may be a tendency for the CQT to produce more false positive than false negative errors, but this trend in the current literature is not particularly strong. Moreover, no tendency towards false positive errors is seen in the decisions of the original examiners. The scientific validity of a properly administered polygraph examination in real-life cases compares favourably with such other forms of scientific evidence as x-ray films, electrocardiograms, fibre analysis, ballistics comparison tests, blood analysis, and is far more reliable than other forms of expert testimony (e.g., medical diagnosis based on radiology, psychiatric, and psychological opinions as to sanity, diminished capacity, dangerousness, and many of the post traumatic stress/recovered memory syndromes; see the discussion in Honts and Perry, 1992, and the recent study by Crewson, 2001).

Controversy regarding the CQT

There is a small group of highly vocal critics who frequently publish negative commentaries attacking the validity of the CQT (e.g., Ben-Shakhar and Furedy, 1990; Iacono and Lykken, 2002; Lykken, 1998). Their positions are generally characterised by the following overarching position: the rationale of the CQT is unreasonable and therefore the test cannot work. Their work is generally characterised by thought experiments that demonstrate that the CQT cannot work and that it is not possible to conduct valid or ethical research on the topic, but their position is generally without empirical support. They selectively rely on poorly conducted research and they fail to reference the high quality empirical studies. In particular they dismiss all laboratory studies as having any value for establishing the validity of the CQT, although they are willing to accept laboratory data when they show the CQT to be fallible.

When the critics do cite empirical studies their presentations are selective and sometimes misleading. For example, they frequently cite two highly flawed field studies as demonstrating that the CQT has low validity. The first of those studies is Horvath (1977). The Horvath study contains a large number of polygraphs on innocent crime victims, not criminal suspects. Moreover, the examiners in that study used global analysis of polygraph data, an approach shown to be low in validity and which is no longer in wide application. It is clearly inappropriate to generalise those data to criminal suspect cases (Honts et al., 2002). The other field study popular with the critics is Kleinmuntz and Szucko (1984). Subjects in that study were employees who were forced to take polygraph examinations as a condition of their employment, a very different type of setting from a criminal investigation. Moreover, students in a polygraph school who were forced to use a scoring system with which they were unfamiliar evaluated the Kleinmuntz and Szucko data. Clearly, neither of these studies can be considered of high quality, but they form the empirical core of the critics' attack on the CQT.

Attitudes of the scientific community towards the CQT

Undoubtedly there is controversy concerning the validity of the CQT in the scientific literature, and not all scientists would agree with the assessment I presented above. However, a legitimate question concerns whether or not the majority of the informed scientific community thinks the CQT is a valid and useful test. Four surveys (Amato and Honts, 1994; Gallup, 1984; Honts et al., 2002; Iacono and Lykken, 1997) of scientific opinion regarding the CQT were made.[2] All of those surveys have included members of the Society for Psychophysiological Research (SPR). The SPR is a professional society of scientists (PhD and MD) who study how the mind and body interact.

The Gallup Organization (1984) undertook the initial survey. That survey was replicated and extended by Amato and Honts (1994). The results of those two surveys were very consistent. Roughly two-thirds of the PhD and MD SPR respondents stated that polygraph tests were a valuable diagnostic tool when considered with other available information or that it was sufficiently reliable to be the sole determinant. In the Amato and Honts survey, when only those respondents who reported they were highly informed about the polygraph literature are considered, the percentage that opine that polygraph tests are a useful diagnostic tool rises to 83 per cent. Of those individuals in the Honts and Amato survey who rated themselves as highly informed, fewer than 10 per cent report being involved in conducting polygraph examinations professionally. Therefore, these results are not suspect on the grounds that the responses were skewed by the financial self-interest of the respondents. These results would seem to indicate that there is a great deal of acceptance of these techniques in the relevant scientific community.

The Iacono and Lykken survey (1997) also addressed the members of the SPR and extended the survey to the members of the American Psychological Association Division 1 (General Psychology). However, the Iacono and Lykken survey is so surrounded by controversy and uncertainty that its value as a valid assessment of scientific opinion is in question. Honts et al. (2002) provide a detailed critique of the problems with the Iacono and Lykken survey. To date Iacono and Lykken have refused all requests to provide their data for independent examination and/or reanalysis. Iacono recently revealed that the data have now been destroyed (*Kevin Lee, et al.,* v. *Honorable Lourdes Martinez, et al.,* 2003).

Honts et al. (2002) reported the most recent survey of scientific opinion regarding the validity of polygraph testing. As well as surveying the members of the SPR, Honts et al. also assessed the opinions of the members of the American Psychology–Law Society (APLS). The APLS is an organisation of scientists and lawyers that study how scientific psychology and the law interact. The members of the APLS are familiar with conducting applied research for use in legal settings and with legal requirements for the admissibility of scientific evidence in the United States. Moreover, in recent years an increasing amount of research on polygraph testing has been presented at the APLS meetings and in psychology and law related journals. Thus, the members of the APLS are also likely to be familiar with much of the current scientific literature on polygraph testing. The Honts et al. (2002) survey found favourable attitudes towards the polygraph among members of both the SPR and the APLS. Those results are typified by the responses to the following question: Do you believe that the accuracy of judicial verdicts about guilt and innocence would be decreased or increased if polygraph experts were allowed to present the results of polygraphs in courts of law? Respondents replied on the following five-point scale. 1 = greatly decreased, 2 = slightly decreased, 3 = unaffected, 4 = slightly increased, and 5 = greatly increased. The modal response for both groups was choice 4: accuracy would be slightly increased. The percentage of respondents who opined that verdicts would either be unaffected, or show increased accuracy was 72 per cent for the APLS and 61 per cent for the SPR. The modal response for both groups was that verdict accuracy would be slightly increased by the introduction of polygraph evidence.

Areas of concern

There are some areas of legitimate concern that could potentially have an impact on the validity of a CQT conducted in a forensic setting.

Field practice standards   The polygraph profession has historically not had strong field practice standards. However, the last several years have seen considerable progress in the area of standards. Raskin and Honts (2002) recently presented a detailed description of how to conduct a CQT properly. Moreover an international standard for conducting forensic polygraph examinations was recently promulgated by the American Society of Testing and Materials, International (ASTM, 2000). Based on Raskin and Honts (2002) and on the ASTM (2000) standard, a properly conducted field polygraph examination should have the following characteristics:

- The examination will not follow an interrogation. Interrogations are likely to sensitise the subject and may lead to an increase in false positive errors.
- The examiner should engage in adequate pretest preparation so that he or she will have formulated a number of alternative hypotheses about what may have happened in the case and a preliminary set of test questions will have been written.
- A recording preserves the entire examination.
- The examination takes place in a non-accusatory environment with an interview that allows the subject to give a free narrative version of the events.
- The examiner displays a willingness to adjust the question wording in response to the narrative and in response to concerns raised by the subject.
- The data are evaluated by one of the validated numerical scoring systems.

Countermeasures   Countermeasures are anything that a subject might do in an effort to defeat or distort an examination. PDD examinations are no different from any other test given in a forensic setting. Guilty suspects are highly motivated to present themselves well and to produce a favourable outcome. The possibility that PDD subjects could engage in countermeasures in an effort to produce a truthful outcome is a legitimate concern and a topic for research. For conceptual purposes polygraph countermeasures can be divided into four categories: Informational Countermeasures concern the impact of subjects knowing about the structure and scoring of PDD tests as well as knowledge of manoeuvres that might serve to inhibit or produce physiological responses. Spontaneous Countermeasures refer to countermeasures that subjects attempt in the absence of formal training. General State Countermeasures are things that a subject does in order to alter his or her general physiological reactivity. General State Countermeasures include such things as ingesting drugs, exercise, or putting antiperspirant on the fingers. The other category of countermeasures is the Specific Point Countermeasures. Specific Point Countermeasures are applied during the PDD examination in an effort to alter the subject's response to specific items. Specific Point Countermeasures include such things as tensing muscles, inducing pain, or engaging in mental activity.

Honts and Amato (2002) provided a recent review of the available research on countermeasures against PDD examinations. Based on the research reviewed by Honts and Amato (2002), several conclusions are possible from the now extensive countermeasure research literature generated over the last twenty years:

- Informational Countermeasures: Two studies have assessed the impact of providing extensive information about the nature and scoring of the CQT and about possible countermeasures (Alloway and Honts, 2002; Rovner, 1986). Neither of those studies produced significant effects of information.
- Spontaneous Countermeasures: There are several studies of the effectiveness of Spontaneous Countermeasures, and the results are consistent and clear: countermeasures attempted without the benefit of hands-on training are ineffective at producing increased false negative or inconclusive outcomes (Honts, Amato, and Gordon, 2001; Honts, Raskin, Kircher, and Hodes, 1988; Otter-Henderson, Honts, and Amato, 2002).
- General State Countermeasures: No research has demonstrated that any General State Countermeasure is effective in increasing false negative or inconclusive rates with the CQT.
- Specific Point Countermeasures: Research demonstrates that some Specific Point Countermeasures can significantly increase false negative rates with both the CQT (e.g., Honts, Hodes, and Raskin, 1985; Honts, Raskin, and Kircher, 1987; 1994) and the CKT (Elaad and Ben-Shakhar, 1991; Honts, Devitt, Winbush, and Kircher, 1996). One study demonstrated that computer evaluation of the PDD data substantially ameliorated the problem of false negatives (Honts et al., 1994). However, those conclusions are qualified by two important caveats:
  - All of this research is conducted in the context of laboratory research. It should be noted that the consequences of failing a forensic polygraph are much higher than the motivations used in laboratory studies. Thus, it seems likely that the error estimates generated by the laboratory studies represent a worst case for the success of countermeasures.
  - The effectiveness of Specific Point Countermeasures was demonstrated only following hands-on training. Research that supplied subjects with extensive information about the CQT and about Specific Point Countermeasures failed to produce significant effects (Rovner 1986; Alloway and Honts, 2002).

In summary, the now extensive scientific literature on countermeasures has not demonstrated any effective Informational, General State or Spontaneous Countermeasures. Providing information about the nature of the CQT and about possible countermeasures does not allow deceptive subjects to beat the CQT. Specific Point Countermeasures following

Table 5.4 *Contingency table of outcomes for a highly accurate PDD test with a low base rate of guilt*

| | | Outcome | | |
		Deceptive	Truthful	Totals
Reality	Guilty	90	10	100
	Innocent	90	810	900
	Totals	180	820	1000

hands-on training enable some subjects to produce false negative outcomes. The laboratory research establishing these findings is likely to represent worst-case scenarios. Moreover, the problem of effective countermeasures seems to be substantially ameliorated by the use of computer-based statistical analysis of the data (Honts et al., 1994).

Polygraphs in national security

In stark contrast to the scientific literature on forensic use of PDD, the use of PDD in employment and for screening, including screening for national security, is the subject of relatively little published research. Initial commentary on the use of polygraphs for national security screening focused on problems that all diagnostic tests experience when attempting to diagnose a rare condition. This difficulty is known as the base-rate problem. For example, consider the situation where there is a technique that correctly classifies subjects at an accuracy of 90 per cent. One thousand subjects are tested and 100 of them are guilty. The classifications resulting from this situation are illustrated in Table 5.4. In this situation, although the test is 90 per cent accurate, because the opportunity for false positive errors is much higher than the opportunity for true positives, half of the deceptive outcomes are incorrect and the confidence in a positive outcome is only 50 per cent. On the other hand, because the opportunity for false negatives is very low compared to the opportunity for true negatives, the confidence in a negative outcome is very high (98.8 per cent). Thought experiments such as this led many commentators in the 1970s and 1980s to expect that national security screening tests would produce many false positive outcomes (e.g., Raskin, 1986).

However, the results of the studies done on screening applications of the polygraph produced very different results from those predicted by base-rate projections and also very different from the PDD research

Table 5.5 *Per cent outcomes in the polygraph screening study reported by Barland, Honts, and Barger (1989)*

	Polygraph outcome		
Reality	Truthful	Inconclusive	Deceptive
Innocent ($n = 116$)	91	3	6
Guilty ($n = 91$)	60	9	31

conducted in forensic contexts. Barland, Honts and Barger (1989) reported the largest of the studies of national security screening. Barland et al. conducted a large mock-espionage study where subjects were recruited from an American military base. Those subjects engaged in complex scenarios that involved committing acts that could be considered as espionage (e.g., removing a 'Secret' document from a secure facility and then selling it to an agent in a bar in the local town). Subjects were subsequently given screening polygraph examinations by government polygraph examiners whose primary duty was to run screening polygraph examinations. Those examiners were instructed to conduct the examinations as if they were real screening tests and to interrogate the subjects if they felt they were deceptive. The results of Barland, Honts, and Barger (1989) were quite surprising. Rather than producing a large number of false positive outcomes, the examinations produced a large number of false negative outcomes. The overall results from the study are illustrated in Table 5.5 and were only slightly better than chance, reflecting a high bias towards truthful outcomes. Subsequent research in the early 1990s replicated and extended the finding that false negative outcomes predominated with the national security screening PPD test. Reviews of that literature are provided by Honts (1991; 1994). It appears that in the last ten years the United States Government has conducted a great deal of research on improving the validity of the national security PDD techniques with some laboratory studies now showing substantial improvements in accuracy (e.g., DoDPI, 1998; also see the recent review by Krapohl, 2002). There is no published research assessing whether or not the accuracy rates demonstrated for such new tests generalise to the field.

Summary

The use of physiological measures for the detection of deception in forensic situations is strongly supported by both high-quality laboratory and high-quality field studies. Although there is controversy about the forensic application of the polygraph, the majority of informed scientists in the United States report positive opinions about the comparison question test. The modal response from American scientists when asked about the impact of polygraph admissibility on judicial verdicts was that accuracy would be slightly increased by admissibility. The situation for the use of the polygraph screening is much different. The scientific literature is small and is generally negative about the validity of the screening uses of the polygraph. Recent research suggests improvement in the screening polygraph techniques, but much additional research is needed in that area. Some countermeasures may pose a threat. Additional research on countermeasures is needed. Researchers are invited to contribute to this growing and interesting area of applied psychology.

REFERENCES

Alloway, W. R., and Honts, C. R. (2002, April). An information countermeasure has no effect on the validity of the Test for Espionage and Sabotage (TES). Paper presented at the annual meeting of the Rocky Mountain Psychological Association, Park City, Utah.

Amato, S. L., and Honts, C. R. (1994). What do psychophysiologists think about polygraph tests? A survey of the membership of SPR. *Psychophysiology, 31,* S22. [Abstract]

Amato-Henderson, S. L., Honts, C. R., and Plaud, J. J. (1996). Effects of misinformation on the Concealed Knowledge Test. *Psychophysiology, 33,* S18. [Abstract]

American Society for Testing and Materials (2000). *Standard guide for PDD examination standards of practice.* ASTM Designation: E 2062_00.

Anderson, C. A., Lindsay, J. J., and Bushman, B. J. (1999). Research in the psychological laboratory: Truth or triviality? *Current Directions In Psychological Science, 8,* 3–9.

Barland, G. H. (1988). The polygraph test in the US and elsewhere. In A. Gale (ed.) *The polygraph test: Lies, truth, and science* (73–95). Beverly Hills, CA: Sage.

Barland, G. H., Honts, C. R., and Barger, S. D. (1989). *Studies of the accuracy of security screening polygraph examinations.* Department of Defense Polygraph Institute, Fort McClellan, Alabama.

Bell, B. G., Raskin, D. C., Honts, C. R., and Kircher, J. C. (1999). The Utah numerical scoring system. *Polygraph, 28, 1–9.*

Ben-Shakhar, G., and Furedy, J. J. (1990). *Theories and applications in the detection of deception.* New York: Springer.

Cook, T. D., and Campbell, D. T. (1979). *Quasi-experimentation: Design & analysis issues for field settings.* Boston: Houghton Mifflin.

Crewson, P. E. (2001). A comparative analysis of polygraph with other screening and diagnostic tools. Report on Contract No. DABT60-01-P-3017 to the Department of Defense Polygraph Institute.

Department of Defense Polygraph Institute Research Division Staff (1998). Psychophysiological detection of deception accuracy rates obtained using the Test for Espionage and Sabotage (TES). *Polygraph, 27,* 68–73.

Driscoll, L. N., Honts, C. R., and Jones D. (1987). The validity of the positive control physiological detection of deception technique. *Journal of Police Science and Administration, 15,* 46–50.

Elaad, E. (1990). Detection of guilty knowledge in real-life criminal investigations. *Journal of Applied Psychology, 75,* 521–9.

Gallup Organization (1984). Survey of the members of the Society for Psychophysiological Research concerning their opinions of polygraph test interpretations, *Polygraph, 12,* 153–65.

Ginton, A., Netzer, D., Elaad, E., and Ben-Shakhar, G. (1982). A method for evaluating the use of the polygraph in a real-life situation. *Journal of Applied Psychology, 67,* 131–7.

Hira, S., and Furumitsu, I. (2002). Polygraphic examinations in Japan: Application of the guilty knowledge test in forensic investigations. *International Journal of Police Science and Management, 4,* 16–27.

Honts, C. R. (1991). The emperor's new clothes: Application of polygraph tests in the American workplace. *Forensic Reports, 4,* 91–116.

(1994). The psychophysiological detection of deception. *Current Directions in Psychological Science, 3,* 77–82.

(1996). Criterion development and validity of the control question test in field application. *Journal of General Psychology, 123,* 309–24.

Honts, C. R., and Amato, S. (2002). Countermeasures. In M. Kleiner (ed.), *Handbook of polygraph testing* (251–64). London: Academic.

Honts, C. R., Amato, S., and Gordon, A. K. (2001). Effects of spontaneous countermeasures used against the comparison question test. *Polygraph, 30,* 1–9.

Honts, C. R., Amato, S., and Gordon, A. K. (2004). Effects of outside issues on the Control Question Test. *Journal of General Psychology, 151,* 53–74.

Honts, C. R., Devitt, M. K., Winbush, M., and Kircher, J. C. (1996). Mental and physical countermeasures reduce the accuracy of the concealed knowledge test. *Psychophysiology, 33,* 84–92.

Honts, C. R., Hodes, R. L., and Raskin, D. C. (1985). Effects of physical countermeasures on the physiological detection of deception. *Journal of Applied Psychology, 70,* 177–87.

Honts, C. R., and Perry, M. V. (1992). Polygraph admissibility: Changes and challenges. *Law and Human Behavior, 16,* 357–79.

Honts, C. R., and Raskin, D. C. (1988). A field study of the validity of the directed lie control question. *Journal of Police Science and Administration, 16,* 56–61.

Honts, C. R., Raskin, D. C., and Kircher, J. C. (1987). Effects of physical countermeasures and their electromyographic detection during polygraph tests for deception. *Journal of Psychophysiology, 1,* 241–7.

(1994). Mental and physical countermeasures reduce the accuracy of polygraph tests. *Journal of Applied Psychology, 79,* 252–9.

(2002). The scientific status of research on polygraph techniques: the case for polygraph tests. In D. L. Faigman, D. Kaye, M. J. Saks, and J. Sanders (eds.), *Modern scientific evidence: The law and science of expert testimony*, Vol. II (pp. 446–83). St. Paul, MN: West.

Honts, C. R., Raskin, D. C., Kircher, J. C., and Hodes, R. L. (1988). Effects of spontaneous countermeasures on the physiological detection of deception. *Journal of Police Science and Administration*, *16*, 91–4.

Honts, C. R., Thurber, S., Cvencek, D., and Alloway, W. (2002, March). General acceptance of the polygraph by the scientific community: Two surveys of professional attitudes. Paper presented at the American Psychology–Law Society biennial meeting, Austin, Texas.

Horowitz, S. W., Kircher, J. C., Honts, C. R., and Raskin, D. C. (1997). The role of comparison questions in physiological detection of deception. *Psychophysiology*, *34*, 108–15.

Horvath, F. S. (1977). The effect of selected variables on interpretation of polygraph records. *Journal of Applied Psychology*, *62*, 127–36.

Iacono, W. G., and Lykken, D. T. (1997a). The validity of the lie detector: Two surveys of scientific opinion. *Journal of Applied Psychology*, *82*, 426–33.

(2002). The scientific status of research on polygraph techniques: The case against polygraph tests. In D. L. Faigman, D. Kaye, M. J. Saks, and J. Sanders (eds.), *Modern scientific evidence: The law and science of expert testimony*, Vol. II (pp. 483–538). St. Paul, MN: West.

Kevin Lee, et al., v. Honorable Lourdes Martinez, et al., Case No. CS-2003-0026. (2003). Transcript of sworn testimony.

Kircher, J. C., Horowitz, S. W., and Raskin, D. C. (1988). Meta-analysis of mock crime studies of the control question polygraph technique. *Law and Human Behavior*, *12*, 79–90.

Kircher, J. C., and Raskin, D. C. (1988). Human versus computerized evaluations of polygraph data in a laboratory setting. *Journal of Applied Psychology*, *73*, 291–302.

Kleinmuntz, B., and Szucko, J. (1984). A field study of the fallibility of polygraphic lie detection. *Nature*, *308*, 449–50.

Krapohl, D. (2002). The polygraph in personnel screening. In M. Kleiner (ed.), *Handbook of polygraph testing*, (pp. 217–36). London: Academic.

Lombroso, C. (1895). *L'Homme Criminel* (2nd edn). Paris: Felix Alcan.

Lykken, D. T. (1998). *A tremor in the blood: Uses and abuses of the lie detector*. New York: Plenum Trade.

Merckelbach, H., Smulders, F., Jelicic, M., and Meijer, E. (2003). Unpublished survey document distributed October 2003. University of Maastricht, the Netherlands.

National Research Council (2003). *The polygraph and lie detection*. Washington, DC: National Academy Press.

Otter-Henderson, K., Honts, C. R., and Amato, S. L. (2002). Spontaneous countermeasures during polygraph examinations: An apparent exercise in futility. *Polygraph*, *31*, 9–14.

Patrick, C. J., and Iacono, W. G. (1989). Psychopathy, threat and polygraph test accuracy. *Journal of Applied Psychology*, *74*, 347–55.

(1991). Validity of the control question polygraph test: The problem of sampling bias. *Journal of Applied Psychology*, *76*, 229–38.

Podlesny, J. A. (1993). Is the guilty knowledge polygraph technique applicable in criminal investigations? A Review of FBI case records. *Crime Laboratory Digest*, 20, 57–61.

Podlesny, J. A., and Raskin, D. C. (1978). Effectiveness of techniques and physiological measures in the detection of deception. *Psychophysiology*, 15, 344–58.

Podlesny, J. A., and Truslow, C. M. (1993). Validity of an expanded-issue (modified general question) polygraph technique in a simulated distributed-crime-roles context. *Journal of Applied Psychology*, 78, 788–97.

Raskin, D. C. (1986). The polygraph in 1986: Scientific, professional, and legal issues surrounding applications and acceptance of polygraph evidence. *Utah Law Review*, 1986, 29–74.

Raskin, D. C., and Hare, R. D. (1978). Psychopathy and detection of deception in a prison population. *Psychophysiology*, 15, 121–36.

Raskin, D. C., and Honts, C. R. (2002). The comparison question test. In M. Kleiner (ed.), *Handbook of polygraph testing* (pp. 1–49). London: Academic.

Raskin, D. C., Kircher, J. C., Honts, C. R., and Horowitz, S. W. (1988). *A study of the validity of polygraph examinations in criminal investigation* (Grant No. 85-IJ-CX-0040). Salt Lake City: University of Utah, Department of Psychology.

Rovner, L. I. (1986). The accuracy of physiological detection of deception for subjects with prior knowledge. *Polygraph*, 15, 1–39.

Verschuere, B., (2003, October). Heart rate orienting to guilty knowledge. Paper presented at the annual meeting of the Society for Psychophysiological Research, Chicago, IL, USA.

NOTES

1. The results excluded the inconclusive outcomes, as they are not decisions.
2. These surveys were made in the context of addressing the legal question of general acceptance of a scientific technique within the relevant scientific community. This issue is a specific criterion for assessing the admissibility of scientific evidence in American jurisprudence. Thus, these surveys were all focused on American scientists.

Part 3

Special issues facing a lie-catcher

6   Lies travel: mendacity in a mobile world

Charles F. Bond, Jr and Sandhya R. Rao

> My Master heard me with great Appearances of Uneasiness in his Countenance, because *Doubting*, or *not believing*, are so little known in his country, that the Inhabitants cannot tell how to behave themselves under such Circumstances. And I remember in frequent Discourses with my Master . . . [when] having Occasion to talk of *Lying*, and *false Representation*, it was with much difficulty that he comprehended what I meant; although he had otherwise a most acute Judgment. For he argued thus; That the Use of Speech was to make us understand one another, and to receive Information of Facts; now if any one *said the Thing which was not*, these Ends were defeated; because I cannot properly be said to understand him; and I am so far from receiving Information, that he leaves me worse than in Ignorance; for I am led to believe a Thing *Black* when it is *White*, and *Short* when it is *Long*. And these were all the Notions he had concerning that Faculty of *Lying*, so perfectly well understood, and so universally practiced among human Creatures.
>
> *Gulliver's travels* Jonathan Swift (1726 emphasis added)

Gulliver travelled to many countries, of which the most peculiar was the land of the *Houyhnhnms* – a land whose equine inhabitants were so honest that 'they had no word in their language to express lying or falsehood'. On those rare occasions when the need arose, the *Houyhnhnms* referred to lying as '*saying the Thing which was not*'.

In the current chapter, we too will travel. Like Gulliver, we will puzzle over the mores and practices in many lands. Our focus will be on deception and cross-cultural differences in deceit. Our evidence will not be literary, but empirical, as we ponder research on three topics: the incidence of '*saying the Thing which is not*', beliefs about lying, and attempts to perpetrate deception across cultures.

Global incidence of deceit

Gulliver found a country where deception was unknown. Having wondered whether such lands exist outside the literary realm, scholars have reached conflicting views. Some maintain that deception is universal

(Saarni and Lewis, 1993), while others contend that the incidence of deceit varies across cultures (Barnes, 1994). Both of these positions are defensible.

Universality

Evolutionary psychologists have offered a universality hypothesis – that every culture involves transactions and exchanges; and in every culture, there are those who would exploit others. Cultural systems of exchange can exist only if people are able to detect those who would cheat the system – by taking the benefits of transactions without paying the price. In every culture, people must detect those who would accept help without giving help. They have to identify those who promise to return favours, but never do.

Having advanced this hypothesis, Sugiyama, Tooby, and Cosmides (2002) examined two starkly different cultures – Harvard undergraduates and Shiwiar hunters. Harvard undergraduates are young, wealthy, and modern. They have gifts of a kind that are valued in American higher education. Shiwiar hunters, by contrast, are illiterate. Their language has no script. The Shiwiar, indigenous to a remote region of Ecuador, have little contact with outsiders. No electricity, no running water, no refrigeration – these are staples of Shiwiar daily life.

To test for universality in the ability to reason about exchanges, Sugiyama, Tooby and Cosmides gave Harvard undergraduates and Shiwiar hunters some very difficult problems in conditional reasoning. The problems concerned one of two topics – either the physical world or unfair transactions. To solve the physical problems, abstract logic was required. To solve the transaction problems, it was sufficient to identify conditions defining an unfair exchange. Thus, these problems functioned as a test for sensitivity to cheaters.

Of interest to evolutionary psychologists Sugiyama, Tooby, and Cosmides was the percentage of logically correct answers to these problems. Results showed that in reasoning about the physical world, both Harvard undergraduates and Shiwiar performed poorly. In fact, both groups of participants offered logically incorrect answers to about three-quarters of the physical problems. In reasoning about cheaters, both were much better, and Shiwiar hunters achieved logical performances that were virtually indistinguishable from the Harvard students. These results suggest that worldwide, people have a special need to think through social contingencies, if they would otherwise be vulnerable to exploitation.

There are many forms of intelligence. There is mathematical, scientific, and technical intelligence (Sternberg, 1985). With these, we have cured infectious diseases and sent people to the moon. There is also another kind of intelligence that allows one *homo sapiens* to gain advantage over another. This is a Machiavellian intelligence – clever, subtle, indirect. We find it in the parsing of language, in political manoeuvring and business tactics. Ambiguity, misdirection, deniability – these are hallmarks of Machiavellian intelligence worldwide. And this form of intelligence is not confined to *homo sapiens*. Mitchell and Thompson (1986) recount the devious exploits of many species.

The size of the primate brain has increased dramatically over evolutionary time, as comparative psychologists know. Many have explained this trend by asserting that primates evolved large brains to cope with the technical challenges of their environment. In this traditional account, there was a natural selection of brains that gave primates an advantage in eluding predators and capturing prey. Other scholars found a flaw in this explanation, arguing that primates had brains far larger than would be needed to master the technical challenges they faced. This problem of 'surplus intelligence' inspired an alternative account of primate evolution. In the newer, now standard view, large brains give primates an advantage in duping their conspecifics, and the natural selection for brain size reflects an evolutionary 'arms race' in which ever-increasing Machiavellian intelligences are pitted against one another (Byrne and Whiten, 1988). From this biological perspective, *Homo sapiens* are distinguished from other species in having the most devious brain of all.

Although all people are equipped to lie, psychologists have assumed that they differ in the willingness to practise deception. While measuring personality, psychologists attempt to identify people who are lying to create a positive image. They do so by embedding 'lie' scales in their self-report personality tests, on which respondents have the opportunity to make implausible self-enhancing claims. Studies indicate that many of these scales do in fact measure the tendency to lie (Paulhus, 1991).

Lie scales have been administered to thousands of people over the years, and the accumulated evidence reveals a strong tendency for lying to run in families. Ahern, Johnson, Wilson, McClearn, and Vandenberg (1982) conducted a relevant study in Hawaii. There the researchers measured fifty-four different personality traits on each member of 415 families. Among the tests was a Lie Scale embedded in the Eysenck Personality Questionnaire (Furnham, 1986). The researchers found that the members of a family have similar personalities. This was expected. Ahern et al. (1982) were surprised, however, to discover that family members resemble one another more in their Lie Scale scores than in *any* of the other fifty-three personality characteristics measured. As the authors reported, 'the minimum of all kinship correlations for this [Lie] scale was, in fact, larger than the maximum for any other scale'.

As this study indicates, family members resemble one another in the tendency to lie, and the degree of resemblance depends on the individuals' biological relationship to one another. Identical twins are most similar to one another in the tendency to lie (Young, Eaves, and Eysenck, 1980); indeed, genetically identical individuals resemble one another in the tendency to lie even if they are separated early in life and reared apart (DiLalla, Carey, Gottesman, and Bouchard, 1996). Children who are adopted into a family are least similar to other family members in the tendency to lie. Specialists tell us that there may be a genetic component to individual differences in lying. From statistical models, they attribute roughly half of those individual differences to genetic factors. For a review, see Bond and Robinson (1988).

Cross-cultural variation

Although Gulliver visited a literary land where deception was unknown, lying has been found in every non-fictional culture ever studied (Saarni and Lewis, 1993). Anthropological descriptions of daily life in rural Lebanon (Gilsenan, 1976), New Guinea (Burridge, 1960), and Venezuela (Chagnon, 1983) graphically illustrate that there are myriad ways of '*saying the Thing which is not*'. What is lacking from the anthropological literature, however, is any quantitative comparison of the incidence of deception in various lands. For the latter, we must turn to recent work on institutional corruption.

Transparency International, based in Berlin, is dedicated to combating corruption. Each year since 1993, this organisation has published a global corruption report and compiled a Corruption Perceptions Index. The index provides a nation-by-nation ranking of levels of corruption worldwide. Of course, it is difficult to measure corruption because the phenomenon is by its nature clandestine. Even so, the Transparency International Corruption Perceptions Index appears to have some validity. It is a composite of indices compiled by the UN, the World Bank, international businesspeople, and risk analysts. Although these organisations assess corruption independently of one another, their measures tend to agree with one another; moreover, the composite Transparency International Index agrees with reports of corruption offered by residents of the ranked countries. Thus, citizens of countries that are ranked as highly corrupt report high levels of corruption in their daily lives (Transparency International, 2003).

A Corruption Perceptions Index published in October 2003 ranked levels of corruption in 133 countries. In this listing, the most corrupt countries in the world were Bangladesh, Nigeria, and Haiti; the least corrupt were Finland, Iceland, Denmark, and New Zealand.

To explain international differences in corruption, social scientists cite economic and political factors. The most corrupt countries are poor and pay their civil servants poorly. Corrupt countries are economically isolated and politically repressed. Few people participate in politics, and there is little media criticism of government. No doubt, these factors play a role in enabling and perpetuating corruption.

Here we discuss a factor of interest to psychologists – the variable of individualism vs. collectivism. In some countries, the focus is on the individual; in others, the focus is on the group. In individualistic cultures, people view the self as autonomous; they exercise individual rights and pursue personal goals. In individualistic cultures, most interpersonal relationships are voluntary, and they tend to be short-lived. In collectivist cultures, by contrast, people see the self as interdependent with an in-group; they fulfil responsibilities to the group and subordinate personal goals to the group's goals. Most interpersonal relationships in collectivist cultures are obligatory, and many are lifelong.

Hofstede (1983) used responses to a large-scale morale survey to rank fifty countries on the dimension of individualism vs. collectivism. According to Hofstede's ranking, the US and Scandinavian countries have some of the most individualistic cultures in the world. The most collectivistic cultures are in Guatemala, Pakistan, and Indonesia.

By comparing Hofstede's ranking of a country's collectivism with the country's Corruption Perceptions Index, we can examine the cross-national relationship between these two variables. A statistical analysis shows that the greater a country's degree of collectivism, the greater is the level of corruption in that country, Pearson's $r = +.67$. Of course, countries differ in a number of ways, and many of these differences may be associated with collectivism. Poor countries, for instance, tend to be more collectivistic than rich countries; and in principle income differences might explain the association between collectivism and corruption. To assess this possibility, we noted the World Bank's 2001 estimate of per capita Gross Domestic Income in various countries and compared these figures with the country's collectivism and level of corruption. Results show that poor countries have high levels of corruption and high levels of collectivism (for relationship of income to corruption and collectivism, $r = -.77$ and $-.69$, respectively). More relevant for present purposes, there is a statistically significant partial correlation between corruption and collectivism, once income has been controlled; for the latter, partial

$r = +.28, p < .05$. As these analyses suggest, income may account for some of the cross-national relationship between collectivism and corruption, but it cannot explain the entire relationship. Perhaps corruption thrives among people who are connected by lifelong relationships – among co-members of an extended family, for instance. Perhaps corruption results when individuals are willing to assume legal risks for the financial welfare of their families.

Collectivism is related to international differences in corruption, as we have seen. But is it related to deception per se? To address the latter question, Triandis and collaborators (2001) conducted research in four individualistic countries (Australia, Germany, the Netherlands, and the United States) and four collectivist countries (Greece, Hong Kong, Japan, and Korea). Students in each country participated in a mock business negotiation. To win a contract for his/her company, the student was given the opportunity to lie by exaggerating the company's production capacity. In the researchers' experimental scenario, this lie was encouraged by the student's boss and would probably go undetected.

Of interest to Triandis and his collaborators was the percentage of students in each country who were completely truthful under these circumstances – the percentage who refused to lie (even a little) to win a business contract. Results show that there are far more truth-tellers in individualistic countries than collectivistic countries (14.25 per cent vs. 4.75 per cent). Thus, collectivism would seem to predispose not only institutional corruption but also individual deception.

These results may be surprising, because the free-enterprise economies of individualistic countries might be expected to invite business deceit. Perhaps individualistic legal institutions anticipate these temptations to lie and are better equipped than their collectivist counterparts to deter deception. People in collectivist cultures may also have little compunction about lying, when lying would benefit an in-group.

Consistent with this latter possibility, evidence suggests that people in different cultures lie for different reasons. Aune and Waters (1994) asked people why they lied, posing this question to participants in both an individualistic culture (the United States) and a collectivist culture (Samoa). Samoans were most willing to lie if the deception would benefit their group whereas Americans were most willing to lie if the deception would protect their own privacy.

Worldwide beliefs about deception

Gulliver marvelled at the Houyhnhnms's naïveté in matters of deception. *Homo sapiens*, by contrast, have elaborate beliefs about deceit. Having learned about the incidence of lying in different lands, we turn now to some of these beliefs – evaluations of the morality of deception and stereotypes about the liar's behaviour.

Moral evaluations

Western philosophers regard lying as wrong. Kant, for example, wrote that lying is always immoral. Although other philosophers may allow for deception under certain circumstances, all agree that there is a strong ethical presumption against lying (Bok, 1989).

Psychologists have studied Western children's evaluations of deceit. In the Western world, children seem to agree with philosophers. Western children believe that lying is wrong, and they acquire this belief at an early age – soon after coming to understand the concept of deception (Bussey, 1992).

To see whether children in Eastern cultures would have similar beliefs, Kang Lee and associates have conducted a number of studies. In one such investigation (Lee, Cameron, Xu, Fu, and Board, 1997), children aged 7, 9, and 11 from Canada and mainland China evaluated lies and truths. Each child was read a vignette in which a schoolboy lost his lunch money. When no one else was in the classroom, one of the boy's classmates (Mark) put some of his own money in the classmate's desk. Upon returning to the classroom and discovering money in the boy's desk, the teacher asked Mark, 'Do you know who put the money there?' In one version of the vignette, Mark answered the teacher's question truthfully, saying 'Yes, I put the money there.' In another version, Mark falsely stated 'No, I don't know who put the money there.' Researchers asked Canadian and Chinese children to evaluate what Mark had done in giving money to his classmate. They also asked the children to evaluate what Mark had said in response to his teacher's question. Children made these evaluations on a scale that ranged from +3 (Very Good) to −3 (Very Naughty).

All of the children in this study believed that it was good for Mark to give money to his needy classmate. However, their evaluations of what Mark said depended on culture and age. The results for Canadian children replicate earlier Western research in showing that truth-telling is evaluated positively and lying is evaluated negatively by seven-year-olds, nine-year-olds, and eleven-year-olds. The Chinese results are of greater interest. Like their Canadian counterparts, Chinese seven-year-olds believe that it was naughty for Mark to tell a lie and good for Mark to tell the truth. However, the older children in China believe that it was *good* for Mark to lie to avoid taking credit for helping a needy classmate. In fact, the eleven-year-olds believed that it was as good for Mark to lie about this pro-social deed as it was for him to tell the truth.

Why do Chinese children approve of lying in these circumstances? Their approval might in principle reflect a political-moral curriculum prescribed by the mainland Chinese government. Beginning in kindergarten, schoolchildren in mainland China are taught to be modest and told that it is permissible not to tell the truth if modesty conflicts with honesty (Lee et al., 1997). This governmental policy builds on the cultural tradition of Confucianism which promotes modesty and self-effacement. To assess the relative importance of Confucianism and the government-mandated curriculum on schoolchildren's moral evaluations, Lee, Xu, and Fu (2001) repeated their study of moral evaluations in Taiwan. Taiwanese children are heirs to the Confucian tradition yet are not required to study any political-moral curriculum in school. Results show that (like their peers in mainland China) Taiwanese eleven-year-olds believe that it is good for a boy to lie in disclaiming credit for a good deed. Thus, the Confucian tradition may best explain Chinese evaluations of deception.

At the conclusion of their study, Lee, Xu, and Fu (2001) asked their child research participants whether Mark had told a 'lie' when he said that he did not know who put money in his classmate's desk. Virtually all of the children responded that Mark's statement was a 'lie'. However, when in subsequent research Chinese adults were read the vignette and asked the same question, nearly half said that Mark's false statement was *not* a 'lie' (Fu, Lee, Cameron, and Xu, 2001). Together with other research (Yeung, Levine, and Nishiyama, 1999), these results suggest that the Chinese have a narrower view than Westerners of what constitutes deception.

Clearly, there are cultural differences in definitions and moral evaluations of lying. Western cultures proscribe false statements that other cultures see as benign. In the Confucian tradition of China, the virtue of modesty may justify statements that are not factually correct. So long as these statements function to maintain group harmony, they may be seen as virtuous and not construed as 'lies'. To the Chinese more than to Americans, the acceptability of a false statement depends on the relationship between the deceiver and the deceived (Seiter, Bruschke, and Bai, 2002). In close relationships, concerns about maintaining 'face' may require that awkward truths be submerged (Ting-Toomey and Oetzel, 2002). For relevant linguistic work, see Sweetser (1987).

For a global perspective on these issues, a World Values Survey supplies pertinent insights. Inglehart, Basañez, and Moreno (2001) present survey data from nationally representative samples of adults in forty-three societies worldwide. Participants were asked a large number of questions about their moral values. One of the questions was 'Is lying in your own interest ever justified?' Of the 43,000 individuals around the world who responded to this question, 48 per cent said that self-interested lying is *never* justified. Answers varied from country to country. The strictest morality was found in Bulgaria as well as South Korea, where 70 per cent of respondents said that self-interested lying is never justified. The least strict moral position was observed in the Netherlands as well as in West Germany, where only 25 per cent of respondents said that self-interested lying is never justified. Inglehart, Basañez, and Moreno also found demographic differences in moral evaluations of deception. Females were more likely than males to condemn self-interested lying; and people over fifty years old were more likely to condemn it than people under thirty. Most striking in survey responses is the relationship between education and moral evaluations. In every single one of the forty-three societies in the World Values Survey, the least educated respondents were more likely than the most educated to say that self-interested lying is never justified. Education may temper moral absolutism on various issues, including deception.

Beliefs about deception cues

Many people imagine that they can tell when others are lying, and have thoughts about how they accomplish this feat. Beliefs about cues to deception have been studied by a number of West European and US researchers (Akehurst, Köhnken, Vrij, and Bull, 1996; Anderson, DePaulo, and Ansfield, 1999; Strömwall, Granhag, and Hartwig, this volume; Zuckerman, Koestner, and Driver, 1981). To complement these Euro-American efforts, the current authors are conducting a worldwide study. Scholars in 150 countries were contacted and invited to participate in a collaborative study of beliefs about deception. Scholars in 45 of the countries accepted our invitation and have graciously provided the preliminary results that we present here.

In each country, our collaborator asked twenty male and twenty female lifelong residents of that country 'How can you tell when people are lying', posing this open-ended question in the dominant language of the country and soliciting written answers in that language. Respondents were allowed to answer the question in any way they wished – by expressing one belief about deception, two beliefs, or many beliefs. The collaborator in each country translated these beliefs into English (if they had been offered in another language), and the resulting English-language translations were coded into one of 100 categories by the second author of this chapter, Sandhya Rao. While coding a particular respondent's beliefs about deception, Rao was unaware of the respondent's nationality. We regard the current results as preliminary, because inter-coder reliability has not yet been assessed.

Here we summarise beliefs about deception in 45 countries: 3 countries in Africa, 11 in Asia, 21 in Europe, 3 in North America, 2 in Oceania, and 5 countries in South America. These data reflect a total of 8,543 beliefs about deception offered in 35 different languages by 1,800 different individuals.

Let us now identify some common beliefs about deception. In response to the question 'How can you tell when others are lying?', eye contact (or direction of gaze) is the most common answer worldwide. In all forty-five of the countries we have studied, more than 5 per cent of all responses refer to eye contact. People mention eye contact more often than everything else in the liar's face combined. Eye contact and other facial cues constitute 16.8 per cent and 8.9 per cent of all beliefs in our study. When mentioning gaze as a cue to deception, most respondents assert that liars *avoid* eye contact with others. An occasional respondent asserts that liars make *more* eye contact than normal, or that a liar's eyes drift in a certain direction (say, downward and to the right).

Our worldwide study reveals some other pancultural beliefs about deception, too. Individuals in these forty-five countries believe that liars make speech errors, by pausing and stuttering more than usual. They believe that liars show signs of nervousness and attribute liars with several forms of inconsistency: inconsistencies in the liar's verbalisations, verbal–non-verbal inconsistencies, and inconsistencies between facts and the liar's assertions. Speech errors, nervousness, and inconsistency constitute 7.4 per cent, 5.2 per cent, and 5.1 per cent of the responses we encountered.

Reading over 8,543 beliefs about deception offered by people worldwide, we were struck by the *infrequency* with which certain beliefs were mentioned. Our sample included many collectivist cultures – including Colombia, Indonesia, and Portugal. Thus, we had imagined that group membership might be mentioned as a cue to others' deceptiveness. Group membership was almost never mentioned. Also conspicuously missing were situational cues to deception. These 1,800 respondents virtually never mentioned incentives to lie or any other motivational factor. Admissions of deceit were rarely mentioned. Together, group membership, situational factors, and admissions comprised less than one-tenth of 1 per cent of all responses offered.

Perhaps some of the findings (and non-findings) of this worldwide survey reflect the wording of our question: 'How can you tell when people are lying?', and maybe a different phrasing would have cued a different set of responses. Even so, this is the largest study to date on this topic, and we are impressed with the consistency among beliefs about deception offered in so many different languages by people from so many different countries.

Cross-cultural deceptions

Cross-cultural deceptions figure prominently in world history – in, for example, Hitler's false promises to Neville Chamberlain (Ekman, 2001). Also historically influential are mistaken inferences of deceit – when (for instance) Saddam Hussein's half-brother disbelieved James Baker's assertion that the United States would invade Iraq unless Hussein left Kuwait (Triandis, 1994). While policy analysts dissect these strategic miscalculations for their impact on international relations (Godson and Wirtz, 2002), psychologists seek a more basic understanding of principles underlying cross-cultural deception.

Psychology of international deception

Lie detection depends on many elements that will be described in other chapters of this volume. Here we focus on factors that are specific to international deceit – language differences, non-verbal differences, and ethnocentrism.

When people from different nations speak different languages, it stands to reason that their ability to detect one another's lies would be affected. However, it is difficult to predict a priori whether language differences would benefit the liar or the lie detector. On the one hand, it might seem that language differences would give the liar an advantage by depriving the would-be detector of speech content that could cue deceit; on the other hand, speech content might be a useful vehicle for perpetrating deception whose absence would force the detector to focus on more reliable cues. Consistent with this latter possibility, American research shows that liars who are highly motivated spin persuasive stories (DePaulo and Kirkendohl, 1989) and that people have little control over their tone of voice (Zuckerman, Larrance, Spiegel, and Klorman, 1981).

In different countries, people display different patterns of non-verbal behaviour. Language differences may, in fact, have less impact on cross-cultural deception judgements than these non-verbal differences. True, attempts at cross-language communication can be frustrating. Still, a language divide is expected in cross-cultural interactions; hence this divide may be discounted when perceivers attempt to divine the veracity of an intercultural claim. International differences in non-verbal behaviour are by contrast unexpected and may be easier to attribute to a speaker's communication goals.

Anderson, Hecht, Hoobler, and Smallwood (2002) describe some cultural dimensions that bear on non-verbal behaviour: immediacy, power distance, and context. Along the dimension of immediacy, there are high-contact cultures (like those in the Arabic world) and low-contact cultures (like many in Asia). People in high-contact cultures make more eye contact, stand closer to one another, and engage in more touching than people in low-contact cultures. Highly intense, Saddam Hussein personifies a high-contact Arabic culture (Davis and Hadiks, 1995). Along the dimension of power distance, there are vertical cultures (e.g., India) and horizontal cultures (e.g., Sweden). In vertical cultures, status-based norms constrain non-verbal interactions by demanding respect to superiors. Downcast eyes, honorific tones, fixed smiles of appeasement – these behaviours are prescribed in vertical cultures but might be seen as insincere by egalitarians. Cultures also differ in the extent to which communications depend on context. In high-context cultures (like Japan), meanings are inferred from interpersonal relationships or the physical surround. Communication hinges on implicit non-verbal codes. In low-context cultures (like Germany), meanings are conveyed by the content of verbal utterances – explicit, logical, and precise.

Like language differences, culturally based non-verbal differences might in principle frustrate attempts at international lie detection. Non-verbal differences would frustrate lie detection if lies are spotted by virtue of their deviation from a culture-specific baseline of truthful communications (Bond, Omar, Mahmoud, and Bonser, 1990). Non-verbal differences might, on the other hand, have just the opposite effect. They would facilitate international lie detection if people in different cultures infer deception from different non-verbal cues, and liars concentrate on controlling those cues that their compatriots associate with deceit. Then attempts at international deception would be exposed by cues that the liar did not bother to hide.

Language and non-verbal differences are objective features of cross-cultural interactions, but their interpretation depends on interactants' views of foreigners. Here social psychological studies are relevant, in showing that most people prefer members of their own group to members of other groups. In cross-cultural contexts, this preference may be fuelled by anxiety and uncertainty induced by the unfamiliar (Gudykunst, 1995). Worldwide, a general suspicion of outsiders may predispose people to be wary of foreigners. Psychologically, it may be natural for people not to believe others whom they cannot understand (Smith and Bond, 1994).

Relevant research

Can lies be detected across cultures? Is deception harder to spot across cultures than within a culture? Having sketched some factors that may bear on the answers to these questions, we are in a position to review relevant empirical research.

Several investigators have reported research on deception between individuals of different cultural origin who are residing in the same country. Thus, Atmiyanandana (1976) examined deception judgements made by American, Asian, and Latin American students – all of whom were studying at a US university. The American and Latin American students were slightly more accurate than Asians in judging Americans' lies. Al-Simadi (2000) showed that Jordanian and Malaysian students at a Jordanian university could identify one another's lies at levels slightly greater than chance. Vrij and Winkel (1994) found that native Dutch police officers were vulnerable to cross-cultural non-verbal communication errors when judging the veracity of black Surinam citizens of the Netherlands. In this research, the white police officers misinterpreted behaviours that are typically displayed by blacks as signs of deception. These investigations yield important information about interactions between the natives of a country and immigrants to that country. Our focus in the current chapter, however, will be elsewhere – on deceptions between native residents of different lands.

Bond et al. (1990) studied American and Jordanian deception judgements. Natives of the United States and Jordan who were attending a university in their home country were videotaped while telling lies and truths about acquaintances. Natives who were residing in the United States and Jordan attempted to detect lies from the resulting videos. Both American and Jordanian judges were able to detect lies told by their compatriots but unable to detect lies told by members of the other culture. Behaviour codings revealed that Jordanians were more likely than Americans to move their head and make eye contact, and that in both cultures judges infer deception from head movements and gaze aversion. No reliable cues to deception were found.

Frustrated by their failure to uncover evidence of cross-cultural lie detection, Bond and Atoum (2000) noted some limitations of their earlier work. Bond et al. (1990) required perceivers to judge deception from a video presentation without sound, studied college students, and solicited low-stakes lies. To complement their earlier project, Bond and Atoum (2000) undertook research on deception judgements across three cultures: the United States, Jordan, and India. Native residents of each of these three countries judged lies and truths told by other native residents

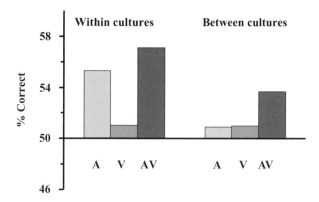

Figure 6.1 Percentage correct lie/truth judgements within and between cultures (Bond and Atoum, 2000)

of these countries from a video-only presentation, an audio-only presentation, or an audiovisual presentation. Bond and Atoum (2000) solicited deception judgements from illiterate farm workers as well as college students and motivated some deceptions with a financial incentive. Here we present results from Bond and Atoum's three-nation study. Some of these findings have been published previously (Bond and Atoum, 2000); others are being presented here for the first time.

Bond and Atoum (2000) conducted their research to determine whether it is possible for Americans, Jordanians, and Indians to detect lies across cultures. Results show that international lie detection is possible. Figure 6.1 displays relevant results: the percentage correct lie/truth discrimination achieved by Americans, Jordanians, and Indians when judging members of their own culture (at left) and members of other cultures (at right). Accuracy is displayed separately for judgements made from an audio-only, a video-only, and an audiovisual presentation of lies (symbolised A, V, and AV, respectively). The results at the left of Figure 6.1 replicate earlier mono-cultural research in showing that people can detect their compatriots' lies to a small, statistically significant degree. Of greater interest are judgements of foreigners' lies. As shown at the right of the figure, Americans, Jordanians, and Indians can achieve statistically reliable cross-cultural lie/truth discrimination when they can see and hear foreigners' lies. Cross-cultural judgements from an audiovisual presentation are superior to judgements from video-only, even when judges cannot understand the liar's language. Thus, lie detection can be facilitated by vocal cues that accompany an unfamiliar language.

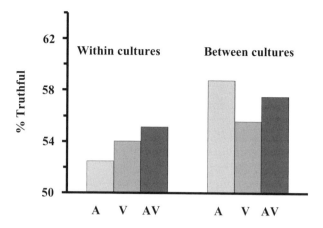

Figure 6.2 Percentage of truth judgements within and between cultures.
(Bond and Atoum, 2000)

Deception judgements can have international consequences even when
the judgements are wrong. Thus, it is important to understand biases that
predispose judges to perceive either too much or too little international
deception. In earlier mono-cultural research, most judges have shown
a truthfulness bias – a tendency to err in the direction of not perceiving
deceit. Prior to conducting their cross-cultural research, Bond and Atoum
(2000) suspected that international deception judgements might evince
the opposite bias – an indiscriminant disbelief of foreigners. Relevant
results appear in Figure 6.2. At the left of the figure are the percentage of
truth judgements Americans, Indians, and Jordanians made of their compatriots. As in earlier research, this percentage exceeds 50 per cent – the
percentage of truths judges in fact saw. Thus, the mono-cultural truthfulness bias evident in earlier research is replicated here. At the right of the
figure are the percentage of truth judgements Americans, Indians, and
Jordanians made of foreigners. All of the percentages there also exceed
50 per cent – the percentage of truthful messages seen. Contrary to expectation, these perceivers show a truthfulness bias when judging *foreigners'*
lies. In fact, the truthfulness bias in cross-cultural deception judgements
is stronger than the corresponding bias in mono-cultural judgements –
at least for lies that can be heard. Apparently, judges give foreigners the
benefit of the doubt if the latter are speaking in an unfamiliar language.
Illiterate farm workers show the strongest tendency to judge foreigners'
lies as truthful. Perhaps this bias reflects the judges' tendency to internalise responsibility for a cross-language communication failure.

Table 6.1 *Inter-judge agreement in Bond and Atoum (2000) by modality and judgement configuration*

Agreement configuration[a]	Audio	Video	Audiovisual
N_1 ↘ N_1 N_1 ↗	.634	.475	.525
N_1 ↘ N_2 N_1 ↗	.392	.589	.643
N_1 ↘ N_1 N_2 ↗	.311	.422	.466
N_1 ↘ N_3 N_2 ↗	.265	.357	.524

Note: [a] Each configuration consists of two judges and a target person. The nationality of the two judges is symbolised to the left of each configuration while the nationality of the target is symbolised to the right. Each entry in the first two rows of the table is a Cronbach's α for agreement among judges from the same nation. Each entry in the last two rows of the table is a Pearson's r for agreement between judges from two different nations.

In international affairs, a statement may be widely scrutinised before a judgement about its truthfulness is reached. Thus, it is important to know how often people agree in their deception judgements. Although mono-cultural research has shown that Americans achieve consensus about which of their compatriots are deceptive (Bond, Kahler, and Paolicelli, 1985), the relevance of these findings for cross-cultural deception judgements was until recently unknown.

Having studied deception judgements across three countries, Bond and Atoum (2000) place us in a position to assess several new forms of inter-judge agreement. Relevant results are presented here for the first time in Table 6.1. We show results for four distinct perceiver-target configurations: agreement among perceivers from a given culture in judging the veracity of targets from that culture (row 1); agreement among perceivers from a given culture in judging targets from a different culture (row 2); agreement between perceivers from two different cultures in judging targets from one of those two cultures (row 3); and agreement between perceivers from two different cultures in judging targets from a third culture (row 4). The entries in Table 6.1 are Cronbach's α-coefficients (rows 1 and 2) and Pearson's rs (rows 3 and 4) for the tendency of perceivers to label a target person deceptive. These are displayed separately for judgements made from audio-only, video-only, and audio-visual presentations.

In all configurations and presentation modalities, judges agree with one another more than would be expected by chance. Of special interest is the pattern of results across the four perceiver-target configurations. When deception must be judged from audio only, levels of inter-judge agreement parallel degrees of similarity among the individuals involved. Agreement is highest among perceivers from a given culture in judging the honesty of a target person from that culture ($\alpha = .634$), and agreement is lowest among perceivers from two different cultures in judging the honesty of a target from a third culture ($r = .265$). Different patterns are evident among judgements that incorporate visual information. When making judgements from video only, perceivers from a given culture achieve at least as much agreement about the honesty of foreigners as compatriots (αs $= .589$ vs. $.475$, respectively). In audiovisual judgements, similarities among individuals have little to do with the levels of agreement achieved; indeed, agreement among perceivers from a given country in judging targets from that country ($\alpha = .525$) is indistinguishable from agreement between perceivers from two different countries in judging targets from a third country ($r = .524$). There are widely shared stereotypes about the ways that liars look, as shown by our worldwide survey of beliefs about deception. Apparently, these beliefs are incorporated into deception judgements and colour judgements of foreigners and compatriots alike.

Often deception is inferred in the middle of face-to-face interactions where the liar can be seen and heard. To ascertain the cues on which such judgements are based, researchers can correlate a target's apparent truthfulness in an audiovisual presentation with the target's apparent truthfulness in (1) an audio-only presentation and (2) a video-only presentation. Here we pursue this analytic strategy to illuminate the impact of culture and language on deception judgements. We examined the four cases depicted in Table 6.2. In all of these instances, we were assessing relationships among judgements made by perceivers from the same culture and language background. The four cases differ in terms of the target's culture and language. In the first row, targets from the perceivers' culture are lying in a language familiar to the perceivers; in the second, they are lying in a language the perceivers do not know. In the third row,

Table 6.2 *Cross-modal consistency of a target's apparent honesty by culture and language*

	Relationship of audiovisual honesty to	
Similarity of target to perceivers	Audio honesty	Video honesty
Same culture – same language	.519	.353
Same culture – different language	.347	.383
Different culture – same language	.516	.347
Different culture – different language	.387	.515

Note: Each entry in the table is a Pearson's *r* for relationships involving judges of a given nationality who speak a common language.

targets from a culture other than the perceivers are lying in a language familiar to the perceivers; in the fourth, they are lying in a language the perceivers do not know.

As the results in Table 6.2 suggest, language differences have a bigger impact than cultural differences on perceivers' use of cues in making audiovisual inferences of deception. The pattern suggests that audiovisual judgements of deception are more strongly based on auditory than visual cues when perceivers understand the target's language; otherwise, they are based as strongly on visual as auditory cues. When perceivers understand a target's language, audiovisual judgements of the target's truthfulness yield mean correlations of .517 and .350 with audio and video judgements of that target, respectively. When perceivers do not understand the target's language, audiovisual judgements yield mean correlations of .367 and .449 with audio and video judgements, respectively. Perceivers are more likely to incorporate auditory information into their deception judgements when they can understand what they are hearing.

Conclusion

No doubt our lives would be transformed if (like Gulliver) we could spend our days in a land of no lies. Alas, it would appear that in every corner of the world people are '*saying the Thing which is not*'. Travelling from one place to another, we may see more or less deception; we hear louder or more muted condemnations of lies. Still, our travels have led us to much that is familiar – beliefs about deception that are shared worldwide, agreements in deception judgement across starkly different cultures. As lies travel, so does the need to detect them. We hope that this chapter will broaden the reader's perspective on mendacity in a mobile world.

REFERENCES

Ahern, F. M., Johnson, R. C., Wilson, J. R., McClearn, G. E., and Vandenberg, S. G. (1982). Family resemblances in personality. *Behavior Genetics, 12*, 261–80.

Akehurst, L., Köhnken, G., Vrij, A., and Bull, R. (1996). Lay persons' and police officers' beliefs regarding deceptive behavior. *Applied Cognitive Psychology, 10*, 461–71.

Al-Simadi, F. A. (2000). Detection of deceptive behavior: A cross-cultural test. *Social Behavior and Personality, 28*, 455–62.

Anderson, D. E., DePaulo, B. M., and Ansfield, M. E. (1999). Beliefs about cues to deception: Mindless stereotypes or untapped wisdom? *Journal of Nonverbal Behavior, 23*, 67–89.

Anderson, P. A., Hecht, M. L., Hoobler, G. D., and Smallwood, M. (2002). Nonverbal communication across cultures. In W. G. Gudykunst and B. Mody (eds.) *Handbook of international and intercultural communication* (pp. 89–106). Thousand Oaks, CA: Sage.

Atmiyanandana, V. (1976). An experimental study of the detection of deception in cross-cultural communication. Unpublished PhD dissertation, Florida State University.

Aune, R. K., and Waters, L. L. (1994). Cultural differences in deception: Motivations to deceive in Samoans and North Americans. *International Journal of Intercultural Relations, 18*, 159–72.

Barnes, J. A. (1994). *A pack of lies: Towards a sociology of lying.* Cambridge: Cambridge University Press.

Bok, S. (1989). *Lying: Moral choice in public and private life.* New York: Vintage Books.

Bond, C. F., Jr, and Atoum, A. O. (2000). International deception. *Personality and Social Psychology Bulletin, 26*, 385–95.

Bond, C. F., Jr, Kahler, K. N., and Paolicelli, L. M. (1985). The miscommunication of deception: An adaptive perspective. *Journal of Experimental Social Psychology, 21*, 331–45.

Bond, C. F., Jr, Omar, A. S., Mahmoud, A., and Bonser, N. (1990). Lie detection across cultures. *Journal of Nonverbal Behavior, 14*, 189–204.

Bond, C. F., Jr, and Robinson, M. A. (1988). The evolution of deception. *Journal of Nonverbal Behavior, 12*, 295–308.

Burridge, K. O. L. (1960). *Mambu: A Melanesian millennium.* London: Methuen.

Bussey, K. (1992). Lying and truthfulness: Children's definitions, standards, and evaluative reactions. *Child Development, 63*, 129–37.

Byrne, R. W., and Whiten, A. (1988). *Machiavellian intelligence: Social expertise and the evolution of intellect in monkeys, apes, and humans.* Oxford, UK: Clarendon Press.

Chagnon, N. (1983). *Yanomano: The fierce people* (3rd edn). New York: Holt, Rinehart, and Winston.

Davis, M., and Hadiks, D. (1995). Demeanor and credibility. *Semiotica, 106,* 5–54.

DePaulo, B. M., and Kirkendohl, S. E. (1989). The motivational impairment effect in the communication of deception. In J. C. Yuille (ed.), *Credibility assessment* (pp. 51–70). Dordrecht, the Netherlands: Kluwer Academic.

DiLalla, D. L., Carey, G., Gottesman, I. I., and Bouchard, T. J., Jr. (1996). Heritability of MMPI indicators of psychopathology in twins reared apart. *Journal of Abnormal Psychology, 105,* 491–9.

Ekman, P. (2001). *Telling lies: Clues to deceit in the marketplace, politics, and marriage.* New York: Norton.

Fu, G., Lee, K., Cameron, C. A., and Xu, F. (2001). Chinese and Canadian adults' categorization and evaluation of lie- and truth-telling about prosocial and antisocial behaviors. *Journal of Cross-Cultural Psychology, 32,* 720–7.

Furnham, A. (1986). Response bias, social desirability and dissimulation. *Personality and Individual Differences, 7,* 385–400.

Gilsenan, M. (1976). Lying, honor, and contradiction. In B. Kapferer (ed.), *Transaction and meaning: Directions in the anthropology of exchange and symbolic behavior* (pp. 191–219). Philadelphia: Institute for the Study of Human Issues.

Godson, R., and Wirtz, J. J. (2002). *Strategic denial and deception: The 21st century challenge.* New Brunswick: Transaction.

Gudykunst, W. B. (1995). Anxiety/uncertainty management (AUM) theory. In R. L. Wiseman (ed.), *Intercultural communication theory* (pp. 8–58). Thousand Oaks, CA: Sage.

Hofstede, G. (1983). Dimensions of national cultures in fifty countries and three regions. In J. Deregowski, S. Dzuirawiec, and R. Annis (eds.) *Explications in cross-cultural psychology.* Lisse: Swets and Zeitlinger.

Inglehart, R., Basañez, M., and Moreno, A. (2001). *Human values and beliefs: A cross-cultural sourcebook.* Ann Arbor, MI: University of Michigan Press.

Lee, K., Cameron, C. A., Xu, F., Fu, G., and Board, J. (1997). Chinese and Canadian children's evaluations of lying and truth-telling. *Child Development, 64,* 924–34.

Lee, K., Xu, F., and Fu, G. (2001). Taiwan and mainland Chinese and Canadian children's categorization and evaluation of lie- and truth-telling: A modesty effect. *British Journal of Developmental Psychology, 19,* 525–42.

Mitchell, R. W., and Thompson, N. S. (1986). *Deception: Perspectives on human and nonhuman deceit.* Albany, NY: State University of New York Press.

Paulhus, D. L. (1991). Measurement and control of response bias. In J. P. Robinson, P. R. Shaver, and L. S. Wrightsman (eds.), *Measures of personality and social psychological attitudes* (pp. 17–59). San Diego: Academic Press.

Saarni, C., and Lewis, M. (1993). Deceit and illusion in human affairs. In M. Lewis and C. Saarni (eds.), *Lying and deception in everyday life* (pp. 1–29). New York: Guilford Press.

Seiter, J. S., Bruschke, J., and Bai, C. (2002). The acceptability of deception as a function of a perceiver's culture, deceiver's intention, and deceiver-deceived relationship. *Western Journal of Communication, 66,* 158–80.

Smith, P. B., and Bond, M. H. (1994). *Social psychology across cultures: Analysis and perspectives*. Boston: Allyn and Bacon.

Sternberg, R. J. (1985). *Beyond IQ: A triarchic theory of intelligence*. New York: Cambridge University Press.

Sugiyama, L. S., Tooby, J., and Cosmides L. (2002). Cross-cultural evidence of cognitive adaptations for social exchange among the Shiwiar of Ecuadorian Amazonia. *Proceedings of the National Academy of Sciences*, 99, 11537–42.

Sweetser, E. E. (1987). The definition of a lie: An examination of folk models underlying a semantic prototype. In D. Holland and N. Quinn (eds.), *Cultural models in language and thought* (pp. 43–66). New York: Cambridge University Press.

Ting-Toomey, S., and Oetzel, J. G. (2002). Cross-cultural face concerns and conflict styles: Current status and future directions. In W. G. Gudykunst and B. Mody (eds.), *Handbook of international and intercultural communication* (pp. 143–63). Thousand Oaks, CA: Sage.

Transparency International (2003). *Global corruption report 2003*. Available online at http://www.globalcorruptionreport.org/

Triandis, H. C. (1994). Culture and social behavior. In W. J. Lonner and R. Malpass (eds.), *Psychology and culture* (pp. 169–73). Boston: Allyn and Bacon.

Triandis, H. C., Carenevale, P., Gelfand, M., Robert, C., Wasti, S. A., Probst, T., Kashima, E. S., Dragonas, T., Chan, D., Chen, X. P., Kim, U., Dreu, C., Vliert, E., Iwao, S., Ohbuchi, K. I., and Schmitz, P. (2001). Culture and deception in business negotiations: A multi-level analysis. *International Journal of Cross Cultural Management*, 1, 73–90.

Vrij, A., and Winkel, F. W. (1994). Perceptual distortions in cross-cultural interrogations: The impact of skin color, accent, speech style and spoken fluency on impression formation. *Journal of Cross-Cultural Psychology*, 25, 284–96.

Yeung, L. N. T., Levine, T. R., and Nishiyama, K. (1999). Information manipulation theory and perceptions of deception in Hong Kong. *Communication Reports*, 12, 1–11.

Young, P. A., Eaves, L. J., and Eysenck, H. J. (1980). Intergenerational stability and change in the causes of variation in personality. *Personality and Individual Differences*, 1, 35–55.

Zuckerman, M., Koestner, R., and Driver, R. (1981). Beliefs about cues associated with deception. *Journal of Nonverbal Behavior*, 6, 105–14.

Zuckerman, M., Larrance, D. T., Spiegel, N. H., and Klorman, R. (1981). Controlling nonverbal displays: Facial expressions and tone of voice. *Journal of Experimental Social Psychology*, 17, 506–24.

7   Coping with suggestion and deception in children's accounts

Graham Davies

Children are increasingly called upon to give evidence in civil and criminal matters in the courts. On many occasions they will appear as victims, typically involving allegations of sexual or physical assault, but also as witnesses, to domestic violence, street incidents or road accidents (Westcott, Davies, and Bull, 2002). In most countries, the law recognises the special status of children as vulnerable witnesses, who require investigative procedures and methods of hearing their evidence that take account of their perceived needs. The United Kingdom has been at the forefront in legislating legal and procedural changes designed to assist children in first eliciting and then giving their evidence in court, the latter a necessary requirement in an adversarial system of justice (Spencer and Flin, 1993).

In England and Wales, the use of closed-circuit television in court and the use of pre-recorded interviews have allowed many children for the first time to have their evidence heard in court and to exercise their rights as citizens to protection under the law (Cashmore, 2002). However, paralleling such procedural innovations has been a growth in predictable concerns over the reliability of children's evidence. Among the issues raised has been the possibility that children may lie or deliberately mislead in the witness box, parental pressures and coaching and vulnerability to suggestive questions during investigative interviews (Besharov, 1985; Coleman, 1990; Pendergrast, 1996; Wakefield and Underwager, 1988). These issues are particularly acute in relation to charges of sexual abuse, where typically, medical evidence is transient or ambiguous, other forensic evidence is lacking, and no other witnesses are present: the courts must choose between the rival accounts of the accused and the child. This chapter summarises some of the factors that are believed to lead to false or misleading accounts by children and the extent to which these can be countered by implementing evidence-based guidelines for investigators. It also considers whether the greater use of experts could assist the courts in reaching sound decisions and revisits cases that illustrate the problems that can arise when investigations miscarry, beginning with two landmark cases in the United Kingdom.

148

When investigations miscarry

The first and best known of these English cases occurred in Middlesbrough, Cleveland in 1987. A team of doctors using a medical technique of unproven validity (anal dilation) diagnosed some 202 children as having suffered sexual abuse. Subsequently, all the children were removed from their carers by Social Services and repeatedly interviewed in an effort to substantiate the diagnosis, a process that produced sometimes bizarre and contradictory evidence. A subsequent official enquiry highlighted shortcomings in the way the interviews were conducted, called for changes in the way that cases of suspected abuse were investigated and for greater cooperation between police and social services (Butler-Sloss, 1988).

The second case is less well known and involved a group of seven children, some with moderate learning difficulties living in an extended family in Broxtowe, Nottingham, in 1987. Following allegations of familial sexual and physical abuse, the children were taken into care by the local authority. The children underwent a medical examination and clear signs of sexual and physical abuse were apparent. Two years later, ten adults were convicted of fifty-three offences against the children, some admitted, some denied, including incest, indecent assault, and cruelty. In the interim, the children had been looked after by foster parents who were encouraged by Social Services to keep diaries of any spontaneous disclosures of abuse made by the children. At first, the children talked about sexual and physical abuse by family members, but this gave way to talk of 'witch parties' and strangers wearing masks who abused the children. These revelations came at a time of heightened concern over 'satanic abuse': sexual and other forms of abuse allegedly taking place within a ritualised setting (Jones, 1991). An American satanic abuse specialist was brought in by Social Services staff, who advised the foster parents on key indicators of satanic involvement. Soon after this, carers reported even more extravagant claims involving members of the local community in the ritualised killing of babies and animals, and in orgies conducted in secret rooms and tunnels beneath local landmarks. The children appeared to corroborate each other's accounts and three adults from the extended family came forward to support the statements of their young relatives.

The police, who had opposed the diary exercise over concerns that the children's evidence might be contaminated prior to the trial, took the allegations sufficiently seriously to explore the named buildings for the rooms and tunnels so graphically described by the children and to search the houses where the children had lived for forensic clues to back up their accounts. However, they could find no evidence to support the children's allegations. The police also uncovered unrecorded meetings between the children involved that readily explained apparent instances of corroboration. Moreover, when the police interviewed the adults, they withdrew their statements, claiming they had been pressurised into making them by social workers. Relations between the police and social workers broke down amid mutual recrimination, and the credibility of the initial, proven, allegations was inevitably overshadowed by these later revelations, which received widespread publicity.

The subsequent official report by a joint enquiry team (Nottinghamshire County Council, 1990) identified issues that had been instrumental in prompting the bizarre statements of the children and adults involved. First, there was the total breakdown of relations between police and social services, with no proper distinction being made between investigative and therapeutic interviewing. The lack of investigative training on the part of the social workers involved led them to become partisan players, caught up in a search for satanic abuse: they sought only confirming evidence and ignored the factual inconsistencies. In their zeal, they repeatedly interviewed children in an effort to gather 'facts' (one child claimed to have been interviewed twenty times) and failed to videorecord these sessions for later analysis. Undue pressure was placed on vulnerable adults and leading questions asked of children in an effort to produce corroboration of the key indicators of satanic abuse. The children responded to these prompts initially haltingly, but later with much spurious detail, which the official investigation attributed to particular television programmes, films, and books with which the children were familiar.

The procedures and official guidance introduced by the British Home Office for the investigative interviewing of children owe much to the lessons learned from Cleveland and Broxtowe. But are such guidelines sufficient to ensure that well-founded cases of abuse are prosecuted and innocent adults protected? And how large is the problem of wholly false allegations of sexual abuse?

False allegations of abuse

Estimating the incidence

False accusations of sexual abuse certainly occur (Campbell, 1992; Green, 1986; Meyer and Geis, 1994), but surveys imply that in general, they are a low-rate phenomenon. In a classic study, Jones and McGraw (1987) investigated 576 cases reported to the social services in Denver, Colorado, and concluded that 6 per cent of all the allegations were fictitious, based upon a mix of clinical judgement and evidential criteria similar to those employed in Criteria-Based Content Analysis or CBCA (see Köhnken, this volume). Of the cases judged fictitious, most were believed to be manipulations by a parent, with only 1 per cent attributed to the child, a common finding as to the relative source of error (Goodwin, Sahd, and Rada, 1989). Approximately 53 per cent of the allegations were judged as reliable, with the remaining 41 per cent unsubstantiated or lacking in sufficient information to make an informed judgement. Everson and Boat (1989), using a similar methodology on a sample of 1,249 US cases, reported comparable rates of false accusations, ranging from approximately 2 per cent at age six or younger to over 10 per cent for adolescents. Somewhat higher figures have been reported for particularly vulnerable groups, such as children involved in divorce and custody disputes, where one parent may seek to use alleged abuse as a means of strengthening their claims against the other (Benedek and Schetky, 1985; Campbell, 1992; Green, 1986).

Published surveys suggest that the frequency with which allegations emerge in disputed cases, while higher than in non-disputed cases, is still relatively low. Thoennes and Tjaden (1990) reported that in a sample of over 9,000 families involved in custody disputes, only 2 per cent involved allegations of sexual abuse, a figure comparable to that reported by McIntosh and Prinz (1993) in a smaller sample from another area of the United States. These surveys also fail to support the view that most allegations made in the course of custody disputes are necessarily false. Thoennes and Tjaden judged that 33 per cent of allegations were false, a further 50 per cent well founded and the remainder indeterminate. Jones and Seig (1988) reported a 20 per cent fictitious rate for a small sample of twenty custody cases seen in Denver. Malicious allegations are certainly a feature of custody disputes, but as Faller (1991) has emphasised, they may also be the point at which true accusations emerge: for instance, sexual or physical abuse of a child by one parent may be the precipitant of the divorce or the absence from the home of one parent may provide sufficient reassurance for a child to disclose a history of abuse to the other.

These figures, and those from other surveys (see Ehrenberg and Elterman, 1995, for a detailed review), provide no support for the view that false accusations are endemic in divorce proceedings and invariably the product of a child's fertile imagination. However, some limitations of all such surveys need to be born in mind. First, in the absence of convincing forensic or documentary evidence, the estimated rates of both true and false accusations are inevitably based upon clinical judgements and the systematic application of evidential criteria, the reliability and validity of which are still in dispute (see Köhnken, this volume). Individual investigators have estimated markedly different base rates for false and substantiated allegations from the same sample of cases, implying that differences in criteria and thresholds will impact upon false allegation rates (Everson and Boat, 1989). Second, all studies show substantial numbers of cases where no decision was made because of the absence of critical information. The migration of such cases into the 'false' columns can have a dramatic impact on the headline rates for false accusations, and these inflated figures are often the source of misleading statements in the media (Spencer and Flin, 1993). However, given the likelihood that at least some of the unsubstantiated cases are indeed false, the commonly quoted rates for malicious allegations should be seen as providing a lower, rather than the upper, boundary for estimates. It is important to stress, however, that where allegations by children prove unfounded, it does not follow that they are made invariably for malicious reasons: children can simply misreport or misunderstand the behaviour of adults, particularly where toileting or other forms of intimate care have taken place. Third, virtually all the survey data have been collected in North America, where mandatory reporting of suspicions of sexual or physical abuse is required of all professionals. It remains to be seen whether similar ratios apply in other parts of the world with different cultural norms and legal procedures.

Varieties of false reports by children

While false statements in abuse cases appear to be a relatively low-rate phenomenon, investigators need to be alert to this possibility and to be able to profile cases where particular care is needed in the interview process. Various typologies of false reports have been proposed, based on proven or suspicious cases. For example, Bernet (1993), an American psychiatrist, listed some seventeen different types of deception, derived from a review of some forty articles and book chapters on the topic, which he grouped into three broad categories. The first was *false statements arising from external influences on the child* including parental pressures fuelled by delusions, deliberate indoctrination, and suggestive questioning by over-zealous interviewers. The second involved *mental mechanisms in the child which are not conscious or purposeful* and included fantasies and delusions, misunderstandings based on misinterpretation of past events or acts by another on the child. The third category focused upon *conscious and purposeful deceptions* and distinguished what Bernet termed 'deliberate lying', where the child set out to deceive and entrap the adult, from 'innocent lying', where a simple 'fib' had unanticipated consequences for the adult concerned. Some of his varieties of deception, such as *pseudologia phantastica* (pathological lying), appear to be very rare indeed and others overlap in their causal mechanisms: parental and interviewer suggestion are placed in the first category, but research emphasises that children influenced by such factors are normally unaware of the basis of their views (Ceci and Bruck, 1995), a characteristic which would place them in his second category. Bernet's typology pays full tribute to the complexity of the factors that can lead to misstatements by children, but as a working system for professionals it may be confusing and over elaborated.

Mikkelson, Gutheil, and Emens (1992) suggest a four-fold typology. According to the authors, in descending order of frequency of occurrence, these are (a) *allegations arising within custody disputes*, (b) *iatrogenic cases* caused by faulty interviewing and diagnostic practices, (c) *deliberate manipulation* by the child, and (d) allegations arising from *psychological disturbance in a carer*. However, their analysis was based on just twenty-two cases and some less frequent causes of false allegation identified by other typologies may consequently have been overlooked.

Another influential typology has been offered by Weir (1996), a British child psychiatrist, on the basis of his extensive professional experience. Weir identified seven principal causes of false reports and these in turn can be subsumed in Bernet's three categories. Bernet's 'external influences on the child' embraces *influences on the child of a hostile witness*, a *disordered adult*, and *post-traumatic stress disorder (PTSD) in an adult*. 'Unconscious' influences include *negative stereotyping of the suspected adult by others, professional bias in the conduct of the interview* by the investigator and *PTSD in the child*. 'Deliberate deception' is illustrated by Weir's category of the *deliberate incrimination of an adult by a child*. While many of the instances identified by Weir overlap with Bernet and Mikkelson et al., the emphasis upon the consequences of PTSD is novel. According to Weir, PTSD in adults caused by their own sexual abuse as children can lead to over-identification with the child involved and the adult consequently confusing their own experiences with those of the child. Likewise, children who suffer PTSD-type flashbacks as a result of their own abuse may subsequently label innocent situations with other carers as abusive. Weir does not place any absolute frequency estimates on his examples, but he views bias by professionals as relatively the most frequent, and deliberate lying by the child as the least frequent cause of false allegations.

One category of deception, which is under-emphasised in all these typologies, is false allegations arising within a group setting, normally involving preschool children or, as in the Broxtowe case, those with learning disabilities. The McMartin case proved to be the most expensive enquiry in Californian legal history. Allegations made in investigative interviews with nursery-school-age children led to charges of sexual abuse being laid against the school superintendent, his sixty-year-old mother, and seven other teachers, but eventually charges were dropped against all defendants. Concerns were expressed that the children's allegations were not credible and that their testimony could have been contaminated by parental pressures exacerbated by poor interviewing practices (Bruck and Ceci, 1995). In another celebrated case, nineteen young children testified that their day-care assistant, Kelly Michaels, had forced them to take part in naked orgies and to eat their own urine and faeces. No forensic evidence was offered at trial and the children's statements were frequently bizarre and contradictory or at odds with the known regime of the nursery. The prosecution relied upon the testimony of the children together with expert evidence that the children were displaying behavioural symptoms typical of abused children. A jury found Miss Michaels guilty and she was sentenced to forty-seven years' imprisonment. This verdict was eventually quashed on appeal after the defence brought forward evidence that the interviews conducted with the children were coercive and suggestive (Bruck and Ceci, 1995). Despite the lack of solid evidence for the existence of satanic sexual abuse (La Fontaine, 1994), there continue to be cases involving similar allegations by young children of bizarre or ritualised abuse in nursery-school settings. Recent examples include Shieldfield in Newcastle (Woffindon and Webster, 2002), Christchurch, New Zealand (Hood, 2002), and a number of cases in Scandinavia described by Scharnberg (1996).

Research on deception and suggestion

Given the diversity of causes of false allegations offered by existing typologies, it is noteworthy that research on false statements by children appears to have been channelled into a very limited number of issues. Two principal areas of research have been (i) developmental studies of children's skills at deception and (ii) research on interviewer suggestion. The indepth study of these areas has had a powerful impact both on clinical and forensic practice and on professional perceptions of the causes of false allegations.

Children's skills at deception

At what age do children start to tell lies? Experimental research has demonstrated that children are surprisingly precocious in their ability both to identify and to tell lies (see Vrij, 2000, for a comprehensive review). Children as young as four years of age are able to classify examples of truthful and deceptive behaviour and appreciate the dangers of telling lies (Bussey and Grimbeek, 2000). Such findings are of obvious significance for the debate over the age at which children may take the oath in those judiciaries where such formalities remain necessary (see Lyon, 2002).

As most parents will readily confirm, the ability of children to tell lies starts rather earlier. Chandler, Fritz, and Hala (1989) reported that children as young as two and a half displayed deceptive behaviour in a board game where it was possible to mislead other players as to the location of treasure. While clearly of academic interest, such demonstrations are of limited relevance to the courts: most experimental research focuses on simple rather than complex lies. As Vrij (2002) emphasises, most experimenters have limited children's responses to brief, often one-word, lies rather than the kind of lengthy statements required to produce a credible false accusation.

One exception to the 'simple lie' approach was a study by Westcott, Davies, and Clifford (1991), in which children aged between seven and ten years who visited a museum were paired with participants who saw only a videotape of the event and were asked to pretend they had taken part. Both groups were then required to answer questions on camera concerning the details of the visit. Adult judges were able to discriminate between the two groups with an overall accuracy of just 59 per cent, a rate significantly above chance, but well below the level of accuracy required by a court.

Adults in the Westcott et al. study showed a 'truth bias'– a tendency to judge children as telling the truth more frequently than was in fact the case – a finding reported in many experimental studies of deception detection in both adults and children (see Bond and DePaulo, forthcoming). Westcott et al. also reported that adult judges were more accurate in discriminating true from false accounts in younger compared to older children, and this again has been widely reported in comparable studies (Vrij, 2002).

Vrij's review (2002) of detection by adults of children's deceptive accounts confirms that they typically perform at chance level or just above on such tasks. Are there certain groups of adults, who by reason of experience or training, might do rather better at this task? Jackson (1996) found no overall difference between barristers and students in their ability to detect which of a group of eleven- to twelve-year-old children were lying about whether they had seen a film, although barristers showed a lower 'truth bias' compared to the students. Chahal and Cassidy (1995) asked groups of social workers, students, and teachers to detect which eight-year-old children were fabricating the details of a film the children had seen previously. They reported no difference in competence across the three groups, but overall, parents outperformed non-parents, suggesting that recent experience of interacting with children may have some facilitative effect on lie detection.

While studies such as these demonstrate that children can deceive adults under questioning, the differences as well as the parallels with child sexual abuse need to be stressed. First, as Vrij (this volume) has emphasised, the penalties involved in being detected and the rewards for successful deception are minimal: these are 'low-stake' lies, rather than 'high-stake' lies typical of the courtroom. Second, in all of these experimental studies the children in the deceptive condition had a good knowledge base from which to derive their narrative – they had seen films – while for a child falsely alleging sexual abuse, his or her knowledge will normally be limited. Even when that knowledge base is supplemented by ready access to pornographic images, knowledge by the child of the abusive process, including grooming and seduction, is likely to be absent.

If such information is present in the false narrative of a child, then it is likely to have come from an external source: an adult who is encouraging the child to lie. The coaching of children forms another area, where allegations are frequently made at court, but where the research knowledge base is lacking. In one oft-quoted study, Tate, Warren, and Hess (1992) asked children aged three to seven years to play a game with an experimenter. Half played with a particular toy, while the remainder were encouraged to pretend that they had played with it, with help from the experimenter as to what they should say to convince another adult. When groups were interviewed, just over half the deceptive children complied with the request to lie and all but three reverted to the truth under simple questioning.

While this result is encouraging from the standpoint of the justice system, it could be that the coaching given was insufficiently thorough or appropriate. Vrij, Akehurst, Soukara, and Bull (2002) reported rather greater success in tutoring children aged between five and fifteen years to include in their deceptive statements some of the 'truth' criteria derived from CBCA (see Köhnken, this volume). Only the youngest children failed to benefit from the training: the older children tutored in CBCA who lied did not differ significantly from truthful children in the number of such criteria contained in their statements, and both groups produced many more criteria than untrained controls. While the children were not questioned on their statements and there was no independent subjective assessment of the credibility of the children's stories, coaching appears to have been successful, at least with the older children's accounts.

Experiments on suggestion: Ceci and after

Ceci has been responsible for some of the most influential research on suggestibility in children. Captured on videotape, his powerful demonstrations of young children's vulnerabilities have had an impact on judicial perceptions of children's evidence, not only in North America but also in the United Kingdom and elsewhere. Ceci's works served as a corrective to the view that children will never tell untruths and are invariably resistant to suggestion. However, his own work has, in turn, been misrepresented as a generalised critique of the testimonial competence of children in general, something that Ceci himself has been quick to deplore (Ceci and Friedman, 2000).

One early study by Leichtman and Ceci (1995) served to underline the deficiencies of previous laboratory research on suggestibility. A stranger, 'Sam Stone', visited a nursery school, spent two minutes chatting briefly with the children, aged 3 to 4 and 5 to 6 years and their teacher before leaving. Over the ensuing ten weeks, a group of children were interviewed four times about the visit, culminating in a final interview by a trained interviewer who had had no previous contact with the children. The memory accuracy of this group was very high, with no spontaneous allegations regarding misbehaviour by Sam Stone. Such a finding of high accuracy and low errors when interviews were conducted in a neutral and non-suggestive manner was entirely consistent with the research literature to date. However, Ceci sought to capture the motivational factors present in real child-abuse investigations which he believed were absent from most previous studies: the negative stereotyping of the alleged abuser and repeated, suggestive questioning. Negative stereotyping was induced by telling another group of children a dozen stories all illustrating Sam Stone's clumsiness in the month prior to the visit. This same group also took part in four interviews in the weeks following the incident that included leading and suggestive questions suggesting that Stone had ripped a book and soiled a teddy. When these children were again interviewed after ten weeks by the trained interviewer, a very different picture of competence emerged. Now, 46 per cent of the younger children and 30 per cent of the older group spontaneously reported that Sam Stone had committed one or other of the misdeeds, a figure that rose under directed questioning to 72 per cent in the younger group and around half that figure among the older group. Suggestive responding showed a very strong age effect, with children aged 5 to 6 years showing only half the levels of suggestiveness of those aged 3 to 4 years. When the children were gently pressed by the interviewer as to whether they had seen Sam Stone commit the deed and were certain of this, the headline percentage dropped to 21 per cent for the younger group and less than 10 per cent for the older group.

In subsequent studies, Ceci and colleagues have demonstrated the impact of committed interviewing on children's testimony. Children aged 3 to 4 and 5 to 6 years were interviewed by different trained interviewers about an incident when they played with a stranger, one and two months afterwards. On each occasion, the interviewer was provided with a brief summary of what had occurred that contained a number of inaccurate details. Some of the inaccurate details were bizarre (e.g., that the child had kissed the researcher or licked his elbow), mimicking allegations in some nursery-school abuse cases (see above). Both the interviewers tended to ask direct questions regarding such details ('Did you kiss the researcher in this game?'). The older group were less ready to confirm the interviewer's preconceptions (18 per cent) compared to the younger children (34 per cent). Children who assented to the non-existent event in the first interview were likely to elaborate falsely upon it in the second, a trend particularly noticeable in the younger group. White, Leichtman, and Ceci (1997) conclude that an interviewer's agenda can unwittingly be conveyed to the child through repeated interviews and direct questions, and this in turn can elicit apparent confirmatory detail from the child.

A feature of many cases involving false allegations is that children have been subject to repeated interviews. Ceci, Loftus, Leichtman, and Bruck (1994) demonstrated the deleterious effect such a process can have on children's recall accuracy. Again, the children involved were aged 3 to 4 and 5 to 6 years and were interviewed once a week over a twelve-week period. The interviews focused on eight significant life events, four of which parents confirmed their children had experienced and four of which they had not. Children were encouraged to visualise each event and were told that their mothers had vouched that all the events were true. The children's memory for events that had actually occurred to them was generally highly accurate. However, rates of false affirmation to fictitious events rose over the interviews so that by the twelfth interview, 45 per cent of the younger and 40 per cent of the older age group agreed that they experienced at least one of the fictitious items. One explanation for this high rate of error may lie in the poor memory-monitoring skills of young children: they increasingly confused the mental images they were encouraged to develop of the fictitious incidents with memories of actual events (see Poole and Lindsay, 2001). The effects, however, appeared to be transient: a follow-up study conducted some two years later found that the number of children who acceded to the false statements had shrunk to just 13 per cent, suggesting that demand characteristics may have played a role in the positive responding (Hoffman, Crossman and Ceci, 1996).

Ceci argues that these and related studies (see Bruck, Ceci, and Hembrooke, 1998; Bruck and Ceci, 1999, for reviews) illustrate a dilemma for many interviewers. On the one hand, direct questions and repeated interviews may be very effective for eliciting the details of abusive events experienced by young children, but on the other hand, they also increase the possibility that non-abused children will produce false allegations. Moreover, children will not merely assent to such suggestions but a minority will go on to provide elaborate, detailed, but totally fictitious, narratives, which Ceci claims adult experts are unable to discriminate accurately from true statements by the same children (Ceci et al., 1994; Leichtman and Ceci, 1995).

Ceci has sought to demonstrate that the effects he has shown are not confined to the laboratory. The amicus brief compiled by Bruck and Ceci (1995) in the Kelly Michaels case highlighted a number of suspect techniques used by the interviewers. These included *Interviewer bias*: interviewers having a pre-set agenda that they pursued single-mindedly, irrespective of the initial responses of the child; eventually, some children complied with the interviewer's agenda; *Differential reinforcement*: any statement made by the child alluding to an abuse was reinforced by the interviewer; *Peer pressure*: the interviewer told children that other children had already mentioned their involvement in various acts and they were simply required to confirm their role, and finally, *Inappropriate use of anatomical dolls*: children aged 4 to 5 years have difficulties using dolls as extensions of themselves and consequently any actions may reflect suggestion rather than mimic real events. In quashing Kelly Michaels' conviction, the court relied heavily upon the Bruck and Ceci brief.

Ceci's work continues to attract criticism from child-care professionals and some lawyers. Lyon (1999) has offered an extensive critique of the generality and applicability of his findings: he argues that the combination of blatant leading questions and peer pressure are rarely found in cases that reach court. Saywitz and Lyon (2002) note the strong age effects present in most of his studies, with the effects much-reduced in 'older' (i.e., 5 to 6-year-old) children. They also note the differences between accusations of abuse and recall of personal events: children appear reluctant to talk about sexual matters in general and to make false accusations against a loved one in particular. Ceci does not accept that his studies are unrepresentative and points to parallels between the effects demonstrable in his studies and the transcripts of actual child testimony. He also

argues that in the United States, the 3 to 5-year age group is dispropor-
tionately represented among complainants of sexual abuse (5.1 per cent
of all cases) (Ceci and Friedman, 2000). By contrast, figures for England
and Wales collected by Davies, Wilson, Mitchell, and Milsom (1995)
suggest that less than 2.6 per cent of all allegations reaching court involve
child witnesses under the aged of six years, the great majority falling in
the 10–14 age group.

Combating suggestion and deception through good interview practice

Reading the details of miscarried investigations, it is easy to forget how
often children and interviewers do 'get it right'. In some cases, the children's allegations will be supported by forensic evidence or the testimony
of others, including the accused, where a confession can provide striking independent confirmation of the child's story (Lyon, 1999). Clearly
to avoid the pitfalls, it is necessary to develop interview protocols that
minimise the risk of interviewer bias and to ensure that the interviewers themselves are properly trained in these procedures and continue to
adhere to them in their professional practice. England and Wales were
among the first countries to introduce national guidelines for the conduct
of investigative interviews.

The memorandum of good practice

The first national guidelines in England and Wales, entitled *The memorandum of good practice on video recorded interviews with child witnesses for
criminal proceedings* (Home Office, 1992) were the result of collaboration
between a psychologist (Professor Ray Bull of Portsmouth University)
and a lawyer (Professor Diane Birch of Nottingham University). The
guidance drew upon the results of recent research to endorse a model of
best practice for interviewing children, which was also compatible with
the requirements of the legal rules of evidence. In accord with the recommendations of the Cleveland Enquiry (Butler-Sloss, 1988), police officers
and social workers were now required to work together to prepare for and
conduct interviews with child complainants of abuse. The 1991 Criminal
Justice Act required that all such interviews were to be videotaped and
could be played at trial as a substitute for the child's live examination at
court (though the 1991 Act still required the child to attend court for live
cross-examination).

The guidance endorsed a phased approach to interviewing, where each
step has a clear purpose. The initial *rapport* phase is designed to settle the

child and reduce anxiety through casual conversation on non-offence-related topics. The rapport phase is also used to impart the *ground rules* of the interview, including the importance of ensuring that children know they have permission to say 'I don't know' or 'I don't understand' in appropriate circumstances and that they are the only source of information as to what occurred; the interviewer was not there and cannot supply the 'right' answer. The reason for the interview is broached with the child. They are also admonished to speak the truth and their understanding of truth and lies explored. In the second, *free narrative*, phase, the child is encouraged to say in their own words what transpired, with no interruptions from the interviewer. Normally this narrative has to be supplemented by a third, *questioning*, phase, where interviewers are expected to seek detail and clarification through questions of increasing explicitness, beginning with open-ended and ending with specific and closed questions. Leading questions are discouraged and reserved only for very reticent children. When the interviewer is satisfied that the child has nothing more to say, the interview is concluded with a *closure* phase, where the interviewer summarises what the child has said, using as far as possible the child's own expressions before reverting to neutral topics designed to ensure the child leaves the interview in as positive a frame of mind as possible (see Bull, 1996, for a more detailed discussion). It has been estimated that some 12–15,000 *Memorandum* interviews have been conducted yearly in England and Wales since the inception of the 1992 Act (Westcott and Jones, 1997).

The *Memorandum* incorporated precautions designed to minimise risks from suggestion that were known from research at the time of drafting. In accord with research supporting increased suggestibility with overt formality and social distance (Tobey and Goodman, 1992), interviews take place away from police stations; police officers wear civilian clothing, and the interview itself is staged in a conventionally furnished room. The rapport phase also acknowledges the need to counter suggestive responding with its emphasis upon children not answering questions that they do not understand or do not know the answer to. The emphasis on the absence of knowledge of the incident by the interviewer is designed to counter egocentricity and the limitations of children's theories of mind which often assume that adults will always know the right answer (see Perner, 1997, for a review). The admonishment to speak the truth and to show an understanding of the truth/lies distinction explores the child's moral maturity and underlines the importance of telling the truth. Interviewers are told not to raise the issue of concern directly with the child, but rather to encourage children to raise it themselves through an indirect question ('Do you know why you are here today?'). The primacy given to the free-narrative phase reflects classic research that demonstrates that free recall is the most accurate source of information available to the interviewer (Binet, 1900). Likewise, the emphasis on open-ended questioning reflects research demonstrating superior accuracy in answering such questions compared to more specific or closed questions (Dent and Stephenson, 1979). In sum, the aim of the *Memorandum* interview is that, as far as possible, the narrative is driven by the child, rather than the interviewer concluding prematurely what must have happened and looking to the child to confirm this, through a mixture of closed and leading questions: a pattern present in some of the more egregious investigative interviews described earlier.

Ceci's research was not available at the time the *Memorandum* was drafted, but the English legislation was prescient in incorporating procedures that countered the dangers it uncovered. First, all interviews are videotaped, so there is a complete record, not only of children's answers but also the form of the question put to them. Under the legislation, judges have the power to order the editing of tapes or to reject a tape in its entirety, if the questioning has been unduly suggestive or oppressive. Second, the *Memorandum* emphasises the importance of minimising the number of interviews conducted with the child. Unlike the position in the United States, where children are interviewed on average nine times prior to trial (Ceci and Bruck, 1995), in England and Wales a single interview is usually sufficient; any parties to the case can view the videotape rather than re-interview the child. Additionally, there is encouragement to interview the child as soon as practicable after the allegation emerges, so that the risk of the child's account being contaminated by discussions with others is minimised.

But do interviewers follow the Memorandum recommendations?

Effective practice requires not only sound guidance but also that interviewers actually adhere to the recommendations. One of the other incidental, but significant advantages of videotaping interviews is that they provide a permanent record which, with the permission of all parties involved, can be audited to assess the interviewer's adherence to guidelines. One of the most extensive audits was performed by Sternberg, Lamb, Davies, and Westcott (2001) on a sample of 119 videotaped interviews with children conducted by trained police officers from thirteen different police forces in England and Wales. The interviewees ranged in age from four to thirteen years and all had made allegations of sexual abuse, ranging from isolated incidents to prolonged intra-familial abuse. The videotaped interviews were systematically analysed for their adherence to

Memorandum guidelines. The setting of ground rules was incompletely realised: while 98 per cent of interviews contained some exploration of truth and lies, only half involved the children being told that 'don't know' was an acceptable response and just 8 per cent contained the warning that the interviewer was not present and must rely upon the child for an accurate account of what occurred. In the evidence-gathering phase, some 65 per cent of interviews began with free narrative, which was followed by the recommended open-ended question in 69 per cent of interviews. However, this initial open-ended question was often the only one used in the whole interview: overall, just 6 per cent of questions asked were categorised as open-ended. Some 47 per cent of questions fell into the 'specific but non-leading' category and a further 29 per cent would be classed as 'closed' questions in *Memorandum* terms. This very low rate of open-ended questions is disturbing, given that research suggests that specific questions can lead to highly erroneous responding from children, where such questions refer to a non-existent event (Waterman, Blades and Spencer, 2001). One positive finding was that use of blatantly leading questions was very low (5 per cent of all questions asked), suggesting a positive impact of training on interviewer behaviour.

Achieving best evidence

This gap between intention and practice was born in mind when new guidelines for interviewers in England and Wales were drawn up recently by a writing team led by the author. The new guidance, 'Achieving best evidence in criminal proceedings: Guidance for vulnerable witnesses including children' (Home Office, 2002), includes a number of significant changes designed to secure greater adherence to good interviewing practice as well as incorporating changes to reflect the growth in knowledge of children's strengths and vulnerabilities as witnesses since the *Memorandum* was published. To assist with training and delivery, matters to be covered in the rapport and closure phases are systematised as bullet points, and sample narratives (or 'verbal formulae') are provided for key issues such as testing the grasp of truth and lies and raising issues of concern. There is a much greater emphasis on the importance of planning and the need to take account of all sources of information regarding the child's intellectual and social development. There is recognition that children may on occasion provide incomplete, erroneous, or deliberately misleading testimony and that investigators need to preserve an open mind in investigations.

While the tried-and-tested principles of the phased interview are preserved in the new guidance, there is recognition that a 'One-size-fits-all' approach needs to be tempered by consideration of the special needs of interviewing intellectually disabled or young children or those from the ethnic minorities. Above all, there is a renewed emphasis upon the value of asking open-ended questions and the importance of reverting to questions of this type when other types of questions have been asked. *Achieving best evidence* is to be complemented by a comprehensive training package, including video clips illustrating good and bad practice (Bull, Davies, Milne and Cherryman, in press). However, there are still no plans to introduce a national training standard or accredited training courses and awards (Davies, Marshall, and Robertson, 1998). Only another extensive audit in a few years' time will establish how successful these new procedures have been in minimising suggestive questioning and deceptive responding.

The use of experts to detect false or misleading reports

If an interview is misleading, what chance is there that a court-appointed expert will be able to assist the court in reaching a sound decision? In the United States and many parts of mainland Europe, psychologists are routinely called as experts by the court to offer an opinion on children's evidence (Ceci and Hembrooke, 1998). The form this evidence takes reflects differing legal traditions. In mainland Europe, where the inquisitorial system is the norm, the expert will comment on the credibility of the evidence of the child witness in the case, using such methods as Statement Validity Analysis (see Köhnken, this volume). In the United States, however, with its adversarial legal tradition, experts are more likely to provide testimony regarding children's general competency as witnesses to aid the jury: case-specific testimony is seen as infringing the prerogative of the jury to reach independent decisions and is normally excluded (Spencer, 1998). There is continuing debate as to whether such didactic testimony, when offered by the defence, merely increases jury scepticism without improving its powers of discrimination between accurate and inaccurate accounts (Lyon, 2002).

The position in the United Kingdom is more complex. In criminal matters, any form of expert testimony on child witnesses, whether case-specific or didactic, is likely to be excluded on the grounds of infringing the prerogatives of the jury. However, in civil matters, where the judge sits alone and no juries are involved, the courts routinely listen to expert testimony in cases involving custody disputes and other matters affecting children. Such testimony covers an eclectic mix of both general pronouncements and case analysis (Spencer, 1998). The attitude is perhaps best summed up by Lady Butler-Sloss in the landmark case of *Re M and R* (minors) (1996), when she affirmed the role of expert witnesses in assisting the civil courts in reaching their decisions, including their opinions on the 'ultimate issue' (the truth or otherwise of a child's statement) (Wall, 1996). It is a role the author has frequently taken as a court-appointed expert and provides opportunities to identify examples of good and poor practice in investigative interviews.

My court reports confirm that while deliberate lying by a child appears rare, interviewer-induced errors are not uncommon. For instance, interviewers frequently fail to appreciate the difficulty children have in dealing with time and number and induce misleading responses as a consequence. In one case, for example, R, aged eight and a half was asked by the interviewer when she had told her foster-carer about an incident. Initially R answered '*a few years ago*', which she then corrected to '*a few weeks after now*' and subsequently modified to '*a few days after I come here*'. The interviewer, who by now appeared thoroughly confused, ended by putting a leading question to the child based on her understanding of the timescale of events, to which the child then acceded. A proper understanding of developmental milestones and a rephrasing of the question could have avoided this damaging exchange.

In my experience, a major problem is inappropriate précis by the interviewer. For instance in another interview, M aged 7y 1m, was asked about an allegation of inappropriate touching. The interviewer began by confusing M with two questions in one: '*When Z has touched you, where have you been, in what places have you been touched by Z?*' When understandably, there was no response, the interviewer led '*What do you call the part of the body that boys keep in their trousers?*' M responded by saying '*privates*', and the interviewer then asked '*Boys have privates at the front and the back, which part would it be that you touched?*' and M responded '*the front*'. At this stage, M had not acknowledged that she had touched any part of Z's body. Fortunately, other independent evidence pointed to the abuse having occurred and the court was not forced to rely solely upon such poor interviewing practice.

Occasionally, the courts will have available a number of interviews with the same child, conducted at different times. Often, these interviews reveal impressive consistency in the child's account over long time intervals. On other occasions, possible interviewer-induced errors of the kind highlighted by Ceci and colleagues can be detected and brought to the attention of the court. In one such case, C alleged in an interview conducted when she was nine years old, that she had been frequently hung from a peg on the wall, with her hands tied behind her with string and forced to watch sexual behaviour involving her carers. The interviewer, very properly, explored the basis of this allegation to see whether it could be possibly based on a pornographic video, but in summarising the child's allegation, she inadvertently referred to C being 'hung from the ceiling by rope'. At the age of fourteen, C was interviewed again and repeated this bizarre allegation, but this time she talked of being tied up with rope rather than string, and hanging from the ceiling rather than secured to the wall, as in the earlier account. Clearly, there is a strong possibility of an interviewer-induced error, though the origins of the original allegation remained a mystery.

My own case files confirm that in child-witness interviews, as in all aspects of forensic investigation, no interview is ever perfect. However, isolated errors or omissions (for instance, omitting aspects of the ground rules) are rarely fatal and may be compensated for by strengths in other parts of the witness's evidence. Occasionally, however, as in the final example above, such errors can raise serious doubts as to the credibility of the child's testimony. The courts appear to appreciate the assistance of experts, but there is no research on the reliability and consistency of their judgements, nor how far they influence the decisions of the court: it is judges who take the final decision in the light of totality of evidence before them.

Conclusions

All witness testimony is prone to error and the special vulnerability of children needs to be taken into account in collecting and hearing their evidence. However, there is no evidence that false reports by children are endemic, though they occur in all judiciaries. Deliberate deception by children can have devastating consequences for an innocent adult when it occurs, though the frequency of such false testimony appears to be low. A great deal of research has focused on the role of interviewer suggestion as an alternative source of error in children's testimony, and there are convincing examples available when this has occurred. The best answer to both sources of error appears to lie in rigorous, but practical guidelines, systematic training of interviewers and proper maintenance of standards through regular audit, backed up by effective advocacy at court. If such training fails, it may be necessary to constrain the interviewer's freedom further through the use of scripted protocols that enforce greater use of open-ended questions (Sternberg, Lamb, Esplin, and Baradaran, 1999).

Inaccurate testimony by children can stem from a range of factors other than interviewer error. For instance, in the Christchurch crèche case referred to earlier, many of the interviews were properly conducted but still resulted in the children volunteering implausible testimony (Davies, 2003). The typologies of Bernet and others demonstrate that other significant influences on children's testimony remain to be explored. These include such subtle factors as the impact of misinterpretation and misconceptions by the child of the behaviour of adults or the role of PTSD in promoting false beliefs in adults and children, highlighted by Weir. Likewise, social factors, in particular the influence of peer and adult suggestion, may also cause distortions in testimony prior to any interview (Poole and Lindsay, 2001; Principe and Ceci, 2002).

Children on occasion do lie in court and can provide misleading testimony. However, all parties seem agreed that adults are more likely to lie in court than children (Ceci and Friedman, 2000): anyone who visits a courtroom will confirm that discrepant testimony by adult witnesses is the norm, rather than the exception. Such discrepant statements have never been regarded as a reason for denying adults their day in court. Likewise, European Human Rights legislation confirms that children have the right to access the court system and to have their evidence heard. That same legislation guarantees the right of a defendant to a fair trial. The psychologist, through relevant research and informed professional advocacy, must assist the courts in preserving the delicate balance between these conflicting demands.

REFERENCES

Benedek, E., and Schetky, D. (1985). Allegations of sexual abuse in child custody cases. In E. Benedek, and D. Schetky (eds.), *Emerging issues in child psychiatry and the law* (pp. 145–56). New York: Brunner Mazel.

Bernet, W. (1993). False statements and the differential diagnosis of abuse allegations. *Journal of the American Academy of Child and Adolescent Psychiatry*, *32*, 903–10.

Besharov, D. J. (1985). Right versus rights: The dilemma of child protection. *Public Welfare*, *43*, 19–27.

Binet, A. (1900). *La suggestibilite*. Paris: Schleicher Freres.

Bond, C. F. Jr., and DePaulo, B. M. (forthcoming). *Accuracy and truth bias in the detection of deception.*

Bruck, M., and Ceci, S. J. (1995). Amicus brief for the case of State of New Jersey v. Michaels, presented by committee of concerned social scientists. *Psychology, Public Policy and Law*, *1*, 272–322.

(1999). The suggestibility of children's memory. *Annual Reviews of Psychology*, *50*, 419–39.

Bruck, M., Ceci, S. J. and Hembrooke, M (1998). Reliability and credibility of young children's reports. *American Psychologist*, *53*, 136–51.

Bull, R. H. C. (1996). Good practice for video recorded interviews with child witnesses for use in criminal proceedings. In G. M. Davies, S. Lloyd-Bostock, M. McMurran, and C. Wilson (eds.), *Psychology, law and criminal justice: International developments in research and practice* (pp. 100–17). Berlin: de Gruyter.

Bull, R. H. C., Davies, G. M., Milne, R., and Cherryman, J. (in press) *Training package to accompany 'Achieving best evidence'*. Cardiff: Welsh Assembly Government.

Bussey, K., and Grimbeek, E. J. (2000). Children's conceptions of lying and truth-telling: Implications for child witnesses. *Legal and Criminological Psychology, 5*, 187–200.

Butler-Sloss, E. (1988). *Report of the enquiry into child abuse in Cleveland, 1987.* (Command 412). London: Her Majesty's Stationery Office.

Campbell, T. W. (1992). False allegations of sexual abuse and their apparent credibility. *American Journal of Forensic Psychology, 10*, 20–35.

Cashmore, J. (2002). Innovative procedures for child witnesses. In H. L.Westcott, G. M Davies, and R. H. C. Bull (eds.), *Children's testimony: A handbook of psychological research and forensic practice* (pp. 203–18). Chichester: John Wiley.

Ceci, S. J., and Bruck, M. (1995). *Jeopardy in the courtroom.* Washington DC: American Psychological Association.

Ceci, S. J., and Friedman, R. D. (2000). The suggestibility of children: Scientific research and legal implications. *Cornell Law Review, 86*, 33–108.

Ceci, S. J., and Hembrooke, H. (1998). *Expert witness in child abuse cases.* Washington, DC: American Psychological Association.

Ceci S. J., Loftus, E. F., Leichtman, M. D., and Bruck, M. (1994). The possible role of source misattributions in the creation of false beliefs among preschoolers. *International Journal of Clinical Experimental Hypnosis, 42*, 304–20.

Chahal, K., and Cassidy, T. (1995). Deception and its detection in children: A study of adult accuracy. *Psychology, Crime and Law, 1*, 237–45.

Chandler, M., Fritz, A. S., and Hala, S. (1989). Small-scale deceit: Deception as a marker of two-, three-, and four-year-olds' early theories of mind. *Child Development, 60*, 1263–77.

Coleman, L. (1990). False accusations of sexual abuse: Psychiatry's latest reign of error. *Journal of Mind and Behavior, 11*, 545–56.

Davies, G. M. (2003). In the footsteps of Varendonck. In L. Kools, G. Vervaeke, M. Vanderhallen, and J. Goethals (eds.), *The truth and nothing but the truth? The relation between law and psychology* (pp. 1–22). Bruges, Belgium: Die Keure.

Davies, G. M., Marshall, E., and Robertson, N. (1998). Child abuse: Training investigative officers (Police Research Series, Paper 94). London: Home Office.

Davies, G. M., Wilson, J. C., Mitchell, R., and Milsom, J. (1995). Videotaping children's evidence: An evaluation. London: Home Office.

Dent, H., and Stephenson, G. M. (1979). An experimental study of the effectiveness of different techniques of questioning child witnesses. *British Journal of Social and Clinical Psychology, 18*, 41–51.

Ehrenberg, M. F., and Elterman, M. F. (1995). Evaluating allegations of sexual abuse in the context of divorce, child custody and access disputes. In T. Ney (ed.), *Allegations in child sexual abuse: Assessment and case management* (pp. 219–40). New York, NY: Brunner Mazel.

Everson, M. D., and Boat, B. W. (1989). False allegations of sexual abuse by children and adolescents. *Journal of the American Academy of Child and Adolescent Psychiatry, 32,* 903–10.

Faller, K. C. (1991). Possible explanations for child sexual abuse allegations in divorce. *American Journal of Orthopsychiatry, 61,* 86–91.

Goodwin, J. M., Sahd, D., and Rada, R. T. (1989). False accusations and false denials of incest: Clinical myths and clinical realities. In J. M. Goodwin (ed.), *Sexual abuse: Incest victims and their families* (pp. 19–36). Chicago: Year Book Medical Publishers.

Green, A. (1986). True and false allegations of child sexual abuse in child custody disputes. *Journal of the American Academy of Child Psychiatry, 25,* 449–56.

Hoffman, M. L., Crossman, A., and Ceci, S. J. (1996). An investigation of the long-term effects of source misattribution error: Are false memories permanent? Paper presented to the APLS Conference, Hilton Head, SC, March.

Home Office, with the Department of Health (1992). Memorandum of good practice on video-recorded interviews with child witnesses in criminal proceedings. London: Home Office.

Home Office (2002). Achieving best evidence in criminal proceedings: Guidance for vulnerable or intimidated witnesses including children. London: Home Office.

Hood, L. (2002). *A city possessed: The Christchurch crèche case.* Dunedin: Longacre Press.

Jackson, J. L. (1996). Truth and fantasy: The ability of barristers and laypersons to detect deception in children's testimony. Paper presented at the American Psychology–Law Society Conference, Hilton Head, SC.

Jones, D. P. H. (1991). Child sexual abuse and satanism (1991). Paper presented at the first National Congress on the Prevention and Treatment of Child Abuse and Neglect, Leicester, UK (September).

Jones, D. P. H., and McGraw, J. M. (1987). Reliable and fictitious accounts of sexual abuse to children. *Journal of Interpersonal Violence, 2,* 27–45.

Jones, D. P. H., and Seig, A. (1988). Child sexual allegations in custody or visitation disputes. In E. B. Nicholson (ed.), *Sexual abuse allegations in custody and visitation cases* (pp. 22–36). Washington, DC: American Bar Association.

La Fontaine, J. (1994). *The extent and nature of organised and ritual abuse.* London: Her Majesty's Stationery Office.

Leichtman, M. D., and Ceci, S. J. (1995). The effects of stereotypes and suggestions on pre-schoolers' reports. *Developmental Psychology, 31,* 568–78.

Lyon, T. D. (1999). The new wave in children's suggestibility research: A critique. *Cornell Law Review, 84,* 1004–87.

(2002). Expert testimony on the suggestibility of children: Does it fit? In B. Bottoms, M. B. Kovera, and B. D. McAuliff (eds.), *Children, social science and the law* (pp. 378–411). New York: Cambridge University Press.

McIntosh, J. A., and Prinz, R. J. (1993). The incidence of alleged sexual abuse in 603 family court cases. *Law and Human Behavior, 17*, 95–101.

Meyer, J. F., and Geis, G. (1994). Psychological research on child witnesses in sexual abuse cases: Fine answers to mostly wrong questions. *Child and Adolescent Social Work Journal, 11*, 209–20.

Mikkelsen, E. J., Gutheil, T. G., and Emens, M. (1992). False sexual abuse allegations by children and adolescents: Contextual factors and clinical subtypes. *American Journal of Psychotherapy, 46*, 556–70.

Nottinghamshire County Council (1990). *The JET report: Revised joint enquiry report*. Nottingham: Nottinghamshire Social Services.

Pendergrast, M. (1996). *Victims of memory: Incest accusations and shattered lives*. London: HarperCollins.

Perner, J. (1997). Children's competency in understanding the role of a witness: Truth, lies and moral ties. *Applied Cognitive Psychology, 11*, 37–54.

Poole, D. A., and Lindsay, D. S. (2001). Eyewitness reports of children exposed to misinformation from their parents. *Journal of Experimental Psychology: Applied, 7*, 27–50.

Principe, G., and Ceci, S. J. (2002) I saw it with my own ears: The effects of peer conversations on preschoolers' reports of nonexperienced events. *Journal of Experimental Child Psychology, 83*, 1–25.

Re M and R (minors) (1996). 2 *Family Law Reports* 195.

Saywitz, K. J., and Lyon, T. D. (2002). Coming to grips with children's suggestibility. In M. Eisen, G. Goodman and J. Quas (eds.), *Memory and suggestibility in the forensic interview* (pp. 85–113). Hillsdale, NJ: Lawrence Erlbaum.

Scharnberg, M. (1996). Textual analysis: A scientific approach for assessing cases of sexual abuse. *Uppsala Studies in Education, 64* (2 vols.). Uppsala, Sweden.

Spencer, J. R. (1998). The role of experts in the common law and the civil law: A comparison. In S. J. Ceci and H. Hembrooke (eds.), *Expert witness in child abuse cases* (pp. 29–58). Washington, DC: American Psychological Association.

Spencer, J. R., and Flin, R. (1993). *The evidence of children: The law and the psychology* (2nd edn). London: Blackstone.

Sternberg, K. J., Lamb, M. E., Davies, G. M., and Westcott, H. W. (2001). The 'Memorandum of Good Practice': Theory versus practice. *Child Abuse and Neglect, 25*, 669–81.

Sternberg, K. J., Lamb, M. E., Esplin, P. W., and Baradaran, L. (1999). Using a scripted protocol to guide an investigative interview: A pilot study. *Applied Developmental Science, 3*, 70–6.

Tate, C., Warren, A., and Hess, T. (1992). Adults' liability for children's lie-ability: Can adults coach children to lie successfully? In S. J. Ceci, M. Leichtman, and M. Putnick (eds.), *Cognitive and social factors in early deception*. (pp. 69–87). New Jersey: Lawrence Erlbaum.

Thoennes, N., and Tjaden, P. G. (1990). The extent, nature and validity of sexual abuse allegations in custody/visitation disputes. *Child Abuse and Neglect, 14*, 151–63.

Tobey, A., and Goodman, G. (1992). Children's eyewitness memory: Effects of participation and forensic context. *Child Abuse and Neglect*, *17*, 807–21.

Vrij, A. (2000). *Detecting lies and deceit.* Chichester: John Wiley.

(2002). Deception in children: A literature review and implications for children's testimony. In H. L. Westcott, G. M. Davies, and R. H. C. Bull (eds.), *Children's testimony: A handbook of psychological research and forensic practice* (pp. 175–94). Chichester: John Wiley.

Vrij, A., Akehurst, L., Soukara, S., and Bull, R. (2002). Will the truth come out? The effect of deception, age, status and coaching on CBCA scores. *Law and Human Behavior*, *26*, 261–83.

Wakefield, H., and Underwager, R. (1988). *Accusations of sexual abuse.* Springfield, IL: Charles C. Thomas.

Wall, N. (1996). Expert evidence on child witness credibility. *Child Psychology and Psychiatry Review*, *1*, 146–50.

Waterman, A. H., Blades, M. and Spencer, C. (2001). Interviewing children and adults: The effect of question format on the tendency to speculate. *Applied Cognitive Psychology*, *15*, 521–32.

Westcott, H. L., Davies, G. M., and Bull, R. H. C. (2002). *Children's testimony: A handbook of psychological research and forensic practice.* Chichester: Wiley.

Westcott, H. L., Davies, G. M., and Clifford, B. L. (1991). Adult's perceptions of children's videotaped truthful and deceptive statements. *Children and Society*, *5*, 123–35.

Westcott, H., and Jones, J. (1997). *Perspectives on the Memorandum: Policy, practice and research in investigative interviewing.* Aldershot: Ashgate.

Weir, I. K. (1996). Evaluating child sexual abuse. *Family Law*, *26*, 673–77.

White, M., Leichtman, M. D., and Ceci, S. J. (1997). The good, the bad and the ugly: Accuracy, inaccuracy and elaboration in preschoolers' reports about past events. *Applied Cognitive Psychology*, *11*, S37–55.

Woffindon, B., and Webster, R. (2002). Cleared. *Guardian*, *G2*, 31 July, pp. 2–5.

8   True or false: 'I'd know a false confession if I saw one'

Saul Kassin

Let me begin with a recent story that already has historic value in the annals of wrongful convictions. This was an infamous case that took place in 1989 in New York City. Known as the 'Central Park jogger case', it involved a young woman, an investment banker, who was beaten senseless, raped, and left for dead. It was a heinous crime that horrified the city. The victim's skull had multiple fractures, her eye socket was crushed, and she lost three-quarters of her blood. Defying the odds, she managed to survive, but she was – and, to this day, still is – completely amnesic for the incident (Meili, 2003). Soon thereafter, solely on the basis of police-induced confessions taken within seventy-two hours of the crime, five African- and Hispanic-American boys, 14 to 16 years old, were convicted of the attack and sentenced to prison. At the time, it was easy to understand why detectives aggressively interrogated the boys, some of whom were 'wilding' in the park that night (Sullivan, 1992). Yet based on a recent confession volunteered from prison by a convicted serial rapist whose DNA was found in semen at the crime scene, the five boys' convictions were vacated, their confessions apparently false (Kassin, 2002; *New York* v. *Wise*, 2002; Saulny, 2002).

Four of the five jogger confessions were videotaped and presented to the juries at trial. The tapes – which showed only the confessions, not the precipitating fourteen to thirty hours of interrogation – were highly compelling. They showed that every one of the boys described in vivid and textured detail how the jogger was attacked, when, where, and by whom, and the role that they played in the process. One boy stood up and physically re-enacted the way he allegedly pulled off the jogger's running pants. A second boy said he felt peer-pressured to take part in his 'first rape', and he expressed remorse for his actions and said it would not happen again. Being a native New Yorker, I followed this case closely in the news. The confessions, portions of which were aired on television, fooled not only two trial juries but an entire city and nation, including myself. It was not until February of 2002, thirteen years later, that Matias Reyes, in prison for three rapes and a murder that he committed subsequent to the jogger attack, stepped forward to give a voluntary, accurate, independently corroborated confession.

The Central Park crime scene betrayed a bloody, horrific, violent act. Yet there were no physical traces of the defendants on the scene and no traces of the scene on them. Semen samples extracted from the victim's body and socks were tested and results conclusively excluded the boys as donors. Solely on the basis of their confessions, however, the district attorney's office prosecuted the defendants and argued to the jury that just because the police did not capture *all* the perpetrators does not mean they did not get *some* of them. The rest, as they say, is history. The Central Park jogger case now stands as a shocking tale of five false confessions resulting from a single investigation.

The jogger case points to a sequence of three serious problems in police investigation: (1) Innocent people are often targeted for interrogation, despite the absence of evidence of their involvement, based solely on an interview-based hunch; (2) under certain circumstances, interrogation can cause innocent people to confess to crimes they did not commit; and (3) afterwards, it is difficult for investigators, attorneys, judges, and juries to distinguish between true and false confessions. In this chapter, I will argue that there are risks of error inherent in each link of this three-step chain of events – from the pre-interrogation interview, to the interrogation itself and the assessment of the confession.

The pre-interrogation interview

The first problem is that innocent people are often targeted for interrogation, despite the absence of any evidence of their involvement, based solely on an investigator's hunch. Consider, for example, the military trial of *US* v. *Bickel* (1999), in which I testified as an expert witness. In this case, the defendant confessed to rape as a result of an interrogation conducted by five agents who used persistent and highly aggressive techniques (e.g., explicit and implied promises and threats, negative feedback on a polygraph test that was described as infallible, and the use of minimisation). There was no independent evidence against the defendant. When asked why they chose to interrogate him and not others, one investigator said that he showed 'signs of deception based on the training we have received'. More specifically, he stated, 'His body language and the way he reacted to our questions told us that he was not telling the whole truth. Some examples of body language is that he tried to remain calm but you could tell he was nervous and every time we asked him a question his eyes would roam and he would not make direct contact, and at times he would act pretty sporadic and he started to cry at one time.' Correctly, I think, this defendant was acquitted by a jury of military officers.

Then there was the case of Tom Sawyer, in Florida, in which investigators accused the defendant of sexual assault and murder, interrogated him for sixteen hours, issued threats, and extracted a confession likely to have been false. The confession was suppressed by the trial judge, so in the absence of other evidence the charges were dropped. But the reason Sawyer became a prime suspect was that his face flushed red and he appeared embarrassed during an initial interview, a behavioural reaction seen as a sign of deception. What the investigators did not know at the time was that Sawyer was a recovering alcoholic and also had a social anxiety disorder that caused him to sweat profusely and blush a deep red in public social situations (Leo and Ofshe, 1998). After spending a year with homicide detectives in Baltimore, Simon (1991) may have captured the essence of the problem: 'Nervousness, fear, confusion, hostility, a story that changes or contradicts itself – all are signs that the man in an interrogation room is lying, particularly in the eyes of someone as naturally suspicious as a detective. Unfortunately, these are also signs of a human being in a state of high stress' (p. 219). Reflecting a common and cynical belief that all suspects are guilty, one detective is quoted as saying, 'You can tell if a suspect is lying by whether he is moving his lips' (Leo, 1996b, p. 23).

I know that most crime investigators are well meaning and well trained, and I have the utmost respect for law-enforcement work, so it is not my intent to paint an unflattering portrait of the profession. Hence, my comments are directed exclusively at those who state, with the confidence that borders on arrogance, that 'I'd know a false confession if I saw one.' Over the years, in talking about the psychology of confessions, I have had many conversations with active and retired detectives, many of whom had been specially trained in the techniques of interviewing and interrogation, who claimed never to have taken a false confession. The conversation would go something like this: 'How do you know that you've never taken a false confession?' Answer: 'Because everyone who has confessed to me was later convicted.' 'But how can you be sure that the powerful methods of interrogation that you are trained to use (methods that are not surgically precise in their impact) do not, at times, lead innocent people to confess?' The answer to this question, which left me scratching my head the first time I heard it, was 'I know because I don't interrogate innocent people.'

To appreciate the basis of this answer fully, one has to know that investigators who are specially trained to take confessions do not commence interrogation until they have made an initial judgement of the suspect's guilt. Sometimes, that judgement is reasonably based on reports from witnesses or informants, or on other forms of extrinsic evidence. At other times, however, that judgement is based on nothing more than a hunch, a clinical impression that detectives form from a pre-interrogation interview. Indeed, many law enforcement professionals believe that, as a function of their training, they can determine from a suspect's interview demeanour whether he or she is being truthful or deceptive – and that they can make these initial judgements at high levels of accuracy (Inbau et al., 2001). According to John E. Reid and Associates, investigators trained in their Behavior Symptom Analysis can learn to distinguish between truth and deception at an extraordinary 85 per cent level of accuracy (http://www.reid.com/service-bai-interview.html) – an average that would substantially exceed human lie-detection performance obtained in any of the world's laboratories. This initial judgement becomes a pivotal choice-point in the life of a case, determining whether a suspect is interrogated or sent home. Hence, it is important to know how – and how well – that judgement is made.

As noted, psychological research has consistently failed to support the claim that groups of individuals can attain such high average levels of performance in making judgements of truth and deception. In fact, most experiments have shown that people perform at no better than chance level when it comes to detecting deception (DePaulo, Lassiter, and Stone, 1982; Memon, Vrij, and Bull, 2003; Vrij, 2000; Zuckerman, DePaulo, and Rosenthal, 1981), that training programs produce, at best, small and inconsistent improvements compared with a control group (Bull, 1989; Bull, this volume; Kassin and Fong, 1999; Porter, Woodworth, and Birt, 2000; Vrij, 1994; Zuckerman, Koestner, and Alton, 1984), and that police investigators, judges, psychiatrists, customs inspectors, poly-graphers, and others with relevant on-the-job experience perform only slightly better than chance, if at all (Bull, 1989; DePaulo, 1994; DePaulo and Pfeifer, 1986; Ekman and O'Sullivan, 1991; Ekman, O'Sullivan, and Frank, 1999; Garrido and Masip, 1999; Garrido, Masip, and Herrero, in press; Köhnken, 1987; Porter, Woodworth, and Birt, 2000).

One might try to argue that performance in laboratory experiments is poor in part because the investigators who participate are asked to detect truths and lies that were given in relatively low-involvement, low-stake situations. Some research has shown that low-stake situations can weaken deception cues and make the statements slightly more difficult to judge (DePaulo, Lindsay, Malone, Muhlenbruck, Charlton, and Cooper, 2003). However, Vrij and Mann (2001) showed police officers videotaped press conferences of family members pleading for help in finding their missing relatives. It turned out that these family members had killed their own relatives, yet even in this high-stake situation the investigators did not exceed chance-level performance. One might also argue that professionals would make more accurate judgements when they personally conduct the interviews than when they merely observe sessions conducted by others. But research does not support this notion. Buller, Strzyzewski, and Hunsaker (1991) had observers watch videotaped conversations between two other participants, one of whom was instructed to lie or tell the truth. They found that the observers were more accurate in their assessments of the target than were those who engaged in the conversation. More recently, Hartwig, Granhag, Stromwall, and Vrij (in press) had some police officers interview college students who were guilty or innocent of committing a mock crime, while other officers observed videotapes of these interviews. Overall levels of accuracy did not exceed chance-level performance, and those who conducted the interviews themselves were not more accurate than those who merely observed them. In short, while the law-enforcement community assumes, often with great confidence, that they regularly make accurate judgements of truth and deception on the basis of verbal and non-verbal behavioural cues, there is little scientific evidence in published studies to support this claim (for a comprehensive meta-analysis of the actual cues to deception, see DePaulo et al., 2003; DePaulo and Morris, this volume).

In a series of studies, my colleagues and I have examined the extent to which special training in deception detection increases judgement accuracy in a specifically forensic context. In one study, Kassin and Fong (1999) trained some student participants, but not others, in the detection of truth and deception, before obtaining their judgements of mock suspects. This study was unique in two ways. First, some of the participants but not others were randomly assigned to receive training in the popular Reid Technique, which has been used in the training of tens of thousands of law-enforcement personnel. Second, judgements were made for a set of videotapes depicting brief interviews and denials by individuals who were truly guilty or innocent of committing one of four mock crimes, which they found moderately stressful: breaking and entering a locked office building, shoplifting in a local giftshop, vandalising a campus building, or breaking into a student's personal computer email account. As in past studies conducted in non-forensic settings, observers were generally unable to differentiate between truthful and deceptive suspects better than would be expected by chance. Moreover, those who underwent training were less accurate than naïve controls – though they were more confident and they cited more reasons as a basis for these judgements. Closer inspection of these data further indicated that the training procedure itself produced a response bias towards guilt. This experiment suggested the disturbing hypothesis that special training in deception detection may lead investigators to make prejudgements of guilt, with high confidence, that are frequently in error. This training may also create a response bias, making people overly sensitive to various non-diagnostic indicators of deception. From a practical standpoint, however, the data are limited by the fact that the observers were college students, not police detectives, and their training was condensed, not offered as part of professional development to those with prior experience.

To address these issues, Meissner and Kassin (2002) conducted a meta-analysis and a follow-up study to examine the performance of real and experienced investigators. First, we used signal-detection theory to examine the literature and to distinguish between accuracy in detecting deception, via a measure of 'discrimination accuracy', and a tendency to perceive targets as overly truthful or deceitful, via a measure of 'response bias'. We identified four studies that compared investigators and naïve participants and two that manipulated training. Across studies, investigators and trained participants, relative to naïve controls, exhibited a proclivity to judge targets as deceptive rather than truthful. Second, we used Kassin and Fong's videotapes to test police samples from the United States and Canada. We found that the investigators – compared to college students – exhibited lower chance-level accuracy, a response bias towards judgements of deception, and significantly more confidence. Within our sample of investigators, both years of experience and special training correlated significantly with the response bias – but not with accuracy. This latter result is not terribly surprising. Using a standardised self-report instrument, Masip, Alonso, Garrido, and Anton (in press) found that police officers harbour a 'generalized communicative suspicion' compared to others. It appears that the pivotal decision to interrogate suspects on the basis of their interview behaviour is based on judgements that are confidently made, but biased and frequently in error.

The interrogation

The second and most obvious problem is that innocent people are sometimes induced to confess to crimes they did not commit. Despite perennial debates and disputes over the numbers (e.g., Bedau and Radelet, 1987; Cassell, 1999; Leo and Ofshe, 2001; Markman and Cassell, 1988), the incidence of false confessions is unknown. Still, there exist a disturbing number of documented cases in which defendants confess and retract the confessions but are convicted at trial and sometimes sentenced to death – only later to be exonerated by DNA or other forms of irrefutable evidence (e.g., Bedau and Radelet, 1987; Gudjonsson, 2003; Leo and Ofshe, 1998; Scheck, Neufeld, and Dwyer, 2000). Looking at known false confessors whose cases had proceeded to trial, Leo and Ofshe (1998) found that 73 per cent were convicted, typically, despite the absence of any physical or other corroborating evidence. As the number of DNA exoneration cases accumulates, researchers for The Innocence Project are finding that roughly a quarter of these wrongful convictions had contained full or partial confessions, which were apparently false, in evidence (http://www.innocenceproject.org/).

Confessions have such powerful and rippling effects within the criminal justice system that many researchers are studying the personal and situational factors that lead people to confess in response to various police interrogation practices. Several years ago, Kassin and Wrightsman (1985) introduced a taxonomy that distinguished three types of false confessions. *Voluntary* false confessions are self-incriminating statements that are offered without external pressure from the police, or anyone else for that matter. When Charles Lindbergh's baby was kidnapped more than sixty years ago, two hundred people confessed. There are several possible reasons why people have volunteered false confessions: to protect a friend or relative, for example, or to satisfy a pathological need for fame, acceptance, recognition, or self-punishment. Coerced-*compliant* false confessions are those in which a suspect confesses in order to escape an aversive interrogation, avoid an explicit or implied threat, or gain a promised or implied reward. In these instances, the confession is a mere act of compliance on the part of a suspect who privately knows that he or she is innocent. That is what happened in the Central Park jogger case, where each of the boys indicated after they had confessed on tape that they did so expecting that they would get to go home. Finally, coerced-*internalised* false confessions are those in which an innocent person – anxious, tired, confused, and subjected to highly suggestive methods of interrogation – comes to believe that he or she committed the crime. In this type of false confession, a suspect's memory of his or her own actions and responsibility may be blurred or altered. In the classic example, eighteen-year-old Peter Reilly returned home one day to find that his mother was murdered. After hours of interrogation, in which Reilly was told that he failed a lie-detector test, Reilly transitioned from denial through the mental states of confusion, self-doubt, and eventual conversion. Independent evidence later revealed that Reilly was innocent and that the confession which even he came to believe was false. This categorisation scheme has provided a useful framework for the study of false confessions and has been both used and refined by others (Gudjonsson, 1992, 2003; Inbau, Reid, Buckley, and Jayne, 2001; McCann, 1998; Ofshe and Leo, 1997; Kassin, 1997).

Techniques of interrogation vary and a number of manuals are available to advise and train police detectives in how to get suspects to confess

(Aubry and Caputo, 1980; O'Hara and O'Hara, 1981; Macdonald and Michaud, 1987; Walkley, 1987; Walters, 2003). The most popular such manual is Inbau et al.'s (2001) *Criminal interrogation and confessions*, which was first published in 1962 and is now in its fourth edition. In the so-called Reid technique, interrogators are advised to dress in civilian clothing and isolate the suspect inside a small, bare, soundproof room. Against this physical backdrop, they describe in operational terms a nine-step procedure in which the interrogator begins by confronting the suspect with assertions of guilt (Step 1), then develops 'themes' that psychologically justify or excuse the crime (Step 2), interrupts all statements of denial (Step 3), overcomes the suspect's factual, moral, and emotional objections (Step 4), ensures that the increasingly passive suspect does not withdraw (Step 5), shows sympathy and understanding, and urges the suspect to cooperate (Step 6), offers a face-saving alternative explanation for the alleged guilty act (Step 7), gets the suspect to recount the details of the crime (Step 8), and converts that statement into a full written confession (Step 9). This technique is designed to get suspects to incriminate themselves by increasing the anxiety associated with denial and reducing the perceived adverse consequences of confession.

It is clear that some individuals more than others are vulnerable to manipulation in the interrogation room, particularly if they are characteristically predisposed to exhibit social compliance or interrogative suggestibility. Youth, naïveté, a lack of intelligence, cultural upbringing, and social anxiety, as well as various psychological disorders that impair cognitive and affective functions, present unique sources of vulnerability. Not surprisingly, large numbers of false confessions have been documented in recent years involving children, juveniles, and people who were mentally retarded (for a comprehensive discussion of individual differences, see Gudjonsson, 2003).

Certain situational factors also increase the risk of a false confession. Research shows that isolation can heighten the stress of custody, especially after extended periods of time, and hence increases the incentive to escape (Zimbardo, 1967), and that fatigue and sleep-deprivation heighten susceptibility to influence and seriously impair complex decision-making ability (Blagrove, 1996; Harrison and Horne, 2000). Research also shows that 'minimisation' tactics – by which interrogators normalise the crime in question and offer moral justification for it – lead people to infer that leniency would follow from confession, even in the absence of an explicit promise (Kassin and McNall, 1991). Other laboratory studies have shown that exaggerating or lying about evidence – such as an eyewitness identification, fingerprint, hair sample, or polygraph results – leads people to take responsibility for acts they did not commit. This deceptive interrogation tactic is both recommended (Inbau et al., 2001) and commonly used (Leo, 1996a) in the United States. Yet it increases the risk that innocent people would confess to acts they did not commit and, at times, internalise an erroneous belief in their own guilt and responsibility (Kassin and Kiechel, 1996). Follow-up studies have replicated this laboratory effect, even when the confession bears consequence (Horselenberg, Merckelbach, and Josephs, 2003), and particularly among juveniles who are more vulnerable to the effect than adults (Redlich and Goodman, 2003).

Over the years, psychologists have proposed theories of motivation, decision-making, and social influence to understand the process of interrogation and the reasons why people confess, sometimes to crimes they did not commit (Davis and O'Donohue, 2003; Hilgendorf and Irving, 1981; Gudjonsson, 1992, 2003; Kassin and Wrightsman, 1985; Kassin, 1997; Leo and Ofshe, 1998; Memon, Vrij, and Bull, 2003; Wrightsman and Kassin, 1993; Zimbardo, 1967). Particularly ironic in this regard is the possibility that *innocence* puts *innocents* at risk. For example, research suggests that innocent people are more likely to waive their rights to silence and counsel, thus exposing themselves to police interrogations out of a naïve faith in the power of truth, justice, and innocence to prevail (Kassin and Norwick, 2004).

Past research has also examined the impact of confession evidence on jurors and others in the criminal justice system. Mock jury studies have shown that confessions have more impact than eyewitness and character testimony, other powerful forms of evidence (Kassin and Neumann, 1997). As a matter of common sense, this result is not surprising. The problem is that people do not fully discount confession evidence even when it is logically appropriate to do so (Kassin and Wrightsman, 1980, 1985). In one series of studies, for example, Kassin and Sukel (1997) found that confessions increase the conviction rate even among mock jurors who see the statements as coerced and who self-report a lack of influence on verdicts. Confessions also tend to overwhelm other information, such as alibis and other evidence of innocence, resulting in a chain of adverse legal consequences – from an arrest through prosecution, conviction, incarceration, and even execution (Leo and Ofshe, 1998). Sometimes, district attorneys refuse to admit innocence in the presence of a confession even after DNA tests unequivocally exonerate the wrongfully convicted. In one case, for example, Bruce Godschalk was exonerated by DNA of two rape convictions after fifteen years in prison when laboratories for both the state and the defendant found that he was not the rapist. Yet the district attorney whose office had convicted Godschalk argued that the DNA tests were flawed and refused to release him from prison. When asked what basis he had for this decision, this district attorney asserted, 'I have no scientific basis. I know because I trust my detective and his tape-recorded confession. Therefore the results must be flawed until someone proves to me otherwise' (Rimer, 2002).

Clearly, confession evidence is powerful in court and hard to overcome. To safeguard against the wrongful convictions such confessions elicit and their consequences, it is therefore vitally important that confessions be accurately assessed prior to the onset of court proceedings. We have seen that people are poor lie detectors and cannot readily distinguish between true and false *denials*. But can people in general, and law-enforcement officers in particular, distinguish between true and false *confessions*?

The narrative confession

I framed the title of this chapter as a true–false question concerning an assertion that I have heard over and over again. The third problem revealed by confession-based wrongful convictions is that police detectives, district attorneys, judges, and juries routinely believe false confessions, which suggests that they cannot separate self-incriminating statements that are true from those that are not. One could argue that even if the process of interrogation is psychologically coercive, and even if innocent people sometimes confess, these problems are solved to the extent that the errors are ultimately detected by authorities and corrected. Essential to this presumed safety net, then, is a commonsense assumption, built on blind faith, that 'I'd know a false confession if I saw one.'

There are four compelling reasons for pessimism on the question of whether people can detect as false the confessions of innocent suspects. First, generalised common sense leads us to trust confessions. Over the years, social psychologists have found in a wide range of contexts that people fall prey to the 'fundamental attribution error' – that is, they tend to make dispositional attributions for a person's actions, taking behaviour at face value, while neglecting the role of situational factors (Jones, 1990). Gilbert and Malone (1995) offered several explanations for this bias, the most compelling of which is that people draw quick and relatively automatic dispositional inferences from behaviour and then fail to adjust or correct for the presence of situational constraints. Common sense also compels the belief that people present themselves in ways that are self-serving, and that self-destructive behaviours, like false confessions, must be particularly diagnostic. Reasonably, most people believe they would never confess to a crime they did not commit and they cannot imagine the circumstances under which anyone would do so.

A second basis for pessimism is that people are typically not adept at deception detection. We saw earlier that neither college students nor police investigators can accurately separate true from false denials. The question remains as to whether they can distinguish true and false confessions. In a two-part study, Kassin, Meissner, and Norwick (2004) examined this question and compared the performance of police investigators and lay people. First, we recruited and paid male prison inmates in a state correctional facility to take part in a pair of videotaped interviews. Each inmate was instructed to give a full confession to the crime for which he was in prison ('Tell me about what you did, the crime you committed, that brought you here'). To ensure that all confessions contained the same ingredients, each free narrative was followed by a standardised set of questions concerning who, what, when, where, how, and other details. In a second videotaped interview, each inmate was provided with a skeletal, one- or two-sentence description of the crime that was committed by the preceding participant and instructed to concoct a false confession ('I'd like you to lie about it and make up a confession as if you did it'). Using this yoked design, the first inmate's true confession became the basis of the second inmate's false confession, the second's true confession became the basis of the third's false confession, and so on. The order in which inmates gave true and false confessions was counterbalanced across sessions.

Using this procedure, we created a stimulus videotape that depicted ten different inmates, each giving a single confession to one of the following five crimes: aggravated assault, armed robbery, burglary, breaking and entering, and automobile theft and reckless driving. The ten statements were not explicitly paired for presentation, but the tape as a whole contained five true confessions and their false confession counterparts. In light of research showing that people are better judges of truth and deception when they use auditory cues rather than misleading visual cues (Anderson, DePaulo, Ansfield, Tickle, and Green, 1999; DePaulo, Lassiter, and Stone, 1982), we also created audiotapes of these same confessions. Two groups of subjects served as judges in this study: sixty-one college students and fifty-seven federal, state, and local investigators, two thirds of whom had received training in interviewing and interrogation. The results closely paralleled those obtained for judgements of true and false denials. From the videotapes, neither students nor the investigators performed significantly better than chance, though once again investigators were far more confident in their judgements. Consistent with research showing that people are more accurate when they attend to the voice than to visual and facial cues, accuracy rates were higher when participants listened to audiotaped confessions than when they watched the videotapes. Importantly, students but not investigators exceeded chance-level performance in this condition – though, once again, the investigators were more confident.

Using a signal-detection theory framework to separate discrimination accuracy from response bias, performance in both subject samples was separated into 'hits' (the proportion of guilty suspects whose confessions were correctly identified as true) and 'false alarms' (the proportion of innocent suspects whose confessions were incorrectly identified as true). This analysis revealed that investigators did not differ from the students in their hit rate, but they exhibited significantly more false alarms. When the estimates were combined into aggregate measures of discrimination accuracy and response bias, the results revealed an investigator bias effect, with police predisposed to believe both the true and false confessions. This bias was particularly evident among those with extensive law-enforcement experience and among those who had received special training in interviewing and interrogation. Importantly, this response bias did not predispose police to see deception per se, but to infer guilt – an inference that rested upon a tendency to believe false confessions.

This overall pattern of results has serious implications for the interrogation of innocent suspects and subsequent assessment of their confessions. There are two possible explanations why investigators were unable to distinguish true and false confessions in this study and why they were generally less accurate than naïve college students. One possibility is that law-enforcement work introduces systematic bias that reduces overall judgement accuracy (Meissner and Kassin, 2004). This hypothesis is consistent with the finding that police investigators as a group are generally and highly suspicious of deception (Masip et al., in press). It is also not terribly surprising in light of the kinds of behavioural deception cues that form part of the basis for training (Vrij, 2000). For example, Inbau et al. (2001) advocate the use of visual cues such as gaze aversion, non-frontal posture, slouching, and grooming gestures that, as an empirical matter, are not diagnostic of truth or deception (DePaulo, et al., 2003). Furthermore, research has shown that people are more accurate when they rely on auditory cues than on visual information (Anderson et al., 1999; DePaulo, Lassiter, and Stone, 1982). Our results replicated this effect, as discrimination accuracy was significantly higher in the audio condition than in the video condition without a significant influence on response bias. In short, it is conceivable that training in the use of visual cues would impair performance, not improve it.

Another possibility is that investigators' judgement accuracy was compromised by our use of a paradigm in which half of the stimulus confessions were false – a percentage that is likely far higher than the real-world base rate for false confessions. To the extent that law-enforcement work leads investigators to presume guilt, and to presume most confessions true, then the response bias they imported from the police station to the laboratory may have proved misleading for a study in which they were told merely that some statements were true and others false. So instructed, investigators judged 65 per cent of the statements to be true, compared to only 55 per cent among students. Hence, our investigators may have performed poorly because of a gross mismatch between the expected and presented base rates for false confessions. To test the hypothesis that investigators' judgement accuracy was depressed relative to students because of differences in their base-rate expectations, Kassin et al. (2004) conducted a second study to neutralise the response bias. In this experiment, all participants were shown the ten videotaped confessions but they were instructed prior to the task that half of the statements were true and that half were false. We predicted that this manipulation would neutralise the dispositional response bias of investigators relative to students – and perhaps increase judgement accuracy in the process. The manipulation was successful, both in reducing the overall number of 'true' judgements that had produced the response bias and in eliminating the differences between participant samples. But on the question of whether this would improve performance, the results were mixed. Compared to their counterparts in the videotape condition of the first experiment, investigators in this study had a comparable hit rate but a much lower false alarm rate. They were still not more accurate than students, however, and they were still over-confident. The response bias was neutralised, but investigators maintained the pattern of low accuracy and high confidence.

A third reason for pessimism is that police-induced confessions, unlike most other types of verbal statements, are corrupted by the very process of interrogation that elicits them – designed for persuasion, even if false. By definition, interrogation is a theory-driven social interaction led by an authority figure who holds a strong a priori belief about the target and who measures success by his or her ability to extract an admission from that target. For innocent people who are initially misjudged, one would hope that investigators would remain open-minded enough to monitor the suspect and situation and re-evaluate their own beliefs. However, research suggests that once people form a belief, they wittingly or unwittingly create behavioural support for that belief. This phenomenon – variously termed self-fulfilling prophecy, interpersonal expectancy effect, and behavioural confirmation – was first demonstrated by Rosenthal and Jacobson (1968) in their classic study of teacher expectancy effects on students' academic performance, with similar results obtained in military, business, and other organisational settings (McNatt, 2000). In the laboratory, researchers have found that behavioural confirmation is the outcome of a three-step chain of events by which a perceiver forms a belief about a target person, behaves towards that person in a manner that conforms to that belief, leading the target to respond in ways that often support the perceiver's initial belief (for reviews, see Darley and Fazio, 1980; Nickerson, 1998; Snyder, 1992; Snyder and Stukas, 1999).

When it comes to criminal confessions, one can imagine the possibility that the presumption of guilt leads interrogators to adopt an approach that is highly aggressive and confrontational, and that leads even innocent suspects to become anxious and defensive – and supportive of the presumption. Illustrating the process, Akehurst and Vrij (1999) found that increased bodily movement among police officers triggered movement among interviewees, behaviour that is interpreted as suspicious. More recently, Kassin, Goldstein, and Savitsky (2003) looked at whether the presumption of guilt shapes the conduct of student interrogators, the behaviour of student suspects, and ultimately the judgements made by neutral observers. This study was conducted in two phases. In Phase I, suspects stole $100 as part of a mock theft or they took part in a related but innocent act, after which they were interviewed via headphones from a remote location. Other subjects, participating as investigators, were led to believe that most of the suspects in the study were truly guilty or innocent. These sessions were audiotaped for subsequent analysis and followed by post-interrogation questionnaires. In Phase II, observers listened to the taped interviews, judged the suspect as guilty or innocent, and rated their impressions of both sets of participants.

The results indicated that student interrogators who were led to expect guilt rather than innocence asked more guilt-presumptive questions, saw the suspects as guilty, used more interrogation techniques, tried harder and exerted more pressure to get a confession, and made innocent suspects sound more defensive and guilty to observers. Consistently, the most pressure-filled interrogation sessions, as rated by all participants, were those that paired investigators who presumed guilt with suspects who were actually innocent. Observers who listened to the tapes later perceived the suspects in the guilty-expectations condition as more defensive and as somewhat more guilty. In short, the presumption of guilt, which underlies all interrogation, may set in motion a process of behavioural confirmation, as it shapes the interrogator's behaviour, the suspect's behaviour, and ultimately the judgements of judges, juries, and other neutral observers.

A fourth reason for pessimism is that real-life false confessions, when elicited through a process of interrogation, contain content cues that people associate with truth-telling. In most documented false confessions, the statements ultimately presented in court are compelling, as they often contain vivid and accurate details about the crime, the scene, and the victim – details that can become known to an innocent suspect through the assistance of leading interview questions, overheard conversations, photographs, visits to the crime scene, and other second-hand sources of information invisible to the naïve observer. To obfuscate matters further, many confessions are textured with what I call 'elective' statements. Often innocent suspects describe not just what they allegedly did, and how, but *why* – as they self-report on revenge, jealousy, desperation, capitulation to peer pressure, and other prototypical motives for crime. Sometimes they add apologies and expressions of remorse. In some cases, innocent suspects find and correct minor errors that appear in the statements that are derived from them, suggesting that they read, understood, and verified the contents. To the naïve spectator, such statements appear to be voluntary, textured with detail, and the product of personal experience. Uninformed, however, this spectator mistakes illusion for reality, not realising that the taped confession is much like a Hollywood drama – scripted by the police theory, rehearsed during hours of unrecorded questioning, directed by the questioner, and enacted on camera by the suspect (Kassin, 2002).

The Reid technique offers advice on how to create these illusions of credibility. Inbau et al. (2001) recommend that interrogators insert minor errors (such as a wrong name, date, or street address) into written confessions so that the suspect will spot them, correct them, and initial the changes. The goal is to increase the perceived credibility of the statement and make it difficult for the defendant later to distance himself or herself from it. Because only guilty suspects should be in a position to spot these errors, this technique has diagnostic potential. However, Inbau et al. (2001) advise that to play it safe, 'the investigator should keep the errors in mind and raise a question about them in the event the suspect neglects to do so' (p. 384). Similarly, Inbau et al. (2001) advise investigators to insert into written confessions irrelevant personal history items known only to the 'offender'. 'For instance, the suspect may be asked to give the name of the grade school he attended, the place or hospital in which he was born, or other similar information' (p. 383). Of course, for the suspect who is not the offender but an innocent person, the insertion of crime-irrelevant biographical details from his or her own life has no diagnostic value. Like the error-correction trick, it merely creates a false illusion of credibility.

Towards a more effective safety net

Despite reasons to be pessimistic, it is possible in theory for investigators, prosecutors, and others to assess suspect statements with some degree of accuracy through a genuine effort at corroboration. A full confession is not a mere admission that 'I did it', but rather it is a post-admission narrative in which suspects recount not just what they did but how, when, where, and with whom.

Evaluating a confession involves a three-step process. The first step requires a consideration of the conditions under which it was made and the extent to which coercive techniques were used. Relevant factors in this enquiry include characteristics of the suspect (e.g., age, intelligence, and mental state); the physical conditions of detention; and the use of stated or implied promises, threats, and other social influence techniques during interrogation. Still, while coercive interrogation increases the risk of false confession, it does not invalidate it. Coerced confessions may be true; innocent people sometimes confess voluntarily, without prompting. The second step requires a consideration of whether the confession contains details that are consistent and accurate in relation to the verifiable facts of the crime. An often overlooked but necessary third step concerns a requirement of *attribution* for the source of the details contained in the narrative confession. A confession has diagnostic value if it contains information knowable only to a perpetrator that was not derivable from such second-hand sources as newspaper accounts, overheard conversations, leading interview questions, photographs, or visits to the crime scene. In short, a confession can prove guilt (or at least guilty knowledge) or it may fail to do so to the extent that it is 'generative', furnishing the police with crime facts that were not already known or leading to evidence that was not already available.

This three-step analysis can be illustrated in the videotaped false confessions from the Central Park jogger case described earlier. On tape, these defendants confessed to a gang rape in statements that seemed vividly detailed, voluntary, and the product of personal experience. But examination of the conditions under which the statements were made reveals the presence of troubling risk factors. The boys were 14 to 16 years old, and at the time of their videotaped statements, they had been in custody and interrogation by multiple detectives for a range of fourteen to thirty hours. The passage of time may not be visible to the naïve consumer of the final product, but it brings heightened pressure, a dogged refusal to accept denials, fatigue, despair, and often a deprivation of sleep and other need states. As to other aspects of the situation, the detectives and suspects disagreed in significant ways about what transpired during the many unrecorded hours of questioning. They disagreed, for example, over whether the parents had access to their boys, whether threats and physical force were used, and whether promises to go home were made. One can only imagine what transpired in a private session between a detective and Kharey Wise that led the boy to request an opportunity to incriminate himself on camera after two non-incriminating handwritten statements and one videotape statement.

The conditions of interrogation contained classic elements of coercion, but that does not absolve the guilty or invalidate their confessions. The Central Park jogger confessions were compelling precisely because the narratives contained highly vivid details, including an on-camera physical re-enactment. From start to finish, however, the narratives were riddled with inconsistencies and factual errors of omission and commission. When asked about the jogger's head injury, one boy said she was punched with fists; then when prompted to recall a blunt object, he said they used a rock; moments later, the rock turned to bricks. Across the defendants, the statements diverged. Each and every defendant minimised his own role in the assault, placing 'them' at centre stage. When two of the suspects were taken to the crime scene and asked to point to the site of the attack, they pointed in different directions. Factual errors were also numerous. One suspect said the jogger wore blue shorts and a t-shirt; she wore long black tights and a long-sleeve jersey. Another said the jogger and clothes were cut with a knife; there were no knife cuts. A third suspect did not seem to know the victim bled; she bled profusely. A fourth said that one of the boys he was with ejaculated; yet no traces of that boy's semen were found. None of the defendants knew the location of the attack, that the jogger was left at the bottom of a ravine, that her hands were tied, or that she was gagged with her own shirt.

Pointing to the presence of accurate details in these statements, the naïve spectator will see the confessional glasses as half full, not half empty. In light of all that is known about the problems with eyewitness memory, it is not reasonable to expect perfection in the accounts of crime suspects. This assertion, however, invites a third analytical step, an attribution as to the source of the accurate details. A confession can prove guilt if it contains details knowable only to the perpetrator, details not derivable by second-hand sources. Yet in the jogger case, after dozens of collective hours of unrecorded questioning, and amidst disputes as to what transpired, there is no way to know whether crime facts were furnished to the defendants, advertently or inadvertently, through the processes of social interaction. One need not stray from the videotaped confessions to hear the prosecutor ask leading questions that functioned not only to elicit information *from* the suspects but also to communicate information *to* suspects. Without apparent regard for the ownership of the facts being extracted, she steered one boy's story through a broken but persistent sequence of leading questions: 'Medical evidence says something other than a hand was used . . . what?' and 'Don't you remember someone using a brick or a stone?' In a move that grossly undermined all opportunity to get a confession diagnostic of guilty knowledge, the detectives inexplicably took one suspect on a supervised visit to the crime scene *before* taking his videotaped confession. The district attorney then showed him graphic photographs of the victim (he was visibly shaken by the pictures, a reaction hard to reconcile with his alleged live presence and participation). For diagnostic purposes, it makes no sense to contaminate a suspect's confession by spoon-feeding him information in these ways, rendering the source of his subsequent knowledge ambiguous. Whether he was there or not, the visit and photographs endowed him with key visual facts about the victim, crime, and place – facts fit for a full confession.

Crime perpetrators have the unique capacity to reveal information about their actions that the police did not already know and produce evidence that police did not already have. Yet the statements of the Central Park jogger defendants – individually and collectively – were not generative in these ways. Lacking such corroboration, the case against the five defendants was like a house of cards, with each boy's confession built squarely and solely upon the foundation of the others' confessions. In December of 2002, this house of cards collapsed under the weight of an imprisoned serial rapist who voluntarily confessed to the attack, who furnished the police with crime facts that were accurate and not previously known, and whose semen was present on the jogger.

Videotaping interrogations: a policy whose time has come

In order to assess the incriminating value of confessions accurately, investigators, prosecutors, and fact-finders must have access to a videotape recording of the entire interview and interrogation. In Great Britain, the Police and Criminal Evidence Act of 1986 (PACE) mandated that all suspect interviews and interrogations be taped. In the United States, however, Inbau et al. (2001) have long opposed the videotaping of interrogations and the FBI prohibits it. To date, only three states have videotaping requirements (Davey, 2003). Still, the practice has many advocates (Cassell, 1999; Drizin and Colgan, 2001; Geller, 1993; Gudjonsson, 2003; Kassin, 1997, 2004; Leo, 1996b; Slobogin, 2003).

There are a number of presumed advantages to a policy of videotaping all interviews and interrogations in their entirety, all of which should provide for a more effective safety net. First, videotaping will deter police from using overly guilt-presumptive and psychologically coercive interrogation tactics. Second, videotaping will deter frivolous defence claims of coercion where none existed. Third, a videotaped record provides an objective and accurate record of all that transpired, which is an all-too-common source of dispute. Questions about whether rights were administered and waived, whether detectives shouted or physically intimidated the suspect, whether promises or threats were made or implied, and whether the details within a confession came from the police or suspect, are among the many issues that become resolvable. This should increase the fact-finding accuracy of judges and juries. It is necessary that entire sessions be recorded and that the camera adopts a 'neutral' or 'equal focus' perspective that shows both the accused and his or her interrogators (Lassiter, Geers, Munhall, Handley, and Beers, 2001; Lassiter and Geers, 2004). Under these circumstances, juries would be likely to make more accurate judgements when they see not only the confession but the conditions under which it was given and the source of the details it contained (Lassiter, Geers, Handley, Weiland, and Munhall, 2002). Indeed, a preliminary study of how people perceive actual cases with videotaped confessions in which the defendant's guilt or innocence is now known suggests that seeing the eliciting interrogation may at times lower the conviction rate among mock jurors who see innocent false confessions without lowering the conviction rate among those exposed to guilty true confessions (Kassin, Leo, Crocker, and Holland, 2003).

The Central Park jogger case reveals a sequence of three serious problems in police investigation: that innocent people are often targeted for interrogation based on judgements of deception that are frequently in error; that the processes of interrogation can cause people to confess to crimes they did not commit; and that it is difficult for investigators, attorneys, judges, and juries to know a false confession when they see one. The risks inherent in this chain of events suggests that there is not a sufficient safety net in criminal justice and that a full videotaping requirement is necessary to provide decision-makers with a full and objective account of the statement and the situation in which it was elicited.

REFERENCES

Akehurst, L., and Vrij, A. (1999). Creating suspects in police interviews. *Journal of Applied Social Psychology*, 29, 192–210.

Anderson, D. E., DePaulo, B. M., Ansfield, M. E., Tickle, J. J., and Green, E. (1999). Beliefs about cues to deception: Mindless stereotypes or untapped wisdom? *Journal of Nonverbal Behavior*, 23, 67–89.

Aubry, A. S., and Caputo, R. R. (1980). *Criminal interrogation* (3rd edn). Springfield, IL: Charles C. Thomas.

Bedau, H. A., and Radelet, M. L. (1987). Miscarriages of justice in potentially capital cases. *Stanford Law Review*, 40, 21–179.

Blagrove, M. (1996). Effects of length of sleep deprivation on interrogative suggestibility. *Journal of Experimental Psychology: Applied*, 2, 48–59.

Bull, R. (1989). Can training enhance the detection of deception? In J. C. Yuille (ed.), *Credibility assessment* (pp. 83–99). London: Kluwer Academic.

Buller, D. B., Strzyzewski, K. D., and Hunsaker, F. G. (1991). Interpersonal deception: II. The inferiority of conversational participants as deception detectors. *Communication Monographs*, *58*, 25–40.

Cassell, P. G. (1999). The guilty and the 'innocent': An examination of alleged cases of wrongful conviction from false confessions. *Harvard Journal of Law and Public Policy*, *22*, 523.

Darley, J. M., and Fazio, R. H. (1980). Expectancy confirmation processes arising in the social interaction sequence. *American Psychologist*, *35*, 867–81.

Davey, M. (2003). Illinois will require taping of homicide interrogations. *New York Times*, July 17, Section A, p. 16.

Davis, D., and O'Donohue, W. (2003). The road to perdition: 'Extreme influence' tactics in the interrogation room. In W. O'Donohue, P. Laws, and C. Hollin (eds.), *Handbook of Forensic Psychology* (pp. 897–996). New York: Basic Books.

DePaulo, B. M. (1994). Spotting lies: Can humans learn to do better? *Current Directions in Psychological Science*, *3*, 83–6.

DePaulo, B. M., Lassiter, G. D., and Stone, J. I. (1982). Attentional determinants of success at detecting deception and truth. *Personality and Social Psychology Bulletin*, *8*, 273–9.

DePaulo, B. M., Lindsay, J. J., Malone, B. E., Muhlenbruck, L., Charlton, K., and Cooper, H. (2003). Cues to deception. *Psychological Bulletin*, *129*, 74–112.

DePaulo, B. M., and Pfeifer, R. L. (1986). On-the-job experience and skill at detecting deception. *Journal of Applied Social Psychology*, *16*, 249–67.

Drizin, S. A., and Colgan, B. A. (2001). Let the cameras roll: Mandatory videotaping of interrogations is the solution to Illinois' problem of false confessions. *Loyola University Chicago Law Journal*, *32*, 337–424.

Ekman, P., and O'Sullivan, M. (1991). Who can catch a liar? *American Psychologist*, *46*, 913–20.

Ekman, P., O'Sullivan, M., and Frank, M. G. (1999). A few can catch a liar. *Psychological Science*, *10*, 263–6.

Garrido, E., and Masip, J. (1999). How good are police officers at spotting lies? *Forensic Update*, *58*, 14–21.

Garrido, E., Masip, J., and Herrero, C. (in press). Police officers' credibility judgements: Accuracy and estimated ability. *International Journal of Psychology*.

Geller, W. A. (1993). Videotaping interrogations and confessions. *National Institute of Justice: Research in Brief*. Washington, DC: US Department of Justice.

Gilbert, D. T., and Malone, P. S. (1995). The correspondence bias. *Psychological Bulletin*, *117*, 21–38.

Gudjonsson, G. H. (1992). *The psychology of interrogations, confessions, and testimony*. London: Wiley.

(2003). *The psychology of interrogations and confessions: A handbook*. West Sussex, England: John Wiley.

Harrison, Y., and Horne, J. A. (2000). The impact of sleep deprivation on decision making: A review. *Journal of Experimental Psychology: Applied*, *6*, 236–49.

Hartwig, M., Granhag, P. A., Strömwall, L. A., and Vrij, A. (in press). Police officers' lie detection accuracy: Interrogating freely vs. observing video. *Police Quarterly*.

Hilgendorf, E. L., and Irving, M. (1981). A decision-making model of confessions. In M. Lloyd-Bostock (ed.), *Psychology in legal contexts: Applications and limitations* (pp. 67–84). London: Macmillan.

Horselenberg, R., Merckelbach, H., and Josephs, S. (2003). Individual differences and false confessions: A conceptual replication of Kassin and Kiechel (1996). *Psychology, Crime, and Law*, 9, 1–18.

Inbau, F. E., Reid, J. E., Buckley, J. P., and Jayne, B. C. (2001). *Criminal interrogation and confessions* (4th edn). Gaithersberg, MD: Aspen.

Jones, E. E. (1990). *Interpersonal perception*. New York: Freeman.

Kassin, S. M. (1997). The psychology of confession evidence. *American Psychologist*, 52, 221–33.

(2002). False confessions and the jogger case, *New York Times*, November 1, p. A-31.

(2004). Videotape police interrogations. *Boston Globe*, April 26, p. A-13.

Kassin, S. M., and Fong, C. T. (1999). 'I'm innocent!' Effects of training on judgements of truth and deception in the interrogation room. *Law and Human Behavior*, 23, 499–516.

Kassin, S. M., Goldstein, C. J., and Savitsky, K. (2003). Behavioral confirmation in the interrogation room: On the dangers of presuming guilt. *Law and Human Behavior*, 27, 187–203.

Kassin, S. M., and Kiechel, K. L. (1996). The social psychology of false confessions: Compliance, internalization, and confabulation. *Psychological Science*, 7, 125–8.

Kassin, S., Leo, R., Crocker, C., and Holland, L. (2003). Videotaping interrogations: Does it enhance the jury's ability to distinguish true and false confessions? Paper presented at the Psychology & Law International, Interdisciplinary Conference, Edinburgh, Scotland.

Kassin, S. M., and McNall, K. (1991). Police interrogations and confessions: Communicating promises and threats by pragmatic implication. *Law and Human Behavior*, 15, 233–51.

Kassin, S. M., Meissner, C. A., and Norwick, R. J. (2004). 'I'd know a false confession if I saw one': A comparative study of college students and police investigators. Unpublished manuscript.

Kassin, S. M., and Neumann, K. (1997). On the power of confession evidence: An experimental test of the 'fundamental difference' hypothesis. *Law and Human Behavior*, 21, 469–84.

Kassin, S. M., and Norwick, R. J. (2004). Why suspects waive their Miranda rights: The power of innocence. *Law and Human Behavior*, 28, 211–21.

Kassin, S. M., and Sukel, H. (1997). Coerced confessions and the jury: An experimental test of the 'harmless error' rule. *Law and Human Behavior*, 21, 27–46.

Kassin, S. M., and Wrightsman, L. S. (1980). Prior confessions and mock juror verdicts. *Journal of Applied Social Psychology*, 10, 133–46.

(1985). Confession evidence. In S. M. Kassin and L. S. Wrightsman (eds.), *The psychology of evidence and trial procedure* (pp. 67–94). Beverly Hills, CA: Sage.

Köhnken, G. (1987). Training police officers to detect deceptive eyewitness statements: Does it work? *Social Behavior*, 2, 1–17.

Lassiter, G. D., and Geers, A. L. (2004). Bias and accuracy in the evaluation of confession evidence. In G. D. Lassiter (ed.), *Interrogations, Confessions, and Entrapment*. New York: Kluwer Academic.

Lassiter, G. D., Geers, A. L., Handley, I. M., Weiland, P. E., and Munhall, P. J. (2002). Videotaped confessions and interrogations: A simple change in camera perspective alters verdicts in simulated trials. *Journal of Applied Psychology, 87*, 867–74.

Lassiter, G. D., Geers, A. L., Munhall, P. J., Handley, I. M., and Beers, M. J. (2001). Videotaped confessions: Is guilt in the eye of the camera? *Advances in Experimental Social Psychology, 33*, 189–254.

Leo, R. A. (1996a). Inside the interrogation room. *Journal of Criminal Law and Criminology, 86*, 266–303.

(1996b). *Miranda's* revenge: Police interrogation as a confidence game. *Law and Society Review, 30*, 259–88.

Leo, R. A., and Ofshe, R. J. (1998). The consequences of false confessions: Deprivations of liberty and miscarriages of justice in the age of psychological interrogation. *Journal of Criminal Law and Criminology, 88*, 429–96.

(2001). The truth about false confessions and advocacy scholarship. *Criminal Law Bulletin, 37*, 293–370.

Macdonald, J. M., and Michauel, D. L. (1987). *The confession: Interrogation and criminal profiles for police officers*. Denver: Apache.

Markman, S. J., and Cassell, P. G. (1988). Protecting the innocent: A response to the Bedau–Radelet study. *Stanford Law Review, 41*, 121.

Masip, J., Alonso, H., Garrido, E., and Anton, C. (in press). Generalized Communicative Suspicion (GCS) among police officers: Accounting for the investigator bias effect. *Journal of Applied Social Psychology*.

McCann, J. T. (1998). Broadening the typology of false confessions. *American Psychologist, 53*, 319–20.

McNatt, D. B. (2000). Ancient Pygmalion joins contemporary management: A meta-analysis of the result. *Journal of Applied Psychology, 85*, 314–22.

Meili, T. (2003). *I am the Central Park jogger: A story of hope and possibility*. New York: Scribner.

Meissner, C. A., and Kassin, S. M. (2002). 'He's guilty!': Investigator bias in judgements of truth and deception. *Law & Human Behavior, 26*, 469–80.

(2004). 'You're guilty, so just confess!' Cognitive and behavioral confirmation biases in the interrogation room. In D. Lassiter (ed.), *Interrogations, confessions, and entrapment*. New York: Kluwer Academic/Plenum.

Memon, A., Vrij, A., and Bull, R. (2003). *Psychology and law: Truthfulness, accuracy and credibility*. London: Jossey-Bass.

New York v. *McCray, Richardson, Salaam, Santana, and Wise* (2002). Affirmation in response to motion to vacate judgment of conviction indictment No. 4762/89.

Nickerson, R. S. (1998). Confirmation bias: A ubiquitous phenomenon in many guises. *Review of General Psychology, 2*, 175–220.

Ofshe, R. J., and Leo, R. A. (1997). The social psychology of police interrogation: The theory and classification of true and false confessions. *Studies in Law, Politics, and Society, 16*, 189–251.

O'Hara, C. E., and O'Hara, G. L. (1981). *Fundamentals of criminal investigation.* Springfield. IL: Charles C. Thomas.

Porter, S., Woodworth, M., and Birt, A. R. (2000). Truth, lies, and videotape: An investigation of the ability of federal parole officers to detect deception. *Law and Human Behavior, 24,* 643–58.

Redlich, A. D., and Goodman, G. S. (2003). Taking responsibility for an act not committed: The influence of age and suggestibility. *Law and Human Behavior, 27,* 141–56.

Rimer, S. (2002). Convict's DNA sways labs, not a determined prosecutor. *New York Times,* February 6.

Rosenthal, R., and Jacobson, L. (1968). *Pygmalion in the classroom: Teacher expectation and pupils' intellectual development.* New York: Holt, Rinehart, and Winston.

Saulny, S. (2002). Why confess to what you didn't do? *New York Times,* December 8, 2002, Section 4.

Scheck, B., Neufeld, P., and Dwyer, J. (2000). *Actual innocence.* Garden City, NY: Doubleday.

Simon, D. (1991). *Homicide: A year on the killing streets.* New York: Ivy Books.

Slobogin, C. (2003). Toward taping. *Ohio State Journal of Criminal Law, 1,* 309–22.

Snyder, M. (1992). Motivational foundations of behavioral confirmation. *Advances in Experimental Social Psychology, 25,* 67–114.

Snyder, M., and Stukas, A. (1999). Interpersonal processes: The interplay of cognitive, motivational, and behavioral activities in social interaction. *Annual Review of Psychology, 50,* 273–303.

Sullivan, T. (1992). *Unequal verdicts: The Central Park jogger trials.* NY: Simon and Schuster.

Vrij, A. (1994). The impact of information and setting on detection of deception by police detectives. *Journal of Nonverbal Behavior, 18,* 117–37.

  (2000). *Detecting lies and deceit: The psychology of lying and the implications for professional practice.* London: John Wiley.

Vrij, A., and Mann, S. (2001). Who killed my relative? Police officers' ability to detect real-life high-stake lies. *Psychology, Crime, and Law, 7,* 119–32.

Walkley, J. (1987). *Police interrogation. Handbook for investigators.* London: Police Review Publication.

Walters, S. B. (2003). *Principles of kinesic interview and interrogation* (2nd edn), Boca Ratan: CRC Press.

Wrightsman, L. S., and Kassin, S. M. (1993). *Confessions in the courtroom.* Newbury Park, CA: Sage.

Zimbardo, P. G. (1967, June). The psychology of police confessions. *Psychology Today, 1,* 17–20, 25–7.

Zuckerman, M., DePaulo, B. M., and Rosenthal, R. (1981). Verbal and nonverbal communication of deception. *Advances in Experimental Social Psychology, 14,* 1–59.

Zuckerman, M., Koestner, R., and Alton, A. O. (1984). Learning to detect deception. *Journal of Personality & Social Psychology, 46,* 519–28.

9   Crime-related amnesia as a form of deception

Sven Å. Christianson and Harald Merckelbach

Much research on deceptive behaviour concerns differences between truthful and deceptive verbal and non-verbal responses. This chapter has a different angle in that we focus on stories that liars don't tell. Thus, this chapter is concerned with lying in the sense of concealing information by evading questions or omitting detail information. More specifically, we focus on homicide offenders who claim memory loss (i.e., amnesia) for their crime, and on whether such memory loss is genuine or feigned.

There are several reasons for investigating offenders' memory of violent crimes. One is that claims of amnesia for violent crimes, including murder, are very common. Obviously, some guilty suspects deny involvement in the crime or claim amnesia to avoid punishment. About 25–40 per cent of those who are found guilty of homicide claim to be amnesic or to have a complete memory loss (Schacter, 1986; Taylor and Kopelman, 1984), and the large majority of these claims are circumscribed to the crime itself (Bradford and Smith, 1979).

In clinical literature, various taxonomies of amnesia can be found. A common distinction is that between amnesia due to organic factors (organic amnesia) and amnesia due to psychological factors (e.g., malingering, emotional stress). As previous research has shown, different memory patterns emerge when amnesia originates from brain trauma, malingering, or severe emotional stress. Thus, the main question here is whether patterns of remembering and forgetting in an offender give hints as to whether his amnesia is genuine or malingered.

According to Schacter (1986), there are two obvious legal reasons why it is important to explore crime-related amnesia. To begin with, amnesia raises the issue of automatism, which refers to criminal behaviour that is executed unconsciously and without intent. The issue of automatism is, of course, critical to establish legal responsibility. We will return to the difference between 'sane' and 'insane' automatism later in this chapter. Secondly, amnesia bears relevance to the issue of competency to stand trial. An accused who has no memory of the crime event cannot plead on his or her own behalf, simply because he or she is unable to inform his or her counsel. Thus, such a person may be incompetent to stand trial.

Research on amnesic homicide offenders has, however, several other, more practical implications. For example, knowledge about an offender obtained by studying crime scene characteristics and the offender's behaviour will generate prerequisites for interrogation strategies. Therefore, the systematic analysis of amnesia claims might help criminal investigators in selecting strategies that might be useful in interviewing perpetrators of impulsive (reactive) or planned (instrumental) homicides (Dodge, 1991; Pollock, 1999) who confess, deny having committed the crime, or claim memory loss. Another implication is related to assessing treatment prognosis for delinquents who have committed serious violent crimes and claim to be amnesic. Still another implication concerns violent recidivism among homicidal offenders, who claimed amnesia throughout their sentence/treatment, and then are released.

The importance of, and need for, an understanding of amnesia claims in homicide suspects is evident in the following two cases. In the mid-sixties, Margaret MacDonald, a 33-year-old citizen of Toronto, stabbed her abusive common-law husband to death. Margaret claimed to be amnesic for the crime. She claimed to have no memory whatsoever of the act of killing but remembered events immediately before and after the killing (Gould and MacDonald, 1987; Porter, Birt, Yuille, and Herve, 2001). The case attracted immense media attention and it was revealed that Margaret had been abandoned and abused as a child, experienced being a sex-slave, prostitute, alcoholic, and drug addict, and exposed to violence throughout her life. Owing to her history of long-standing abuse, Margaret herself and the women's movement in Canada regarded her as a victim rather than a perpetrator. Eventually, she was acquitted of murder and received a probation sentence. Less than a year later, she killed her second husband and was sentenced to life imprisonment.

In a Swedish case from the late eighties, a young man left his hometown by car and, after several hours driving, stopped to call his parents-in-law to tell them that something terrible had happened at their daughter's home and that they must go there. The parents soon found their daughter stabbed to death in her apartment. During the police investigation, the man claimed to have no memory of what had happened to his fiancée. He could not provide any details, he could not deny or confess to the crime. He served a sentence of eight years in jail and claimed to be amnesic throughout that period. After being released, he soon moved together with a woman, who was found shortly thereafter strangled to death in his apartment. As in the first murder, he claimed to be amnesic. In the second investigation, however, an interrogator who used an empathetic style (characterised by cooperation, an obliging manner, a positive attitude, helpfulness, and personal interest in his case) interviewed him. Owing to this positive contact, the offender revealed that he had remembered both acts of killing from the beginning. As to his motive for simulating amnesia, he said that even a murderer should not be treated as he had been during the police investigations in the first murder case (see also Holmberg and Christianson, 2002).

These two cases suggest that amnesic offenders may be at risk for repeated violence. Obviously, using amnesia as a calculated defence strategy enables the offender to avoid emotional memories of the crime. That such memories might have a far-reaching impact is illustrated by the fact that perpetrators who are fully aware of what they did sometimes develop Post Traumatic Stress Disorder (PTSD; see, e.g., Pollock, 1999). Amnesia also prevents the offender from working through the factors underlying the homicidal behaviour. Thus, in our opinion, claims of crime-related amnesia represent a risk factor. Indeed, in their large-scale study involving 308 forensic patients in high-security settings, Cima, Nijman, Merckelbach, Kremer, and Hollnack (in press, b) found that such claims were especially prominent among recidivists.

In the Swedish case that we cited, the perpetrator eventually admitted that he had simulated amnesia. But what about all the other cases in which perpetrators claim amnesia? Are their claims bona fide? Or is it clinical folklore that we easily accept, and even nurse, in order to have some kind of understanding of or excuse for a perpetrator's post-homicidal behaviour? 'Well, he shows no regret, but on the other hand, he is amnesic.' Or, amnesia may be used as an explanation, when we fail to get a statement (narrative) from a suspect/client. In this chapter, we will review the literature in this area and describe various forms of amnesia. We will present the perspectives of offenders and lay people, as well as what science says about crime-related amnesia. Finally, we will discuss the complexity of remembering and telling about homicidal experiences.

Types of crime-related amnesia

Offenders who claim amnesia for their crime are by no means rare. In an older study of Leitch (1948), 51 murderers were interviewed and 14 (27 per cent) of them claimed amnesia for their crime. Taylor and Kopelman (1984) replicated this study by interviewing 34 murderers and found that 9 (26 per cent) of them claimed amnesia. In a study by Gudjonsson, Petursson, Skulason, and Sigurdardottir (1989) on 64 convicted criminals, 21 (32 per cent) of them claimed amnesia for their crime. As a rule of thumb, then, one can say that 20 to 30 per cent of offenders of violent crimes claim amnesia. While these claims are often raised in the context of murder or manslaughter cases, there are other crime categories in which claims of amnesia do occur. For example, claims of amnesia regularly occur in sexual crime cases (Bourget and Bradford, 1995), domestic violence cases (Swihart, Yuille, and Porter, 1999), and fraud cases (Kopelman, Green, Guinan, Lewis, and Stanhope, 1994).

In the literature, several taxonomies have been proposed to distinguish between different types of amnesia (e.g., Schacter, 1986; Loewenstein, 1991; Kopelman, 1995; Kihlstrom and Schacter, 1995). Most of them agree that at least three amnesia types should be considered: *dissociative amnesia* (formerly termed psychogenic or functional amnesia), *organic amnesia*, and *feigned amnesia* (or simulated or malingered amnesia). Dissociative amnesia for criminal behaviour is thought to originate from extreme emotions that accompany such behaviour. Several authors have argued that dissociative amnesia is typical for crimes that are unplanned, involve a significant other, and are committed in a state of strong agitation (see, e.g., Loewenstein, 1991; Kopelman, 1995). Thus, dissociative amnesia would typically occur in the context of what has been termed 'reactive homicide' (Pollock, 1999; see below). The idea behind this is that extreme levels of arousal during the crime may hamper memory at a later point in time. Thus, a failure in retrieval processes would underlie dissociative amnesia: the offender, who eventually has come to his senses, finds it impossible to access memories stored during a moment of turbulence. A term often used in the Anglo-Saxon literature to describe amnesia as a consequence of strong emotions (e.g., rage) is 'red-out'. In the words of Swihart, Yuille, and Porter (1999): 'Apparently, an individual can get so angry with his/her intimate partner that s/he can severely beat or kill that partner and then not remember doing so: that is, they can experience a red-out resulting in circumscribed amnesia' (p. 200).

Organic amnesia is always caused by a neurological defect. This defect may be structural (e.g., epilepsy, brain trauma), but it may also be transient (e.g., alcohol or drug intoxication). Kopelman (1995) assumes that memory loss in organic amnesia has to do with storage problems rather than retrieval problems: due to epileptic seizure, brain damage, or intoxication, offenders would not be able to store their memories in the first place, which would eventually lead to a total 'blackout' for their crime.

A number of authors have emphasised that excessive alcohol use may contribute to dissociative amnesia for crime (Kopelman, 1995; Bourget and Bradford, 1995; Swihart, Yuille, and Porter, 1999). Bower's (1981) 'state-dependent memory theory' is often invoked to account for the combination of dissociative amnesia and alcohol (Swihart, Yuille, and Porter, 1999). In short, this theory states that when memories are stored in an exceptional context (e.g., strong emotions and under the influence of alcohol), subsequent retrieval of these memories is facilitated when a similar context is reinstated. However, in a different context (e.g., when the person is relaxed and sober), the pertinent memories would be inaccessible and so dissociative amnesia would occur. The case of Sirhan Sirhan, who was held responsible for the murder of Robert Kennedy, is often presented as an example of state-dependent memory. Sirhan claimed that he was unable to remember the murder. However, when he was hypnotised and brought into an agitated state, he suddenly remembered details of the murder (Swihart, Yuille, and Porter, 1999).

As for feigned amnesia, offenders may simulate amnesia for a crime in an attempt to obstruct police investigation and/or to avoid responsibility for their acts. In an older study, Hopwood and Snell (1933) found that 20 per cent of the offenders who claimed amnesia were malingerers. However, there are good reasons to believe that the rate of malingering is much higher (see below). The literature provides clear examples of defendants who feigned amnesia in order to gain tactical advantage in legal procedures. A fascinating example is that of Rudolf Hess who at the start of the 'Nuremberg' trials claimed to be amnesic for his role in the Third Reich period. A group of prominent psychiatrists examined Hess and concluded that his amnesia was genuine. When it became clear to Hess that the amnesic role confers a disadvantage in the sense that one cannot respond to allegations, he suddenly announced during one of the trial sessions that he had fooled the psychiatrists (Gilbert, 1971). A more recent example of how malingering might surface during legal proceedings is provided by the 'three strikes and you're out' law that has been adopted by some American States. Under this law, the third crime that a defendant commits will lead to a severe sentence. Thus, even if one's third offence consists of stealing a slice of pizza, one may face a sentence of twenty-five years in prison. Several psychiatrists have noted that defendants who are charged under this law often simulate amnesia in combination with bizarre symptoms. For example, Jaffe and Sharma (1998) described how in some Californian prisons there is a true epidemic of amnesia claims along with Lilliputian hallucinations (i.e., hallucinations of little green men). Of course, offenders report these symptoms so as to be held incompetent to stand trial.

What homicide offenders say

One way to understand crime-related amnesia is to ask offenders themselves about the occurrence of amnesia and their evaluation of other homicide offenders. In a study by Christianson, Bylin, and Holmberg (2003), a total of 182 convicted homicide and sexual offenders serving their sentences in Swedish prisons were contacted by post and asked to complete a written interview. The questionnaires were distributed to all inmates by the Swedish Prison and Probation Administration. More than 50 per cent were willing to participate (N = 83). More specifically, half of the homicide offenders and half of the sexual offenders, with ages ranging from 20 to 63 years, and with sentences ranging from 1.3 years to life imprisonment volunteered to provide information. The questionnaire consisted of items about offenders' experiences with Swedish police interviews, about their attitudes towards allegations of these serious crimes (see Holmberg and Christianson, 2002), but also about memory and amnesia. To increase confidentiality and the inmates' trust in participating in the study, and to avoid censorship from the correctional staff, the prestamped envelopes were preaddressed to a public authority (Stockholm University). The Swedish Law on treatment of offenders in prison (§25, The Swedish Law, SFS 1974:203) states that letters from inmates to public authorities should be forwarded without any censorship, accordingly the offenders were expected to be truthful in their anonymous answers to the questions. One item in the questionnaire asked about their estimation of how often offenders generally deliberately feign loss of memory for the crime in order to avoid conviction. Only 2 per cent of the homicide offenders thought that perpetrators of this type of crime never feign memory loss to some degree.

Another question asked whether they had ever felt that they truly wanted to forget the crime event. Fifty-three per cent of the homicide offenders against 35 per cent of the sexual offenders answered positive to this item. These results tell us that homicide offenders are highly motivated to forget their offences. Overall, the results showed higher proportions of homicide offenders who claimed to be amnesic or to have a vague memory for the crime as compared to sexual offenders. This difference between homicide and sexual offenders has probably to do with the fact that sexual offences are planned (instrumental), which is less frequently associated with amnesia than are reactive offences (see below). To the specific question of whether they had experienced a complete or partial loss of memory for the crime event, 58 per cent of homicide and 45 per cent of sexual offenders claimed that they had. A subsequent question pertained to the vividness of their memory for the crime event. Among the homicide offenders, only 23 per cent claimed to have a very vague memory for the crime event. Keeping in mind that 58 per cent claimed to have a complete or partial amnesia at some point for their crime, and that only 23 per cent had a vague memory at the time of the interview, one must assume that 35 per cent (58 − 23) have had some sort of recovery of memory. Note that the 23 per cent rate is similar to what other studies found with respect to the prevalence of amnesia for homicide. Later in this chapter, we will return to the issue of whether this percentage reflects genuine memory loss among homicide offenders.

As part of a large, on-going research project on homicidal crimes, Christianson and Von Vogelsang (2003) reviewed records of offenders who had committed at least one homicide. Among those few offenders who had committed more than one homicide, the first homicide was coded. A distinction was made between instrumental/proactive and reactive/expressive homicide offenders (Dodge, 1991; Pollock, 1999), excluding homicides committed by inner-city gangs, organised criminals, or terrorists. In reactive homicide, the violence leading to the death of another person can be construed as some sort of impulsive response. The attack is spontaneous, immediate, and emotion-driven. Victim provocation is evident, but there is no apparent external goal other than to harm the victim following a provocation/conflict (e.g., rage and despair associated with crimes of passion). A purely reactive homicide is an immediate, rapid, and powerful affective response. However, in some cases, the crime may contain some degree of planning. For example, the offender may leave to get a weapon and return for revenge, but without a 'cooling off' period between provocation and attack. Victims are typically a spouse or someone well known to the offender. The offender experiences a high level of angry arousal at the time of the violent event.

In instrumental homicide, the violence leading to death is planned and proactive. A homicide is purely instrumental when the murder is clearly goal directed (e.g., to fulfil sexual or material needs or to obtain a thrill), with no evidence of an immediate emotional or situational provocation, and when the victim has little personal significance to the offender. Self-reported lack of arousal and anger during the offence are common in this group of offenders.

A distinction between reactive and instrumental homicide may oversimplify a highly complex behaviour with multiple motivations and manifestations. However, it is possible to classify with some degree of accuracy whether homicidal behaviour is predominantly reactive or instrumental. This distinction is relevant for several reasons. For example, the reactive versus instrumental dichotomy appears to be useful for predicting recidivism and treatment prognosis, and it is associated with specific psychological characteristics of offenders (e.g., PTSD; see Pollock, 1999). Woodworth and Porter (2001) found in their sample of 125 Canadian offenders that 27 per cent of them could be classified as psychopaths. Over 90 per cent of the psychopaths were instrumental offenders. Because psychopaths would be expected to exhibit a general lack of affective interference and absence of empathy and remorse, and because of the pre-homicide fantasies among psychopaths, genuine dissociative memory reactions (amnesia) are unlikely to occur in this group of killers.

Because there is a high degree of premeditation and preparation in instrumental homicides, one may expect that such offences are easier for the offender to remember. In cases of sexual murder – especially in offenders who plan to commit subsequent homicides – the act of killing (own actions, sexual components, victim's actions and reactions) is often compared to a script fantasy that foregoes the murder. Premeditated fantasies and the act of murder are replayed over and over in the offender's mind, and the more the offender goes over the event in his/her mind (i.e., elaborative rehearsal; Craik and Lockhart, 1972), the more firmly will the event be stored. Furthermore, instrumental offenders are expected to experience a more optimal level of intra-crime arousal as opposed to a state of extreme arousal (cf. red-outs, see below), which thus will facilitate remembering the offence.

To test whether rates of amnesia are lower among instrumental than among reactive homicide offenders, Christianson and Von Vogelsang (2003) collected data from 88 homicide cases. Of these, 54 were coded as reactive and 34 were coded as instrumental. Rage and relational themes were the two most common crime motives among reactive offenders, whereas sexual and thrill themes were the most common motives among instrumental offenders. All reactive offenders reported negative emotions at the time of the crime and 91 per cent reported such emotions for the period after the crime. In the instrumental group, 59 per cent experienced negative emotional arousal during and 44 per cent after the crime. This pattern is in line with previous research (e.g., Pollock, 1999) revealing that 58 per cent of those who had committed reactive homicide showed PTSD symptoms compared to 36 per cent among the instrumental murderers. In the reactive group, 56 per cent claimed amnesia as opposed to 30 per cent in the instrumental group.

In comparing the offenders' memory before, during, and after the crime, it was more common to have complete memory loss for what happened during the crime than for information immediately before and after the crime. This pattern was evident for both groups but was most pronounced in the reactive group. Note that this pattern is opposite to what is normally found when studying memory for emotional events (Christianson, 1992). That is, subjects typically remember the emotion-inducing event quite well, but show impaired memory for information preceding and/or succeeding the highly arousing event. Christianson and Von Vogelsang also compared the proportions of offenders who had specific memories of the act of killing, were amnesic, or denied crime at the end

Table 9.1 *Percentages of reactive and instrumental homicide offenders who at the end of the police investigation remember the act of killing, are amnesic, or deny crime*

| | Homicide offender | |
	Reactive(%)	Instrumental(%)
Vivid memory	20	56
Partial memory	30	12
Vivid memory, later deny	7	8
Amnesic	26	12
Deny crime	17	12

of the police investigation. As can be seen in Table 9.1, 57 per cent of the reactive offenders described at some point in time during the police investigation detail memories of the act of killing, compared to 76 per cent of the instrumental offenders.

Twenty-six per cent (14 offenders) of the reactive offenders against 12 per cent (4 offenders) of the instrumental offenders consistently claimed to be amnesic for the act of killing throughout the investigation. Averaged across the two groups, this percentage is 21 per cent, which is highly similar to the 23 per cent rate found in the Christianson, Bylin, and Holmberg (2003; cf. above) study. These rates are also highly similar to those reported by other studies on amnesia for homicide (see, e.g., Cima, Nijman, Merckelbach, Kremer, and Hollnack, in press b; Guttmacher, 1955; Leitch, 1948; Parkin, 1987).

The question arises whether these rates reflect true proportions of genuine amnesia for homicidal violence. In assessing the validity of the amnesia claims raised by 21 per cent of the offenders, characteristics that are often associated with malingering were scrutinised. Drawing on a review by Porter and Yuille (1995), some clues will be listed. First, many amnesic offenders say that they recall events immediately preceding and following the crime, with a circumscribed memory loss for the act of killing itself. This typical pattern of remembering and forgetting was also claimed by Margaret MacDonald, whose case was described earlier. It is a pattern that is very unusual in clinical cases of both organic and dissociative amnesia, where more blurred demarcations between remembering and forgetting are found. Second, Schacter (1986) argued that false claims of amnesia are characterised by a sudden onset and low ratings on feeling-of-knowing judgements. If, for example, a murder suspect is asked about the possibility of recurrence of memories after being provided with cues, recognition alternatives, more time to think about the event, additional interrogation, visit the crime scene, etc., the malingerer is usually dogmatically negative. On a related note, malingerers typically report that they are not helped by an interviewing method known as the Cognitive Interview (Fisher and Geiselman, 1992). This method incorporates (a) reinstatement of both environmental and personal context, (b) reporting everything regardless of its perceived importance, (c) recounting the line of events in a variety of orders, and (d) reporting events from a variety of perspectives. Although the Cognitive Interview may not break a suspect who intentionally wishes to withhold information, one should expect him or her to retrieve more information as a result of these well-established memory-enhancing techniques. Malingerers usually say that they do not profit from these techniques.

Third, Porter and Yuille (1995) pointed out that malingerers are also more likely to relate symptoms of extreme specificity (e.g., 'I cannot recall anything from noon until midnight') and to recount symptoms of extreme severity. Doubt should also arise when suspects with a diagnosis of psychopathy claim amnesia. Psychopaths do not experience the extreme emotions that may undermine encoding of information, but they do have a tendency for pathological lying and malingering (Porter and Yuille, 1995). In keeping with this, Cima et al. (in press, b) found in their sample of psychiatric prison inmates that those who claimed amnesia displayed more antisocial characteristics but also scored higher on an instrument tapping malingering tendencies.

Fourth, suspects often blame their amnesia on intoxication. Yet, as pointed out by Parwatiker, Holcomb, and Menninger (1985; see also below), amnesia for crime is unlikely to be purely dependent on an intoxicated state. In their study on drivers arrested during large traffic-control actions by the Dutch police, Van Oorsouw, Merckelbach, Ravelli, Nijman, and Pompen (in press) found that claims of alcohol amnesia (blackout) were predominantly raised by those involved in an accident. More specifically, 85 per cent of the drivers who claimed amnesia were involved in a serious motor vehicle accident against 35 per cent of those not claiming amnesia. Interestingly, during the time of the arrest, blood-alcohol concentrations (BACs) in those who claimed amnesia were not higher than the BACs of arrested drivers without amnesia. This illustrates that the combination of amnesia and intoxication claims may serve face-saving purposes.

In evaluating the 21 per cent claiming amnesia in the Christianson and Von Vogelsang study, certain characteristics were found to be common in this group. To begin with, the offenders in this group were dogmatic about their amnesia (e.g., 'It doesn't matter if you ask me five, ten or even more times, I will never remember anything about what happened that evening'). A second feature was that they claimed to have total memory loss: 'My memory is like a black hole, everything is gone.' In clinical cases of both organic and dissociative amnesia, patients have islands of memories from the amnesic part of the event rather than total memory loss. Further, offenders' claims of sharp limits for beginning and end of the amnesia were quite common (e.g., 'from the moment I stepped out of the restaurant door, until I sat in the police car, everything is lost'). As noted above, this is an atypical pattern in clinical settings. Finally, references to intoxication were also quite common. However, a closer look at the total sample revealed that 65 per cent of the offenders who were intoxicated by alcohol remembered the murder quite well, whereas only 19 per cent of them claimed amnesia.

Given these characteristics, one may assume that forensic experts are well advised to consider the possibility of malingering in these 21 per cent claimants of amnesia. Perhaps we nurse a myth when we believe that people can be amnesic for such a unique, emotional, often once-in-a-lifetime event as murder. Of course, offenders can forget about certain details of the event, but if the question is whether an offender can be amnesic with respect to the complete act of killing, the present data suggest they cannot.

What lay people say

At the beginning of this chapter, we mentioned two legal reasons why it is important to explore crime-related amnesia. One issue was that of automatism (criminal behaviour that is executed unconsciously and without intent), which is critical for establishing legal responsibility. The other issue was that memory loss implicates that the suspect cannot plead on his or her own behalf and is therefore incompetent to stand trial.

For the Anglo-Saxon situation, Parwatiker, Holcomb, and Menninger (1985) noted that 'no court has found a defendant incompetent to stand trial solely because of amnesia' (p. 202; see also Hermann, 1986). And, indeed, in Anglo-Saxon countries amnesia does not figure in the list of disorders that typically contribute to 'not guilty by reason of insanity' trial outcomes. Most of the times, such outcomes involve schizophrenia and mood disorders, especially in combination with alcohol or drug use (Lymburner and Roesch, 1999).

Still, according to some leading Anglo-Saxon authors, claims of amnesia may have far-reaching legal implications (e.g., Bradford and Smith, 1979). In the legal context, it is not amnesia per se that is considered to be informative, but what amnesia reveals about the state of the defendant at the moment he or she committed the crime. More specifically, amnesia may indicate a state of 'automatism', which refers to unconscious, non-intentional, and therefore uncontrollable, behaviour. In the literature, eccentric examples of 'automatic' crimes committed during sleepwalking, epileptic seizures, or hypoglycaemia states abound.

In countries like Canada and Australia, automatism has been divided into 'sane' and 'insane' types. For both categories of automatism, it is assumed that the *mens rea* (i.e., 'wicked mind') aspect of the crime is at stake (Hermann, 1986). 'Sane' automatism refers to a crime committed by someone who is essentially healthy, but who is in a temporary state of madness due to some external agent (e.g., insulin). Such a scenario may lead to acquittal. 'Insane' automatism refers to a crime originated from structural brain dysfunction. The prototypical example is the man who killed his neighbour during an epileptic seizure (Fenwick, 1993). Such a scenario can lead to a 'not guilty by reason of insanity' verdict. Kopelman (1995) noted that offenders who commit an 'automatic' crime always would become amnesic. However, the opposite does not hold: when a defendant claims crime-related amnesia, it does not necessarily imply that the crime came about automatically (Kalant, 1996). Curiously enough, this is nevertheless what, for example, the highest German court (Bundesgerichtshof; BGH) seems to think, because this court ruled that 'a verified amnesia for the criminal act – alone or in combination with other factors – is a sign of an emotionally based disorder of consciousness' (BGH 4 Str 207/87; Barbey, 1990).

The distinction between sane and insane automatism is more problematic than it may appear to be at first glance. Referring to several case examples, McSherry (1998) showed that this distinction is highly dependent on arbitrary judgements made by expert witnesses and especially their opinion as to what counts as a structural brain dysfunction. McSherry described two similar cases of domestic murder. Owing to expert witness testimonies, one case was classified as 'sane' automatism leading to full acquittal, whereas the other case was classified as an example of 'insane' automatism, leading to a 'not criminally responsible' verdict and admission to a psychiatric hospital. With these interpretational problems in mind, Yeo (2002) argued that automatism has little to do with memory problems and that it is better to conceptualise automatic states in terms of uncontrollable behaviour.

Merckelbach, Cima, and Nijman (2002) explored popular ideas about crime-relate amnesia. The authors made a summary of a real case in which an offender, after a night out visiting various cafés, stabbed someone to death. The offender claimed amnesia for the homicide. The court appointed a mental health professional, who after two interviews with the defendant, concluded that his crime-related amnesia was a result of 'alcohol and drug use in combination with strong emotions'. This case vignette was administered to fifty-four laypersons. They were asked whether they thought that genuine amnesia would be a plausible scenario in this type of crime. The majority of them (82 per cent) indicated that it was a plausible scenario. A majority (76 per cent) also felt that the court was very wise to appoint a forensic expert. As well, respondents had very strong opinions about the origins of the amnesia. A large majority of the respondents (70 percent) agreed that alcohol and emotions were responsible for the offender's amnesia. Apparently, offenders who claim crime-related amnesia do not need to worry that their claims meet widespread disbelief.

Naïve ideas about crime-related amnesia would be of little or no concern to us were it not that judges and lawyers are lay people who in some cases have to decide about the plausibility of crime-related amnesia. One could argue that in such cases, triers of fact consult an expert witness precisely to overcome their own lack of technical knowledge. On the other hand, in cases of claimed amnesia expert witnesses often rely on notions that come dangerously close to those of lay people. Meanwhile, expert witnesses should base their opinions on what psychological literature says about dissociative amnesia, simulated amnesia, and organic amnesia.

What science says

For the expert witness, it is difficult to differentiate between dissociative, organic, or feigned amnesia. This has to do with the fact that simulators can give a compelling imitation of someone with a dissociative or organic amnesia. It is only with the help of tests, tasks, and structured interviews focusing on certain memory characteristics, that an expert will be able to identify simulators. Nevertheless, our impression is that experts in cases where amnesia claims are raised often use clinical interviews with the defendant as their sole source for making diagnostic judgements. This state of affairs is hardly surprising. After all, the average mental health professional is not a memory expert and has no specialised knowledge about tests that might be helpful in discriminating between dissociative, organic, and feigned amnesia. Below, we will take a closer look at this issue.

Dissociative versus feigned amnesia

Dissociative amnesia is defined as 'an inability to recall important personal information, usually of a traumatic or stressful nature, that is too extensive to be explained by ordinary forgetfulness' (American Psychiatric Association, 1994, p. 477). A number of authors have argued that the term dissociative amnesia is quite confusing (Pope, Hudson, Bodkin, and Oliva, 1998). It not only suggests that the cause of the memory loss is a dissociation between consciousness and memory, but also assumes that memory loss for emotional trauma does exist. Although lay people believe that it is perfectly possible that an emotionally provocative event like murder can lead to complete memory loss, specialists have not yet reached a consensus about this. Some authors (e.g., Kopelman, 1995) opine that dissociative amnesia does exist and their most important argument is that defendants who claim amnesia often inform the police about the crime: 'This makes an account of amnesia as simulation to avoid punishment less plausible' (p. 435; for a similar reasoning, see Porter, Birt, Yuille, and Herve, 2001). However, this line of reasoning is not very convincing. A defendant who knows that there is extensive forensic evidence against him may speculate that he will make a more sympathetic impression on triers of fact when he simulates amnesia than when he provides them with a lucid description of crime details. Thus, Sadoff (1974) argued that most cases of dissociative amnesia are actually feigned. Apart from the atypical memory features that often accompany amnesia claims (e.g., sharp demarcations, total memory loss), there are three good reasons to take Sadoff's point seriously.

The first is that there is quite some knowledge about the psychological characteristics of those who claim dissociative amnesia for a crime. Older studies reported that criminals who raise such claim can be distinguished from other criminals by their relative low intelligence and their hysterical traits (O'Connel, 1960; Parwatiker, Holcomb, Menninger, 1985). In this context, hysterical traits refer to manipulative behaviour, including the tendency to feign symptoms (O'Connel, 1960). While the concept of hysteria has largely disappeared from psychiatric vocabulary, more recent studies point in the same direction. For example, Lynch and Bradford (1980) reported that claims of amnesia are often raised by defendants with an antisocial personality disorder. A hallmark feature of this disorder is, of course, manipulative behaviour (Porter et al., 2001). Similarly, Cima, Merckelbach, Hollnack, and Knauer (in press, a) noted that criminals who claimed amnesia had low intelligence and displayed antisocial personality features. The picture emerging from these studies is that defendants who claim dissociative amnesia often rely on a simple form of denial in an attempt to minimise their responsibility.

A second reason to adopt a sceptic attitude towards claims of dissociative amnesia is that the whole idea of amnesia for crime is based on the dubious assumption that 'the majority of crimes which are followed by amnesia are those accompanied by strong emotional reactions' (Hopwood and Snell, 1933, p. 32). By this view, strong emotions lead to repression or, to use a more recent notion, to dissociation and this would produce retrieval problems. If this line of reasoning is correct, one expects that, for example, concentration-camp survivors also display amnesia for the horrifying events they have experienced. However, this is not the case (e.g., Kuch and Cox, 1992; Yehuda, Elkin, Binder-Brynes, Kahana, Southwick, Schmeidler, and Giller, 1996; Merckelbach, Dekkers, Wessel, and Roefs, 2003a, b). On a related note, eyewitnesses to extreme violence only rarely report that they are amnesic for the events they have witnessed (Porter et al., 2001). In short, the notion that people may develop amnesia for highly emotional events is very controversial (Pope et al., 1998). In the forensic context, it is therefore wise to consider dissociative amnesia as a rare phenomenon (Christianson and Nilsson, 1989).

A third reason to be sceptical about claims of dissociative amnesia is that recent psychiatric literature shows that a non-trivial minority of people tend to feign a variety of symptoms and to confabulate stories if this serves their interests. For example, it is estimated that as much as 20 per cent of closed-head injury patients pursuing financial compensation exaggerate their symptoms (Binder and Rohling, 1996). Likewise, in the United States there are now many well-documented cases of Vietnam veterans who have never served in Vietnam and who fake their PTSD symptoms (Burkett and Whitley, 1998; for other examples, see Gold and Frueh, 1998; Rosen, 1995). When motor vehicle accidents victims feign neurological complaints and when military personnel invent a complete autobiography to qualify for disability payments, why should the criminal who simulates amnesia be a rarity? Laypersons as well as many expert witnesses tend to view dissociative amnesia as the rule and feigned amnesia as the exception. Given the considerations discussed above, we think that it would be wise to reverse these probability estimates. This conclusion is further supported by studies in which normal subjects are instructed to play the role of a murderer who during interrogation is confronted with abundant evidence. The most frequently chosen strategy of these subjects is to claim amnesia for the criminal act and to attribute it to an internal force that they cannot control (Spanos, Weekes, and Bertrand, 1986; Merckelbach, Devilly, and Rassin, 2002).

The role of alcohol   Excessive alcohol or drug use is often said to precede criminal acts for which dissociative amnesia is claimed. At least, that is what criminals who claim such memory loss tell researchers and expert witnesses. As said before, the 'state-dependent memory' hypothesis is often invoked to explain the apparent link between alcohol and amnesia (Swihart et al., 1999). Yet, a closer look at the literature shows that this hypothesis is not based on solid evidence. For example, in a study of Wolf (1980), a substantial amount of alcohol was given to criminals who had committed murder under the influence of alcohol and who claimed to be amnesic. The 'state-dependent memory' hypothesis would lead one to predict that alcohol results in recovery from the amnesia. This is not what Wolf (1980) found. Although his subjects became emotional, they maintained that they could not remember the crime details.

Of course, the phenomenon of 'alcohol-blackout' exists. However, it is best viewed as an organic form of amnesia resulting from an excessive amount of alcohol consumed within a very short time span (e.g., 5 glasses of whisky or 20 glasses of beer within four hours; Goodwin, 1995). Even when subjects consume such a large dose, only some of them will develop an alcohol-blackout. And when they do, they are not capable of the fine motor operations that are needed to carry out a criminal act (Kalant, 1996). In most cases where dissociative amnesia is claimed, alcohol doses do not reach such an extreme level. This suggests that in these cases, defendants' reference to their alcohol or drug use may serve a different function, namely that of the 'partial excuse for the essentially inexcusable' (Room, 2001, p. 194). That is, for those who have seriously violated the law, an appeal to alcohol or drug intoxication may give an explanation for the crime that has been committed as well as for the memory loss that is claimed. The example of the Canadian Supreme Court shows that courts are not insensitive to such 'intoxification defence'. In the case of a rapist who argued not to remember the crime because he was in a state of alcohol intoxication, the Court ruled that the crime had been committed in a state of 'drunken automatism' (Kalant, 1996). Laypersons not only seem to have strong opinions about the plausibility of dissociative amnesia, they also have strong opinions about the behavioural and memory effects of alcohol or drugs. Again, these opinions are not always in line with what is actually known about these effects.

The role of expectations Experiments show that the behavioural effects of alcohol are to some extent guided by expectancies that people have about these effects: 'Things that are believed real are real in their consequences' (Thomas and Thomas, 1928, p. 572). A straightforward procedure to demonstrate this phenomenon is the 'balanced placebo design'. The rationale behind this design is that some subjects are given a non-alcoholic drink that they believe to contain alcohol, whereas other persons consume an alcoholic drink that they believe is a non-alcoholic refreshment. Under these circumstances, extravert behaviour, tension reduction, and other positive as well as negative effects that people associate with alcohol do not depend on actual alcohol intake but on the belief that one has consumed alcohol (Critchlow, 1986). In a recent study, Assefi and Garry (2003) demonstrated that the mere suggestion to subjects that they have consumed alcohol makes these subjects more susceptible to misleading information. These findings underline that people have strong ideas about the effects of alcohol, ideas that in turn may guide their behaviour.

Is it possible that a similar expectancy effect occurs in cases of dissociative amnesia? In other words, is it possible that some defendants really believe that they are amnesic because they assume that this is a probable outcome given the traumatic character of the event and/or their large consumption of alcohol? The case of Gudjonsson, Kopelman, and MacKeith (1999) demonstrates that there is such a thing as imaginary amnesia. In this case, a defendant was convicted for the murder of a little girl. During the police interrogations, the defendant was encouraged to distrust his own memory, which made him more susceptible to what police officers told him about his involvement in the crime. The fact that he had no memories of the crime was interpreted as a manifestation of dissociative amnesia, an interpretation in which the defendant himself came to believe. Subsequently, it became clear that he was innocent.

Germane to the issue of expectancies is also an experiment by Christianson and Bylin (1999). These authors gave their subjects a case vignette of a murder. Subjects were instructed to identify themselves with the offender. Next, one group of subjects was told to play the role of an amnesic offender during a task that consisted of a series of questions about the case. The control group was encouraged to perform as well as they could on this task. After a week, subjects returned to the lab and, again, answered questions about the case. This time, all subjects were instructed to perform as well as they could. During the first session, subjects who played an amnesic role gave fewer correct answers than control subjects, which is not remarkable. It only shows that the 'amnesic' subjects took their role seriously. However, at the one-week follow-up test, ex-simulators were still performing under the level of control subjects. This is remarkable, because it shows that simulating amnesia has memory-undermining effects.

The memory-undermining effect of simulating amnesia is a robust phenomenon (Van Oorsouw and Merckelbach, in press). There are several explanations for this phenomenon. One emphasises rehearsal of crime details. The first test occasion may serve as an act of repetition from which control subjects, but not simulators, benefit. Another possibility is that simulators think of a new version that better fits their wish of being less responsible for the crime. This type of processing would imply that subjects who feign amnesia confuse their own version with the original event and subsequently have difficulties understanding how their own memory has changed. This might result in source-monitoring errors (Johnson, Hashtroudi, and Lindsay, 1993). Still another explanation is that expectancies are the driving force behind the memory-undermining effect of simulating amnesia. People who initially played the role of an amnesic person may have a strong expectation that they will perform poorly on subsequent memory tasks. This, in turn, may give rise to a 'self-fulfilling prophecy' when the person is given such a memory task. This phenomenon is also known from studies on placebo effects. Subjects who receive a placebo in combination with the story that it is a memory-undermining substance, later on perform less well on memory tasks than do control subjects (Kvavilashvili and Ellis, 1999).

The memory-undermining effects of simulating suggest that a simulated amnesia may sometimes develop into a real memory problem. Referring to such mixtures of simulated and real memory problems, Kopelman (2000) argued that the various forms of amnesia 'form end-points along a continuum rather than discrete categories' (p. 608).

Organic versus feigned amnesia

Unlike dissociative amnesia, organic amnesia is a relatively unproblematic phenomenon. In many cases, organic amnesia will be a persistent symptom due to brain damage as a result of chronic alcohol abuse, epilepsy, tumours, encephalitis, or traumatic injury. Note that in this context, the word trauma has a circumscribed meaning. Whereas in psychiatric literature, it refers to emotional shock (e.g., witnessing a shooting), here it refers to an external agent that caused brain dysfunction (e.g., closed-head injury from an accident or fight; Hacking, 1996). Even in cases of mild traumatic brain injury, acute loss of consciousness and subsequent Post Traumatic Amnesia (PTA) may occur. PTA refers to a disoriented state and a serious memory problem immediately after the incident that caused the brain injury. When loss of consciousness exceeds thirty minutes and PTA duration is longer than twenty-four hours, traumatic brain injury is said to be severe (Faust, 1996).

Regardless of whether brain injury is mild or severe, in the period after the PTA, the patient usually reports all kinds of complaints that vary from concentration difficulties to depressive feelings. These complaints are sometimes referred to as the 'post-concussion' syndrome, but this impressive term suggests more clarity than the neurological literature really offers. For example, Lees-Haley, Fox, and Courtney (2001) noted that most symptoms associated with this syndrome are surprisingly aspecific and are also highly prevalent among people who never sustained a brain injury. However, an inability to recall important details surrounding the trauma (e.g., an accident or a fight) – organic amnesia – is a rather specific symptom of the post-concussion syndrome. Organic amnesia follows a fixed course that was first described by the nineteenth-century French memory psychologist Theodule Ribot (Haber and Haber, 1998) and is therefore known as Ribot's Law. This law refers to the phenomenon that organic amnesia pertains to the traumatic incident itself and events that immediately preceded and/or followed it, rather than events that took place long before the trauma. If such older memories have nevertheless become inaccessible, they will return sooner in the weeks following the trauma than more recent memories that have become inaccessible (e.g., Christianson, Nilsson, and Silfvenius, 1987). Eventually, the amnesia will largely disappear and will be limited to the traumatic event itself and the few seconds that preceded it.

There are reasons to believe that the vague, aspecific symptoms of the post-concussion syndrome are sensitive to simulation. This is mostly the case in civil law suits, in which, for example, vehicle accident victims require financial compensation. In such cases, it is relatively easy to feign atypical symptoms (Youngjohn, Burrows, and Erdal, 1995). Meanwhile, organic amnesia is considerably more difficult to simulate – at least for naïve malingerers – because of its typical course. That is, organic amnesia requires the specific sequence of trauma, loss of consciousness, PTA, memory loss pertaining to recent rather than old memories, and memory recovery in such a way that old memories come back more readily than recent ones. In addition, organic amnesia goes hand in hand with subtle attentional difficulties that are not easy to fake (e.g., Cochrane, Baker, and Meudell, 1998). When complaints about organic amnesia do not follow this pattern, there is every reason to be sceptical and to consider the possibility of malingering.

What tests say

When a defendant claims crime-related amnesia, how should an expert witness determine what type of amnesia the defendant suffers from? One possibility is that the defendant sustained brain injury and consequently developed an organic amnesia. The expert may explore this by examining if and how the defendant's amnesia disappears over time. If the defendant's amnesia follows Ribot's Law, that information might be crucial for the defendant's counsel. Consider a defendant charged with murder. If the defendant has an organic amnesia and it can be shown that this amnesia originates from the victim hitting the defendant on his head before he was murdered, then a self-defence interpretation of the murder case might be considered.

Another possibility is that a defendant honestly believes that he suffers from amnesia. As far as we know, there is no valid test to explore this possibility. However, with the findings of Kvavilashvili and Ellis (1999) in mind, the expert might consider giving the defendant a placebo along with the instruction that it is a memory-enhancing drug. In a way, such a manipulation is deceptive. On the other hand, it is highly similar to forensic hypnosis, because that technique also capitalises on expectancies (Kebbell and Wagstaff, 1998).

A third possibility is that a defendant feigns his amnesia. Again, this possibility warrants serious attention and can be explored in several ways, for example by using Symptom Validity Testing, self-report scales, or other techniques.

Symptom Validity Testing

Symptom Validity Testing (SVT) has been found to be useful in identifying defendants who simulate amnesia (Frederick, Carter, and Powel, 1995; Denney, 1996; Rosen and Powel, 2002). Basically, SVT procedures consist of a forced-choice recognition test, where the defendant is asked a series of dichotomous (true–false) questions about the crime and the circumstances under which it took place. The defendant is instructed to guess in case he does not know the right answers because of his amnesia. Typically, 15 to 100 items are presented, each followed by a forced-choice recognition task. With any number of items, chance performance (guessing) can be determined fairly precisely. This has to do with the fact that purely random responding will result in about 50 per cent of the answers being correctly answered. Individuals who perform significantly below chance strategically avoid correct alternatives (for a review, see Bianchini, Mathias, and Greve, 2001). This means that they must possess knowledge about the correct answers and this implies that they feign memory impairment. SVT is based on binomial statistics, which has the clear advantage that one can quantify memory performance.[1] Thus, one can determine the exact probability that someone with genuine memory loss gives only 3 right answers to 15 true–false questions. On the basis of chance alone, such a person should have 6, 7 or 8 correct answers. The probability that someone with genuine memory loss produces only 3 correct answers is smaller than 5 per cent[1].

Some researchers have argued that a clever defendant who attempts to simulate amnesia will readily recognise the rationale behind SVT. By this view, defendants would quickly realise that they have to perform at chance level (half of the answers correct and the other half incorrect). A recent study by Merckelbach, Hauer, and Rassin (2002) tested this idea. In this study, twenty students were instructed to steal an envelope containing money. Next, students were told to simulate amnesia in a way that would convince experts. To explore how well the SVT could identify this feigned amnesia, students took a 15 true–false item SVT. About half of the students (53 per cent) had less than 4 correct answers and were identified as malingerers. The other students succeeded in performing at chance level and thus seemed to be able to simulate in a convincing way. However, post-experiment interviews with these subjects made it clear that only a minority of them were able to verbalise the rationale behind SVT. These results were replicated in follow-up studies that relied on other types of mock crimes and other samples (Jelicic, Merckelbach, and Van Bergen, in press, a; b).

Given the fact that a small majority of students fails to beat the SVT, the efficacy of the SVT in identifying malingering should be considerably better with less educated defendants who simulate amnesia. This is especially true when the number of SVT items is increased. The studies cited above relied on a relatively small number of test items (i.e., 15). However, with more SVT items, say 30, it becomes more and more difficult for defendants to monitor whether they perform at chance level. And even when defendants succeed in doing so, there is an appropriate test to examine whether the pattern of correct and incorrect answers is truly random (as it should be in the case of genuine amnesia) or strategic (as is the case when deliberate attempts are made to simulate chance level). A discussion of this 'runs'-test falls beyond the scope of this chapter, but the principle behind it can be summarised as follows (Cliffe, 1992). Suppose you have a coin and on 15 consecutive trials you throw heads, while on the next 15 consecutive trials you throw tails. That would be nicely at chance level. However, there must be something wrong with the coin, because too few so-called 'runs' have been made (namely 2) to assume that the pattern of heads and tails is random. The same is true for SVT performance at chance level. For example, subjects who answer the first 15 questions of a 30 items SVT correctly and the last 15 items incorrectly perform nicely at chance level but are identified as malingerers by the 'runs'-test.

SVT does not require technical facilities. All one needs is a pencil, a paper, and basic knowledge of statistics. It is essential, though, that the correct and incorrect alternatives are first evaluated by a panel of naïve subjects. When this panel judges the incorrect alternatives as more plausible than the correct alternatives, it is possible that someone with a genuine amnesia performs below chance level. With this restriction in mind, we would like to recommend the SVT to experts who have to examine cases in which defendants claim amnesia.

Self-report scales

Another way to examine claims of amnesia is provided by self-report questionnaires that capitalise on the tendency of malingerers to exaggerate their memory complaints (Smith, 1997; Jaffe and Sharma, 1998). A promising questionnaire is the Structured Inventory of Malingered Symptomatology (SIMS; Smith and Burger, 1997). The SIMS consists of 75 dichotomous (i.e., true–false) items that can be grouped into 5 subscales, each subscale containing 15 items. Subscales correspond to symptoms domains that are sensitive to malingering and include low intelligence (LI), affective disorder (AF), neurological impairment (N), psychosis (P), and amnesic disorder (AM). Items of the subscales refer to bizarre experiences (e.g., 'At times I've been unable to remember the names or faces of close relatives so that they seem like complete strangers') or to unrealistic symptoms (e.g., 'When I can't remember something, hints do not help'). Other items explicitly allude to a certain syndrome (e.g., amnesia) in such a way that specialists recognize that highly atypical symptoms are listed (e.g., 'My past and important events became a blur to me almost overnight'). The idea is that malingerers will tend to exaggerate and in doing so will endorse bizarre, unrealistic, and atypical symptoms. Answers indicating malingering are summed to obtain a total SIMS score.

So far, a number of studies have looked at the accuracy with which the SIMS detects malingered symptomatology (Rogers, Hinds, and Sewell, 1996; Smith and Burger, 1997; Edens, Otto, and Dwyer, 1999). Although these studies came up with promising results, most of them relied on laboratory set-ups. In this type of study, undergraduate students are instructed to feign, in a convincing way, certain psychiatric symptoms (e.g., amnesia). Performance of these instructed malingering groups on the SIMS is then compared to the SIMS scores of control (i.e., uninstructed) groups responding honestly. It is evident that this approach is subject to a number of limitations, not the least of which is that for undergraduates instructed to feign symptoms there are hardly any risks or incentives. Nevertheless, the results of these studies are encouraging in that the SIMS appears to be able to identify subjects instructed to feign, say, amnesia with a high degree of precision. For example, Merckelbach and Smith (2003) reported that more than 90 per cent of the subjects instructed to malinger amnesia are identified by the SIMS (sensitivity) and more than 90 per cent of the control subjects are classified by the SIMS as honest respondents (specificity).

Other techniques

Traditional tests (e.g., IQ tests, memory tests, MMPI, polygraph methods) may provide useful background information in evaluating amnesia claims (for reviews, see Allen and Lacono, 2001; Hall and Poirier, 2000; Lynch and Bradford, 1980; Rogers, 1997). For example, one could rely on well-validated tests to examine whether there are indications for clear irregularities in the suspect's memory (e.g., autobiographical memories, childhood memories, new learning capacity). One could also look for a history of memory loss due to stress, alcohol, skull injury, epilepsy, or sleepwalking ('automatism'). Along with objective tests, information can be gathered from social authorities, medical history, journal notes, legal documents, interrogation reports, and interviews with relatives, friends, and work-mates. Assessment of personality traits (psychopathy, dissociative tendencies, fantasy proneness, and suggestibility) might also provide important information. Hypnosis is controversial (Porter and Yuille, 1995) but could be useful if the amnesic suspect is clearly motivated to participate in such a procedure. The traditional explanation for positive results obtained with hypnosis is that the altered mental state during hypnosis will break down the suspect's defences and that he or she is more willing to verbalise what is already unconsciously known. However, it is important to be aware of the heightened suggestibility of the person in this state and to avoid leading questions, which otherwise can confuse original memories, or even worse, implant false memories or confessions (Kebbell and Wagstaff, 1998).

Still another technique, although controversial, is that of 'symptom suggestion' (Porter and Yuille, 1995). Here, the suspect is provided with false characteristics of amnesia and his behaviour is then monitored for possible incorporation of the symptoms, which would be indicative of malingered amnesia. While in general we do not want to recommend misinformation techniques, the first author of this chapter has used symptom suggestion with some success. In one case, he told a suspect who was charged with murder and who claimed amnesia about the true characteristics of amnesia. During an interview, the suspect was informed that his presentation of amnesia was atypical because in most cases there are islands of memories pertaining to certain points in the amnesic period. In the next interview, when the suspect was taken to the scene of crime, he claimed to have suddenly recovered an island of memory (a 'flashback') and described how he stabbed the victim in the left side. He maintained, however, to have no further memories about the events preceding or following this specific act of stabbing.

Searching for and telling about homicidal memories

Are perpetrators who claim amnesia liars? Instead of giving a straight-forward answer, let us consider the complexity of remembering and sharing homicide offences. Not only victims and bystanders but also per-petrators, display an aversion to remembering traumatic events. People in general have the tendency to remove stressful thoughts, feelings, and memories from their conscious awareness. Cognitive aversion is not static, however, but is dependent on the amount of psychological stress that is experienced. Of course, to tell about a strong emotional event such as having committed a murder is very different from a typical conversation. After all, murder is one of the most severe forms of antisocial behaviour a human being can produce. There are many obstacles to report about such an event. First, the individual has to be motivated even to start to search for memory details that have been vigorously avoided. It is common among sexual and homicide offenders, as well as among victims of repeated sexual and physical abuse, to develop strategies to avoid think-ing about the event – an event for which they have no explanation as to why it occurred. Over time, active avoidance, such as stop-thinking activity, suppression, and other strategies, may make links and associa-tions to specific details of the event less robust (e.g., Wegner, Quillian, and Houston, 1996). A second problem is confronting and telling about memories of the crime. This is a matter of confronting not only one's own feelings and the victim's reactions, but also the past (e.g., strong neg-ative childhood memories of being rejected, abused, alone, and deeply secluded). Most homicide offenders do not have a background of sharing personal negative experiences and have developed skills from childhood that involve avoidance of thinking about negative experiences (e.g., dis-tortion, displacement, stop-thinking activity). This will result in fewer cues to other types of autobiographical memories and experiences and thus the offender will not easily retrieve detailed memories of the crime.

A third factor concerns the offender's need to have a recipient of trau-matising memories, someone who is skilled in listening to and prepared to receive reports of gruesome, shocking experiences from other people. Details of murder are not easy to listen to and many listeners disclose, either verbally or non-verbally, that they are receiving horrible informa-tion, and that they are not prepared to hear about all the gruesome details. Police officers often seek a confession, which, from their perspective, is an ideal starting point for a perpetrator to tell his story about the crime.

Most offenders, however, are not focused on the crime. They do not want to confess. They want to be understood and to understand how it all could have happened. This is especially true for reactive homicide offenders, who often themselves have been traumatised by the crime (Pollock, 1999). Against this background, it is counterproductive when police officers are preoccupied with confessions rather than truth seeking. Police officers should try to understand what has happened and in doing so, treat the suspect with respect and empathy. A dominant interviewing style marked by impatience, aggression, brusqueness and obstinacy, haste, and condemnation will often turn the suspect's attention away from the crime. Instead the suspect will focus on the interrogators and the experience of having been insulted and provoked by them. An aggressive and provocative police interrogation will thus promote an avoidance approach in the offender (Holmberg and Christianson, 2002). With this in mind, it is not surprising that some offenders claim amnesia. Such a claim could be construed as a strategy for psychological survival, as a way to handle both the past, which has led to the act of crime, and the immediate present, being a murderer and being interviewed by a confronting police officer.

Conclusions

It is not uncommon that defendants claim amnesia for the crime of which they are accused. In this chapter, we have focused on amnesia for homicide and the issue of whether this is genuine or feigned memory loss. Among lay people, a large majority believe that it is perfectly possible for an offender to develop complete amnesia for his crime and that in certain types of homicide, dissociative amnesia is a highly plausible scenario. Mental health professionals who appear as expert witnesses in such cases often assume that this type of memory loss is the joint effect of strong emotions and excessive drug or alcohol use. It is also common to seek arguments for this interpretation by interviewing the defendant. In this chapter, we have presented arguments for why this approach is dubious. To begin with, our empirical data from interviews with homicide offenders show that they have a strong motivation for feigning amnesia and also that their memory loss possesses the typical features of malingered amnesia. Second, dissociative amnesia is not the only or even the most prevalent form of crime-related amnesia. Experts should at least take the possibility of other types of amnesia into account. These other types include simulated and imagined amnesia. Third, the diagnostic differentiation between these types of amnesia cannot be made solely on the basis of interviews. To make this differentiation, experts should rely on tests (e.g., the SIMS), tasks (e.g., the SVT), and clues that are typical for malingering memory dysfunctions (e.g., sharp boundaries between remembering and forgetting). Although this may seem simple, such an approach requires sophisticated knowledge about diagnostic quality parameters. For example, an important technical issue is that false positives (i.e., classifying a suspect as a malingerer, when he in fact suffers from bona fide amnesia) are highly dependent on base rates (Rosenfeld, Sands, and Van Gorp, 2000). Many psychologists and psychiatrists do not possess such knowledge and therefore their competence to act as expert witnesses in cases in which claims of crime-related amnesia are raised is doubtful. A main question in this chapter is whether homicide offenders who claim amnesia are liars. A yes-or-no answer does not do justice to the complexities of the whole issue. Rather, in considering all the obstacles a homicide offender has to meet in remembering and telling about the crime, it is not surprising that offenders often claim amnesia.

REFERENCES

Allen, J. J. B., and Iacono, W. G. (2001). Assessing the validity of amnesia in dissociative identity disorder. *Psychology, Public Policy, and Law, 7*, 311–44.

American Psychiatric Association. (1994). *Diagnostic and Statistical Manual of Mental Disorders* (4th edn). Washington, DC: Author.

Assefi, S. L., and Garry, M. (2003). Absolut® memory distortions: Alcohol placebos influence the misinformation effect. *Psychological Science, 14*, 77–80.

Barbey, I. (1990). Postdeliktische Errinerungsstorungen: Ergebnisse einer retrospektiven Erhebung [Post-offence amnesia: results of a retrospective study]. *Blutalkohol, 27*, 241–59.

Bianchini, K. J., Mathias, C. W., and Greve, K. W. (2001). Symptom Validity Testing: A critical review. *Clinical Neuropsychologist, 15*, 19–45.

Binder, L. M., and Rohling, M. L. (1996). Money matters: A meta-analytic review of the effects of financial incentives on recovery after closed-head injury. *American Journal of Psychiatry, 153*, 7–10.

Bourget, D., and Bradford, J. M. W. (1995). Sex offenders who claim amnesia for their alleged offense. *Bulletin of the American Academy of Psychiatry and Law, 23*, 299–307.

Bower, G. H. (1981). Mood and memory. *American Psychologist, 36*, 129–48.

Bradford, J. W., and Smith, S. M. (1979). Amnesia and homicide: The Padola case and a study of thirty cases. *Bulletin of the American Academy of Psychiatry and Law, 7*, 219–31.

Burkett, B. G., and Whitley, G. (1998). *Stolen valor: How the Vietnam generation was robbed of its heroes and its history*. Dallas, TX: Verity Press.

Christianson, S.-Å. (1992). Emotional stress and eyewitness memory: A critical review. *Psychological Bulletin, 112*, 284–309.

Christianson, S.-Å., and Bylin, S. (1999). Does simulating amnesia mediate genuine forgetting for a crime event? *Applied Cognitive Psychology, 13*, 495–511.

Christianson, S.-Å., Bylin, S., and Holmberg, U. (2003). Homicide and sexual offenders' view of crime-related amnesia. Unpublished manuscript.

Christianson, S.-Å., and Nilsson, L.-G. (1989). Hysterical amnesia: A case of aversively motivated isolation of memory. In T. Archer and L.-G. Nilsson (eds.), *Aversion, avoidance, and anxiety: Perspectives on aversively motivated behavior* (pp. 289–310). Hillsdale, NJ: Lawrence Erlbaum.

Christianson, S.-Å., Nilsson, L.-G., and Silfvenius, H. (1987). Initial memory deficits and subsequent recovery in two cases of head trauma. *Scandinavian Journal of Psychology, 28*, 267–80.

Christianson, S.-Å., and von Vogelsang, E. (2003). Homicide offenders who claim amnesia for their crime. Unpublished manuscript.

Cima, M., Merckelbach, H., Hollnack, S., and Knauer, E. (in press, a). Characteristics of psychiatric prison inmates who claim amnesia. *Personality and Individual Differences*.

Cima, M., Nijman, H., Merckelbach, H., Kremer, K., and Hollnack, S. (in press, b). Claims of crime-related amnesia in forensic patients. *International Journal of Law and Psychiatry*.

Cliffe, M. J. (1992). Symptom-validity testing of feigned sensory or memory deficits: A further elaboration for subjects who understand the rationale. *British Journal of Clinical Psychology, 31*, 207–9.

Cochrane, H. J., Baker, G. A., and Meudell, P. R. (1998). Simulating a memory impairment: Can amnesics implicitly outperform simulators? *British Journal of Clinical Psychology, 37*, 31–48.

Craik F. I. M., and Lockhart, R. S. (1972). Levels of processing: A framework for memory research. *Journal of Verbal Learning and Verbal Behavior, 11*, 671–84.

Critchlow, B. (1986). The powers of John Barleycorn: Beliefs about the effects of alcohol on social behavior. *American Psychologist, 41*, 751–64.

Denney, R. L. (1996). Symptom validity testing of remote memory in a criminal forensic setting. *Archives of Clinical Neuropsychology, 11*, 589–603.

Dodge, K. A. (1991). The structure and function of reactive and proactive aggression. In D. J. Pepler and K. H. Rubin (eds.), *The development and treatment of childhood aggression*, (pp. 224–53). Hillsdale, NJ: Lawrence Erlbaum.

Edens, J. F., Otto, R. K., and Dwyer, T. (1999). Utility of the Structured Inventory of Malingered Symptomatology in identifying persons motivated to malinger psychopathology. *Journal of the American Academy of Psychiatry and the Law, 127*, 387–96.

Faust, D. (1996). Assessment of brain injuries in legal cases: Neuropsychological and neuropsychiatric considerations. In B. S. Fogel, R. B. Scheffen and S. M. Rao (eds.). *Neuropsychiatry* (pp. 973–90). Pennsylvania: Williams and Wilkins.

Fenwick, P. (1993). Brain, mind, and behaviour: Some medico-legal aspects. *British Journal of Psychiatry, 163*, 565–73.

Fisher, R. P., and Geiselman, R. E. (1992). *Memory-enhancing techniques for investigative interviewing. The cognitive interview.* Springfield, IL: Charles C. Thomas.

Frederick, R. I., Carter, M., and Powel, J. (1995). Adapting symptom validity testing to evaluate suspicious complaints of amnesia in medicolegal evaluations. *Bulletin of the American Academy of Psychiatry and the Law, 23*, 227–33.

Gilbert, G. M. (1971). *Nürnberger Tagebuch: Gespräche der Angeklagten mit dem Gerichtspsychologen.* Frankfurt am Main: Fischer.

Gold, P. B., and Frueh, B. C. (1998). Compensation-seeking and extreme exaggeration of psychopathology among combat veterans evaluated for Posttraumatic Stress Disorder. *Journal of Nervous and Mental Disease, 187*, 680–4.

Goodwin, D. W. (1995). Alcohol amnesia. *Addiction, 90*, 315–17.

Gould, A., and MacDonald, M. (1987). *The violent years of Maggie MacDonald.* Scarborough, Ontario: Prentice-Hall.

Gudjonsson, G. H., Kopelman, M. D., and MacKeith, J. A. C. (1999). Unreliable admissions to homicide: A case of misdiagnosis of amnesia and misuse of abreaction technique. *British Journal of Psychiatry, 174*, 455–9.

Gudjonsson, G. H., Petursson, H., Skulason, S., and Sigurdardottir, H. (1989). Psychiatric evidence: A study of psychological issues. *Acta Psychiatrica Scandinavica, 80*, 165–9.

Guttmacher, M. S. (1955). *Psychiatry and the law.* New York, NY: Grune & Stratton.

Haber, L., and Haber, R. N. (1998). Criteria for the admissibility of eyewitness testimony of long past events. *Psychology, Public Policy, and Law, 4*, 1135–59.

Hacking, I. (1996). *Rewriting the Soul: Multiple Personality and the Sciences of Memory.* Princeton, NJ: Princeton University Press.

Hall, H. V., and Poirier, J. G. (2000). *Detecting Malingering and Deception: Forensic Distortion Analysis.* London: CRC Press.

Hermann, D. H. J. (1986). Criminal defenses and pleas in mitigation based on amnesia. *Behavioral Sciences and the Law, 4*, 5–26.

Hopwood, J. S., and Snell, H. K. (1933). Amnesia in relation to crime. *Journal of Mental Science, 79*, 27–41.

Holmberg, U., and Christianson, S. Å. (2002). Murderers' and sexual offenders' experience of police interviews and their inclination to admit or deny crimes. *Behavioral Sciences and the Law, 20*, 31–45.

Jaffe, M. E., and Sharma, K. K. (1998). Malingering uncommon psychiatric symptoms among defendants charged under California's 'three strikes and you're out' law. *Journal of Forensic Sciences, 43*, 549–55.

Jelicic, M., Merckelbach, H., and van Bergen, S. (in press, a). Symptom validity testing of feigned amnesia for a mock crime. *Archives of Clinical Neuropsychology.*

    (in press, b). Symptom validity testing of feigned crime-related amnesia: A simulation study. *Journal of Credibility Assessment and Witness Psychology.*

Johnson, M. K., Hashtroudi, S., and Lindsay, D. S. (1993). Source monitoring. *Psychological Bulletin, 14*, 3–28.

Kalant, H. (1996). Intoxicated automatism: Legal concept vs. scientific evidence. *Contemporary Drug Problems, 23*, 631–48.

Kebbell, M. R., and Wagstaff, G. F. (1998). Hypnotic interviewing: The best way to interview the eyewitness? *Behavioral Sciences and the Law, 16*, 115–29.

Kihlstrom, J. F., and Schacter, D. L. (1995). Functional disorders of autobiographical memory. In A. D. Baddeley, B. A. Wilson, and F. N. Watts (eds.). *Handbook of memory disorders* (pp. 337–64). New York: Wiley.

Kopelman, M. D. (1995). The assessment of psychogenic amnesia. In A. D. Baddeley, B. A. Wilson, and F. N. Watts (eds.). *Handbook of memory disorders* (pp. 427–48). New York: Wiley.

(2000). Focal retrograde amnesia and the attribution of causality: An exceptionally critical review. *Cognitive Neuropsychology, 17*, 585–621.

Kopelman, M. D., Green, R. E. A., Guinan, E. M., Lewis, P. D. R., and Stanhope, N. (1994). The case of the amnesic intelligence officer. *Psychological Medicine, 24*, 1037–45.

Kuch, K., and Cox, B. J. (1992). Symptoms of PTSD in 124 survivors of the Holocaust. *American Journal of Psychiatry, 149*, 337–40.

Kvavilashvili, L., and Ellis, J. A. (1999). The effects of positive and negative placebos on human memory performance. *Memory, 7*, 421–37.

Lees-Haley, P. R., Fox, D. D., and Courtney, J. C. (2001). A comparison of complaints by mild brain injury claimants and other claimants describing subjective experiences immediately following their injury. *Archives of Clinical Neuropsychology, 16*, 689–95.

Leitch, A. (1948). Notes on amnesia in crime for the general practitioner. *Medical Press, 26*, 459–63.

Loewenstein, R. J. (1991). Psychogenic amnesia and psychogenic fugue: A comprehensive review. *American Psychiatric Press Review of Psychiatry, 10*, 189–222.

Lymburner, J. A., and Roesch, R. (1999). The insanity defense: Five years of research (1993–1997). *International Journal of Law and Psychiatry, 22*, 213–40.

Lynch, B. E., and Bradford, J. (1980). Amnesia: Its detection by psychophysiological measures. *American Academy of Psychiatry and Law, 8*, 288–97.

McSherry, B. (1998). Getting away with murder: Dissociative states and criminal responsibility. *International Journal of Law and Psychiatry, 21*, 163–76.

Merckelbach, H., Cima, M., and Nijman, H. (2002). Daders met geheugenverlies [Offenders with memory loss]. In P. J. van Koppen, D. J. Hessing, H. Merckelbach, and H. Crombag (eds.). *Het Recht van Binnen: Psychologie van het Recht.* (pp. 667–85). Deventer: Kluwer Academic.

Merckelbach, H., Dekkers, Th., Wessel, I., and Roefs, A. (2003a). Dissociative symptoms and amnesia in Dutch concentration camp survivors. *Comprehensive Psychiatry, 44*, 65–9.

(2003b). Amnesia, flashbacks, nightmares, and dissociation in aging concentration camp survivors. *Behaviour Research and Therapy, 41*, 351–60.

Merckelbach, H., Devilly, G. J., and Rassin, E. (2002). Alters in dissociative identity disorder: Metaphors or genuine entities? *Clinical Psychology Review, 22*, 481–97.

Merckelbach, H., Hauer, B., and Rassin, E. (2002). Symptom validity testing of feigned dissociative amnesia: A simulation study. *Psychology, Crime, and Law, 8*, 311–18.

Merckelbach, H., and Smith, G. P. (2003). Diagnostic accuracy of the Structured Inventory of Malingered Symptomatology (SIMS) in detecting instructed malingering. *Archives of Clinical Neuropsychology*, *18*, 145–52.

O'Connell, B. A. (1960). Amnesia and homicide. *British Journal of Delinquency*, *10*, 262–76.

Parkin, A. J. (1987). *Memory and amnesia*. New York: Blackwell.

Parwatiker, S. D., Holcomb, W. R., and Menninger, K. A. (1985). The detection of malingered amnesia in accused murderers. *Bulletin of the American Academy of Psychiatry and Law*, *13*, 97–103.

Pollock, Ph. H. (1999). When the killer suffers: Post-traumatic stress reactions following homicide. *Legal and Criminological Psychology*, *4*, 185–202.

Pope, H. G., Hudson, J. L., Bodkin, J. A., and Oliva, P. (1998). Questionable validity of dissociative amnesia in trauma victims. *British Journal of Psychiatry*, *172*, 210–15.

Porter, S., Birt, A. R., Yuille, J. C., and Herve, H. F. (2001). Memory for murder: A psychological perspective on dissociative amnesia in legal contexts. *International Journal of Law and Psychiatry*, *24*, 23–42.

Porter, S., and Yuille, J. C. (1995). Credibility assessment of criminal suspects through statement analysis. *Psychology, Crime, and Law*, *1*, 319–31.

Rogers, R. (1997). *Clinical Assessment of Malingering and Deception*. New York: Guilford Publications.

Rogers, R., Hinds, J. D., and Sewell, K. W. (1996). Feigning psychopathology among adolescent offenders: Validation of the SIRS, MMPI-A, and SIMS. *Journal of Personality Assessment*, *67*, 244–57.

Room, R. (2001). Intoxication and bad behaviour: Understanding cultural differences in the link. *Social Science and Medicine*, *53*, 189–98.

Rosen, G. M. (1995). The Aleutian Enterprise sinking and Posttraumatic stress disorder: Misdiagnosis in clinical and forensic settings. *Professional Psychology: Research and Practice*, *26*, 82–7.

Rosen, G. M., and Powel, J. E. (2002). Use of Symptom Validity Test in the forensic assessment of Post Traumatic Stress Disorder. *Journal of Anxiety Disorders*, *420*, 1–7.

Rosenfeld, B., Sands, S. A., and van Gorp, W. G. (2000). Have we forgotten the base rate problem? Methodological issues in the detection of distortion. *Archives of Clinical Neuropsychology*, *15*, 349–59.

Sadoff, R. L. (1974). Evaluations of amnesia in criminal-legal situations. *Journal of Forensic Sciences*, *19*, 98–101.

Schacter, D. L. (1986). Amnesia and crime: How much do we really know? *American Psychologist*, *41*, 286–95.

Smith, G. P. (1997). Assessment of malingering with self-report instruments. In R. Rogers (ed.). *Clinical Assessment of Malingering and Deception* (pp. 351–70). New York: Guilford Publications.

Smith, G. P., and Burger, G. K. (1997). Detection of malingering: Validation of the Structured Inventory of Malingered Symptomatology (SIMS). *Journal of the Academy of Psychiatry and the Law*, *25*, 180–9.

Spanos, N. P., Weekes, J. R., and Bertrand, L. D. (1986). Multiple personality: A social psychological perspective. *Journal of Abnormal Psychology*, *94*, 362–76.

Swihart, G., Yuille, J., and Porter, S. (1999). The role of state-dependent memory in red-outs. *International Journal of Law and Psychiatry*, 22, 199–212.

Taylor, P. J., and Kopelman, M. D. (1984). Amnesia for criminal offences. *Psychological Medicine*, 14, 581–8.

Thomas, W. I., and Thomas, D. S. (1928). *The child in America: Behavior problems and programs*. New York: Knopf.

Van Oorsouw, K., and Merckelbach, H. (in press). Feigning amnesia undermines memory for a mock crime. *Applied Cognitive Psychology*.

Van Oorsouw, K., Merckelbach, H., Ravelli, D., Nijman, H., and Pompen, I. (in press). Alcohol black-out voor een delict: bestaat dat? [Alcohol black-out for crime: Does it exist?]. *De Psycholoog*.

Wegner, D. M., Quillian, F., and Houston, C. E. (1996). Memories out of order: Thought suppression and the disturbance of sequence memory. *Journal of Personality and Social Psychology*, 71, 680–91.

Wolf, A. S. (1980). Homicide and blackout in Alaskan natives. *Journal of Studies on Alcohol*, 41, 456–62.

Woodworth, M., and Porter, S. (2001). Historical and current conceptualizations of criminal profiling in violent crime investigations. *Expert Evidence*, 7, 241–64.

Yehuda, R., Elkin, A., Binder-Brynes, K., Kahana, B., Southwick, S. M., Schmeidler, J., and Giller, E. L. (1996). Dissociation in aging Holocaust survivors. *American Journal of Psychiatry*, 153, 935–40.

Yeo, S. (2002). Clarifying automatism. *International Journal of Law and Psychiatry*, 25, 445–58.

Youngjohn, J. R., Burrows, L., and Erdal, K. (1995). Brain damage or compensation neurosis? The controversial post-concussion syndrome. *Clinical Neuropsychologist*, 9, 112–23.

NOTE

1. The Binomial formula is as follows: $z = [(x \pm .5) - Np)]/\sqrt{Npq}$, in which z is the test statistic (value and corresponding p can be looked up in a table), N is the number of items, x the number of correctly answered items, p the probability of a correct answer when one has to guess (ideally .5), and q is 1-p. For the example described in the text, the exact probability can be calculated as follows: $z = (3 + .5 - (15 \times .5)/\sqrt{(15 \times .5 \times .5)} = 2.1$, which corresponds to a *p*-value of ≤ 0.02.

Part 4

Enhancing lie-detection accuracy

10   Practitioners' beliefs about deception

Leif A. Strömwall, Pär Anders Granhag,
and Maria Hartwig

The aim of this chapter is to provide an overview of research on beliefs about deception – especially practitioners' beliefs. Specifically, we will outline which beliefs on deception professionals hold and compare these with what is known about actual (objective) differences between liars and truth-tellers. Then we will discuss how these beliefs have arisen, why they survive, how they spread, and to what they might lead. Finally, we will suggest how one might come to terms with misconceptions and false beliefs.

In the present chapter we define *belief* as a (strong or weak) feeling or conviction that something is true or real. The beliefs that a person holds, irrespective of whether these are correct or not, are often reflected in his or her behavioural disposition (Eichenbaum and Bodkin, 2000). Since beliefs often guide action, it is important to study people's beliefs about deception in order to learn more about why people fail and succeed in their endeavour to catch lies.

In the deception literature, there are an abundance of studies on deception detection accuracy. Many studies report low accuracy in human lie detection (Kraut, 1980; Vrij, 2000). The most commonly given reason for the low accuracy is that there is a mismatch between what actually is indicative of deception and what people *believe* is indicative of deception (Vrij, 2000).

Beliefs about deception

How does one find out people's beliefs about deception? The most straightforward approach is to just ask them to describe the cues they believe to occur more or less often when people are lying, compared to when they are telling the truth. These answers can be given on a series of rating scales (as in most survey studies). This method does not give the respondents the opportunity to provide their own beliefs; they are forced to respond to the researcher-defined items. Alternatively, the answers are responses to open-ended questions such as: 'Which verbal or non-verbal

Table 10.1 *The most common subjective non-verbal cues to deception (laypersons)*

• Liars are more gaze aversive	• Liars blink more often
• Liars shift position more often	• Liars have a higher-pitched voice
• Liars make more illustrators	• Liars make more speech disturbances
• Liars make more self-manipulations	• Liars have a slower speech rate
• Liars make more arm/hand movements	• Liars have a longer latency period
• Liars make more leg/feet movements	• Liars take more and longer pauses

cues do you think are indicative of deception? Which verbal or non-verbal cues do you use to decide whether someone is lying or not?'

Another way to gain insight into beliefs about deception is to ask people to judge the veracity of videotaped interviews, and then ask them to justify their judgements. The downside of this method is that people may not be aware of the reasons for their judgements (Nisbett and Wilson, 1977), and hence may provide cues in line with stereotypical notions.

A third alternative is for the researcher to code the non-verbal and/or verbal behaviour of the liars and truth-tellers, and correlate these scores with the veracity judgements to see which cues to deception observers used (see Anderson, DePaulo, Ansfield, Tickle, and Green, 1999, and Vrij, 2000).

Lay people's beliefs

Beliefs about non-verbal behaviour   Research on subjective non-verbal indicators of deception has shown that people tend to associate lying with an increase in speech disturbances such as hesitations and speech errors, a slower speech rate, longer and more frequent pauses, more gaze aversion, and an increase in smiling and movements such as self-manipulations, hand/finger and leg/foot movements (Vrij, 2000). In Table 10.1 we present the most commonly expressed beliefs about liars' non-verbal behaviour. Generally, these subjective deception cues are indicators of nervousness. It seems as if people believe that a liar will feel nervous and act accordingly; however, not all liars feel nervous or act nervously (Köhnken, 1989; in Vrij and Semin, 1996). In other words, since people tend to believe that liars are more nervous than truth-tellers, they infer deception from signs of nervousness. The most commonly and strongly expressed cue to deception is a decrease in eye contact, also called gaze aversion.

Table 10.2 *The most common subjective verbal cues to deception (laypersons)*

• Lies seem less plausible	• Lies are less detailed
• Lies are less consistent	• Lies are shorter
• Liars give more indirect answers	• Lies contain more negative statements
• Lies make fewer self-references	• Lies contain more irrelevant information

The beliefs presented in Table 10.1 are clear and unanimous; Zuckerman, DePaulo, and Rosenthal (1981) and Vrij (2000) have presented reviews of a multitude of studies, with very clear-cut overall results. What emanates from the studies of beliefs about deception is a set of stereotypical beliefs; these cues are preferred over people's idiosyncratic behaviour.

According to Anderson et al. (1999), when people are asked to describe the cues they think are indicative of deceit, they do little more than recount the accepted cultural wisdom about such matters. Even with experience of a friend's idiosyncratic non-verbal behaviour (i.e., when the beliefs were not confined to the quite uncommon setting of judging the veracity of someone you have never met before being interviewed in a research laboratory), the participants in that study did not change their initially stated stereotypical beliefs.

Beliefs about verbal content Turning to the beliefs about verbal content and behaviour, we first of all notice that research is quite scarce, at least compared with the abundance of studies of non-verbal behaviour. Zuckerman, DePaulo and Rosenthal (1981), and Vrij (2000) review the existing literature and conclude that people believe that, for example, short statements, indirect responses, and implausible-sounding answers are indicative of deception. Table 10.2 contains these and other expressed beliefs about verbal deception.

The validity of the beliefs The purpose of this section is not to provide an overview of the huge literature on actual indicators of deception. We refer the reader to DePaulo and Morris (this volume), DePaulo, Lindsay, Malone, Muhlenbruck, Charlton, and Cooper (2003), and Vrij (2000), for such reviews and meta-analyses. In Table 10.3, the most reliable non-verbal indicators of deception are given – and there are not many of them. Almost all of the non-verbal beliefs do not find support in the literature on actual indicators of deception and truth. For example, the most commonly expressed belief – liars are more gaze aversive – does not fit with reality.

Table 10.3 *The most reliable objective non-verbal cues to deception*

• Liars speak in a higher pitch	• Liars take longer pauses
• Liars make fewer movements with arms/hands/fingers	• Liars make fewer movements with legs/feet
• Liars make fewer illustrators	

Table 10.4 *The most reliable objective verbal cues to deception*

• Liars' answers are less plausible and convincing	• Liars tell the story more chronologically correct
• Liars' stories contain fewer details	• Lies contain more negative statements
• Liars give more indirect answers	• Lies contain less temporal information
• Liars provide shorter answers	• Lies contain less spatial information
• Liars make fewer self-references	• Lies contain less perceptual information

Above we noted that it seems as if people believe that a liar is nervous, and has a very hard time controlling this inner state, resulting in, for example, increases in different bodily movements. Many of the beliefs concern behaviours that do not reliably discriminate between the truthful and deceptive, such as gaze aversion and self-manipulations. For other expressed beliefs, the opposite of the expected pattern has been found in studies on actual behaviour. In this category, behaviours such as illustrators, hand/arm, and leg/feet movements are found. Liars actually make fewer of these movements than truth-tellers.

In Table 10.4, the most reliable verbal content differences are given. In contrast to the non-verbal behaviours, people's beliefs about verbal content are more in tune with what research on actual differences has shown (DePaulo et al, 2003; Vrij, 2000).

The reliable indicators of truth and deception, that is those cues to deception that actually work, are to a large extent consequences of deceivers' strategies. Those lying avoid presenting themselves in the manner of the stereotypical liar (hence they make fewer illustrators and body movements) and do not want to give away information they later may have a hard time remembering (hence shorter, less-detailed answers). Other typical findings are that those lying are perceived as less personal and forthcoming in that they make fewer self-references, provide less plausible and convincing answers, and give a more negative impression (DePaulo et al., 2003; Vrij, 2000). Furthermore, there is evidence that the memory reports of liars are different from those of truth-tellers, hence the differences in amount of perceptual, temporal, and spatial information,

Table 10.5 *The most common subjective beliefs as expressed by practitioners*

• Liars are more gaze aversive	• Liars fidget more
• Liars make more self-manipulations	• Liars shift position more
• Liars make more head movements/nods	• Liars make more body movements in
• Liars' speech is less fluent	general
• Liars make more arm/hand movements	• Lies are less consistent
• Liars make more leg/feet movements	• Liars' stories are less plausible
	• Lies contain fewer details

which fits well with the Reality Monitoring framework (see Sporer, this volume, for a review of Reality Monitoring as a deception detection tool).

Across non-verbal and verbal behaviour, research has found only weak support for the correctness of lay people's beliefs about deception. When analysing the relation between people's beliefs and objective cues to deception, Zuckerman, Koestner, and Driver (1981) found an average correlation of only .11. Despite much research activity in the area since that time, there is no reason to believe that the relationship should be any stronger. People's beliefs about deception cues simply are not very realistic.

Practitioners' beliefs

In line with commonsense ideas, it could be argued that certain categories of people, such as professional lie detectors (e.g., working in the legal field), describe different cues to deception from laypersons, and that these cues correspond more closely with the reliable and valid cues that exist. The laypersons that the research reviewed so far is based on are generally college students, without any special experience or interest in the subject. Certain groups of professionals are faced with the problem of deciding whether someone is lying or not every day. In this chapter we refer to them as practitioners. It sounds plausible that this everyday experience, coupled with these practitioners' education and, probably, special interest in these issues, could affect their beliefs about cues to deception. A few studies, mostly surveys, have examined this issue. Table 10.5 summarises the beliefs stated by the various groups of practitioners examined.

Akehurst, Köhnken, Vrij, and Bull (1996) examined beliefs about both non-verbal and verbal cues to deception of a United Kingdom sample of police officers, and compared their beliefs with those of laypersons (not students). Akehurst and her colleagues found no differences in beliefs between lay people and police officers.

In the Netherlands, Vrij and Semin (1996), examining beliefs about non-verbal behaviour only, compared professional lie-catchers (police officers, customs officers, prison guards, and patrol police officers) with students and prisoners. The beliefs of the professional lie-catchers and the students were very similar to each other. The prisoners expressed different beliefs, which we will discuss later in this chapter.

In Sweden, Strömwall and Granhag (2003), examining beliefs about verbal and non-verbal cues to deception as well as the effect of some situational factors, compared the beliefs of police officers, prosecutors, and judges. Some differences between the practitioner groups were found, including police officers believing more strongly in the value of relying on non-verbal cues rather than verbal cues. For example, the police officers were convinced of liars being more gaze aversive and making more body movements than truth-tellers to an even greater extent than were the prosecutors and judges.

Granhag, Strömwall, and Hartwig (in press) investigated the beliefs about verbal and non-verbal cues to deception and cross-cultural aspects of deception, as expressed by Migration Board officers handling asylum cases, and compared them with lay people's beliefs. Overall, this particular kind of practitioners did not differ in their beliefs from lay people. A notable exception was that the Migration Board officers believed verbal cues to be much more reliable than the lay people did.

In Spain, Masip and Garrido (2001) collected data from police officers and police students on their beliefs about deception. In general, the two samples expressed the same beliefs, although the experienced police officers' beliefs were more pronounced (e.g., an even stronger belief in increased leg movement frequency as a lie indicator for the experienced officers).

Greuel (1992) examined the beliefs of German police officers with special focus on rape cases. Inconsistency of statements and lack of plausibility were mentioned by a majority of the officers as lie indicators. However, Greuel also analysed actual police interviews and found that they did not use these verbal cues very often; instead, they reported relying on (their own stereotypical reading of) the victim's behaviour when assessing credibility in a particular case.

Kraut and Poe (1980) compared customs officers' (predominantly non-verbal) beliefs with those of laypersons and found no significant differences.

Furthermore, there are studies of beliefs about cues to deception and perceived deception cues in more experimental settings. Vrij (2000) reviewed a number of studies looking at practitioners' accuracy in detecting deception. The practitioners examined were federal law-enforcement personnel, Secret Service agents, federal polygraphers, and, mostly, police officers and detectives. The overall accuracy in these studies was not very impressive (54 per cent correct judgements), and it appears that these groups of practitioners do not subscribe to any set of beliefs that makes them better deception detectors than the average layperson.

Vrij (1993) examined the accuracy and perceived cues to deception of police detectives. The police officers were very similar in their veracity judgements (which were correct about half of the time) as well as in their perceived cues. They were affected by the level of comfort in the situation of the senders, whether the senders were untidily dressed, and by a number of non-verbal behaviours such as smiles and hand movements. Not one of the indicators the police officers had used to make their final veracity judgements was a reliable lie indicator.

In the perhaps most ecologically valid study of police officers' beliefs (and their deception detection accuracy), Mann, Vrij, and Bull (2004) showed British police officers fragments of real-life police interviews with suspects. A majority of the police officers claimed that searching for a decrease in eye contact is useful in detecting deception. Those police officers who were more correct used this cue to a lesser extent, and furthermore used more verbal content cues ('story cues') than those who performed less well. The authors suggested that police officers rely upon cues that are general rather than idiosyncratic (Mann et al., 2004).

The practitioners have basically the same beliefs as laypersons (cf Tables 10.1 and 10.2): In general these beliefs are incorrect, especially the beliefs concerning non-verbal behaviour. Just like laypersons, the presumed experts consider nervous behaviours to indicate deception (Vrij, 2000). The indicator that experts and lay people alike rely most upon is a decrease in eye contact when lying, which is not a reliable predictor (DePaulo et al., 2003).

The small differences in signs of nervousness between liars and truth-tellers might be explained by liars not being nervous enough (Miller and Stiff, 1993; Vrij and Taylor, 2003) or that high-stake situations increase the pressure on both liars and truth-tellers (Strömwall, Hartwig, and Granhag, 2004). When more is at stake, in theory, the liars should be easier to identify. Taylor and Vrij (2001) found that the cues people (both police officers and students) associate with deception are those that typically occur in high-stake situations. It seems as if participants in deception studies (practitioners and laypersons), when stating their beliefs about how a liar behaves, visualise a highly motivated liar, and if the liars in the studies are not as nervous as in real-life high-stake situations, the beliefs expressed are bound to be wrong.

On a more positive note, it seems as if practitioners and laypersons have more accurate beliefs concerning the verbal content than the non-verbal behaviours (Mann, Vrij, and Bull, 2004; Masip and Garrido, 2001).

Origins and consequences of wrongful beliefs

About the origin of false beliefs

An important question is where the stereotypical beliefs of practitioners come from. Below, we will discuss a number of possible origins of these beliefs. First, we will examine the role of police interrogation manuals in the creation of stereotypical beliefs. Second, we will provide a brief overview of some cognitive mechanisms that help create and perpetuate wrongful beliefs. Finally, we will discuss the role of feedback in the perpetuation of wrongful beliefs.

Police interrogation manuals   In 1986, the book *Criminal interrogation and confessions* (Inbau, Reid, and Buckley, 1986) was published. It was based upon the two first authors' previous work and incorporated a number of practical guidelines on how to conduct interrogations with suspects. These methods, which were in part already in use, gained practice by police forces all over the world, and a number of interrogation manuals have been produced since, similar in content to the work by Inbau and colleagues (e.g., Gordon and Fleisher, 2002; Hess, 1997; MacDonald and Michaud, 1992; Rabon, 1992; Zulawski and Wicklander, 1993). A new and updated edition of the manual was published in 2001 (Inbau, Reid, Buckley, and Jayne, 2001).

In interrogation manuals such as the one by Inbau and colleagues, interrogators are often advised to rely on the suspect's non-verbal behaviour in order to detect deceit and assess the likelihood of guilt. For example, Inbau and colleagues suggest the following: 'During an interview the investigator should closely evaluate the suspect's behavioral responses to interview questions. The suspect's posture, eye contact, facial expression, and word choice, as well as response delivery may each reveal signs of truthfulness or deception' (2001, p. 1). This assumption is invalid for two reasons. First, people in general are not skilled in distinguishing between truthful and deceptive behaviour (Vrij, 2000). In studies examining human lie detection ability, accuracy rates above 57 per cent are rarely achieved, which is not an impressive performance level, since an accuracy rate of 50 per cent is expected by chance alone (Vrij, this volume). According to commonsense notions, professional lie detectors such as police officers ought to outperform lay people in terms of lie-detection accuracy, due to their more extended experience of making these judgements. However, research has shown that this commonsense expectation is faulty; the accuracy levels obtained by these presumed lie experts are similar to those obtained by college students (Ekman and O'Sullivan, 1991; Ekman, O'Sullivan, and Frank, 1999; Köhnken, 1987; Vrij, 1993; Vrij and Graham, 1997; Vrij and Mann, 2001a; Vrij and Mann, 2001b).

Second, the manuals recommend relying on non-verbal and verbal cues that research has not identified as valid cues to deception (Vrij, 2000; Vrij, 2003). As for non-verbal behaviour, Inbau and colleagues mention posture shifts, grooming gestures, and placing hand over mouth as cues to deception. Zulawski and Wicklander (1993) claim that liars' movements are jerky, abrupt, and swift, and that their hands are cold and clammy. They also state that liars are gaze aversive, that they stutter and mumble, and that liars fidget and scratch themselves. Gordon and Fleisher (2002) are even more specific and claim that women and gay males who experience an increase in tension often put their hands to their throats, gently touching it with their fingers, while heterosexual men tend to finger the collar of their shirts. It is interesting to note that there are both similarities and differences in the cues that these manuals mention. For example, several of them (Inbau et al., 2001; Gordon and Fleisher, 2002; Zulawski and Wicklander, 1993) state that liars exhibit a large number of self-manipulations. Crossed arms are also considered a sign of defensiveness and deception (Gordon and Fleisher, 2002; Zulawski and Wicklander, 1993). The feet and leg are said to provide valuable cues to deception; however, Gordon and Fleisher (2002) claim that the guilty person often extends his or her feet towards the interrogator to create a physical distance between them, while Zulawski and Wicklander (1993) state that legs suddenly pulled under the chair may indicate deception.

Concerning verbal behaviour, the manuals claim that liars are less talkative, use mild and evasive terms, and try to distance themselves from the crime, while truth-tellers will admit that they had the opportunity to commit the crime (Gordon and Fleisher, 2002). Moreover, liars are said to offer qualified and well-rehearsed responses (Inbau et al., 2001). Liars are also vague and stammering in their responses, they often voice complaints and can be excessively polite towards the interrogator (Zulawski and Wicklander, 1993).

There is simply no empirical support for the claims made in these manuals; instead, research suggests that the cues reported in the manuals reflect common misconceptions about the link between demeanour and deception (Akehurst et al., 1996; Strömwall and Granhag, 2003; Vrij and Semin, 1996).

Not only are stereotypical beliefs provided in police interrogation manuals; it has also been argued that the learning process within the police culture is characterised by transference of sets of beliefs from the older generation to the younger (Ainsworth, 1995). In other words, through this inter-individual inheritance, stereotypical beliefs can survive within the police culture. (For cultural inspired theories and discussions on why certain beliefs survive and spread, while others do not, see Fraser and Gaskell (1990).)

Creation and perpetuation of wrongful beliefs from a psychological perspective

Psychological research has attempted to examine the formation and maintenance of wrongful beliefs (Cooper, Kelly, and Weaver, 2004), and the findings resulting from this research are highly relevant for the area of deception. Research has shown that people have a tendency to create beliefs about and explanations for ambiguous events. This tendency to create order and predictability has evolved in order to facilitate perception and processing of the environment (Gilovich, 1991). For example, the observations of Charles Darwin, and his ability to spot patterns in the distribution of species of birds in the Galapagos made him start thinking about evolution and natural selection. However, when over-applied, this tendency can cause people to create wrongful or simplified beliefs concerning random or very complex events. For example, some people believe in the so called 'hot hand' in basketball, meaning that a successful shot is likely to lead to another successful one, while a miss is likely to be followed by other misses. The explanation for this belief, which research has proven to be faulty, is partly that people do not know what random sequences look like (Gilovich, Vallone, and Tversky, 1985). Thus, people will seek an explanation and try to find a pattern in the sequences of hits and misses that are seemingly too ordered to be random, and hence the belief in the 'hot hand' has been created. The same processes are relevant for people's beliefs about deceptive behaviour, and below we will give a brief overview of some of the characteristics of human reasoning. These intra-individual processes can cause wrongful and stereotypical beliefs about cues to deception to be created and cemented.

The representativeness heuristic   This heuristic is a rule of thumb used for making judgements that assume that a given sample is representative of the larger population from which it is drawn (Nevid, 2003;

Tversky and Kahneman, 2002). This can be transferred into the context of deception; and can then explain, for example, why people believe that liars are gaze aversive, and that they fidget and stutter (Vrij, 2000). Since people tend to believe that liars are more nervous than truth-tellers, they infer deception from signs of nervousness. Without doubt, some liars are nervous, but it is the over-application of this notion that presents a problem. Far from all liars feel and act nervously, and many truth-tellers may also feel nervous when being suspected of trying to deceive.

Confirmation bias   When trying to assess whether a certain belief is correct, people have a tendency to seek confirming rather than disconfirming information, a tendency called confirmation bias. In one study (Snyder and Cantor, 1979), people were asked to read a story about a woman who acted in a number of typically extroverted and introverted ways. Later, these people were asked to judge the suitability of the woman for a job. Half of the participants were asked to assess her suitability for a job demanding a certain degree of extroversion (real estate sales) and half to judge her suitability for a more introversion-oriented job (librarian). The participants were then asked to recollect examples of her extroversion and introversion. Interestingly, the participants who were asked to deem the woman's suitability for an extroverted job reported more examples of her extroversion than of her introversion, while the opposite was true for those who deemed her suitability for an introverted job (Snyder and Cantor, 1979). In parallel, if people are asked the question of why they hold the belief that liars are gaze aversive, it is likely that they search their memory for instances where they indeed have encountered a gaze-aversive person who turned out to be lying. Seldom would people instead try to think of instances that would disconfirm their belief, such as when they have met a liar who looked them in the eyes. This tendency will then help uphold the belief that liars are gaze aversive.

Not only do people have a tendency to recall evidence confirming their beliefs, people also have a biased evaluation of new information (Lord, Ross, and Lepper, 1979). In other words, people tend to see what they expect to see, while discounting information that contradicts their preconceptions. In one study (Gilovich, 1991), proponents and opponents of the death penalty read summaries of two studies examining the effectiveness of capital punishment. One of the studies indicated that the death penalty had a deterring effect, while one indicated that there was no such effect. It was found that people's evaluation of the two studies differed depending on their initial position. The study that was in line with their prior opinion was deemed to be a solid and reliable piece of work, while the study opposing their view was considered flawed and associated with numerous problems. People's opinions were even polarised by reading these studies: both proponents and opponents became more convinced of the correctness of their beliefs after reading this mixed body of evidence (Gilovich, 1991). In a deception context, the same tendency may well cause people to discount evidence that their beliefs about liars' behaviour may be wrongful while attending to confirmatory information.

The 'feedback hypothesis'   One explanation that has been proposed to account for the stereotypical beliefs and poor deception detection performance of presumed lie experts is that outcome feedback on their veracity judgements is rarely available. The notion of the importance of feedback on veracity judgements (henceforth referred to as the 'feedback hypothesis') suggests that mere experience of judging veracity is not enough for changing stereotypical beliefs about deception, let alone for improving lie-detection accuracy (DePaulo and Pfeifer, 1986; Ekman and O'Sullivan, 1991; Granhag, Andersson, Strömwall, and Hartwig, 2004; Vrij, 2000; Vrij and Semin, 1996). DePaulo, Stone and Lassiter (1985; in DePaulo and Pfeifer, 1986) suggested that feedback often is inadequate and unsystematic in occupations where lie detection is a central task. One example of such an occupational group is customs officers, who do not always find out whether their decisions are correct. From travellers whom they decide not to search, they get no feedback at all. Einhorn (1982) has stressed the importance of feedback on learning from experience but points out that positive feedback actually can hamper the learning of valid decision-making rules by undermining people's motivation to investigate exactly how the success was achieved. If a customs officer finds out that the traveller he decided to search indeed did smuggle goods, he may regard this as a validation of his theories about the relation between verbal and non-verbal behaviour and deception. In fact, it might be the case that he relied on the wrong cues but managed to catch a smuggler by pure coincidence. He may also have relied on cues without any conscious awareness. In cases like this, erroneous beliefs can be cemented rather than corrected through experience. For feedback to be helpful in developing accurate decision-making rules, it thus has to be frequent and reliable, and preferably immediate (Allwood and Granhag, 1999; Einhorn, 1982). We will return to the feedback issue later.

Consequences of wrongful beliefs

The consequences of wrongful beliefs about cues to deception can be serious. Researchers agree that wrongful convictions do occur, and that they pose a threat to legal systems (Gudjonsson, 2003; Victory, 2002; Wagenaar, van Koppen, and Crombag, 1993; Walker and Starmer, 1999). Although it is impossible to estimate how frequently it happens, misconceptions about deceptive behaviour may be one of the starting points for such wrongful convictions. For example, misinterpretation of a suspect's nervous behaviour as a cue to deception during an interrogation may convince the police that the suspect has committed the crime. Such an assumption can lead to a suspect-driven investigation (Wagenaar, van Koppen, and Crombag, 1993), where the police become increasingly convinced of the guilt of the suspect and blind to the possibility that other people may have committed the crime. Such an investigation may be the starting point for a process that ultimately can lead to the conviction of an innocent person.

At least two studies have pointed to the deteriorating effect of following the Inbau and Reid technique in the process of assessing veracity. In an experimental study, Kassin and Fong (1999) trained students in using the technique outlined by Inbau and his associates. The deception detection performance of the trained group was compared against the performance of an untrained group. The important finding was that the untrained group outperformed the trained group in terms of lie detection accuracy. In line with these results, Mann, Vrij, and Bull (2004) found, using a sample of real police interviews, that the more the officers endorsed the views recommended by Inbau et al. (2001), the worse their lie detection accuracy was.

Intuition and a look ahead

So far we have shown that not only lay people, but also presumed lie-catching experts, hold stereotypical beliefs about deceptive behaviour. Furthermore, we have speculated on possible sources of these misconceptions, why false beliefs survive, how they might spread and to where they might lead. This section contains a discussion on two possible ways to come to terms with the problem of misconceptions about deceptive behaviour. First, we will turn our attention to the question of whether it is possible to educate one's intuition, and in the next instance, to correct wrongful beliefs. Second, we will highlight the fact that the research on deception conducted to this date has almost exclusively employed designs which have confined the lie-catchers to belief-driven decision processes. We will discuss to what extent designs that enforce belief-driven processes – and that deprive the lie-catcher of knowledge-driven processes – can be trusted in order to measure experts' lie detection performance.

To educate one's intuition and correct wrongful beliefs

Hogarth (2001) presents a thought-provoking theoretical framework for intuition, including principles for how one's intuition can be educated. Importantly, human intuition is not viewed as something mystical or esoteric, instead it is seen as a part of our normal information processing system. According to Hogarth, the core of intuitive judgements is that they are reached with little apparent effort, without conscious awareness, and that they involve little or no conscious deliberation (see also DePaulo and Morris, this volume).

Critically, Hogarth views intuition as a result of experience. But how then can it be explained that experienced police officers, judges, customs officers, together with others who assess veracity on a daily basis hold wrongful beliefs about deceptive behaviour? Why is it that their experience has not taught them the right lessons? To answer this question, Hogarth (2001) introduced the term of *learning structures*, and below we will apply this concept in order to try to increase our understanding of why professionals hold wrongful beliefs about deceptive behaviour, and what might be done to correct these false beliefs.

Hogarth uses the concept of learning structures to explain how different elements in the environment affect the validity of intuition, and he makes a distinction between 'kind' and 'wicked' learning structures. In essence, kind learning structures allow people to learn the right lessons from experience, while wicked learning structures do not. Hence, in environments characterised by kind learning structures, intuitive judgements will be reliable. As discussed above, feedback has been stressed as an important component in learning from experience (Allwood and Granhag, 1999; Einhorn, 1982). However, Hogarth expands on this idea, and proposes a two-dimensional model that can help explain when we learn the valid lesson from experience, and when we do not. The two dimensions are (a) quality of feedback and (b) consequences of faulty judgements. It is easier to learn from experience when feedback is clear. When feedback is ambiguous, it is difficult to challenge one's beliefs or improve one's decision rules since it is unclear whether one has made a correct judgement. Moreover, when the consequences of mistakes are serious (i.e., when the environment is exacting) and it is necessary to make correct judgements, intuition needs to be developed. An example of an environment in which feedback is both clear and exacting is the one of brain surgeons. Their judgements need to be correct, because the consequences of faulty judgements are very serious. Moreover, errors have often obvious consequences, thus clear feedback is provided.

If the idea put forth above is placed in a deception detection context, it is clear that the environment of, for example, police officers lacks certain important features in order for it to be a kind learning structure. Critically, it is far from easy for the police officer to find out whether he has made a correct or incorrect veracity judgement of a suspect. However, and as outlined above, the consequences of wrongful decisions can be serious. Wicked learning structures and high demands on accuracy are also true for decisions made by, for example, judges, customs officers, and migration board officers. In sum, Hogarth proposes that in order to educate one's intuition, the ability to learn from experience is the key factor. If the learning structure is kind, the feedback received is accurate and valid learning can occur. If the learning structure is wicked, the feedback received is misleading, and learning may be invalid.

In terms of deception detection, is there any group of people that live in an environment characterised by kind learning structures, and whose experience may have equipped them with more proper intuition? One such group may be experienced criminals. Speculatively, criminals live in a more deceptive environment than most other people, something that may make them aware of the deceptive strategies that work. For example, being repeatedly interrogated by the police and thus receiving feedback on deception success and failure might increase one's knowledge about which deceptive strategies are useful in convincing others. In addition, and importantly, survival in a deceptive culture is also dependent on a general alertness not to be deceived by others.

The idea that criminals might have more accurate beliefs about deception was first tested in a study by Vrij and Semin (1996). Indeed, the results from this study showed that prison inmates had a better notion about the relationship between non-verbal behaviour and deception compared to other presumed lie experts (customs officers, police detectives, patrol police officers, and prison guards). This finding was further supported by a study by Granhag et al. (2004) who found that criminals' beliefs on verbal as well as non-verbal cues to deception were less stereotypical compared to the ones held by prison personnel and students.

Further support for the idea that feedback is of importance to achieve a certain degree of expertise in the deception area, is that criminals have been shown to detect lies significantly more accurately than chance (Hartwig, Granhag, Strömwall, and Andersson, 2004), and on demand, and with little or no time for preparation, produce very convincing false confessions (Norwick, Kassin, Meissner, and Malpass, 2002). Also, Bugental, Shennum, Frank, and Ekman (cited in Ekman, 2001) showed that abused children living in an institutional environment were better at detecting lies from demeanour than were other children. In sum, these studies indicate that living in an environment that demands high alertness against betrayal and deceit can improve one's knowledge about cues to deception. In short, these findings support Hogarth's notion on the importance of learning structures.

Is it possible to correct wrongful beliefs? And if so, how should one go about doing this? First, we believe it is fair to say that the different attempts made to train observers in order to improve their deception detection ability have so far shown some, but rather limited, success (Bull, this volume). In the studies showing an improvement, it is usually small (Frank and Feeley, 2003).

It has been found that both students' (DeTurck, Harszlak, Bodhorn, and Texter, 1990) and parole officers' (Porter, Woodworth, and Birt, 2000) deception detection performance improved after receiving outcome feedback. However, we are somewhat sceptical of whether this increased ability to detect deception (achieved after relatively few instances of feedback) will generalise to types of lies and situations other than those studied, and of whether such brief training will generate any positive long-terms effects. Instead, our contention is that people's beliefs about cues to deception are rather resistant to correction, and we believe that changing such beliefs in order to improve people's ability to detect deception may be a very slow and complex process. In short, we do not believe that there is a simple antidote against false beliefs about deceptive behaviour. However, we do have some advice to offer.

We believe that it is possible to build in elements of feedback into the legal system. For example, one could make sure that developments in later stages of the legal process (in terms of, for example, evidence, confessions, etc.) are systematically fed back to those who handled the case in the initial stages; in other words to construct loops of feedback. Moreover, systematically scrutinising one's own judgements after such feedback, and the beliefs upon which one based one's veracity judgement, may be one fruitful way to question stereotypical and wrongful beliefs. For most professionals it is possible to actively seek situations that offer information that might challenge (or support) previous beliefs about how liars and truth-tellers behave. For example, in cases where ground truth is known, police officers could profit from analysing videotaped interrogations, viewing both liars' and truth-tellers' behaviour. Furthermore, a customs officer with whom we collaborate told us that he for many years made sure to get notification as soon as customs were tipped off that a certain person on a certain flight was about to try to smuggle goods into Sweden (in the absolute majority of cases this often anonymous information turned out to be correct). As often as possible he watched how the smuggler acted, and he had a particular interest in those situations where it was decided that the smuggler should be allowed to pass customs without visitation, only to be followed and arrested at his or her final destination. In short, the customs officer used these situations to observe how real smugglers behaved in crowds. In support of this line of reasoning, O'Sullivan and Ekman (this volume) show that real lie experts (people with an ability to make correct judgements the vast majority of times they assess veracity) have high levels of motivation to improve their ability and seek feedback about their performance. Finally, in line with Hogarth (2001) we recommend that programmes designed to train people to be better at detecting deception should, in addition to myth dissolution and awareness training, explicitly target people's skill of imagination and observation.

To detect deception: belief- vs. knowledge-driven processes

To make a clear distinction between belief and knowledge is a far from easy task. However, for the present context it suffices to say that although both belief and knowledge often are products of experience, *belief* is a disposition to behave in a manner that is rather resistant to correction by experience, whereas *knowledge* is a disposition to behave in a manner that is more open to corrective modification and updating by experience (Eichenbaum and Bodkin, 2000).

Translated into the context of deception detection, a lie-catcher who is asked to assess veracity solely on the basis of a video clip of a suspect must resort to a belief-driven decision process. That is, in order to assess veracity he or she is forced to match his or her beliefs on (often non-verbal) cues to deception against perceptions of the suspect's behaviour. In contrast, a lie-catcher who is given both case-specific evidence and background information about the suspect, and then is set free to interrogate the suspect in his or her own manner, can employ knowledge-driven decision processes. That is, he or she can plan and prepare different strategies, in terms of both the order in which the questions are asked, and how and when to disclose the evidence. Obviously, such strategies can be employed more or less effectively in order to detect deceit (for a recent study on this topic see Hartwig, Granhag, Strömwall, and Vrij, 2004).

Our point is not to argue that there exist pure belief-driven and pure knowledge-driven decision processes. In the context of deception detection, as well as in any other context, the processes at play are often mixed. For example, the point of time and the way in which a police officer chooses to disclose case-specific evidence to a suspect reflects the *beliefs* that the officer holds about how best to use the evidence. Instead our point is the following: the paradigmatic study in which people's ability to detect deception is examined does only to a very limited extent allow for knowledge-driven processes. We believe that this limits the generalisability of the deception research conducted so far. Furthermore, we believe it is reasonable to argue that this limitation has particular bearing on studies investigating presumed experts' deception detection performance. Most real-life police investigations, and other forensic investigations, generate case-specific facts (Wagenaar, van Koppen, and Crombag, 1993); these facts and evidence, if used properly, can be of paramount importance in the process of assessing the veracity of a suspect. Hence, placing a presumed lie-catching expert in an unfamiliar context (e.g., where he or she must resort to belief-driven strategies only) might hide structures with which the expert is actually quite familiar and deprive him or her of the opportunity to employ knowledge-driven processes (e.g., strategic disclosure of case-specific evidence).

Put differently, what the research conducted to this date tells us is that people (both lay-people and presumed experts) are mediocre at detecting lies in situations where they are forced to base their judgements on their beliefs about how liars and truth-tellers behave (i.e., when they are confined to the use of belief-driven decision processes). Interestingly, this is mirrored in the most commonly mentioned reason why people are poor at detecting deception: that there is a poor match between what people believe is indicative of deception (subjective cues) and actual (objective) cues to deception (Vrij, 2000). This research finding is important and should be acknowledged in those situations where there is no background information, nor case-specific evidence (Kassin, this volume), nor opportunity for the lie-catcher to ask questions (or when such information and opportunity exists but is used ineffectively). However, it might be a mistake to generalise the results obtained so far to situations where experienced professionals have access to case-specific information and hold knowledge about how to use this information properly while interrogating a suspect.

Summary

While our review of the literature on beliefs on deception has not been exhaustive, we believe that it is sufficient to make the following concluding remarks.

First, the available research paints a picture of presumed lie experts having stereotypical beliefs about deception and deceptive behaviour. Especially for the non-verbal behaviours did we find clear-cut results: practitioners have the same wrongful beliefs about deception as lay-persons. These beliefs are a part of our cultural mythology (Anderson et al., 1999; Bond and Rao, this volume).

Second, stereotypical beliefs can originate from, among other things, police interrogation manuals. The cues described in these manuals are spread and kept alive within the police culture, partly through the transference of beliefs from older generations to younger, a process that can be described as inter-individual. Moreover, these stereotypical beliefs can be perpetuated through a number of different intra-individual processes, for example via cognitive heuristics and biases.

Third, there is no simple cure for wrongful beliefs about deceptive behaviour. However, by actively seeking feedback that might challenge previous beliefs, professional lie-catchers might be able to educate their intuition and become better at detecting deceit.

Finally, we believe that future research would profit from investigating situations where the lie-catchers under examination are given access to information (e.g., case-specific evidence) that allows them to distance themselves from their wrongful beliefs; and which instead encourages them to employ knowledge-driven processes. It is a challenge for future research on deception to suggest and empirically test ways in which facts and evidence should be disclosed most effectively in order to detect deceit.

REFERENCES

Allwood, C. M., and Granhag, P. A. (1999). Feelings of confidence and the realism of confidence judgements in everyday life. In P. Juslin and H. Montgomery (eds.), *Judgement and decision making: Neo-Brunswikian and process-tracing approaches* (123–46). Mahwah, NJ: Lawrence Erlbaum.

Ainsworth, P. B. (1995). *Psychology and policing in a changing world*. Chichester: Wiley.

Akehurst, L., Köhnken, G., Vrij, A., and Bull, R. (1996). Laypersons' and police officers' beliefs regarding deceptive behaviour. *Applied Cognitive Psychology*, *10*, 461–71.

Anderson, D. E., DePaulo, B. M., Ansfield, M. E., Tickle, J. J., and Green, E. (1999). Beliefs about cues to deception: Mindless stereotypes or untapped wisdom? *Journal of Nonverbal Behavior*, *23*, 67–89.

Cooper, J., Kelly, K. A., and Weaver, K. (2004). Attitudes, norms, and social groups. In M. B. Brewer and M. Hewstone (eds.), *Social Cognition* (pp. 244–67). Oxford: Blackwell.

DePaulo, B. M., Lindsay, J. J., Malone, B. E., Muhlenbruck, L., Charlton, K., and Cooper, H. (2003). Cues to deception. *Psychological Bulletin*, *129*, 74–118.

DePaulo, B. M., and Pfeifer, R. L. (1986). On-the-job experience and skill at detecting deception. *Journal of Applied Social Psychology*, *16*, 249–67.

DeTurck, M., Harszlak, J., Bodhorn, D., and Texter, L. (1990). The effects of training social perceivers to detect deception from behavioural cues. *Communication Quarterly*, *38*, 189–99.

Eichenbaum, H., and Bodkin, J. A. (2000). Belief and knowledge as distinct forms of memory. In D. L. Schacter and E. Scaryy (eds). *Memory, brain, and belief* (pp. 176–207). Cambridge, MA: Harvard University Press.

Einhorn, H. J. (1982). Learning from experience and suboptimal rules in decision making. In D. Kahneman, P. Slovic, and A. Tversky (eds.), *Judgement under uncertainty: heuristics and biases* (pp. 268–83). Cambridge: Cambridge University Press.

Ekman, P. (2001). *Telling lies: Clues to deceit in the marketplace, politics and marriage.* New York: Norton.

Ekman, P., O'Sullivan, M. (1991). Who can catch a liar? *American Psychologist,* *46,* 913–20.

Ekman, P., and O'Sullivan, M., and Frank, M. G. (1999). A few can catch a liar. *Psychological Science, 10,* 263–6.

Frank, M. G., and Feeley, T. H. (2003). To catch a liar: Challenges for research in lie detection training. *Journal of Applied Communication Research, 31,* 58–75.

Fraser, C., and Gaskell, G. (1990). *The social psychological study of widespread beliefs.* Oxford. Clarendon Press.

Gilovich, T. (1991). *How we know what isn't so: The fallibility of human reason in everyday life.* New York: Free Press.

Gilovich, T., Vallone, R., and Tversky, A. (1985). The hot hand in basketball: On the misperception of random sequences. *Cognitive Psychology, 17,* 295–314.

Gordon, N. J., and Fleisher, W. L. (2002). *Effective interviewing and interrogation techniques.* London: Academic Press.

Granhag, P. A., Andersson, L. O., Strömwall, L. A., and Hartwig, M. (2004). Imprisoned knowledge: Criminals' beliefs about deception. *Legal and Criminological Psychology, 9,* 103–19.

Granhag, P. A., Strömwall, L. A., and Hartwig, M. (in press). Granting asylum or not? Migration Board personnel's beliefs on deception. *Journal of Ethnic and Migration Studies.*

Greuel, L. (1992). Police officers' beliefs about cues associated with deception in rape cases. In F. Lösel, D. Bender, and T. Bliesener (eds.), *Psychology and Law – International Perspectives* (pp. 234–9). Berlin: Walter de Gruyter.

Gudjonsson, G. H. (2003). *The psychology of interrogations and confessions: A handbook.* Chichester: Wiley.

Hartwig, M., Granhag, P. A., Strömwall, L. A., and Andersson. L. O. (2004). Suspicious minds: Criminals' ability to detect deception. *Psychology, Crime, and Law, 10,* 83–95.

Hartwig, M., Granhag, P. A., Strömwall, L. A., and Vrij, A. (2004). Deception detection via strategic disclosure of evidence. Manuscript submitted for publication.

Hess, J. E. (1997). *Interviewing and interrogation for law enforcement.* Cincinnati: Anderson Publishing.

Hogarth, R. M. (2001). *Educating intuition.* Chicago: University of Chicago Press.

Inbau, F. E., Reid, J. E., and Buckley, J. P. (1986). *Criminal interrogation and confessions.* Baltimore, MD: Williams and Wilkins.

Inbau, F. E., Reid, J. E., Buckley, J. P., and Jayne, B. C. (2001). *Criminal interrogation and confessions.* Gaithersburg: Aspen Publishers.

Kassin, S. M., and Fong, C. T. (1999). 'I'm innocent!': Effects of training on judgments of truth and deception in the interrogation room. *Law and Human Behaviour*, *23*, 499–516.

Köhnken, G. (1987). Training police officers to detect deceptive eyewitness statements. Does it work? *Social Behaviour*, *2*, 1–17.

Kraut, R. E. (1980). Humans as lie detectors. Some second thoughts. *Journal of Communication*, *30*, 209–16.

Kraut, R. E., and Poe, D. (1980). Behavioral roots of person perception: The deception judgements of customs inspectors and laymen. *Journal of Personality and Social Psychology*, *39*, 784–98.

Lord, C. G., Ross, L., and Lepper, M. R. (1979). Biased assimilation and attitude polarization: The effects of prior theories on subsequently considered evidence. *Journal of Personality and Social Psychology*, *37*, 2098–109.

Macdonald, J. M., and Michaud, D. L. (1992). *Criminal interrogation*. Denver: Apache Press.

Mann, S., Vrij, A., and Bull, R. (2004). Detecting true lies: Police officers' ability to detect suspects' lies. *Journal of Applied Psychology*, *89*, 137–49.

Masip, J., and Garrido, E. (2001, June). Experienced and novice officers' beliefs about indicators of deception. Paper presented at the 11th European Conference of Psychology and Law, Lisbon, Portugal.

Miller, G. R., and Stiff, J. B. (1993). *Deceptive communication*. Newbury Park, CA: Sage.

Nevid, J. S. (2003). *Psychology: Concepts and applications*. Boston: Houghton Mifflin.

Nisbett, R. E., and Wilson, T. D. (1977). Telling more than we can know: Verbal reports on mental processes. *Psychological Review*, *84*, 231–59.

Norwick, R. J., Kassin, S. M., Meissner, C. A., and Malpass, R. A. (2002, March). 'I'd know a false confession if I saw one': A comparative study of college students and police investigators. Paper presented at the Biennial Meeting of the American Psychology–Law Society in Austin, Texas.

Porter, S., Woodworth, M., and Birt, A. R. (2000). Truth, lies and videotapes: An investigation of the ability of federal parole officers to detect deception. *Law and Human Behavior*, *24*, 643–58.

Rabon, D. (1992). *Interviewing and interrogation*. Durham: Carolina Academic Press.

Snyder, M., and Cantor, N. (1979). Testing hypotheses about other people: The use of historical knowledge. *Journal of Experimental Social Psychology*, *15*, 330–42.

Strömwall, L. A., and Granhag, P. A. (2003). How to detect deception? Arresting the beliefs of police officers, prosecutors and judges. *Psychology, Crime, and Law*, *9*, 19–36.

Strömwall, L. A., Hartwig, M., and Granhag, P. A. (2004). To act truthfully: Nonverbal behavior during a police interview. Manuscript submitted for publication.

Taylor, R., and Vrij, A. (2001). The effects of varying stake and cognitive complexity on the beliefs about the cues to deception. *International Journal of Police Science and Management*, *3*, 111–23.

Tversky, A., and Kahneman, D. (2002). Extensional versus intuitive reasoning: The conjunction fallacy in probability judgements. In T. Gilovich, D. Griffin, and D. Kahneman (eds.), *Heuristics and biases: The psychology of intuitive judgement* (pp. 19–48). Cambridge: Cambridge University Press.

Victory, P. (2002). *Justice and truth: The Guildford Four and the Maguire Seven*. London: Sinclair-Stevenson.

Vrij, A. (1993). Credibility judgements of detectives: The impact of non-verbal behavior, social skills and physical characteristics on impression formation. *Journal of Social Psychology, 133,* 601–11.

(2000). *Detecting lies and deceit. The psychology of lying and the implications for professional practice.* Chichester: John Wiley.

(2003). We will protect your wife and child, but only if you confess. In P. J. van Koppen and S. D. Penrod (eds.), *Adversarial versus inquisitorial justice: Psychological perspectives on criminal justice systems* (pp. 55–79). New York, NJ: Kluwer Academic.

Vrij, A., and Graham, S. (1997). Individual differences between liars and the ability to detect lies. *Expert Evidence: The International Digest of Human Behaviour, Science and Law, 5,* 144–8.

Vrij, A., and Mann, S. (2001a). Telling and detecting lies in a high-stake situation: The case of a convicted murderer. *Applied Cognitive Psychology, 15,* 187–203.

Vrij, A., and Mann, S. (2001b). Who killed my relative? Police officers' ability to detect real-life high-stake lies. *Psychology, Crime, and Law, 7,* 119–32.

Vrij, A., and Semin, G. R. (1996). Lie experts' beliefs about nonverbal indicators of deception. *Journal of Nonverbal Behavior, 20,* 65–80.

Vrij, A., and Taylor, R. (2003). Police officers' and students' beliefs about telling and detecting trivial and serious lies. *International Journal of Police Science and Management, 5,* 1–9.

Wagenaar, W. A., van Koppen, P. J., and Crombag, H. F. M. (1993). *Anchored narratives. The psychology of criminal evidence.* New York: St Martin's Press.

Walker, C., and Starmer, K. (eds.). (1999). *Miscarriages of justice: A review of justice in error.* London: Blackstone Press.

Zuckerman, M., DePaulo, B. M., and Rosenthal, R. (1981). Verbal and nonverbal communication of deception. *Advances in Experimental Social Psychology, 14,* 1–59.

Zuckerman, M., Koestner, R., and Driver, R. (1981). Beliefs about cues associated with deception. *Journal of Nonverbal Behavior, 6,* 105–14.

Zulawski, D. E., and Wicklander, D. E. (1993). *Practical aspects of interview and interrogation.* Boca Raton: CRC Press.

11   Training to detect deception from behavioural cues: attempts and problems

Ray Bull

Fifteen years ago at the beginning of a book chapter on training to detect deception (Bull, 1989) I noted that:

An advertisement urging people to join a British police force recently appeared in a Sunday newspaper. Part of it stated that, 'Most people speak the truth most of the time. When they lie they experience stress and it usually shows'. Accompanying the words in the advertisement were a number of photographs of people. One of these showed a man touching the side of his nose with the index finger of his left hand. The caption for this stated that, 'The man with his finger to his nose is showing one of the signals associated with lying'. The advertisement continued by saying that, 'After training, you'll register the particular things a person does when conversing normally. When a change of topic brings about significant changes in their actions you'll notice that too'.

Another similar advertisement stated, 'If you're interviewing a suspect, how do you know if he's telling the truth? You'll be taught the rudiments of body language, gesticulation and body movements that indicate stress and nervousness'.

In closing that chapter I made the point that:

Until a number of publications in refereed journals appear demonstrating that training enhances the detection of deception, it seems that some police recruitment advertisements and police training books are deceiving their readers.

This chapter will focus on attempts to train groups of people to detect deception from non-verbal behaviour. It will not address training in Criteria-Based Content Analysis (CBCA) since this analysis of what has been said is usually done by relatively few experts. (However, we should note that attempting to train police and social workers in CBCA has been found problematical (Akehurst, 1997).)

The effects of training

Focusing on certain cues

One of the first studies specifically designed to examine the possible effects of training to detect deception was conducted just over twenty years ago by Druckman, Rozelle, and Baxter (1982) who suggested, with regard to non-verbal cues to deception, that training would seem to be in order. They informed trainees of the cues their research had found (by discriminant analysis) to be valid guides to deception (e.g., gaze time at interviewer, leg movements) in a prior experiment involving students as liars and as observers. In their training study an actor was asked to play the role of an honest, or deceptive, or evasive Soviet ambassador. The actor was instructed to vary his behaviour across the roles in line with the findings of their prior study. That is:

For the deceiver role, the actor fidgeted with his glasses, gazed away from the moderator occasionally, made several speech hesitations, and showed occasional rocking movements. The evasive enactment consisted of frequent leg and foot movements, looking around the room, occasional fidgeting with glasses, and head-shaking during the early part of the interview. For the honest enactment the actor looked at the interviewer frequently, showed occasional illustrators and head-shakes, and made few facial displays (smiles or frowns). (Druckman, Rozelle, and Baxter, 1982, p. 180)

Each of the three resulting videotapes was observed by members of workshops on communication for training officers from various government agencies who were asked to indicate for each interview whether the actor had been truthful, lying, or evasive. Before viewing the interviews the observers were given one of three training procedures:

1. Group 1 'were given an orientation lecture on non-verbal communication. Topics covered included the meaning of non-verbal behaviour (NVB), the relation between NVB and psychological states, ways in which NVB can be used to diagnose intentions, multiple-channel displays, leakage, types of deception, the distinction between encoding and decoding, and the advantages of a technical approach to the study of non-verbal behaviour. This lecture was introduced as an attempt to sensitise workshop members to the importance of NVB' (ibid., p. 182).
2. Group 2 'were given a technical briefing on experimental results. The briefing consisted of a graphic presentation of findings obtained in the prior experiment. Differences in condition frequencies of leg movements, object-fidgeting, gaze direction, looking around the room, and speech hesitations were illustrated. Discriminant analysis results were also presented' (*ibid.*).
3. Group 3 were asked to assess the truthfulness or otherwise of each of the three interviews solely by listening to what was said. They 'were given inference training prior to viewing the tapes. The procedure consisted of three parts. The first part entailed a briefing, with viewcharts, on key experimental results, including the comparison of

discriminant and expert predictions. Findings were then translated into signals and noise, the distinction turning on whether an NVB discriminated among the experimental conditions. Third, the procedure for inferring intentions from non-verbal displays was demonstrated' (ibid., p. 183).

The results demonstrated that group one achieved the chance performance level of 33 per cent. Group two achieved 52 per cent, and group three 77 per cent. However, group three's circumstances differed from the other two groups in that the effects of being instructed to listen to what was said seem to be confounded with training. However, in this group pre-training performance was assessed and found to be 50 per cent (i.e., above the 33 per cent chance level); so the within-participant effect of the training raised performance from 50 per cent to 77 per cent, which itself is confounded by a practice effect. Nevertheless, the results are interesting.

Few subsequent publications seem to mention this study, possibly because the design is far from neat.

In the same year as the Druckman et al. study was published De Paulo, Lassiter, and Stone (1982) asked students to attend to videotapes of people giving brief accounts of persons they liked/disliked. The students, who were attempting to detect truth/lies, were in one of four groups and were in each:

1. told to 'pay particular attention to how the speakers are saying what they have to say rather than to what they are saying or how they look when they are saying it;
2. told to attend (similarly to above) to how speakers look;
3. told to attend (similarly to above) to what the speakers are saying;
4. not given any attentional instructions.

A significant difference in accuracy was found between groups 1 and 4. While the deceptiveness rating scores varied little across groups for false accounts, it decreased for true accounts across groups 4, 3, 2, and 1. (The weakness of the effects De Paulo et al. ascribe to the small sample sizes of 11 'observers' per group.)

The next training study to be published focused on the effect of telling participants where to devote their attention (Köhnken, 1987). (In the intervening years a few studies of the effects of providing feedback on truth/lies decisions were published, but these will not be reviewed here – see Strömwall, Granhag, and Hartwig's chapter in this volume.) Köhnken's study examined the ability of police officers to discriminate between truthful and deceptive eyewitness statements. Unlike some previous studies, his videotapes contained statements concerning observed facts rather than private feelings or attitudes, and the samples of observed material were complete, fairly long statements rather than a small portion of a message.

Köhnken noted that it is important to assess the ecological validity of research in this area. In some previous studies the senders were instructed to describe truthfully and deceptively persons they like or dislike. He pointed out that in terms of assessing the credibility of witnesses, it is usually their factual statements rather than reports of their feelings which are the focus of enquiry. The making of deceptive factual statements may well be a more difficult task than lying about internal emotions since such statements have to fit in with a scenario, some aspects of which may already be known, say, to the police, whereas in the description of private feelings the observers may rarely know something about the senders' true feelings.

Köhnken suggested that detection accuracy in a study like his could be higher than the rather low rates commonly found in previous studies. In addition, he argued that, as observers, police officers could have considerable relevant on-the-job experience in assessing credibility. The rather low rates of accuracy found by previous studies among observers who were students need not be taken to suggest, as did DePaulo and Pfeifer (1986), that the skill profile of the human lie detector is not a very impressive one, if experience and/or training could enhance these skills. (Studies of 'professional' lie detectors are covered in the chapters by Strömwall et al., and by Vrij.)

In Köhnken's study psychology students were videorecorded giving an account of a film (theft or kidnap) that they had previously been shown. Some of these students were instructed to say what they had seen in the film as completely and accurately as possible (truth) and others were instructed in their account to change one specified important component of what had happened (lie). The observers were in one of four groups:

1. told to pay particular attention to the contents of the statements;
2. told to attend to the senders' speech behaviour;
3. instructed to devote their attention to the senders' non-verbal behaviour;
4. given no instructions regarding which cues they should use.

Each of groups 1, 2 and 3 was given relevant information including:

- group 1 the criteria from criteria-based content assessment;
- group 2 speech behaviours found in Köhnken's prior study to differ between truth/lies;
- group 3 aspects of non-verbal behaviour including e.g., foot movements, gaze, head movements, illustrators, body movements, adaptors, eyeblinks, illustrators.

The observers were not students but police officers of various lengths of service. They were drawn from police training courses and were told that the outcome of the study would be used to help develop a training package for police officers to detect deception. Each group received the same initial general information about witness testimony, accuracy, and credibility. The 'no particular cues' group (i.e., group 4) received no further information, whereas to each of the other three groups a further forty-five minutes were devoted to their instructions regarding where to devote their attention. All observers were presented firstly with a statement from a sender and were correctly informed that this was a truthful statement about a short film that the experimenter had shown to the sender. Next they saw the same sender making a statement (mean length just over four minutes) about a second film which may or may not have been truthful, and about which they were required to make a truthful/lying decision, and to rate their confidence in this decision. Each observer saw a total of four different senders.

The mean overall accuracy score was 45 per cent, which did not differ significantly from the chance level of 50 per cent. No effect of focus of observers' attention was found. That is, those not told to pay particular attention to certain cues did as well as the other three groups, who did not differ among themselves. Length of police service did not correlate positively with detection accuracy. However, the partial correlation of accuracy and length of police service (controlling for age) was significantly negative.

The mean of the confidence ratings was fairly high. More important was the finding that although overall there was not a significant correlation between confidence and accuracy, there was a significant negative correlation for the detection of deceptive statements between confidence and accuracy.

This was a pioneering study that sought to have higher ecological validity than previous studies. However, one reason why the performance in the lie detection was poor may have been that what much of the senders were saying was true – this is an important difference from many prior and subsequent studies. However, this is probably common in police interviews with suspects, especially some guilty ones, and in other aspects of life. Future research should demonstrate awareness of this point.

In 1990 deTurck, Harszlak, Bodhorn, and Texter said that 'It is disturbing . . . that researchers studying deception detection . . . have not studied whether social perceivers can be trained to use a social actor's behaviour (verbal and non-verbal cues) when judging his/her veracity' (p. 190). Their unawareness of the previous psychological research highlights a difficulty in research on deception which is that people from different disciplines (deTurck et al. were professors and students in departments of communication), who read different journals, can be unaware of findings outside their discipline.

They had noted Zuckerman, Koestner, and Alton's (1984) study of the effects of the provision of feedback but they pointed out that in that kind of study there are no aversive consequences for being detected and, as a result, it is likely that the liars in Zuckerman et al. did not experience deception-induced arousal.

In the deTurck et al. (1990) study some of the student observers received training involving practice plus feedback with regard to six cues identified in an earlier study by deTurck and Miller (1985) to be 'unique to deception induced arousal' (p. 191), these being

- adaptors
- hand gestures
- pauses
- response latency
- speech errors
- message duration.

The students' task was to detect deception in video recordings of senders being interviewed about whether they had cheated in a task. They were all first exposed to an interview of the person telling the truth before judging their second interview for truth/lie. A main effect of training was found. (However, the training did not improve females' detection of those half of the senders who themselves received training regarding the above cues.) Training also had an effect of reducing the students' over-confidence in their detections.

deTurck and Miller (1990) found that training very similar to that in deTurck et al. (1990) improved detection accuracy even for rehearsed liars, a group whose deception is especially difficult to detect. In addition, deTurck and Miller (1990) noted that the:

deception detection training also served to minimise the accuracy-certainty discrepancy in deception judgements which is an added bonus. It seems that training does not necessarily lead to overconfidence in social judgements. The pattern of accuracy–certainty judgements indicates that training seems to affect accuracy more than it does certainty. (p. 616)

Another important point made by deTurck and Miller is that when people are trying to detect deception they may become aroused themselves. Such arousal, they suggested, could result in observers narrowing their field of attention. This narrowing could result in more reliance on commonsense beliefs (which the literature has shown to be erroneous). deTurck and Miller also noted that: 'When observers are informed of the reliable indices of deception and provided with an opportunity to practice deception detection, they may experience less arousal when judging communicators' veracity. This may enhance their ability to focus on reliable cues' (p. 618).

This could be an important point, though Köhnken (1987) suggested that training could result in cognitive overload during the detection task.

In 1991 deTurck again reported a positive effect of training but noted that his research had not determined whether the observers used some or all the cues in their judgements or, we might add, any. In 1997 deTurck, Feeley, and Roman published data concerning observers reporting what cues they used during the experiment. To do so, their participants were given a checklist of eight training cues. DeTurck et al. noted that participants may have reported that they used the instructed cues in an effort to please the experimenter. Training was again reported to have a positive effect but only for those trained regarding both visual cues (adaptors, hand gestures, head movements, hand shaking) and vocal cues (speech errors, pauses, response latency, message duration), or visual cues alone. Those whose training involved only vocal cues performed no better than the control group.

deTurck et al. offered a number of possible reasons for the lack of a training effect for the vocal cues group. However, one explanation they seem not to have considered is, as they note in their introduction, 'Research on modality indicates that observers make more accurate veracity judgements using vocal cues' (p. 250). If the people in the untrained group already knew that the vocal cues assist, then their performance (which was 57 per cent, not the chance 50 per cent) might not be worse than the trained group who were told this.

An important point made by deTurck et al. is that trained observers may be put on their guard by the very subject of the experiment. If prior to the training a truth bias exists (i.e., believing most messages/accounts to be true) then participants may correctly classify most of the truthful accounts (usually 50 per cent of the sample) as true but mis-classify many of the deceptive accounts (the other 50 per cent of the sample) also as true. If training reduces the truth bias, could this raise the accuracy rate not by virtue of the particular contents of the training (which cues and so on) but merely by it making people more suspicious?

In their own study deTurck et al. noted that inspection of the pattern of lie and truth judgements does not lend itself to this explanation. Nevertheless, this general point may be very important regarding the training of professionals. If interviewers (e.g., the police in some countries) believe that the vast proportion of suspects they have chosen to interrogate are guilty, and if deception training does not reduce this proportion to whatever is the actual realistic proportion, then how large an effect can deception training have? Perhaps for deception training to have its greatest effect the interviewers really do need to have an open mind as to whether the suspect is guilty or not (Milne and Bull, 1999).

In 1993 another study was published on the effects of giving participants detailed instructions about valid non-verbal cues to deception. In this complex study Fiedler and Walka (1993) asked students to lie and tell the truth about everyday delinquency or sub-criminal behaviour of the kind that most people have occasionally shown and about their beliefs concerning topical issues (e.g., drug use). Other students saw video clips of the lies/truths. These observers were in one of three groups:

1. informed condition in which details were given of 'seven most frequent concomitants of lying' (p. 208) (drawn from the previous literature but also found in this study to discriminate),
2. same information as group 1 but also feedback given on each of the earlier clips as to whether the observers' own decision was correct or not,
3. control/uninformed.

Fiedler and Walka (1993) overall found better discrimination of true and feigned messages in the informed groups than in the uninformed group, but no extra effect of feedback. This information effect, however, just reached 'a conventional level of statistical significance'.

In the following year Horvath, Jayne, and Buckley (1994) reported a study in which evaluators trained in 'The Behaviour Analysis Interview' were able to detect truthfulness/deception at levels substantially above chance. However, since this study seems not to have employed a pre- versus post-training comparison nor a control group it will not be reviewed here. (Indeed, Horvath et al. concluded that research is necessary to determine the effects of such training.)

In 1994 Vrij noted that deTurck and Miller (1990) had suggested that instructing trainees to focus on six behavioural cues, which slightly improved their accuracy rate, may have resulted in processing overload. He therefore instructed his participants to focus only on the cue of hand and arm movements. He found that giving police detectives the following information (p. 124) significantly improved accuracy:

Research shows that deception is associated with a decrease in movements, especially subtle hand and finger movements. The explanation is that deceivers think that every single movement will give their lies away. Therefore, they think the safest strategy is not to make any movement at all, resulting in an inhibition and decrease in movements.

However, further analysis revealed that this was caused by the effect of such information only in the 'hands only' video condition in which only the senders' hands were visible and the sound was turned off. There was no effect of such information in the 'total image' condition. (Separate analysis confirmed a decrease in hand/finger movements in the lying condition.)

In 1999 Kassin and Fong attempted to train some introductory psychology students in the technique recommended in 1991 by John E. Reid and associates (see Kassin and Fong for more on this). Essentially, half the students were shown two Reid training videotapes that focus on (i) the verbal cues and (ii) the non-verbal cues that the Reid technique says characterise deception.

Both the trained and untrained groups of students were provided with videotapes of the five-minute interviewing/interrogation of eight other students who were denying involvement in a mock crime, half of whom were telling the truth. It was found that the *un*trained group outperformed the trained group in terms of deception detection accuracy.

One reason Kassin and Fong suggested for this finding was that the training materials focus attention on cues that have not been shown to be diagnostic in past research. They also discuss some limitations of their study, but not really the possibility that even training with appropriate content can prove counterproductive, or ineffective, if it is not delivered properly (see below).

Overview of cue training

The studies reviewed above seem, on the surface at least, to contradict each other in terms of cue training. While some found that this improved performance, others did not, perhaps because they failed to address the 'problems' to be mentioned below.

Parole officers

The year 2000 saw the publication of one of the most comprehensive studies of possible training effects. Porter, Woodworth, and Birt used as participants both Canadian federal parole officers and students. The parole officers had former experience of parole interviews with offenders that consider them for possible release from detention into the community. In such interviews, the honesty of reports offered by offenders concerning their current offence, degree of remorse, level of rehabilitation, and plans for life in the community are assessed. The parole officers had volunteered to participate in a workshop on the detection of deception.

The videorecordings used in this study were (unfortunately) not of real-life parole interviews but were from the research team's prior study in which students gave true or fabricated accounts of a variety of childhood experiences. To determine the parole officer's base-line ability, they assessed, prior to training, some of these recordings for truthfulness/lying and this produced a level of accuracy of close to 40 per cent, which was significantly below the chance accuracy of 50 per cent (whereas, the students' baseline accuracy was much closer to 50 per cent). To explain this, Porter et al. suggested that the officers were probably relying on false cues and/or had a bias that the majority of offenders had lied during parole hearings – but these interviews were not drawn from such a setting (nevertheless, the officers' poor base-line performance confirms their need for effective training).

The training the officers received initially consisted of a day involving:
• myth dissolution;
• information provision, including empirically based cues to deception;
• practice, feedback and knowledge testing.

At the end of the first day, they assessed some further recordings. Five weeks later the officers returned for another day. First of all, they assessed some more recordings. Then the day focused on:
• refresher of first day's training;
• analysing and discussing actual and fictional cases;
• feedback on these cases.

Finally, the officers assessed another sample of recordings drawn from the prior study. Across the four samples of interviews assessed, the officers' performance was as follows:
• baseline = 39%;
• end of day one = 60%;
• beginning of day two = 62%;
• end of day two = 77%.

This rate of improvement is impressive. However, Porter et al. were wise enough to consider that it might merely be the result of factors such as practice. Therefore, their study also involved three groups of students assessing the interviews, namely:
1. control group;
2. feedback group that received feedback on accuracy following each judgement;
3. feedback and cue information group that also received information on empirically based cues.

While, as stated above, the students' overall base-line accuracy was close to 50 per cent, for those students who happened to be in the control group it was close to 40 per cent. At the end of four assessment sessions, the control group's performance was 60 per cent – an impressive rise that is, perhaps, difficult to attribute solely to practice (without feedback). The feedback group's performance rose from 54 per cent to 64 per cent.

The feedback plus cues group's increased from 52 per cent to 70 per cent – suggesting a positive benefit for them of the training.

One major difference between the parole officers' base-line performance and that of the student control group was that while these were somewhat similar for deceptive messages, they differed for truthful messages (at 20 per cent and 42 per cent respectively) – thus, at base-line the officers were prone to judging truthful messages as lies. Why the control group of students achieved base-line performance rather below chance for truth and lies is not clear.

Porter et al. concluded that their research offers an important and original demonstration of factors contributing to deception detection by both professionals and non-professionals and that it is also important that even a brief training session (such as theirs) can improve detection performance.

Porter et al. noted that among their students the feedback group improved almost as much as did the feedback plus cues information group, which suggests that feedback alone, might be important.

While the study by Porter et al. has several strengths, it was a pity that the observed interviews were not from the parole setting but merely laboratory-based interviews with students. However, it is as yet extremely rare for published research on the detection of deception to involve real-life investigative interviews such as with police suspects (as was achieved by Mann, Vrij, and Bull, 2002; in press). One rarely, if ever, mentioned strength of deception research involving real-life interviews with (alleged) criminals is that such research would permit the examination of a number of problems, such as the widespread belief that it is only ugly people who commit crimes (and therefore lie).

Facial appearance

In psychology there now exists (i) a vast literature on the effects of facial appearance (Bull and Rumsey, 1988) – for example its possible relationship with criminality (Memon, Vrij, and Bull, 2003) – and (ii) a large number of publications on the detection of deception (Vrij, 2000). However, very few studies seem to have been designed specifically to examine the possible effects of people's facial attractiveness on judgements of whether they are telling the truth or lying. Many years ago one of our early studies of the effects of facial appearance found that people with attractive faces are assumed to be more honest (Bull, 1979). (However, Masip, and Garrido (2001) did not find such a relationship.)

In 1988 in a thought-provoking article on the evolution of deception and the possible role of genes in the tendency to lie, Bond and Robinson

(1988) theorised that genetically transmitted anatomical features prefigure human success at deceit.

Some years later Bond, Berry, and Omar (1994) investigated the possible relationship between people's honest appearance and their willingness to engage in deception. (Earlier Berry and McArthur (1986) had confirmed our finding that facial attractiveness influences impressions of honesty.) Bond et al. found that people who were judged to have an honest facial appearance (which they found to be significantly correlated with attractiveness) were less likely to agree to deceive other people. They therefore concluded that there might be a kernel of truth in the belief that ugly people may be more likely to lie. Zebrowitz, Voinescu, and Collins (1996) also found a relationship between facial appearance and impressions of honesty and they cautioned that people who are attempting to ascertain others' veracity should be aware that their judgements may be biased by the attractiveness of those they are judging. However, they did not directly test the hypothesis that facial attractiveness may bias decisions about lying/truth telling.

This hypothesis may have been directly tested only once prior to our own study (to be described below). In that study by Aune, Levine, Ching, and Yoshimoto (1993), from the Department of Speech at the University of Hawaii, a woman was video-recorded answering questions about her personal likes, work, hobbies, and dating preferences. Her responses (which were scripted) did not reflect her actual beliefs. There were two versions of the recording which were similar except they varied in terms of her appearance by altering her makeup, hairstyle, and clothing. In both recordings, in which she behaved similarly, she displayed several cues stereotypically associated with deception.

Aune et al. found that the male undergraduates' judgements of her deceptiveness were significantly influenced by her appearance. The female students seemed not to be affected in this way. However, it was noted that the way her physical appearance was manipulated had a much stronger effect on the males' judgements of her attractiveness than it did on the females'. Nevertheless, when (for both male and female participants) a correlation was performed between how attractive they rated her and how deceptive they judged her this was significant and negative not only for males but also for females.

Though the findings of the study by Aune et al. are thought-provoking, their study suffers from having only one person as the 'observed', from her only being deceptive, and from her deception being scripted.

For years I have wanted to find the time to conduct a better study. Fortunately, one of my students was willing to conduct a research project on this topic. In our study (Bull and Vine, 2003) video clips of twelve young adults (six male) lying or telling the truth were shown to a group of other young adult observers (n = 40) who did not know the video-recorded persons. (These 'stimulus' persons were an opportunity sample whose facial photographs were rated for attractiveness by a further group of young adult observers. There was statistically significant inter-judge agreement concerning the attractiveness ratings even though the range of rated attractiveness was not great. In addition, faces rated as attractive were also rated as more trustworthy.)

With regard to judgements of lying/truth-telling in the main study, when the six stimulus persons were more attractive (decided by median split) and lying, the mean accuracy rate was close to chance (50 per cent) at 52 per cent. Similarly, for the six stimulus persons who were less attractive, the observers' truth detection accuracy for each of the persons was sometimes below and sometimes above chance level averaging 57 per cent; this was also found when these persons were lying (mean = 59 per cent). However, when the more attractive persons were telling the truth the observers' mean success rate for each of the faces (separately) always exceeded 50 per cent, ranging from 60 per cent to 90 per cent with a mean of 76 per cent (this set of mean scores significantly differing from chance using a binomial test). This score of 76 per cent could be the result of observers' assumptions that good-looking people do nice things (Memon, Vrij, and Bull, 2003). Thus, our study, though in need of replication, does suggest the possibility that people may take cognitive short-cuts in this decision-making situation. Aune et al. (1993) suggested that effects of a person's appearance on decisions as to whether he or she is lying may be explainable through receivers' heuristic processing (e.g., 'she is attractive, she must be honest').

Indeed, Fiedler and Walka (1993), while not mentioning facial appearance, did emphasise in their paper on training people to detect deception that people's use of global heuristics (i.e., easy-to-employ rules) probably is a major explanation of why training (which is necessarily detailed and complex) may have limited or no effect.

Problems for training

So, one of the problems confronting training might be the widespread assumption that good looking people don't do bad things (Bull and Rumsey, 1988).

Another problem is the 'demeanour bias', by which I mean that some people's natural behaviour fits observers' (false) assumptions concerning cues to deception. In 1994 Vrij noted that 'some people (expressive people for instance) impress observers as more credible, regardless of whether they are telling the truth or not . . . , while others (introverted people for instance) impress others as less credible' (p. 120). Given that there may well be a relationship between facial attractiveness and extraversion/ expressivity (Bull and Rumsey, 1988), this is an especially useful notion.

Truth/lie bias

Another factor that affects detection accuracy rate is whether observers have a general truth or lie bias. For example, some (but not all) studies have found that investigators assume that most people are liars (Porter et al., 2000) and lay people assume that most people tell the truth. Given that their assumptions may not fit the rate of lying used in research studies (which is often 50 per cent), such biases may reduce accuracy. This has been known for a while now. What is more recent is the idea (mentioned above) that there is another type of truth/lie bias, which is based on the observed person's appearance.

Furthermore, any type of truth or lie bias may actually affect the cues observers choose to look for. Amongst the myriad of behavioural cues available to observers, do they choose to focus on those that will lead them to a decision that confirms the 'correctness' of their bias? Fiedler and Walka (1993) hinted at the possibility of this. There are certainly findings in social psychology and in the psychology of policing (Bull, Bustin, Evans, and Gahagan, 1983; Milne and Bull, 2003; Mortimer and Shepherd, 1999) that interviewers (i) seek out information that confirms their hypotheses and (ii) may actually 'choose' to behave in ways that cause the very behaviours in others they then take to justify their hypotheses (Bull, 2002; Winkel, Koppelaar, and Vrij, 1988). More research is needed on such biases in the detection of deception, especially their interaction with the narrowing of observers' attentional focus, particularly when the detection situation is high stakes for the observer.

Confidence

The idea that observers focus on those cues that will lead them to a decision that confirms their bias might explain why several studies have found no relationship between professionals' confidence in their detection of deception and their accuracy (e.g., Vrij, 1994). Indeed, it might explain why with greater professional experience comes more confidence in one's ability to detect deception but no more accuracy (Köhnken, 1987). Also, professionals' personality is likely to affect their confidence.

'Personality'

The work of Vrij (2000) and others has made it clear that the 'personality' of the liar/truth-teller will affect the cues they actually demonstrate when lying. Vrij and Graham (1997) built this important notion into their 'training' study and found students who received the 'training' improved their performance. (However, police officers did not.) Training programmes will need to address this topic.

Training programmes will also need to address the issue of personality differences among those seeking to detect deception. Recently as part of her doctoral studies one of our students found that personality differences affect people's beliefs about their own lying (Gozna, Vrij, and Bull, 2001). She also found that personality/individual differences among professionals (i.e., police and customs officers) were related to the cues they believed to be indicative of deception and (for customs officers) to their lie-detection accuracy (Gozna, 2003).

Quality of the training

For any training programme to stand a chance of being effective it will need to demonstrate awareness of the points made in this chapter and the many relevant points from other chapters in this book. The human ability successfully to deceive others has evolved over the millennia and it would be foolish to assume that a simple training programme could be effective. However, when given confidential access to some professional groups' training programmes I am constantly amazed at how simple-minded they usually are. The simple-minded approach to detecting deception that characterises many of the professional groups responsible for our safety is a cause for concern. However, in England and Wales the Association of Chief Police Officers' Investigative Interviewing Strategic Steering Group has very recently set up a subcommittee on the detection of deception to produce a (probably unpublished) report on the effectiveness of all known procedures designed to detect deception.

Conclusion

Even if the contents of training programmes were of the complexity that research on this topic demonstrates is necessary, crucial obstacles will have to be overcome for training to stand a chance of being effective. These have to do with requiring those being trained (e.g., police officers) to detect deception from behavioural cues.

1. to stop relying on false beliefs about cues
2. to be willing to acknowledge that researchers on this topic have relevant and important information available, and
3. to be prepared to accept that some of them (especially the more experienced) are poor at this task and therefore will have made crucial mistakes in the past (e.g., that certain crime suspects were, in fact, telling the truth).

For professionals who have to be confident in their abilities, accepting that they have performed poorly in the past and that psychologists may know better is far from easy. This may well explain why even well-informed training programmes (say on investigative interviewing, Aldridge and Cameron, 1999; Memon, Bull, and Smith, 1995; Milne and Bull, 1999) have rarely been successful.

I began this chapter by reiterating the point I made in 1989 that some police training books are deceiving their readers. In many countries this may still be the case. However, due to the praiseworthy efforts put in to organise this seminal book, I do believe things will change.

REFERENCES

Akehurst, L. (1997). Deception and its detection in children and adults via verbal and nonverbal cues. Unpublished doctoral dissertation, Department of Psychology, University of Portsmouth.
Aldridge, J., and Cameron, S. (1999). Interviewing child witnesses: Questioning techniques and the role of training. *Applied Developmental Science, 3,* 136–47.
Aune, R. K., Levine, T., Ching, P., and Yoshimoto, J. (1993). The influence of perceived source reward value and attributions of deception. *Communication Research Reports, 10,* 15–27.
Berry, D., and McArthur, L. (1986). Perceiving character in faces: The impact of age-related craniofacial changes on social perception. *Psychological Bulletin, 100,* 3–18.
Bond, C., Berry, D., and Omar, A. (1994). The kernel of truth in judgements of deceptiveness. *Basic and Applied Social Psychology, 15,* 523–34.
Bond, C., and Robinson, M. (1988). The evolution of deception. *Journal of Nonverbal Behavior, 12,* 295–307.
Bull, R. (1979). The psychological significance of facial deformity. In M. Cook and G. Wilson (eds.) *Love and attraction.* Oxford: Pergamon.
    (1989). Can training enhance the detection of deception? In J. Yuille (ed.) *Credibility assessment.* Deventer: Kluwer Academic.
    (2002). Applying psychology to crime investigation. The case of police interviewing. In I. McKenzie and R. Bull (eds.), *Criminal justice research.* Ashgate: Aldershot.
Bull, R., Bustin, R., Evans, P., and Gahagan, D. (1983). *Psychology for police officers.* Chichester: Wiley.

Bull, R., and Rumsey, N. (1988). *The social psychology of facial appearance.* New York: Springer.

Bull, R., and Vine, M. (2003). Attractive people tell the truth: Can you believe it? Poster presented at the Annual Conference of the European Association of Psychology and Law, Edinburgh.

De Paulo, B. M., and Pfeifer, R. L. (1986). On-the-job experience and skill at detecting deception. *Journal of Applied Social Psychology, 16*, 249–67.

De Paulo, B., Lassiter, G., and Stone, J. (1982). Attentional determinants of success at detecting deception and truth. *Personality and Social Psychology Bulletin, 8*, 273–9.

DeTurck, M. (1991). Training observers to detect spontaneous deception: Effects of gender. *Communication Reports, 4*, 81–9.

DeTurck, M., Feeley, T., and Roman, L. (1997). Vocal and visual cue training in behavioural lie detection. *Communication Research Reports, 14*, 249–59.

DeTurck, M., Harszlak, J., Bodhorn, D., and Texter, L. (1990). The effects of training social perceivers to detect deception from behavioural cues. *Communication Quarterly, 38*, 189–99.

DeTurck, M., and Miller, G. (1990). Training observers to detect deception: effects of self-monitoring and rehearsal. *Human Communication Research, 16*, 603–20.

DeTurck, M., and Miller, G. (1985). Perception and arousal: Isolating the behavioural correlates of deception. *Human Communication Research, 12*, 181–201.

Druckman, D., Rozelle R., and Baxter, J. (1982). *Nonverbal communication: Survey, theory and research.* Beverly Hills: Sage.

Fiedler, K., and Walka, I. (1993). Training lie detectors to use nonverbal cues instead of global heuristics. *Human Communication Research, 20*, 199–223.

Gozna, L. (2003). Individual differences and the detection of deception. Unpublished doctoral dissertation, Department of Psychology, University of Portsmouth.

Gozna, L., Vrij, A., and Bull, R. (2001). The impact of individual differences on perceptions of lying in everyday life and in a high stake situation. *Personality and Individual Differences, 31*, 1203–16.

Horvath, F., Jayne, B., and Buckley, J. (1994). Differentiation of truthful and deceptive criminal suspects in Behaviour Analysis Interviews. *Journal of Forensic Sciences, 39*, 793–807.

Kassin, S., and Fong, C. (1999). 'I'm innocent!': Effects of training on judgments of truth and deception in the interrogation room. *Law and Human Behavior, 23*, 499–516.

Köhnken, G., (1987). Training police officers to detect deceptive eyewitness statements: Does it work? *Social Behaviour, 2*, 1–17.

Mann, S., Vrij, A., and Bull, R. (2002). An analysis of authentic high-stake liars. *Law and Human Behavior, 26*, 365–76.

(in press). Detecting true lies: Police officers' ability to detect suspects' lies. *Journal of Applied Psychology.*

Masip, J., and Garrido, E. (2001). Is there a kernel of truth in judgments of deceptiveness? *Anales de Psicologia, 17*, 101–20.

Memon, A., Bull, R., and Smith, M. (1995). Improving the quality of the police interview: Can training in the use of cognitive techniques help? *Policing and Society*, 5, 53–8.

Memon, A., Vrij, A., and Bull, R. (2003). *Psychology and law: Truthfulness, accuracy and credibility* (2nd edn). Chichester: John Wiley.

Milne, R., and Bull, R. (1999). *Investigative interviewing: Psychology and practice.* Chichester: John Wiley.

   (2003). Police interviewing. In D. Carson and R. Bull (eds.). *Handbook of psychology in legal contexts* (2nd edn). Chichester: John Wiley.

Mortimer, A., and Shepherd, E. (1999). Frames of mind: Schemata guiding cognition and conduct in the interviewing of suspected offenders. In A. Memon and R. Bull (eds.), *Handbook of the psychology of interviewing*. Chichester: John Wiley.

Porter, S., Woodworth, M., and Birt, A. (2000). Truth, lies and videotape: An investigation of the ability of federal parole officers to detect deception. *Law and Human Behavior*, 24, 643–58.

Vrij, A. (1994). The impact of information and setting on detection of deception by police detectives. *Journal of Nonverbal Behavior*, 18, 117–36.

Vrij, A. (2000). *Detecting lies and deceit.* Chichester: John Wiley.

Vrij, A., and Graham, S. (1997). Individual differences between liars and the ability to detect lies. *Expert Evidence*, 5, 144–8.

Winkel, F. W., Koppelaar, L., and Vrij, A. (1988). Creating suspects in police-citizen encounters. *Social Behaviour*, 3, 307–18.

Zebrowitz, L., Voinescu, L., and Collins, M. (1996). 'Wide-eyed' and 'crooked-faced'. Determinants of perceived and real honesty across the life span. *Personality and Social Psychology Bulletin*, 22, 1258–69.

Zuckerman, M., Koestner, R., and Alton, A. (1984). Learning to detect deception. *Journal of Personality and Social Psychology*, 46, 519–28.

12   The wizards of deception detection

Maureen O'Sullivan and Paul Ekman

Wizard . . . a sage . . . a person of amazing skill or accomplishment

For many years we have studied individual differences among people in their ability to detect deception from demeanour. Most people do rather poorly in making such judgements. In experimental situations in which someone is either lying or telling the truth half the time, people do little better than chance (i.e., they get average accuracy scores of 50 per cent). This has been found not only in our studies (Ekman and O'Sullivan, 1991), which examined high-stake lies, but also in a wide range of other studies (Malone and DePaulo, 2001).[1] By doing an idiographic analysis, we have discovered some individuals who are highly accurate across different types of deception. This report describes our beginning research with a small group of such 'wizards' of deception detection.

In the late 1980s, we started to administer a test of the ability to detect deception, based on our early work with a group of nurses who had lied or been truthful about their feelings as they watched either a gruesome surgical film or a pleasant nature film (Ekman and Friesen, 1974). When we analysed group performance, we found that most groups – police officers, CIA and FBI agents, lawyers, college students, therapists, judges, etc. – did little better than chance. Yet our objective measurements had demonstrated that there were discernible clues that could have been used to distinguish lying from truthfulness accurately (Ekman, Friesen, O'Sullivan, and Scherer, 1980; Ekman, Friesen, and O'Sullivan, 1988).

We (Ekman and O'Sullivan, 1991) did find one group – Secret Service agents – who as a group, scored significantly better than chance, and slightly more than half of them were highly accurate, scoring 70 per cent or better on the test. At that time, we speculated that there were at least two reasons that the Secret Service agents were better at detecting deception than other groups we had tested. The Secret Service has two different jobs. One is to protect public officials, especially in public venues such as giving speeches in front of many people. We speculated that their practice at scanning crowds sensitised them to the non-verbal clues to deception contained in our deception task.

The other job the Secret Service does is to evaluate threats made against public officials. Most of these threats are made by mentally ill individuals. Secret Service agents must decide whether a threat is the precursor to action or merely the outward manifestation of a pathology that is unlikely to lead to behaviour. Unlike many police officers who seek evidence to support their belief in the guilt of the suspect they have arrested, the Secret Service must keep an open mind about the guilt or innocence of the person whose threat they are investigating. Premature closure about the truthfulness or deceptiveness of others is one of the cognitive drawbacks involved in inaccurate lie detection (O'Sullivan, 2003). Another aspect, of course, is the low base rate of occurrence of assassins. Other law-enforcement personnel deal with groups in which the base rate of crime and guilt is much higher. The relative infrequency of the threats the Secret Service deals with may heighten their sensitivity to relevant cues to truthfulness.

The publication of Ekman's book *Telling lies* (1985), and subsequent media publicity, drew the attention of law-enforcement officers who were interested in improving training on interrogation. Among these was J. J. Newberry, an agent in charge of interview training for the department of Alcohol, Tobacco, and Firearms. He scored 100 per cent on the test available at that time on the ability to discern deception and truthfulness. Over the next few years, Ekman and Newberry formed the Institute for Analytic Interviewing which provides training for a wide variety of law-enforcement agencies and which gives us access to many highly specialised and highly motivated populations.

During this period, Frank and Ekman (reported in 1997) were in the process of developing two other deception scenarios (in addition to Ekman and Friesen's scenario of nurses lying or telling the truth about emotion). In one scenario, men lied or told the truth about their opinion; in the other, men lied or told the truth about whether they had stolen $50. These scenarios appear to have more applicability to law enforcement training than the earlier emotion scenario. In 1999, Ekman, O'Sullivan, and Frank reported their identification of three different professional groups, each of which was significantly better than chance in recognising truthfulness and deception. These groups were: (1) law-enforcement officials from a variety of agencies who had shown special interest in improving their lie-detection abilities and who had been nominated by their agencies as superior interviewers, (2) federal judges, and (3) forensic psychologists. Because two of these groups had volunteered for such training and one of them was willing to lose pay and to travel some distance from home, we speculated that what all three groups had in common was a high level of interest in the topic of lie detection and unusual motivation to improve their ability in this area.

Other 'wizards' of deception detection were discovered when a very large group (approximately 1,200) of psychotherapists were given the opinion deception scenario. About 10 per cent of the therapists scored 90 per cent or better on the test. Having data on such a large sample substantiated our impression from the earlier studies of smaller groups that this kind of lie detection 'wizardry' is as statistically infrequent as any kind of genius or talent. We believe it is likely that less than 1 or 2 per cent of selected populations will achieve great accuracy in detecting deception from demeanour. Our report focuses on what we have learned so far about the characteristics of these highly talented lie-catchers.

First, let us provide more detail about the three lie-detection accuracy measures we have used in identifying our wizards.

The Lie-detection measures

The Emotion Deception Judgement Task

The task is based on a black and white videotape of ten Euro-American women lying or telling the truth about the feelings they are having at that moment (Ekman and Friesen, 1974; Ekman, Friesen, and O'Sullivan, 1988). In each of the ten items, the woman is shown being interviewed by a female interviewer, who is not visible on screen and who did not know which film the woman she was interviewing was watching. Each woman said she was watching a pleasant nature film, but only about half of them actually were. The others were watching a man with third-degree burns over much of his body intermixed with close-up views of another person undergoing surgery on his arms.

Extensive behavioural measurements of the videotapes identified a variety of behavioural clues in both verbal and non-verbal channels that distinguish lying from truthfulness (Ekman et al., 1980; Ekman, O'Sullivan, Friesen, and Scherer, 1991), establishing that the honest and deceptive interviews can be discriminated from the information available. The women shown on the videotape were students entering the University of California at San Francisco Nursing School who had received a letter from the Dean of the Nursing School inviting them to participate in the research. To motivate them further, the student nurses were told that their ability to control their emotional reactions would be related to their future success as nurses. And, indeed, there was a significant positive correlation between how detectable the lies of each woman were and the ratings made of her by her clinical supervisor three years later (Ekman, 1985).

The emotion video was taped in 1970 and the women's hairstyles are dated, but participants have not responded negatively to completing this task, other than to comment on the difficulty of determining whether the women are lying or telling the truth. Although accuracy is close to chance for most occupational groups on all three tests, we have found that the emotion task is the most difficult. It yields the smallest proportion of individuals who are highly accurate in their judgements.

The Opinion Deception Judgement Task

This test was developed by Frank and Ekman (1997) from colour video-tapes of twenty men who volunteered to be research subjects in a study about human communication. The men in the opinion test were 18 to 28 years of age and included African-, Asian-, and Euro-Americans. Based on the false opinion paradigm suggested by Mehrabian (1971), the men were asked about their opinions before they were told that the experiment involved lying or telling the truth. The opinion that each man felt most strongly about was the one he was then asked to discuss with an interviewer (Ekman). Some men described their opinion truthfully; others lied, claiming to believe the opposite of their true opinion. Truth-tellers who were believed by the interviewer received a $10 bonus. Liars who were believed received a $50 bonus. Liars or truth-tellers who were disbelieved received no money and half of them faced an additional punishment. (See Frank and Ekman, 1997, for more details.)

To verify that the men actually did manifest different behaviours when lying or telling the truth, their facial muscle movements were analysed using the Facial Action Coding System (Ekman and Friesen, 1978) which demonstrated that '80% of the participants . . . could be successfully classified as liars or truth tellers on the basis of the presence or absence of fear or disgust' (Frank and Ekman, 1997, p. 1433). The Opinion Deception Judgement Task consists of one-minute segments from each of ten video-taped interviews. Each item shows a different man. The ten interview segments selected were chosen so as to represent equal numbers of pro and con positions on each of the opinions represented. Half of the interview segments are of men who truthfully described their strongly held opinion; half lied about it. (The opinions discussed were either 'Convicted cold-blooded murderers should be executed', or 'Smoking should be banned in all public places'.) The videotapes showed face-and-shoulder close-ups with full audio. The interviewer could be heard but not seen.

As with the emotion videotape, the merit of this detection task is that each of the interviews contains behavioural and/or verbal content clues to either honesty or deception. The interviewees were highly motivated by money rewards and the threat of a noxious punishment. In addition, they were interviewed about opinions they were passionately interested in. Consequently, the subjects displayed emotions consistent or inconsistent with what they were saying, so there were sufficient clues in the videotaped interviews to allow honesty or lying to be detected. (Most previous lie-detection research by other investigators has focused on low-stakes lies (e.g., polite, 'white' lies) that may not cause any emotional arousal in those telling them, thereby providing few, if any, clues for observers to detect (DePaulo, Lindsay, Malone, Muhlenbruck, Charlton, and Cooper, 2003).) Moreover, most investigators have not taken the necessary step of obtaining behavioural measures to document that there are discernible clues that could be used to distinguish lies from truthfulness.

The Crime Deception Judgement Task

This deception judgement task was also developed by Frank and Ekman (1997). Ten men (different from the ten men used in the Opinion Deception Judgement Task) lied or told the truth about whether they had stolen $50. As in the opinion task, the men received a significant reward if they were believed. If they lied and the interviewer believed their protestations of innocence, they kept the $50 they had stolen. If they were innocent and the interviewer believed them, they received $10. If they were disbelieved (whether they were innocent or stole the money), they did not get to keep the $50, and they were threatened with a noxious punishment. (See Frank and Ekman, 1997, for more details.) As in the Opinion Deception Judgement Task, the men were highly motivated to succeed at the task, whether it was lying or telling the truth. Those who lied showed visible and measurable behavioural signs of cognitive and emotional arousal. Each man was shown being interviewed for about one minute. Half the men were lying and half were telling the truth.

How were the experts identified?

We disseminate our research findings for use by law-enforcement and other professionals through workshops on behavioural cues to deceit and the precautions necessary in interpreting such cues. These workshops vary in length from one hour to five days. The content of the presentation for the longer workshops includes techniques for interviewing developed by J. J. Newberry based on Fisher and Geiselman's (1992) cognitive interviewing paradigm. The section on detecting deceit is based on Ekman's research on behavioural clues to deception. The one-hour workshops focus on the pitfalls involved in detecting deception. The Opinion Deception Judgement Task is administered at the start of the workshop so participants can gauge their own lie detection ability. We believe this has served to motivate their attention to the training that is offered.

After completing the opinion task, which takes about fifteen minutes, the workshop participants are given the correct answers and asked to report to the group (by a show of hands) how many items they got right. Usually, only one participant in a hundred indicates that he or she got a score of 90 per cent or better. We then ask those who got scores of 90 per cent or better, and who are willing to help in our research, to give us their names and contact information.

Not everyone who is highly accurate has agreed to take further tests as described below. In subsequent reports, we will describe the differential volunteer rate of different occupational groups and the reasons that may explain those differences.

Who are the experts?

Individuals in groups such as those reported in our earlier lie detection accuracy research (Ekman and O'Sullivan, 1991; Ekman et al., 1999) are not included in the Wizards Project because, at that time, we did not identify the participants as individuals. We only gathered group data. The groups in the current research containing highly accurate lie-catchers, who are being studied individually, include therapists, law-enforcement personnel, judges, lawyers, arbitrators, and artists.

The qualification process

Each of the three lie-detection measures described earlier contains ten items, each having a binary choice – lying or truthful. By chance alone, an observer should be able to identify five of the ten items correctly. Based on the binomial distribution, a score of nine out of ten correct, by chance alone, will occur about 1 per cent of the time. A score of eight out of ten will occur, by chance alone, 5 per cent of the time.

We decided that initial qualification for the Wizards Project would require achieving the very high score of 90 per cent on the Opinion Deception Judgment Task. Having achieved that cut-off score, the crime and emotion videotapes were then mailed to the participants. At first we set the criterion very high. If the participants achieved scores of 80 per cent on *both* the crime and the emotion tests, they would be classified as 'expert' lie detectors or 'wizards'. An additional consent form was then sent to them in which they agreed to be interviewed about their answers to the tests, to talk with us about aspects of their life and work, and to complete a battery of psychological tests.

What is the probability that wizards selected by the criteria described above could have achieved their scores by chance alone? Essentially non-existent. On the basis of chance alone, the combinatorial probability that any single individual would achieve a score of 90 per cent on the first lie-detection test and scores of 80 per cent or better on two other tests is twenty-five in a million. So, it is highly unlikely that we have any false positives, that any of our wizard lie-catchers are incorrectly classified as highly accurate. It is quite likely, however, that we have many false negatives, that other expert lie detectors were falsely categorised as non-experts. The false negatives may be attributed to the fact that we do not provide our participants with many of the opportunities that are normally available in an interview – a longer sample of behaviour, the ability to formulate the questions and follow-ups, the opportunity to use role-playing and other behavioural stratagems, etc. Note, however, that the experts we have identified are able to detect deception, even with these restrictions.

Professional experience and accuracy in detecting deception

At first, we used the very stringent criteria described above for identifying our experts. One in which for all three tests (90 per cent on the opinion test and at least 80 per cent on both the crime and emotion tests) the odds of being classified as an expert by chance alone were extraordinarily low. Using these criteria, we identified fourteen 'ultimate' wizards.

We first started identifying potential experts using our large group of therapists. We found that some of them failed to qualify as experts because, although they scored 90 per cent on the opinion tests, and 80 per cent or above on the emotion test, they failed to achieve a score of 80 per cent or better on the crime tape.

As the study progressed, and we received data from other professional groups, we noticed a complementary pattern among law-enforcement personnel (police, judges, and lawyers) who scored 80 per cent or higher on the crime tape but failed to reach criterion on the emotion tape. Fifteen participants (in addition to the fourteen 'ultimate' experts) achieved scores of 80 per cent or better on two of the deception scenarios, but not on the third. Table 12.1 shows the frequencies with which these participants, classified as therapist or law enforcement[2] failed to achieve a similarly high score on either the crime or the emotion test.

Table 12.1 *Deception detection inaccuracy of two professional groups on two tasks*

	Deception detection task	
Profession	Crime	Emotion
Therapists	8	1
Law professionals	0	6

Notes: Values are the number of professionals in each group who obtained scores of 70% or less on each test, having scored 80% or higher on the other test, i.e., 6 law professionals achieved scores of 80% or higher on the crime task, but all of them received 70% or less on the emotion task.

The chi-square ($\chi^2 = 11.429$ $p < .00072$; with Yates' correction $\chi^2 = 8.136$ $p < .0043$) is highly statistically significant. It appears that the type of lie one least often encounters is the one that is responsible for failure to qualify – therapists on crime, law enforcement on emotions.

Therapists, while keenly observing their clients for areas of emotional and personal significance would not ordinarily have reason to be concerned about whether their clients were criminal, nor would they have experience with the kinds of stratagems people might use to avoid having their crimes detected. Conversely, law-enforcement personnel are in the business of detecting lies about crimes and would have more familiarity with that kind of deception. Lies about feelings would be less important in their day-to-day professional lives. (Recall, however, that our fourteen original 'ultimate' experts were able to identify all three kinds of lies accurately and that the ultimate experts include therapists and law-enforcement personnel.) This finding of seeming professional relevance for the lies correctly identified encouraged us to study this second group of experts as well, to try to understand what differentiates their expertise. By October, 2003, we had identified fourteen 'ultimate' experts, who had obtained 80 per cent or better on all three deception detection tasks, and fifteen 'penultimate' experts who had scored 90 per cent or better on the opinion test and 80 per cent or better on either the crime or the emotion test. We continue to assess potential wizards.

Although we believe that the pattern of differential accuracy shown in Table 12.1 reflects differences in professional experience with different kinds of lies, other hypotheses need to be ruled out. One alternative explanation is that it is not the type of lie that is important, but the

Table 12.2 *Deception detection inaccuracy by sex of target and sex of expert*

	Sex of liar or truth-teller	
Sex of expert	Males interviewed about stealing money (Crime video)	Females interviewed about film viewing (Emotion video)
Female	2	2
Male	5	6

Notes: Values are the numbers of male and female 'penultimate' experts who scored 70% or lower on either the crime or the emotion video. Penultimate experts obtained 90% on the Opinion Deception Detection Task and 80% on either the emotion or crime task. Table 12.2 shows the distribution, by sex, of the penultimate experts on the video on which they did **not** achieve criterion. As can be seen, there is no relationship between the sex of the target and the sex of the expert.

gender of the liar and the lie-catcher. Most of the therapists and all of the people lying about their feelings are female; most of the law-enforcement personnel and all of those lying about stealing money are male. This explanation is less satisfactory, however, since all the penultimate experts, male and female, were highly accurate in detecting lies about opinions told by males (the initial screening task). Further, a chi-square partitioning the penultimate expert data in terms of the gender of the liars and truth-tellers and the gender of the lie-catchers ($\chi^2 = 0.024 \; p < .877$) was not significant. These data are given in Table 12.2.

The protocol

After the experts are identified, they meet with one or both of the experimenters (O'Sullivan and Ekman) to review their responses to each of the three videos. They are instructed to say aloud anything that occurs to them as they watch the video. They are encouraged, in other words, to 'think aloud' (Ericsson and Simon, 1998). This procedure was usually the first activity we did with the experts since we did not want to influence their recall or their reporting of the process they used in detecting deception. We said very little during this initial phase, interrupting only to encourage the expert to 'talk aloud' if they were merely watching the tape, or asking clarifying questions when remarks were made which we did not understand. After reviewing all three tapes, we sometimes went back over the tapes and called the experts' attention to aspects of the tape that they had not mentioned, aspects of the interviews that we knew contained important information about the truthfulness of what was being said, and asked them for their comments on that part of the videotaped interview. This initial review procedure lasted from one to two hours and was tape-recorded and transcribed, a lengthy and difficult procedure since there are four or five voice sources.[3]

Ordinarily, the next step is to conduct a semi-standardised interview about personal and life history information. Early on, we found that this interview was adequate for gaining factual biographical information and, occasionally, information about career choices, mentors, and the like. But, often, the experts were overly humble about their skills or provided only biographical facts. This information was also tape-recorded and transcribed.

The experts who were interviewed first were law enforcement personnel with whom we were conducting week-long training courses. During this time, we would eat and drink together and the police officers would talk about each other, tell 'tall tales' about their police exploits, and be far more revealing of themselves and their colleagues than they had been in the formal semi-structured interview. Because of the richness of the data gathered in this way, we are trying to obtain more naturalistic observations for all of our experts, by visiting them at home, or at their job, and by talking with colleagues and family members who might be more forthcoming. In the course of these social interactions with the experts, we make detailed notes as soon after our encounters as possible.

In addition to the think-aloud procedure and the gathering of interview and observational data about their personal and professional lives, a series of standardised psychological tests will be administered to the experts. These will include a personality inventory such as the NEO, a short measure of verbal comprehension as an indirect measure of IQ, a measure of attributional or cognitive complexity, and perhaps measures of cognitive style and life themes.

Limitations of the identification protocol and this report

We are aware that our procedure will select for a particular kind of lie-catcher. Our task limits the lie detector to watching a one-minute videotape of a liar or truth-teller being interviewed by someone else. The sample of behaviour is quite limited (one minute), the observer does not have the opportunity to obtain a baseline sample of behaviour that is known to be honest to use as a comparison, the observer is limited to merely watching the behaviour on the videotape. Highly skilled interviewers who have learned over the years how to use their appearance and personality to best effect, or how to interview different personality types with different techniques, or who have developed particularly effective interview strategies for use in detecting deception may be handicapped by the protocol we use which does not allow them to use these talents and techniques. On the other hand, in earlier research (Ekman et al., 1999) interviewers identified by their agencies as superior interviewers also were identified as superior lie detectors by one of the measures used in the present study. Although not all kinds of expert lie detectors will be detected by our methods, many of them will be.

We have only started interviewing the wizards. As of July, 2003, only half of the ultimate experts and none of the penultimate experts have been interviewed. We can offer no definitive findings (other than the relationship between professional experience and differential expertise described above), but a description of the demographic characteristics of the experts, beginning evidence for some of our hypotheses and some overall impressions of these wizards may be of interest.

Demographic characteristics of the ultimate and penultimate experts

Sex

Although we did not collect precise data on the gender composition of our samples, in most of our samples the number of males was notably greater than the number of females. Nonetheless, 10 of the 29 experts are female, which is a larger proportion of women than would be expected by chance alone. This finding is surprising since neither we (Ekman and O'Sullivan, 1991) nor others (Anderson, DePaulo, and Ansfield, 2002) have found a sex difference in lie-detection accuracy. On the other hand, women often perform better than men on non-verbal accuracy tasks (Hall, 1990) and one kind of non-verbal ability, recognising micro momentary facial expressions, is correlated with lie detection accuracy (Ekman and O'Sullivan, 1991; Frank and Ekman, 1997). The seeming over-representation of women in our expert group may be the result of women being more likely to volunteer to participate in a research project and to be more conscientious in completing their agreement to participate. The issue of sex differences in expert levels of accurate lie detection is one of the many questions we hope to address in future analyses of this data set.

Age

Consistent with the data described earlier suggesting that experience is important in recognising a wide variety of lies, most of our accurate lie-catchers are middle aged. The youngest is a female law student in her twenties; all the others are between 40 and 60. Given the depth of information and understanding of the personalities and behaviours of our widely varying truth-tellers and liars, this age range is understandable. Our young expert may provide a unique glimpse of ways in which a sophisticated understanding of others develops early in life.

Hypotheses suggested by previous research

Non-verbal behavior

In previous work (Ekman and O'Sullivan, 1991; Frank and Ekman, 1997) we found a significant correlation between accuracy in lie detection and accuracy in interpreting micro momentary facial expressions of emotion. We also found (Ekman and O'Sullivan, 1991; O'Sullivan, 2000) that more accurate lie detectors report using non-verbal as well as both verbal and non-verbal cues more frequently than less accurate lie detectors.

Based on these findings, we predicted that the experts who were accurate on the deception detection tasks would use non-verbal cues in making their assessments of truthfulness. In all of the think-aloud interviews we have conducted so far, the experts spontaneously refer to the non-verbal behaviour of the people they are watching 'He looks like a deer in the headlight of a car' (and the expert showed on his face the open, transfixed look of a deer). 'At that point, he smirked, and it didn't make sense that he would do that.' Every expert interviewed so far has described the non-verbal behaviour of the liar or the truth-teller, as well as the consistency or inconsistency between verbal and non-verbal behaviour on some, if not all, of the individuals they are assessing.

One of the things we hope to achieve with this study is a description of the non-verbal paradigms that expert lie detectors use in understanding others. Do they have a single strategy that they tailor for each person? Or do they use different strategies for different kinds of lies? Are there some non-verbal (and verbal cues) that experts use more than non-experts, or use in a different way, or in different combinations?

Verbal behaviour

For many years, many researchers (O'Sullivan, Ekman, Friesen, and Scherer, 1985; Köhnken, 1987; Sporer, 1997; Yuille, Marxman, and Cooper, 1999; Ekman, 2001; DePaulo et al., 2003; Newman, Pennebaker, Berry, and Richards, 2003) have argued that the verbal content of speech is important in differentiating deception and truthfulness. This occurs because the cognitive difficulty of constructing an alternative reality is revealed in reduced word complexity, less immediacy, more distancing, as well as vague and general language. In addition to their nonverbal facility many of the expert lie-catchers show an exquisite sensitivity to the nuances of language use.

Childhood experiences

Another consistency among the handful of experts who have been interviewed so far is that most of them have had unusual childhoods. Some of them did not speak English until grade school, some are children of alcoholics, some had working mothers, when not many children their age did. Most of them report being aware of changes in the emotional levels of those around them from a very early age.

Motivation

In our early studies of groups of experts (Ekman and O'Sullivan, 1991; Ekman et al., 1999), we speculated that superior lie-catchers were distinguished by their motivation to do well at the task as evidenced by their taking a workshop on the topic of detecting deception when others in their professions did not. All the experts in the Wizard Project are like the well-motivated lie detectors in our earlier studies. They, however, are even more highly motivated or, perhaps, more responsible and/or conscientious. Most attendees at our workshops are very enthusiastic about participating in the project at the beginning. But time and distance dampens their ardour. Although some groups had high response rates, in all the professional groups, many well-meaning, but busy, professionals failed to respond to our request for their help, although they had initially agreed to do so. The ultimate and penultimate experts did respond. We hypothesise that they will be more conscientious than a control group on a standardised personality measure.

Habitual practice

Ericsson (1996) in his review of expertise in professions as widely varying as grand master chess champions and concert violinists argued that the one characteristic that distinguishes the highly expert from the merely good was an extended period of intensive practice, usually lasting ten years, at the start of their careers. Recently, Brassington (2003) reported similar findings with prima ballerinas and members of the corps de ballet. Prima ballerinas reported more practice, visualising more about their performance, more planning. We will be assessing these planful, intellectual habits in our experts as well. Our observation, at this point, having interviewed only a third of them, is that an intense focus and investment in their performance, and concentrated attempts to improve it, are characteristic of most, if not all, of the wizards.

Other hypotheses

As noted above, our protocol has limitations. Those limitations may have skewed our sample. Our experts certainly do not represent all the possible kinds of expert lie detectors there are. Champion poker players, for example, might be different in personality characteristics as well as in their lie-detection strategies. Nevertheless, even with such limitations, the interviews conducted so far provide some interesting preliminary observations. These include the following:

- Many of our experts seem to be introverted and observant, rather than extroverted and active. Although some of our experts are extraordinarily, even excessively outgoing, most are not. Most are quiet, reserved, and observant. This hypothesis will be evaluated with a standardised personality inventory.
- When necessary, a surprising number of our experts report acting as a situation demands, whether that means being low-key and inoffensive or dominant and take-charge. Their ability to understand others seems to coexist with an ability to act the role or the behaviour that is required in a given situation. The understated, low-key, observant lie detectors ride Harleys, wear ten-galloon hats and high-heeled cowboy boots, or dress the part of the sailor-boy or the army captain when necessary. We hypothesise that the expert lie detectors will relate examples of noteworthy role-playing in their professional and personal lives significantly more often than the members of the control group will.
- Although a few of our experts do not have college degrees, most of them do and some have postgraduate degrees. The group, as a group, is surely above the mean in intelligence, but this will be assessed through objective measures.
- The experts interviewed so far seem to observe and describe people in a more complex fashion and with a thoroughness that others do not. Not only do they seem to have their own personality theories, but they also show a nuanced understanding of social, racial, and individual differences. Although some of the experts expressed many of the same stereotypic beliefs of non-experts, the wizards seem able to put these beliefs aside as they attempt to understand this particular young white woman, this particular black man.

- Most of the experts have had a familiarity with a wide array of very different types of people. One Los Angeles County Sheriff worked with psychiatric patients early in his career, as well as with prostitutes of many sexual persuasions, including transsexuals, but he goes to garage sales with his daughter and helps her find Daisy Duck collectibles. A labour attorney has dealt over the course of his career with people having the lowest level of education and intellectual capacity to the highest, from ore boat captains or wildcat coal-mine operators in the Appalachians to CEOs of multinational corporations.
- So far, our expert lie detectors show no discernible pattern with respect to political and religious beliefs. At this point, an equal number of them are Republicans and Democrats. Similarly, although many are extremely religious or very active in their church, some are agnostic, atheistic, or non-practising.
- How do the experts construe the personalities of the people they observe? What dimensions characterise their observation? How important is their assessment of the kind of person they are observing as a base-line for evaluating the non-verbal cues they are so sensitive to? How do they know when to attend to a non-verbal cue and when to ignore it? These are questions we are exploring.
- Some of the wizard lie-catchers have hobbies or vocations that either honed their acute sensitivity to non-verbal cues or became hobbies because of their inherent talent in that area. One expert is a bird watcher, another is an artist who does detailed paintings of facial expressions of emotion, another is a hunter known for his tracking ability and his persistence. We do not yet have the control group information to know, however, whether these observations are relevant or serendipitous. Which brings us to our final consideration: What is the control group?

The control group

One of the dilemmas of this project has been the problem of defining an adequate control group. Given the age, professional accomplishments, and talents of our wizard lie-catchers, the task of finding an adequate control group was daunting. The members of the control group would have to be non-expert lie detectors, by our criterion, but also be interested to participate in the research project. They would have to be similar to the experts in terms of social class, educational level, geographic location, and age.

There was no pre-existing group that met these requirements, so we decided to use each expert's spouse or close family member as his or her control. In most cases, the family member is interested in the project, and in their spouse's involvement. In some cases, before we had decided to use spouses as controls, husband or wives of the potential expert took the test too, out of personal interest. In one case, the wife was the target and did not qualify. Her husband took the test and did qualify!

The reasons recommending this strategy of using the spouses as the control group are that the spouse would usually be similar in age, as well as social and educational level. And since they are still married, they would both be living in the same part of the country. Also, since most of the experts are at least middle-aged, they would have been married for some time. There is anecdotal speculation, as well as research evidence, that married people become more similar over time, at least in terms of emotional convergence (Anderson, Keltner, and John, 2003). This similarity provides a strong comparison group, so that any differences we find are likely to be meaningful ones. We will, however, be exploring the utility of other control groups as well.

Conclusion

For Olympic athletes, talent is a necessary, but not a sufficient, condition for athletic excellence. The development of even the greatest gifts takes practice, feedback, and motivation. We speculate that the same is true for the development of the ability to understand others. Almost all the experts we have interviewed have exhibited high levels of motivation to improve their ability to understand others and to seek feedback about their performance. These characteristics are integrated into the everyday professional lives and personalities of the experts we have interviewed so far. They are not 'tricks' that can be taught in a four-hour seminar. Hopefully, however, our study of the wizards of deception detection will enrich our understanding of how human beings communicate and understand truthful and deceptive behaviour and provide information to those of us seeking to detect deception more accurately. We have suggested to government officials that these wizards are a resource that might be consulted on cases of extraordinary importance when there are few other means of evaluating truthfulness in a limited time frame.

REFERENCES

Anderson, C., Keltner, D., and John O. P. (2003). Emotional convergence between people over time. *Journal of Personality and Social Psychology*, *84* (5), 1054–68.
Anderson, D. E., DePaulo, B. M., and Ansfield, M. E. (2002). The development of deception detection skill: A longitudinal study of same-sex friends. *Personality and Social Psychology Bulletin*, *28* (4), 536–45.

Brassington, G. (2003). Mental skills distinguish elite soloist ballet dancers from corps dancers. Paper presented at the annual meeting of the Western Psychological Association Convention, Vancouver, B. C., May, 2003.

DePaulo, B. M., Lindsay, J. J., Malone, B. E., Muhlenbruck, L., Charlton, K., and Cooper, H. (2003). Cues to deception. *Psychological Bulletin, 129* (1), 74–118.

Ekman, P. (1985). *Telling lies: Clues to deceit in the marketplace, politics, and marriage.* New York: Norton.

(2001). *Telling lies: Clues to deceit in the marketplace, politics, and marriage* (3rd edn). New York: Norton.

Ekman, P., and Friesen, W. V. (1974). Detecting deception from body or face. *Journal of Personality and Social Psychology, 29,* 288–98.

Ekman, P., and Friesen, W. V. (1978). *Facial action coding system.* Palo Alto, CA: Consulting Psychologists Press.

Ekman, P., Friesen, W. V., O'Sullivan, M., and Scherer, K. R. (1980). Relative importance of face, body, and speech in judgments of personality and affect. *Journal of Personality and Social Psychology, 38* (2), 270–7.

Ekman, P., Friesen, W. V., and O'Sullivan, M. (1988). Smiles when lying. *Journal of Personality and Social Psychology, 54,* 414–20.

Ekman, P., and O'Sullivan, M. (1991). Who can catch a liar? *American Psychologist, 46* (9), 913–20.

Ekman, P., O'Sullivan, M., and Frank, M. G. (1999). A few can catch a liar. *Psychological Science, 10* (3), 263–6.

Ekman, P., O'Sullivan, M., Friesen, W. V., and Scherer, K. R. (1991). Invited article: Face, voice, and body in detecting deceit. *Journal of Nonverbal Behavior, 15* (2), 125–35.

Ericsson, K. A. (1996). The acquisition of expert performance: An introduction to some of the issues. In K. A. Ericsson (ed.), *The road to excellence: The acquisition of expert performance in the arts and sciences, sports, and games* (pp. 1–50). Hillsdale, NJ: Lawrence Erlbaum.

Ericsson, K. A., and Simon, H. A. (1998). How to study thinking in everyday life: contrasting think-aloud protocols with descriptions and explanations of thinking. *Mind, Culture and Activity, 5* (3), 178–86.

Fisher, R. P., and Geiselman, R. E. (1992). *Memory enhancing techniques for investigative interviewing: The cognitive interview.* Springfield, IL: Charles C. Thomas.

Frank, M. G., and Ekman, P. (1997). The ability to detect deceit generalizes across different types of high-stake lies. *Journal of Personality and Social Psychology, 72* (6), 1429–39.

Hall, J. A. (1990). *Nonverbal sex differences: Accuracy of communication and expressiveness.* Baltimore, MD: Johns Hopkins University Press.

Köhnken, G. (1987). Training police officers to detect deceptive eyewitness statements: Does it work? *Social Behavior, 1,* 1–17.

Malone, B. E., and DePaulo, B. M. (2001). Measuring sensitivity to deception. In J. A. Hall and F. J. Bernieri (eds.), *Interpersonal sensitivity: theory and measurement* (pp. 103–24). Mahwah, NJ: Lawrence Erlbaum.

Mehrabian, A. (1971). Nonverbal betrayal of feeling. *Journal of Experimental Research in Personality, 5* (1), 64–73.

Newman, M. L., Pennebaker, J. W., Berry, D. S., and Richards, J. M. (2003). Lying words: Predicting deception from linguistic styles. *Personality and Social Psychology Bulletin, 29* (5), 665–75.

O'Sullivan, M. (2000). Why I think you're lying. Paper presented at the International Congress of Psychology. Stockholm, Sweden, July 2000.

(2003). The fundamental attribution error in detecting deception: The boy-who-cried wolf effect. *Personality and Social Psychology Bulletin, 29,* 1316–27.

(in press). Detecting deception and nonverbal communication: Why most people can't 'read' others, but a few can. In R. Riggio, and R. Feldman (eds.), *Applications of Nonverbal Communication.* Mahwah, NJ. Erlbaum.

O'Sullivan, M., Ekman, P., Friesen, W., and Scherer, K. R. (1985). What you say and how you say it: The contribution of speech content and voice quality to judgments of others. *Journal of Personality and Social Psychology, 48* (1), 54–62.

Sporer, S. L. (1997). The less traveled road: Verbal cues in deception detection in account of fabrication and self experiences events. *Applied Cognitive Psychology, 11* (5), 373–97.

Yuille, J. C., Marxman, D., and Cooper, B. (1999). Training investigative interviewing: Adherence to the spirit as well as the letter. *International Journal of Law and Psychiatry. Special issue: Current Issues in Law and Psychiatry, 22* (3–4), 323–36.

NOTES

We wish to thank Leora Lubliner for her extraordinary contributions to the administrative organisation and data analysis involved in the initial phase of the Wizard Project. We also offer our sincere gratitude to the wizards who have been so generous with their time and talent.

1. We (Ekman, 1985; 2001; O'Sullivan, 2003; O'Sullivan, in press) have described numerous reasons for most people's inability to detect deception.
2. One law professor, who had a master's in counselling and taught an interviewing/self-knowledge class in a law school, was classified as a therapist rather than as law enforcement because the bulk of his work was psychological rather than legal.
3. The voice of the expert lie-catcher, the interviewer or interviewers, and, in the background, the voice of the liar/truth-teller and the person interviewing him or her.

13 Guidelines to catch a liar

Aldert Vrij

A Warning

The guidelines which will be presented in this chapter are based upon psychological principles and research regarding deception and lie detection (I will use the words 'lying' and 'deception' interchangeably throughout this chapter). Most studies are conducted in university laboratory situations where people are asked to lie for the sake of the experiment. This might be seen as a serious limitation, as lying for the sake of the experiment might well be totally different from lying in police interviews. This issue will be addressed throughout the guidelines where relevant.

Introduction

Research has convincingly demonstrated that catching liars is a difficult task and that people, including professional lie-catchers, frequently make mistakes when they attempt to detect deceit (Vrij, 2000a). In scientific studies concerning the detection of deception, observers are typically given videotaped or audiotaped statements of a number of people who are either lying or telling the truth. After each statement, observers (typically college students) are asked to judge whether the statement is truthful or false. In such tasks, guessing whether someone is lying or not gives a 50 per cent chance of being correct. Vrij (2000a) has reviewed thirty-seven lie-detection studies in which the observers were college students. The total accuracy rate, the percentage of correct answers, was 56.6 per cent, which is only just about the level of chance. The review further revealed that people are to some extent capable of detecting truths (i.e., correctly judging that someone is telling the truth: 67 per cent accuracy rate) but particularly poor at detecting lies (i.e., correctly judging that someone is lying: 44 per cent accuracy rate). In fact, 44 per cent is below the level of chance. In other words, people would be more accurate at detecting lies if they simply guessed. The superior accuracy rate for truthful messages is caused by the *truth bias*: judges are more likely to consider that messages are truthful than deceptive and, as a result, truthful messages are identified with more accuracy than are deceptive messages.

It could be argued that college students are not habitually called upon to detect deception. Perhaps professional lie-catchers, such as police officers or customs officers, would obtain higher accuracy rates than laypersons. It might be that their experience in interviewing people and catching liars has had a positive influence on their abilities and skills in detecting deceit. In several studies published to date professional lie-catchers' ability to detect lies has been tested (DePaulo and Pfeifer, 1986; Ekman and O'Sullivan, 1991; Ekman, O'Sullivan, and Frank, 1999; Köhnken, 1987; Meissner and Kassin, 2002; Porter, Woodworth, and Birt, 2000; Vrij, 1993; Vrij and Mann, 2001a, b). Three findings emerged from these studies (Vrij and Mann, 2001b, in press, b). First, most accuracy rates were similar to the accuracy rates found in studies with college students as observers (most were in the 45–60 per cent range), suggesting that professional lie-catchers are no better than laypersons in detecting deceit. Second, some groups (members of the Secret Service, US Federal officers (police officers with a special interest and experience in deception and demeanour), and sheriffs (police officers identified by their department as outstanding interrogators)) seem to be better than others (Ekman and O'Sullivan, 1991; Ekman, O'Sullivan, and Frank, 1999). Third, the truth bias, consistently found in studies with students as observers, is much less profound or perhaps even lacking in studies with professional lie-catchers. It might be that their jobs make professional lie-catchers naturally more suspicious.

However, the poor ability to detect deceit that emerged from all these detection of deception studies might be the result of an artefact. Deception research has almost exclusively been conducted in university laboratories where participants (mostly college students) tell the truth or lie for the sake of the experiment. Perhaps in these laboratory studies the stakes (positive consequences of getting away with the lie and negative consequences of getting caught) are not high enough for the liar to elicit clear cues to deception (Miller and Stiff, 1993). In order to raise the stakes in laboratory experiments, participants have been offered money if they successfully get away with their lies (Vrij, Akehurst, Soukara, and Bull, 2002; Vrij, Edward, and Bull, 2001b). In other studies, participants are told that they will be observed by a peer who will judge their sincerity (DePaulo, Stone, and Lassiter, 1985b). In a series of experiments in which the stakes were manipulated (although the stakes were never really high), it has been found that high-stake lies were easier to detect than low-stake lies (DePaulo, Kirkendol, Tang, and O'Brien, 1988; DePaulo, Lanier, and Davis, 1983; DePaulo, LeMay, and Epstein, 1991; DePaulo,

Stone, and Lassiter, 1985b; Lane and DePaulo, 1999; Vrij, 2000b; Vrij, Harden, Terry, Edward, and Bull, 2001).

In some laboratory studies the stakes were even further increased (see Frank and Ekman, 1997, and Tye, Amato, Honts, Kevitt, and Peters, 1999, for examples of 'high-' stakes laboratory scenarios). However, one might argue that in all these laboratory studies the stakes are still not comparable with the stakes liars face in some real-life situations, such as suspects during police interviews. Laboratory studies are not suitable for examining the responses in high-stake situations, as raising the stakes really high is not possible in laboratory settings for ethical reasons. In addition to this high-stakes argument, one might further argue that police officers are familiar with detecting lies which are related to crime issues, whereas in most lie-detection studies people lied about other issues than crime. For example, in a typical experiment (Ekman, O'Sullivan, and Frank, 1999), professional lie-catchers watched video clips of twenty people who gave a statement about a number of current controversial issues (such as the death penalty) which was either their true opinion (truth) or an opinion opposite to their true opinion (lie). For each statement, the professional lie-catchers were asked to indicate whether it was a truth or a lie.

Therefore, a better way to test police officers' true ability to detect truths and lies is to examine their skills when they attempt to detect real truths and lies told by suspects during police interviews. Mann, Vrij, and Bull (2004) have done exactly this. They showed 99 police officers a total of 54 video clips of suspects who were lying and telling the truth during their police interviews. The suspects were all being interviewed in connection with serious crimes such as murder, rape, and arson. After each clip the police officers were requested to indicate whether the suspect was truthful or not. None of the sample of police officers belonged to one of the specific groups which have been identified by Ekman and his colleagues as being superior lie detectors. However, the study revealed accuracy rates which were higher than generally found in previous studies. The total accuracy rate was 65 per cent, with a 64 per cent truth accuracy rate and a 66 per cent lie accuracy rate. All these accuracy rates were significantly higher than the 50 per cent level of chance. Moreover, both the total accuracy and the lie accuracy rates were higher than the accuracy rates which have been found in most previous studies (see Vrij, 2000a, for a review). However, although these ordinary police officers seemed to be better at detecting truths and lies than has been found in previous research, many incorrect decisions were still made. I believe that people will become better lie detectors if they avoid some common pitfalls and employ some alternative lie-detection strategies. I will present fifteen guidelines aimed to provide insight into these pitfalls and alternative techniques. They are based upon our understanding of the findings of more than three decades of deception research.

(1)   There is no single obvious sign to deceit like Pinocchio's growing nose

DePaulo, Lindsay, Malone, Muhlenbruck, Charlton, and Cooper (2003) and Vrij (2000a, in press) recently reviewed more than a hundred scientific studies regarding indicators of deceit. Those three reviews revealed one conclusive outcome. There is no typical cue that indicates deception. Not a single behavioural pattern, verbal response, or physiological reaction is uniquely related to deception. In other words, there is no giveaway clue like Pinocchio's growing nose. For example, it is simply not true that as soon as people start lying they raise an eyebrow, move a finger, develop a trembling voice, shuffle their feet, look away or up to the right.[1]

Despite the absence of a Pinocchio's growing nose, at least in white Western cultures, there is a strong belief among many people, including professional lie-catchers, that liars look away and make grooming gestures (Akehurst et al., 1996; Mann, Vrij, and Bull, 2004; Strömwall and Granhag, 2003; Taylor and Vrij, 2000; Vrij and Semin, 1996; Vrij and Taylor, 2003). Research has revealed that 75 per cent of police officers believe that liars look away[2] (Mann, Vrij, and Bull, 2002; Vrij and Semin, 1996) and that they make grooming gestures (Vrij and Semin, 1996). These findings are not surprising given that police manuals typically promote the idea that liars look away and fidget (Gordon, Fleisher, and Weinberg, 2002; Hess, 1997; Inbau, Reid, and Buckley, 1986; Inbau, Reid, Buckley, and Jayne, 2001; Yeschke, 1997; Zulawski and Wicklander, 1993).

Stereotypical, but incorrect, views about how liars behave may result in incorrect interpretations of behaviour during encounters between people belonging to different ethnic groups. Research in various countries such as Germany, the United Kingdom, the Netherlands, and the United States has shown that black citizens make a more suspicious impression on white police officers than white citizens do (Brown, 1995; Ruby and Brigham, 1996). The latter effect is, in part, triggered by the fact that non-verbal behaviour is culturally determined. For example, looking into the eyes of the conversation partner is regarded as polite in Western cultures but is considered to be rude in several other cultures (Vrij and Winkel, 1991; Vrij, Winkel, and Koppelaar, 1991). Therefore, not surprisingly, Afro-American people display more gaze aversion than white American people do (LaFrance and Mayo, 1976), and people living in the

Netherlands originally from Surinam, Turkey, and Morocco show more gaze aversion than native Dutch people do (Vrij, 2000a; Vrij, Dragt, and Koppelaar, 1992; Vrij and Winkel, 1991). Also, compared to Caucasian Dutch citizens, Dutch citizens originating from Surinam make more speech disturbances (speech fillers such as 'ah', 'um', 'er', and stutters), smile more often, and make more self-manipulations (scratching the head, wrists, and so on) and illustrators (hand and arm movements designed to modify and/or supplement what is being said verbally). These behaviours show an overlap with the behaviours Western white people believe liars display (Akehurst et al., 1996; Strömwall and Granhag, 2003; Taylor and Vrij, 2000; Vrij and Semin, 1996; Vrij and Taylor, 2003). Indeed, several experimental studies conducted in the Netherlands have revealed that behaviours typical for some ethnic groups living in the Netherlands make a suspicious impression on white Dutch police officers, a phenomenon which has been labelled *cross-cultural non-verbal communication errors* (Vrij and Winkel, 1992, 1994; Vrij, Winkel, and Koppelaar, 1991; Vrij, Dragt, and Koppelaar, 1992). That is, non-verbal behavioural patterns that are typical for certain ethnic groups may be interpreted by Caucasian observers as revealing attempts to hide the truth. People have stereotypical views not only on how liars respond, but also typical views about how they look. For example, Bull and Vine (2003) showed video clips of people lying or telling the truth. These people differed in their facial attractiveness. Observers of the video clips more frequently ascribed truth-telling to the attractive faces. Similarly, Aune, Levine, Ching, and Yoshimoto (1993) found that when a woman looked more attractive, she was rated as less deceptive.

(2)   **In order to reveal cues to deceit, liars should experience emotions or cognitive load, or should attempt to control themselves**

Despite the absence of giveaway clues such as Pinocchio's growing nose, sometimes signs of deceit do occur. Some responses are more likely to occur during deception than others, depending on three processes that a liar may experience: emotion, content complexity, and attempted behavioural control (DePaulo, Stone, and Lassiter, 1985a; Vrij, 2000a; Zuckerman, DePaulo, and Rosenthal, 1981). The mere fact that a person is lying will not result in any particular behaviour, but liars might be nervous (emotional), might have to think hard to come up with a plausible and convincing answer (content complexity), and might try to control their behaviour in order to give a credible impression (attempted behavioural control). Each of these three processes may elicit specific responses. The distinction between them is artificial. Lies may well feature all three aspects simultaneously, and so they should not be considered as in opposition.

Telling a lie might evoke three different emotions: fear, guilt, or duping delight (Ekman, 1985/2001). A liar might feel *guilty* because he or she is lying, might be *afraid* of getting caught, or might be *excited* about having the opportunity to fool someone. The strength of these emotions depends on the personality of the liar and on the circumstances under which the lie takes place (Ekman, 1985).

Sometimes liars find it difficult to lie, as they have to think of plausible answers, avoid contradicting themselves and tell a lie that is consistent with everything which the observer knows or might find out, whilst avoiding making slips of the tongue. Moreover, they have to remember what they have said, so that they can remain consistent when asked to repeat their story (Burgoon, Buller, and Guerrero, 1995; Vrij, 2000a). This might be more difficult than truth telling, especially when liars are unprepared and have to make up their stories instantly (DePaulo et al., 2003). Also, liars continuously have to monitor their speech and non-verbal behaviour so that they appear convincing throughout their statement. This probably becomes increasingly difficult as statements increase in length and complexity (see also Guideline 8).

Liars may worry that several cues will give their lies away and therefore will try to suppress such signs, engaging in *impression management* in order to avoid getting caught (Buller and Burgoon, 1996; Burgoon and Buller, 1994; Burgoon, Buller, Floyd, and Grandpre, 1996; Burgoon, Buller, White, Afifi, and Buslig, 1999; Krauss, 1981), that is, trying to make a convincing impression. However, this is not easy. The liar needs to suppress his or her nervousness effectively, masking evidence that they have to think hard, should know how they normally respond in order to make an honest and convincing impression, and should show which responses they want to show. It may well be the case that, when attempting to control their behaviour, liars may exhibit 'overcontrol', displaying a pattern of behaving that will appear planned, rehearsed, and lacking in spontaneity. For example, liars may believe that movements will give their lies away (Hocking and Leathers, 1980; Vrij and Semin, 1996) and will therefore move very deliberately and tend to avoid any movements that are not strictly essential. This will result in an unusual degree of rigidity and inhibition, because people do normally make movements which are not essential (DePaulo and Kirkendol, 1989).

It is also likely that liars will think that the use of speech hesitations and speech errors sound dubious (Hocking and Leathers, 1980; Vrij and Semin, 1996). Therefore they will try to avoid making such non-fluencies. This, however, may result in a speech pattern which sounds unusually smooth, as it is normal for most people to make some errors in speech (Vrij and Heaven, 1999). Impression management might also result in liars being reluctant to say certain things (for example, they might be reluctant to admit spontaneously that what they previously said was incorrect) as they will fear that this will make their stories appear less convincing.

Another possible cue that may result from inadequate control of behaviour is that performances may look flat due to a lack of involvement (Burgoon and Buller, 1994; Burgoon, Buller, and Guerrero, 1995; DePaulo et al., 2003). Charles Ingram, who was found guilty in the United Kingdom of trying to cheat his way to the top prize in the popular TV quiz *Who wants to be a Millionaire*, might have experienced this. Staff working for the TV programme became suspicious when Ingram and his wife, after winning the top prize of £1 million, 'had not appeared as jubilant as the newly rich might' (*Independent*, 8 April 2003, p. 9). Ekman (1985) pointed out that emotional facial expressions are often different when emotions are actually felt compared to when they are not actually felt. Felt smiles include all smiles in which the person actually experiences a positive emotion and presumably would report that emotion. Felt smiles are accompanied by the action of two muscles, the *Zygomatic Major*, which pulls the lip corners upwards towards the cheekbone, and the *Orbicularis Oculi*, which raises the cheek and gathers skin inwards from around the eye socket, producing a bagged skin below the eyes and crow's-feet wrinkles beyond the eye corners. False smiles are deliberately made to convince another person that a positive emotion is felt whereas, in fact, it isn't. The action of the Orbicularis Oculi is often absent in a false smile.

(3)   Some cues are more likely to occur during deception than others

The combined reviews of DePaulo et al. (2003) and Vrij (2000a, in press) revealed that six behavioural patterns and seventeen verbal patterns in particular were to some extent associated with deception.[3]

Non-verbal behaviour and deception

Liars tend to speak with a *higher pitched voice* which might be the result of experienced arousal (Ekman, Friesen, and Scherer, 1976). However, differences in pitch between liars and truth-tellers are usually very small and therefore only detectable with sophisticated equipment. Also, sometimes liars' *voices sound more tense* than truth-tellers' voices, another result of arousal. The results concerning *speech errors* (word and/or sentence repetition, sentence change, sentence incompletions, slips of the tongue, and so on) and *speech hesitations* (use of speech fillers such as 'ah', 'um', 'er', and so on) show a conflicting pattern. In most studies an increase in such errors (particularly word and phrase repetitions) and in hesitations during deception have been found. This might have been the result of liars having to think hard about their answer. Alternatively, the increase might be the result of nervousness. In some studies, however, a decrease in speech errors and speech hesitations occurred. There is some evidence that variations of lie complexity are responsible for these conflicting findings (Vrij and Heaven, 1999). Lies which are difficult to tell result in an increase in speech errors and speech hesitations (in line with the content complexity approach), whereas lies which are easy to tell result in a decrease in speech hesitations and speech errors (in line with the attempted control approach).

Liars tend to make *fewer illustrators* (hand and arm movements designed to modify and/or supplement what is being said verbally) and *fewer hand and finger movements* (non-functional movements of hands and fingers without moving the arms) than truth-tellers. The decrease in these movements might be the result of lie complexity. Increased cognitive load results in a neglect of body language, reducing overall animation (Ekman and Friesen, 1972). Ask people what they ate three days ago, and observe their behaviour while they try to remember. Most people will sit still while thinking about the answer. The decrease in movements might also be the result of an attempt to control behaviour. Liars may believe that movements will give their lies away and will therefore move very deliberately and tend to avoid any movements which are not strictly essential. An unusual degree of rigidity and inhibition (i.e., an overcompensation of behaviour) will be the result, because people normally make movements which are not essential (DePaulo and Kirkendol, 1989) even if they are not aware that they do so. Finally, the decrease in movements might be the result of a lack of emotional involvement (see the Charles Ingram example mentioned before).[4]

Verbal behaviour and deception

Compared to non-verbal indicators ($N = 6$), many more verbal indicators ($N = 16$) have been found to be associated with deception (DePaulo et al., 2003; Vrij, 2000a, in press). Compared to stories told by truth-tellers, liars' stories sound *less plausible*, and *more ambivalent*. This may all be the result of the difficulties liars face when they tell their stories.

Another verbal indicator is called *unstructured production*. Liars tend to tell their stories in chronological order (this happened first, and then this, and then that, and so on), whereas truth-tellers sometimes tend to give their account in unstructured ways, particularly when they talk about emotional events. Sometimes, when a person is clearly upset, he or she may tell you what has happened in a chaotic and incomprehensible way. In fact, the story can be so incomprehensible that a listener has to ask the person to sit down for a while, to calm down, and to repeat exactly what has happened, beginning with the start of the event. This unstructured production effect disappears when someone has already told the story a couple of times or frequently thought about the event, rehearsing it in their head, as this will result in telling a story in a more chronological order (Vrij, 2000a). Liars tend to tell their stories in a logical time sequence (Zaparniuk, Yuille, and Taylor, 1995), perhaps because this is easier to do. We return to this in Guideline 10.

Truth-tellers tend to *speak for longer* than liars do. This is probably because they include *more details* in their statements than liars (Vrij, in press). In particular, truth-tellers include *more visual details* (describe things they saw) and *more auditory details* (describe things they heard) into their accounts. They also tend to *repeat literally what has been said* more frequently (e.g., Then he said: 'How are your parents?' whereas liars would be more inclined to say: 'Then he asked me about my parents'). Moreover, truth-tellers mention *more spatial details* ('He stood behind me', 'The book was on the table under the window', 'We were in the living room') and *more temporal details* ('He switched on the TV first and then the video recorder', 'Approximately fifteen minutes later the phone rang again', 'He stayed with me for about three hours'). There are several reasons for these differences between liars and truth-tellers (Vrij, 2000a). Liars sometimes do not have enough imagination to invent such details, or they may sometimes be too difficult to fabricate. Moreover, liars sometimes do not want to provide many different details, because they are afraid that they will forget what they have said and therefore will not be able to repeat these details when asked to do so. Finally, differences might occur because memories of experienced events differ in quality from memories of imagined events (Johnson and Raye, 1981, 1998). Unlike memories of imagined events, memories of real experiences are obtained through perceptual processes and are therefore more likely to contain perceptual information when relayed (information about what someone saw, heard, said, and so on).

Moreover, compared to truth-tellers, liars tend to sound vocally *less expressive*, *more passive*, *more uncertain*, and *less involved*. This might all be the result of an overcontrol of behaviour. They also come across as being *less cooperative* and they make *more negative statements* (message includes negative comments or complaints). Both might be caused by a negative emotion felt by the liar.

Perhaps the most remarkable outcome from the literature reviews is that several signs of nervousness, such as gaze aversion and fidgeting, are unrelated to deception. This is remarkable because, as mentioned before, many people believe that those behaviours are associated with deception (Akehurst et al., 1996; Mann, Vrij, and Bull, 2002; Strömwall and Granhag, 2003; Taylor and Vrij, 2000; Vrij and Semin, 1996; Vrij and Taylor, 2003). One reason why cues of nervousness do not seem to be related to deception is that truth-tellers could be nervous as well (see Guideline 5). Secondly, the absence of cues of nervousness might be the result of an artefact. As discussed before, most deception studies are laboratory studies in which people are requested to lie or tell the truth for the sake of the experiment, and in such studies liars might not be nervous enough to elicit cues of nervousness. Different outcomes may therefore emerge when researchers investigate the reactions of liars in high-stake situations.

Vrij and Mann (2001a) and Mann, Vrij, and Bull (2002) are amongst the very few researchers who have investigated liars' behavioural responses in high-stake situations. For example, Mann, Vrij, and Bull, (2002) examined the behavioural responses of sixteen suspects during their police interviews. The police interviews were videotaped and the tapes have been made available to us for detailed scoring of the suspects' behavioural responses. All interviews were clear high-stake situations. The suspects were interviewed in connection with serious crimes such as murder, rape, and arson, and were facing long prison sentences if found guilty. Results revealed that the suspects in these high-stake situations did not show the nervous behaviours typically believed to be associated with lying, such as gaze aversion and fidgeting. In fact, they exhibited an increase in pauses, a decrease in eye blinks, and (male suspects) a decrease in finger, hand, and arm movements. This is more in agreement with the content-complexity and attempted-control approaches than with the emotional approach. The strongest evidence that content complexity affected suspects' behaviour more than nervousness was the finding regarding eye blinks. Suspects made fewer eye blinks when they lied. Research has shown that nervousness results in an increase in eye blinking (Harrigan and O'Connell, 1996), whereas increased cognitive load results in a decrease in eye blinking (Bagley and Manelis, 1979; Bauer, Strock, Goldstein, Stern, and Walrath, 1985; Wallbott and Scherer, 1991).

The apparent predominance of cognitive-load processes compared to emotional processes in those suspects is perhaps not surprising. Many of the suspects included in Mann, Vrij, and Bull's (2002) study have had regular contact with the police. Therefore, they were probably familiar with police interviews which might decrease their nervousness during those interviews. However, suspects in police interviews are often less intelligent than the average person (Gudjonsson, 1992). There is evidence that less-intelligent people will have particular difficulty in inventing plausible and convincing stories (Ekman and Frank, 1993).

Although several cues to deception are presented in this guideline, we do not suggest that looking at any of these cues individually will make people good lie detectors. In fact, we know that people who look at individual cues are typically poor lie detectors (Mann, Vrij, and Bull, 2004; Vrij, Edward, Roberts, and Bull, 2000; Vrij and Mann, 2001a). Generally, looking at a cluster of cues simultaneously is necessary, as will be discussed in Guideline 4.

(4)   The more diagnostic cues that are present, the more likely it is that the person is lying

As Pinocchio's growing nose does not exist, lie detectors should not rely just upon one cue to detect deceit. The fact that a person just shows one suspicious behavioural cue, or just one suspicious speech-related cue, does not justify labelling that person as a liar. The lie detector should therefore search for more cues, and the more cues that are present, the more likely it is that the person is lying (Ekman, O'Sullivan, Friesen, and Scherer, 1991; Vrij, Akehurst, Soukara, and Bull, 2004; Vrij, Edwards, Roberts, and Bull, 2000; Vrij and Mann, 2004). In other words, when someone decreases his or her movements during a conversation, this is not enough to conclude that he or she is lying. However, when a decrease in movements is associated with speech content that becomes less detailed and in which specific characteristics are all of a sudden lacking (someone who until that moment repeats literally what has been said, stops doing that; the person becomes all of a sudden less cooperative; no references are any longer made about the duration of events, etc.), the likelihood increases that the person is lying at that particular time.

(5)   Avoid the Othello-error

A common error in lie detection is to judge some cues too quickly as cues of deception. This happens in particular with signs of nervousness. The mistake lie detectors then make is not considering that truth-tellers can be nervous too and so may show nervous behaviours (Bond and Fahey, 1987). Such a wrong decision, mistakenly interpreting signs of nervousness displayed by truth-tellers as signs of deceit, is called the *Othello-error* (Ekman, 1985) because in Shakespeare's play, Othello made such an error. Othello falsely accuses Desdemona (his wife) of infidelity. He tells her to confess since he is going to kill her for her treachery. Desdemona asks Cassio (her alleged lover) to be called so that he can testify to her innocence. Othello tells her that he has already murdered Cassio. Realising that she cannot prove her innocence, Desdemona reacts with an emotional outburst. Othello misinterprets this outburst as a sign of her infidelity.

Polygraph examiners are vulnerable to the Othello-error (A. Vrij, 2001). In a polygraph test which is frequently used, the directed lie test (Iacono and Lykken, 1997; Raskin, 1989), examinees are asked 'control questions' such as 'Have you ever told a lie before in your life?' and 'Have you ever done anything which was not according to the rules?' Examinees are encouraged to lie to these questions with a simple 'No' and to think about situations in which they told a serious lie or in which they seriously broke the rules. In this way, the examiner establishes someone's *'base-line-arousal'* in 'serious situations'. The examiner also asks 'relevant questions' which are specifically about the crime. A relevant question in a murder investigation could be: 'On March 12, did you shoot Scott Fisbee?' (Iacono and Patrick, 1997). Polygraph examiners assume that guilty examinees will show a stronger response to the relevant question than to the control questions, as by denying the allegation, they are telling a serious lie which imposes a serious threat (in case the lie is detected). Innocent suspects are believed to show a weaker response to the relevant question than to the control questions, as they could answer the relevant question truthfully and have nothing to fear. However, it is not unreasonable to believe that even some innocent suspects will show a strong response when they answer the crucial question: 'On March 12, did you shoot Scott Fisbee?' (Ofshe and Leo, 1997). Polygraph research has revealed that this indeed happens (Vrij, 2000a). See Kleiner (2002), MacLaren (2001), Vrij (2000a), and the report written by the Committee to Review the Scientific Evidence on the Polygraph (2003) for recent reviews of polygraph research.

The Othello-error implies that lie detectors should be very cautious interpreting a given response as an indication of deception. Instead, lie detectors should always consider alternative explanations before deciding that someone is lying. For example, they should consider questions such as: 'Is my questioning likely to evoke emotions in the respondent, regardless of whether they are guilty?', 'Is the present situation likely to evoke emotions in the respondent anyway?', 'Is this a type of person who is likely to be emotional in this situation anyway?', and so on (Ekman, 1985).

Given its importance, looking for alternative explanations is explicitly mentioned in Guidelines 6 and 7.

(6) Pay attention to mismatches between speech content and non-verbal behaviour and try to explain these mismatches

As mentioned in endnote 4, strong emotions may result in almost automatic facial expressions. Since certain patterns of facial expressions are so specifically related to certain emotions, it is highly likely that the person actually feels the emotion when a specific facial expressions pattern emerges, even when he or she denies feeling the emotion. However, other cues are less diagnostic. Although perhaps most people will show clear signs of distress when they experience a negative event, some others don't (Baldry, Winkel, and Enthoven, 1997; Burgess, 1985; Burgess and Homstrom, 1974; Vrij and Fischer, 1995). In other words, not showing distress during an interview about an upsetting event is not a valid indicator of deceit (Littmann and Szewczyk, 1983). Moreover, as already mentioned in Guideline 1, non-verbal behaviour is culturally defined, and incorrect interpretations of behaviours displayed in cross-cultural interactions are easily made. Therefore, when lie detectors notice a mismatch between someone's non-verbal behaviour and speech content they should be careful about how they interpret this difference, and a final judgement that the person is lying should not be made too easily. Keep in mind the possibility that the person is lying, but consider this as only one possibility for this mismatch.

(7) Attention should be directed at deviations from a person's 'Normal' or usual patterns of behaviour and speech, when these are known. Try to explain the deviations

There are large individual differences in people's speech, behaviour, and physiological responses. Some expressive people typically make many movements, others don't; some people are very talkative, others are not, etc. Owing to these individual differences, a given response is often difficult to interpret, as it leaves the observer with a dilemma: Is a particular response a sign of deceit or is it someone's natural truthful response? Therefore, it might facilitate lie detection if someone's natural truthful speech style, behaviour, and physiological response is known to the observer so that behaviour, speech style, or physiological response under investigation could be compared with that person's natural truthful speech style, behaviour, or physiological response. A deviation from the natural truthful response might indicate that a person is lying.

Research has shown that this so-called *base-line method* works and that people are better lie detectors when they have seen somebody's natural truthful behaviour (Brandt, Miller, and Hocking, 1980a, b, 1982; Feeley, deTurck, and Young, 1995).

However, people behave differently in different situations (DePaulo, 1992; DePaulo and Friedman, 1998). Therefore, crucial in applying the base-line method is that parts of the interview are compared *which are truly comparable*. It is important to avoid comparing apples with oranges. Unfortunately, comparing the wrong parts of an interview is common practice in police interviews (Moston and Engelberg, 1993), and police detectives are even taught to make an incorrect comparison (Horvath, Jayne, and Buckley, 1994; Inbau et al., 1986/2001). For example, comparisons are typically made between someone's responses during small talk at the beginning of the interview and their responses during the actual interrogation. This is an incorrect way of employing the technique as small talk and the actual investigative part of the police interview are totally different situations. The actual interview matters to suspects as there might be severe negative consequences when they are not believed. In other words, this is a high-stake situation. Although the suspect might generally be feeling anxious about the coming interview, the small talk has no such consequences and is therefore a low-stake situation. People tend to behave differently during low-stake and high-stake situations and both guilty and innocent suspects tend to change their behaviour the moment the actual interview starts (Ekman, 1985; Vrij, 1995). (The reason why the base-line method worked in previous deception studies (Brandt, Miller, and Hocking, 1980a, b; Feeley, deTurck, and Young, 1995) is that both the initial small talk and the actual interviews were low-stake situations and therefore comparable.)

A better comparison was made in the following murder case (Vrij and Mann, 2001a). During a videotaped real-life police interview, a man suspected of murder (and later convicted of murder) was asked to describe his activities during a particular day. The murder suspect gave descriptions of his activities during the morning, afternoon, and evening. Detailed analyses of the videotape revealed a sudden change in behaviour as soon as he started to describe his activities during the afternoon and evening. One possible reason for this may have been that he was lying. Evidence supported this view. Police investigations could confirm his story with respect to his morning activities but revealed that his statement about the afternoon and evening was fabricated. In reality, he met the victim in the afternoon and killed her later on that day.

In the case of the murderer, we were able to make a good comparison. There are no good reasons why different behaviours would emerge while describing different parts of the day. When such differences do emerge, they are remarkable and worth investigating. Interestingly, the question on which we based the base-line method 'What did you do that particular day?' could be asked in many interviews.

Even when appropriate comparisons are made, the lie detector should be careful about drawing conclusions. A difference in response between two comparable parts of the interview does not necessarily indicate that someone is lying; it is only a possibility. Other explanations for the change in response should be taken into consideration as well. For example, there is some evidence that some behaviours are topic related. ('Topic' is not a synonym of 'stake'. During a high-stake interview, different topics can be discussed.) While analysing the behaviour shown by Saddam Hussein when he was interviewed by Peter Arnett during the First Gulf War (the interview was broadcast by CNN), Davis and Hadiks (1995) found that the illustrators Hussein made were to some extent related to the topic he discussed. When discussing Israel he made specific movements with his left forearm. This behavioural pattern emerged only when he was discussing Israel and Zionism. The lie detector therefore should consider whether different response patterns shown during a high-stake interview might be topic-related.

(8) Encourage a person to talk

It might be beneficial to encourage a person who is suspected of lying to talk. Cognitive load, one of the reasons why cues to deception might occur, will increase when people talk a lot, as liars then have to think continuously of plausible answers without contradicting themselves, and tell a lie that is consistent with everything which the observer knows or might find out, and continuously have to monitor their speech and non-verbal behaviour so that they appear convincingly throughout their statement. In case a lie detector suspects a certain statement to be a lie, he or she might encourage the alleged liar to elaborate on their statements.

(9) Let the person repeat what he or she has said

A common reason why liars get caught is that they have not fully prepared themselves (Ekman, 1985; Vrij, 2000a). Therefore, they may be taken by surprise by a certain question and immediately have to invent an answer in order not to appear suspicious. Lie detectors could benefit from such poor preparation by asking people to repeat what they have just said.

Some liars would not be able to remember in detail what they have just said and thus could be easily caught. This technique can be used in almost all circumstances, including during short interactions ('You just gave me your date of birth, address, and postcode. Could you please give me this information again?').

(10)   Let the person tell his or her story in a non-chronological order

As discussed under Guideline 2, lying is sometimes cognitively difficult. Under Guideline 3 it was pointed out that it is difficult for people to recount an invented story in a non-chronological order. Lie detectors could exploit this by asking people to tell their stories in a non-chronological order. This should increase the cognitive load on interviewees and might put a real strain on liars, thus enhancing the likelihood of occurrence of cognitive-load cues in liars. Asking people to tell their stories in a non-chronological order, particularly asking them to recount the story in reverse order, is currently employed in police interviews as it is part of the Cognitive Interview procedure (Fisher, Brennan, and McCauley, 2002; Fisher and Geiselman, 1992). However, the Cognitive Interview is used as a memory-enhancing technique while interviewing *witnesses* (the technique results in interviewees recalling more information about an event they have witnessed), rather than a technique to detect lies in *suspects* (but see Colwell, Hiscock, and Memon, 2002, and Hernandez-Fernaud and Alonso-Quecuty, 1997, for exceptions).

(11)   Be suspicious/on guard

One important reason why lie detectors are not good at catching liars is that they have a tendency to believe other people (Levine, McCornack, and Park, 1999). Credulity is an important reason why lies remain often undetected between romantic partners (Levine and McCornack, 1992). Credulity is sometimes caused by conversation rules. In conversations with acquaintances or colleagues it is 'odd' or 'paranoid' to be suspicious and uncommon to express this suspicion. Conversation partners will probably not appreciate utterances such as 'Could you elaborate on this?', 'Could you back this up with evidence?', 'Could you repeat what you have just said?' in daily-life conversations and might object to it. However, it is more accepted to be suspicious during police interviews and other situations such as customs interviews and security checks.

Although lie detectors should be suspicious at any time (they should always be aware that someone may be trying to dupe them and has the capability of fooling them), they should not actually show any suspicion, as this may in itself change a person's behaviour (see Guideline 5, the Othello-error). Showing suspicion could also result in other undesirable reactions from the alleged liar, such as refusing to talk any longer ('Why should I speak to you? You don't believe me anyway!'), or starting a 'counter-attack'. When a wife accuses her husband of lying about an affair she believes he has with another woman, he might respond with 'Why don't you trust me?'

Inbau and his colleagues (Inbau et al., 1986/2001) advise police detectives to confront suspects with pieces of evidence they have already gathered. Pearse and Gudjonsson (1996) who listened to 161 police interviews with suspects in two London police stations found that this tactic was employed in three-quarters of the interviews. This interview style will hamper lie detection. One of the difficulties for liars is that they do not know what the observer knows. They therefore do not know what they can say without running the risk of being caught out. By disclosing to suspects the facts they know, police officers make lying easier for suspects. Also, not knowing what the lie detector knows might elicit fear in the liar: Fear of saying the wrong thing, which may result in the lie being exposed.

(12)   Pay attention to speech content and vocal aspects when attempting to detect deceit

A popular belief is that lie detection is easiest when the lie detector has access to the full picture of the potential liar and that just reading a textual version of a statement, or just listening to someone's voice hampers lie detection. However, research has shown that this is not the case. Lie-detection experiments have revealed that people become better lie detectors when they pay attention to speech content cues (plausibility, contradictions, etc.) and vocal aspects (tone of voice, etc.) (Anderson, DePaulo, Ansfield, Tickle, and Green, 1999; Feeley and Young, 2000; Mann, Vrij, and Bull, 2004; Vrij and Mann, 2001a). Other research has revealed that people become better lie detectors as soon as they are not exposed to someone's face (DePaulo et al., 1985a; Wiseman, 1995). The reason for this is that lie detectors are inclined to look at someone's eye movements when these are available to them (Mann, Vrij, and Bull, 2004; Vrij and Mann, 2001a), whereas in fact eye movements are quite easy to control and not related to deception.[5]

(13)   Employ implicit lie-detection techniques

There is evidence that people know more about deception than it first appears, when they are asked indirectly whether they think someone is lying (Burgoon and Buller, 1994; DePaulo, 1994). In Vrij, Edward, and Bull's (2001a) study, participants lied or told the truth about a staged event. In an attempt to simulate what liars experience in police interviews, they had created a situation in which the task was more difficult for the liars than for the truth-tellers, and, as a result of this, liars showed signs of cognitive load such as a decrease in hand and finger movements. The interviews were videotaped and shown to police officers. Some were asked whether each of the people were lying (explicit lie detection), others were asked to indicate for each person whether that person 'had to think hard' (implicit lie detection, they were not informed that some people were actually lying). Police officers could distinguish between truths and lies, but only by using the implicit method. An explanation for this finding is that, when detecting deceit explicitly, police officers rely on their stereotypical views about deceptive behaviour, such as 'liars look away' and 'liars make many movements'. As mentioned previously, these stereotypical views are mostly incorrect. While detecting deceit in an implicit way, however, the participants might have been implicitly directed to look at more valid cues. Indeed, the findings showed that only officers using the indirect method paid attention to the cues which actually discriminated between truth-tellers and liars on the videotape, such as a decrease in hand and finger movements. See DePaulo (1994) and A. Vrij (2001) for overviews of implicit lie-detection studies.

(14)   Detecting deceit might be easiest during the first interview

Lie detection is perhaps easier during the first interview than during subsequent interviews. During the first interview, interviewees may not yet be fully prepared and may not have worked out their interview strategy, or rehearsed their story in their head. During the Second World War, members of the resistance who were caught by the Germans and subsequently interviewed by German police were often poorly prepared for those interviews (J. Vrij, 2001). All their precaution activities were focused on avoiding getting caught by the German police, and the equally important aspect of what to say if they were captured was ignored.

In addition, after the initial phase of the interview, interview dynamics are probably going to play an important role which makes interpreting the responses of the alleged liar more complex. For example, the interview may create suspicion in the interviewer and this suspicion, in turn, may affect the interviewee's behaviour (Bond and Fahey, 1987; Buller, Stiff, and Burgoon, 1996; Burgoon, Buller, Dillman, and Walther, 1995; Burgoon, Buller, Ebesu, White, and Rockwell, 1996).

Also, it is known that when people communicate with each other, behavioural matching and behavioural synchrony takes place (Akehurst and Vrij, 1999; Bargh and Chartrand, 1999; Burgoon et al., 1995, 1996, 1999; Chartrand and Bargh, 1999). People may mirror each other's posture or they may converge in how quickly and how loudly they speak. This effect can occur quite unconsciously. They may also reciprocate each other's gazing, nodding, and smiling behaviour, and even accents can converge (DePaulo and Friedman, 1998). This effect, recently labelled 'the chameleon effect' (Chartrand and Bargh, 1999) emerges even when total strangers interact with each other and it happens within a few minutes (Akehurst and Vrij, 1999; Chartrand and Bargh, 1999). Akehurst and Vrij (1999) carried out an experiment where the experimenter (a retired police detective) was instructed to make grooming gestures. Within a minute the people who were interviewed (the 'suspects') mimicked these mannerisms. As a result, the behaviour of the interviewee might become influenced by the behaviour of the interviewer as the interview progresses. This complicates interpreting the behaviour of the interviewee considerably.[6]

(15)   Check the information provided

Probably the most definite way of detecting lies is to compare what has been said with the evidence available. If a person claims that he stayed at home all night, clear CCTV evidence showing that he walked in a street at the time he claimed to be at home reveals that he was lying with a level of certainty often not obtained by other lie-detection tools. It is therefore important to check as much as possible the information which has been provided by the potential liar. This guideline sounds obvious, but it is an important guideline. Introducing improved lie-detection techniques during police interviews may result in police officers focusing more on such interviews and putting less effort in searching for conclusive evidence, as interviewing might be easier and less time consuming than finding decisive evidence. This guideline reminds police officers that lie-detection techniques can never be an appropriate substitute for corroborating evidence.

Conclusion

Police officers make mistakes when they attempt to distinguish between lies and truths during police interviews. That mistakes occur is not surprising. Detecting deceit is a difficult task, as there is nothing like Pinocchio's growing nose. As a result, there is no valid cue a lie detector can rely upon. In this chapter I have presented fifteen guidelines pointing out several pitfalls in lie detection and several suggestions for improved interview techniques. I believe that police officers will become better lie detectors if they follow these guidelines. However, we are aware that many of these guidelines have not been employed yet in police interviews or tested in laboratory research. I hope that introducing these guidelines will stimulate practitioners and researchers to test them, as we believe that their feedback will be of much value for the further development of lie-detection techniques.

REFERENCES

Akehurst, L., Köhnken, G., Vrij, A., and Bull, R. (1996). Lay persons' and police officers' beliefs regarding deceptive behaviour. *Applied Cognitive Psychology*, *10*, 461–73.

Akehurst, L., and Vrij, A. (1999). Creating suspects in police interviews. *Journal of Applied Social Psychology*, *29*, 192–210.

Anderson, D. E., DePaulo, B. M., Ansfield, M. E., Tickle, J. J., and Green, E. (1999). Beliefs about cues to deception: Mindless stereotypes or untapped wisdom? *Journal of Nonverbal Behaviour*, *23*, 67–89.

Aune, R., Levine, T., Ching, P., and Yoshimoto, J. (1993). The influence of perceived source reward on attributions of deception. *Communication Research Reports*, *10*, 15–27.

Bagley, J., and Manelis, L. (1979). Effect of awareness of an indicator of cognitive load. *Perceptual and Motor Skills*, *49*, 591–4.

Baldry, A. C., Winkel, F. W., and Enthoven, D. S. (1997). Paralinguistic and nonverbal triggers of biased credibility assessments of rape victims in Dutch police officers: An experimental study of 'Nonevidentiary' bias. In S. Redondo, V. Garrido, J. Perze, and R. Barbaret (eds.), *Advances in psychology and law* (pp. 163–74). Berlin: Walter de Gruyter.

Bargh, J. A., and Chartrand, T. L. (1999). The unbearable automaticity of being. *American Psychologist*, *54*, 462–79.

Bauer, L. O., Strock, B. D., Goldstein, R., Stern, J. A., and Walrath, L. C. (1985). Auditory discrimination and the eyeblink. *Psychophysiology*, *22*, 629–35.

Bond, C. F., and Fahey, W. E. (1987). False suspicion and the misperception of deceit. *British Journal of Social Psychology*, *26*, 41–6.

Brandt, D. R., Miller, G. R., and Hocking, J. E. (1980a). The truth-deception attribution: Effects of familiarity on the ability of observers to detect deception. *Human Communication Research*, *6*, 99–110.

(1980b). Effects of self-monitoring and familiarity on deception detection. *Communication Quarterly*, *28*, 3–10.

(1982). Familiarity and lie detection: A replication and extension. *Western Journal of Speech Communication*, *46*, 276–90.

Brown, R. (1995). *Prejudice: Its social psychology*. Cambridge: Blackwell.

Bull, R., and Vine, M. (2003). Are judgements of who is lying influenced by their facial attractiveness? Manuscript in preparation.

Buller, D. B., and Burgoon, J. K. (1996). Interpersonal deception theory. *Communication Theory*, *6*, 203–42.

Buller, D. B., Stiff, J. B., and Burgoon, J. K. (1996). Behavioral adaptation in deceptive transactions: Fact or fiction. Reply to Levine and McCornack. *Human Communication Research*, *22*, 589–603.

Burgess, A. W. (1985). *Rape and sexual assault: A research book*. London: Garland.

Burgess, A. W., and Homstrom, L. L. (1974). *Rape: Victims of crisis*. Bowie: Brady.

Burgoon, J. K., and Buller, D. B. (1994). Interpersonal deception, III: Effects of deceit on perceived communication and nonverbal dynamics. *Journal of Nonverbal Behavior*, *18*, 155–84.

Burgoon, J. K., Buller, D. B., Dillman, L., and Walther, J. B. (1995). Interpersonal deception, IV: Effects of suspicion on perceived communication and nonverbal behaviour dynamics. *Human Communication Research*, *22*, 163–96.

Burgoon, J. K., Buller, D. B., Ebesu, A. S., White, C. H., and Rockwell, P. A. (1996). Testing interpersonal deception theory: Effects of suspicion on communication behaviors and perception. *Communication Theory*, *6*, 243–67.

Burgoon, J. K., Buller, D. B., Floyd, K., and Grandpre, J. (1996). Deceptive realities: Sender, receiver, and observer perspectives in deceptive conversations. *Communication Research*, *23*, 724–48.

Burgoon, J. K., Buller, D. B., and Guerrero, L. K. (1995). Interpersonal deception, IX: Effects of social skill and nonverbal communication on deception success and detection accuracy. *Journal of Language and Social Psychology*, *14*, 289–311.

Burgoon, J. K., Buller, D. B., White, C. H., Afifi, W., and Buslig, A. L. S. (1999). The role of conversation involvement in deceptive interpersonal interactions. *Personality and Social Psychology Bulletin*, *25*, 669–85.

Chartrand, T. L., and Bargh, J. A. (1999). The chameleon effect: The perception-behavior link and social interaction. *Journal of Personality and Social Psychology*, *76*, 893–910.

Colwell, K., Hiscock, C. K., and Memon, A. (2002). Interviewing techniques and the assessment of statement credibility. *Applied Cognitive Psychology*, *16*, 287–300.

Committee to Review the Scientific Evidence on the Polygraph (2003). *The polygraph and lie detection*. Washington, DC: National Academies Press.

Davis, M., and Hadiks, D. (1995). Demeanor and credibility. *Semiotica*, *106*, 5–54.

DePaulo, B. M. (1992). Nonverbal behavior and self-presentation. *Psychological Bulletin*, *111*, 203–43.

(1994). Spotting lies: Can humans learn to do better? *Current Directions in Psychological Science, 3,* 83–6.

DePaulo, B. M., and Friedman, H. S. (1998). Nonverbal communication. In D. T. Gilbert, S. T. Fiske, and G. Lindzey (eds.), *The handbook of social psychology* (pp. 3–40). Boston, MA: McGraw-Hill.

DePaulo, B. M., Kashy, D. A., Kirkendol, S. E., Wyer, M. M., and Epstein, J. A. (1996). Lying in everyday life. *Journal of Personality and Social Psychology, 70,* 979–95.

DePaulo, B. M., and Kirkendol, S. E. (1989). The motivational impairment effect in the communication of deception. In J. C. Yuille (ed.), *Credibility assessment* (pp. 51–70). Dordrecht, the Netherlands: Kluwer Academic.

DePaulo, B. M., Kirkendol, S. E., Tang, J., and O'Brien, T. P. (1988). The motivational impairment effect in the communication of deception: Replications and extensions. *Journal of Nonverbal Behaviour, 12,* 177–201.

DePaulo, B. M., Lanier, K., and Davis, T. (1983). Detecting the deceit of the motivated liar. *Journal of Personality and Social Psychology, 45,* 1096–103.

DePaulo, B. M., LeMay, C. S., and Epstein, J. A. (1991). Effects of importance of success and expectations for success on effectiveness at deceiving. *Personality and Social Psychology Bulletin, 17,* 14–24.

DePaulo, B. M., Lindsay, J. L., Malone, B. E., Muhlenbruck, L., Charlton, K., and Cooper, H. (2003). Cues to deception. *Psychological Bulletin, 129,* 74–118.

DePaulo, B. M., and Pfeifer, R. L. (1986). On-the-job experience and skill at detecting deception. *Journal of Applied Social Psychology, 16,* 249–67.

DePaulo, B. M., Stone, J. L., and Lassiter, G. D. (1985a). Deceiving and detecting deceit. In B. R. Schenkler (ed.), *The self and social life* (pp. 323–70). New York: McGraw-Hill.

DePaulo, B. M., Stone, J. I., and Lassiter, G. D. (1985b). Telling ingratiating lies: Effects of target sex and target attractiveness on verbal and nonverbal deceptive success. *Journal of Personality and Social Psychology, 48,* 1191–203.

Ekman, P. (1985). *Telling lies: Clues to deceit in the marketplace, politics and marriage.* New York: Norton.

Ekman, P., and Frank, M. G. (1993). Lies that fail. In M. Lewis and C. Saarni (eds.), *Lying and deception in everyday life* (pp. 184–201). New York, NJ: Guilford Publications.

Ekman, P., and Friesen, W. V. (1972). Hand movements. *Journal of Communication, 22,* 353–74.

Ekman, P., Friesen, W. V., and Scherer, K. R. (1976). Body movement and voice pitch in deceptive interaction. *Semiotica, 16,* 23–7.

Ekman, P., and O'Sullivan, M. (1989). Hazards in detecting deceit. In D. C. Raskin (ed.), *Psychological methods in criminal investigation and evidence.* New York: Springer.

(1991). Who can catch a liar? *American Psychologist, 46,* 913–20.

Ekman, P., O'Sullivan, M., and Frank, M. G. (1999). A few can catch a liar. *Psychological Science, 10,* 263–6.

Ekman, P., O'Sullivan, M., Friesen, W. V., and Scherer, K. (1991). Face, voice, and body in detecting deceit. *Journal of Nonverbal Behavior, 15,* 125–35.

Feeley, T. H., deTurck, M. A., and Young, M. J. (1995). Baseline familiarity in lie detection. *Communication Research Reports, 12,* 160–9.

Feeley, T. H., and Young, M. J. (2000). The effects of cognitive capacity on beliefs about deceptive communication. *Communication Quarterly, 48,* 101–19.

Fisher, R. P., Brennan, K. H., and McCauley, M. R. (2002). The cognitive interview method to enhance eyewitness recall. In M. L. Eisen, J. A. Quas, and G. S. Goodman (eds.), *Memory and suggestibility in the forensic interview* (pp. 265–86). Mahwah, NJ: Lawrence Erlbaum.

Fisher, R. P., and Geiselman, R. E. (1992). *Memory-enhancing techniques for investigative interviewing: The cognitive interview.* Springfield, IL: Charles C. Thomas.

Frank, M. G., and Ekman, P. (1997). The ability to detect deceit generalizes across different types of high-stake lies. *Journal of Personality and Social Psychology, 72,* 1429–39.

Gordon, N. J., Fleisher, W. L., and Weinberg, C. D. (2002). *Effective interviewing and interrogation techniques.* San Diego, CA: Academic Press.

Granhag, P. A., and Strömwall, L. A. (2002). Repeated interrogations: Verbal and nonverbal cues to deception. *Applied Cognitive Psychology, 16,* 243–57.

Gudjonsson, G. H. (1992). *The psychology of interrogations, confessions and testimony.* Chichester, England: Wiley.

Harrigan, J. A., and O'Connell, D. M. (1996). Facial movements during anxiety states. *Personality and Individual Differences, 21,* 205–12.

Hernandez-Fernaud, E., and Alonso-Quecuty, M. (1997). The Cognitive Interview and lie detection: A new magnifying glass for Sherlock Holmes? *Applied Cognitive Psychology, 11,* 55–68.

Hess, J. E. (1997). *Interviewing and interrogation for law enforcement.* Reading, UK: Anderson Publishing.

Hirsch, A., and Wolf, C. J. (2001). Practical methods for detecting mendacity: A case study. *Journal of the American Academy of Psychiatry and the Law, 29,* 438–44.

Hocking, J. E., and Leathers, D. G. (1980). Nonverbal indicators of deception: A new theoretical perspective. *Communication Monographs, 47,* 119–131.

Horvath, F., Jayne, B., and Buckley, J. (1994). Differentiation of truthful and deceptive criminal suspects in behavior analysis interviews. *Journal of Forensic Sciences, 39,* 793–807.

Iacono, W. G., and Lykken, D. T. (1997). The validity of the lie detector: Two surveys of scientific opinion. *Journal of Applied Psychology, 82,* 426–33.

Iacono, W. G., and Patrick, C. J. (1997). Polygraphy and integrity testing. In R. Rogers (ed.), *Clinical assessment of malingering and deception.* 2nd edn (pp. 252–81). New York: Guilford Publications.

Inbau, F. E., Reid, J. E., and Buckley, J. P. (1986). *Criminal interrogation and confessions* (3rd edn). Baltimore, MD: Williams & Wilkins.

Inbau, F. E., Reid, J. E., Buckley, J. P., and Jayne, B. C. (2001). *Criminal interrogation and confessions* (4th edn). Gaithersburg, MA: Aspen Publishers.

Johnson, M. K., and Raye, C. L. (1981). Reality Monitoring. *Psychological Review, 88,* 67–85.

Johnson, M. K., and Raye, C. L. (1998). False memories and confabulation. *Trends in Cognitive Sciences, 2*, 137–45.

Kleiner, M. (ed.). (2002). *Handbook of polygraph testing*. San Diego, CA: Academic Press.

Köhnken, G. (1987). Training police officers to detect deceptive eyewitness statements. Does it work? *Social Behaviour, 2*, 1–17.

Krauss, R. M. (1981). Impression formation, impression management, and non-verbal behaviors. In E. T. Higgins, C. P. Herman, and M. P. Zanna (eds.), *Social cognition: The Ontario Symposium*, Vol. I (pp. 323–41). Hillsdale, NJ: Lawrence Erlbaum.

LaFrance, M., and Mayo, C. (1976). Racial differences in gaze behaviour during conversations: Two systematic observational studies. *Journal of Personality and Social Psychology, 33*, 547–52.

Lane, J. D., and DePaulo, B. M. (1999). Completing Coyne's cycle: Dysphorics' ability to detect deception. *Journal of Research in Personality, 33*, 311–29.

Levine, T. R., and McCornack, S. A. (1992). Linking love and lies: A formal test of the McCornack and Parks model of deception detection. *Journal of Social and Personal Relationships, 9*, 143–54.

Levine, T. R., McCornack, S. A., and Park, H. S. (1999). Accuracy in detecting truths and lies: Documenting the 'veracity effect'. *Communication Monographs, 66*, 125–44.

Littmann, E., and Szewczyk, H. (1983). Zu einigen Kriterien und Ergebnissen forensisch-psychologischer Glaubwürdigkeitsbegutachtung von sexuell misbrauchten Kindern und Jugendlichen. *Forensia, 4*, 55–72.

MacLaren, V. V. (2001). A quantitative review of the Guilty Knowledge Test. *Journal of Applied Psychology, 86*, 674–83.

Mann, S., Vrij, A., and Bull, R. (2002). Suspects, lies and videotape: An analysis of authentic high-stakes liars. *Law and Human Behaviour, 26*, 365–76.

(2004). Detecting true lies: Police officers' ability to detect suspects' lies. *Journal of Applied Psychology, 89*, 137–49.

Meissner, C. A., and Kassin, S. M. (2002). 'He's guilty!': Investigator bias in judgments of truth and deception. *Law and Human Behavior, 26*, 469–80.

Miller, G. R., and Stiff, J. B. (1993). *Deceptive communication*. Newbury Park, CA: Sage.

Moston, S., and Engelberg, T. (1993). Police questioning techniques in tape recorded interviews with criminal suspects. *Policing and Society, 3*, 223–37.

Ofshe, R. J., and Leo, R. A. (1997). The decision to confess falsely: Rational choice and irrational action. *Denver University Law Review, 74*, 979–1112.

Pavlidis, J., Eberhardt, N. L., and Levine, J. A. (2002). Seeing through the face of deception. *Nature, 415*, 35.

Pearse, J., and Gudjonsson, G. (1996). Police interviewing techniques of two south London police stations. *Psychology, Crime, and Law, 3*, 63–74.

Porter, S., Woodworth, M., and Birt, A, R. (2000). Truth, lies, and videotape: An investigation of the ability of federal parole officers to detect deception. *Law and Human Behaviour, 24*, 643–58.

Raskin, D. C. (1989). Polygraph techniques for the detection of deception. In D. C. Raskin (ed.), *Psychological methods in criminal investigation and evidence* (pp. 247–96). New York: Springer.

Ruby, C. L., and Brigham, J. C. (1996). A criminal schema: The role of chronicity, race, and socioeconomic status in law enforcement officials' perceptions of others. *Journal of Applied Social Psychology, 26*, 95–112.

Strömwall, L. A., and Granhag, P. A. (2003). How to detect deception? Arresting the beliefs of police officers, prosecutors and judges. *Psychology, Crime, and Law, 9*, 19–36.

Taylor, R., and Vrij, A. (2000). The effects of varying stake and cognitive complexity on beliefs about the cues to deception. *International Journal of Police Science and Management, 3*, 111–24.

Tye, M. C., Amato, S. L., Honts, C. R., Kevitt, M. K., and Peters, D. (1999). The willingness of children to lie and the assessment of credibility in an ecologically relevant laboratory setting. *Applied Developmental Science, 3*, 92–109.

Vrij, A. (1993). Credibility judgments of detectives: The impact of nonverbal behavior, social skills and physical characteristics on impression formation. *Journal of Social Psychology, 133*, 601–11.

(1995). Behavioral correlates of deception in a simulated police interview. *Journal of Psychology: Interdisciplinary and Applied, 129*, 15–29.

(2000a). *Detecting lies and deceit: The psychology of lying and its implications for professional practice*. Chichester: John Wiley.

(2000b). Telling and detecting lies as a function of raising the stakes. In C. M. Breur, M. M. Kommer, J. F. Nijboer, and J. M. Reintjes (eds.), *New trends in criminal investigation and evidence II* (pp. 699–709). Antwerpen, Belgium: Intersentia.

(2001). Liegen en het ontmaskeren van leugenaars: Leugens en waarheden over de polygraaf. In M. Bockstaele (ed.), *De Polygraaf* (pp. 11–33). Uitgeverij Politeia.

(in press). Criteria-Based Content Analysis: A qualitative review of the first 37 studies. *Psychology, Public Policy, and Law*.

Vrij, A., Akehurst, L., Soukara, S., and Bull, R. (2002). Will the truth come out? The effect of deception, age, status, coaching, and social skills on CBCA scores. *Law and Human Behavior, 26*, 261–83.

(2004). Detecting deceit via analyses of verbal and nonverbal behavior in children and adults. *Human Communication Research, 30*, 8–41.

Vrij, A., Dragt, A. W., and Koppelaar, L. (1992). Interviews with ethnic interviewees: Nonverbal communication errors in impression formation. *Journal of Community and Applied Social Psychology, 2*, 199–209.

Vrij, A., Edward, K., and Bull, R. (2001a). Police officers' ability to detect deceit: The benefit of indirect deception detection measures. *Legal and Criminological Psychology, 6, 2*, 185–97.

(2001b). Stereotypical verbal and nonverbal responses while deceiving others. *Personality and Social Psychology Bulletin, 27*, 899–909.

Vrij, A., Edward, K., Roberts, K. P., and Bull, R. (2000). Detecting deceit via analysis of verbal and nonverbal behaviour. *Journal of Nonverbal Behaviour, 24*, 239–63.

Vrij, A., and Fischer, A. (1995). The expression of emotions in simulated rape interviews. *Journal of Police and Criminal Psychology, 10*, 64–7.

Vrij, A., Harden, F., Terry, J., Edward, K., and Bull, R. (2001). The influence of personal characteristics, stakes and lie complexity on the accuracy and confidence to detect deceit. In R. Roesch, R. R. Corrado, and R. J. Dempster (eds.), *Psychology in the courts: International advances in knowledge* (pp. 289–304). London: Routledge.

Vrij, A., and Heaven, S. (1999). Vocal and verbal indicators of deception as a function of lie complexity. *Psychology, Crime, and Law, 4*, 401–13.

Vrij, A., and Lochun, S. (1997). Neuro-linguistic programming and the police: Worthwhile or not? *Journal of Police and Criminal Psychology, 12*, 25–31.

Vrij, A., and Mann, S. (2001a). Telling and detecting lies in a high-stake situation: The case of a convicted murderer. *Applied Cognitive Psychology, 15*, 187–203.

(2001b). Who killed my relative? Police officers' ability to detect real-life high-stake lies. *Psychology, Crime, and Law, 7*, 119–32.

(2003). Telling and detecting true lies: Investigating and detecting the lies of murderers and thieves during police interviews. In M. Verhallen, G. Verkaeke, P. J. van Koppen, and J. Goethals (eds.), *Much ado about crime: Chapters on psychology and law* (pp. 185–208). Brussels: Uitgeverij Politeia.

(2004). Detecting deception: The benefit of looking at a combination of behavioral, auditory and speech content related cues in a systematic manner. *Group Decision and Negotiations, 13*, 61–79.

Vrij, A., and Semin, G. R. (1996). Lie experts' beliefs about nonverbal indicators of deception. *Journal of Nonverbal Behaviour, 20*, 65–80.

Vrij, A., and Taylor, R. (2003). Police officers' and students' beliefs about telling and detecting little and serious lies. *International Journal of Police Science and Management, 5*, 1–9.

Vrij, A., and Winkel, F. W. (1991). Cultural patterns in Dutch and Surinam nonverbal behaviour: An analysis of simulated police/citizen encounters. *Journal of Nonverbal Behaviour, 15*, 169–84.

(1992). Social skills, distorted perception and being suspect: Studies in impression formation and the ability to deceive. *Journal of Police and Criminal Psychology, 8*, 2–6.

(1994). Perceptual distortions in cross-cultural interrogations: The impact of skin color, accent, speech style and spoken fluency on impression formation. *Journal of Cross-Cultural Psychology, 25*, 284–96.

Vrij, A., Winkel, F. W., and Koppelaar, L. (1991). Interactie tussen politiefunctionarissen en allochtone burgers: twee studies naar de frequentie en het effect van aan- en wegkijken op de impressieformatie. *Nederlands Tijdschrift voor de Psychologie, 46*, 8–20.

Vrij, J. (2001). Verzet tegen angst. *Kontakt door Aantreden, 56*, 4.

Wallbott, H. G., and Scherer, K. R. (1991). Stress specifics: Differential effects of coping style, gender, and type of stressor on automatic arousal, facial expression, and subjective feeling. *Journal of Personality and Social Psychology, 61*, 147–56.

Wiseman, R. (1995). The megalab truth test. *Nature, 373*, 391.

Yeschke, C. L. (1997). *The art of investigative interviewing: A human approach to testimonial evidence.* Boston, MA: Butterworth Heinemann.

Zaparniuk, J., Yuille, J. C., and Taylor, S. (1995). Assessing the credibility of true and false statements. *International Journal of Law and Psychiatry, 18,* 343–52.

Zuckerman, M., DePaulo, B. M., and Rosenthal, R. (1981). Verbal and nonverbal communication of deception. In L. Berkowitz (ed.), *Advances in experimental social psychology,* vol. XIV (1–57). New York, NJ: Academic Press.

Zulawski, D. E., and Wicklander, D. E. (1993). *Practical aspects of interview and interrogation.* Boca Raton: CRC Press.

NOTES

1. Some researchers claim that they have found 'Pinocchio's growing nose' and such studies generally attract large media attention. Hirsch and Wolf (2001) took Pinocchio's growing nose literally and claimed that Clinton's nose actually swelled up when he lied during his televised testimony in the Monica Lewinsky trial. We have doubts about this claim. Apart from the fact that it is difficult to establish whether, and if so, exactly when Clinton was lying during that testimony (Vrij and Mann, 2003), we wonder whether this physiological reaction would be found with other liars or even with Clinton himself in another situation. Obviously, both consistency between liars and consistency within the same liar is necessary to make an appropriate claim about having found Pinocchio's growing nose.

   In a more recent study (Pavlidis, Eberhardt, and Levine, 2002), published in the prestigious journal *Nature,* it was claimed that liars could be detected by recording thermal warming around the eyes. The technique, which does not allow physical contact with the examinees, has, according to Pavlidis et al., 'potential for application in remote and rapid security screening, without the need for skilled staff or physical contact' (p. 35). However, such security checks are likely to cause errors. Thermal warming is likely to be the result of physiological arousal rather than deception. In other words, those people who are physiologically aroused are likely to be highlighted by the thermal cameras, and hence accused of wrongdoing, and yet these people are not necessarily liars. On the one hand, experienced liars might not be aroused at all, and, on the other hand, some truth-tellers might be very aroused. We return to this issue in Guideline 5.

2. Sometimes professional lie-catchers tell us that they believe that eye movements are associated with deception. They then typically refer to the neuro-linguistic programming (NLP) model. However, not a single scientific study has demonstrated that eye movements are related to deception in the way described in the NLP model (Vrij and Lochun, 1997). NLP teachers who claim the opposite therefore are engaged in deceiving their pupils.

3. Not included in the present review are the cues listed by DePaulo et al. (2003, Appendix B) which were based on a small number of estimates (but see end-note 4 for an exception). In addition to the cues mentioned in the present section, DePaulo et al.'s (2003) review revealed some additional cues which cannot be easily classified as verbal or non-verbal behaviours: pressed lips, raised chin, facial pleasantness, nervous appearance, and dilated pupils.

4. Ekman's work (1985) has revealed that observing *emotional micro-expressions* in the face might reveal valuable information about deception. Strongly felt emotions almost automatically activate muscle actions in the face. For example, eyebrows which are raised and pulled together and a raised upper eyelid and tensed lower eyelid typically denote fear. If a person denies an emotional state which is actually being felt, this person will have to suppress these facial expressions. Thus, if a scared person claims not to be afraid, that person has to suppress the facial micro-expressions which typically indicate fear. This is difficult, especially because these emotions can arise unexpectedly. For instance, people do not usually deliberately choose to become frightened, this happens automatically as a result of a particular event that took place, or as the result of a particular thought. The moment fright occurs, a fearful facial expression may be shown which may give the lie away. People are usually able to suppress these expressions quickly and they can easily be missed by an observer. Detecting these micro-expressions is difficult for untrained observers, but Ekman (1985) contends that it is a skill that can be learned.

   Ekman's observations could well be of value. For example, in one of our lie detection studies (Vrij and Mann, 2001b) we showed lie detectors, amongst other video clips, a video clip of a person who held a televised press conference asking for information about his missing girlfriend. Later it turned out that he had killed his own girlfriend. A detailed analysis of the video clip revealed that he showed a micro-expression of a (suppressed) smile during that press conference. His smile was in the given context interesting. Why did the man smile? And why did he attempt to suppress that smile? Although his smiling at a press conference cannot be interpreted as a definite indication of deceit, it made the man suspicious at least.

5. A possible argument against this guideline is that by applying this rule micro facial expressions of emotions will remain unnoticed. However, micro-expressions are difficult to spot and it requires special training to notice them (Ekman, 1985). Also, they are likely to occur only when emotions are strongly and suddenly felt (Ekman, 1985). Since most people do not feel strong emotions when they lie (DePaulo, Kashy, Kirkendol, Wyer, and Epstein, 1996), most lies in daily life would remain unnoticed when lie detectors rely solely upon micro-expressions of emotions.

6. I acknowledge that this guideline needs further testing. For example, Ekman and O'Sullivan (1989) suggest that the first meetings are especially likely to lead to errors in judgements, as in their first encounters people may carefully control their behaviour and follow well-learned rules about how to act. However, Granhag and Strömwall (2002), measured truth-tellers' and liars' behaviours in repeated interviews and did not find differences in responses over time.

Part 5

Conclusions

14 Research on Deception detection: intersections and future challenges

Pär Anders Granhag and Leif A. Strömwall

This volume has offered a collection of state-of-the-art chapters on deception detection. The focus has been set on the different types of deception taking place in forensic contexts, and the different methods proposed in order to detect these attempts. In this closing chapter we will highlight a few, as we believe, important intersections and we will offer hints about some future challenges. We will end by a brief note on how to view and use the knowledge presented in the volume.

Intersections

When juxtaposing the chapters in this volume, several common themes can be noted, and below we will highlight three such intersections. All three mirror the recent shift in research focus: from studies examining people's ability to detect deception, to studies on how people's deception detection performance can be enhanced (Granhag and Vrij, in press). We consider these intersections to have immediate practical implications, as well as laying common ground for future research.

Combining different methods

In his preface to the Maratea volume, Yuille (1989) noted that each of the three traditional approaches to deception detection (psychophysiological, non-verbal, and verbal content) 'has developed and remained independent of the others' (p. viii). One of the Maratea conference's goals was to examine possible and potential relationships between the different approaches. Judging from its proceeding volume, the meeting did not result in any integrated method for detecting deception. Nevertheless, Yuille expressed optimism for the future when it came to bringing together the different approaches, for example combining non-verbal cues and psychophysiological measures, or combining non-verbal cues and statement analysis techniques. Fifteen years later, has the situation changed, in terms of integrating different approaches?

After thoroughly reviewing the literature, Vrij (2000) concluded that the research on deception detection is still very much divided into camps, and that the attempts to combine different approaches are rare. We agree, and conclude that the current volume does not contain any attempts of merging two (or more) methods into one integrated approach either. However, we do believe that there is an increased awareness of and interest in *combining different cues*, especially verbal and non-verbal cues. It is noteworthy that several of the chapters in the current volume intersect on this particular issue. In this context it is possible to distinguish between two ways of combining verbal and non-verbal cues, complementary and simultaneous.

At the more basic level, cues can be combined in a *complementary* way, where veracity is assessed on the basis of at least two different types of cues (e.g., 'I think he is telling the truth because he is relaxed and tells a story rich in detail'). As noted by Vrij (Chapter 13) research shows that people become better lie-catchers when paying attention to both speech content (e.g., plausibility) and vocal aspects (e.g., tone of voice). At a (perhaps) more sophisticated level, cues can be *simultaneously* combined, where veracity is assessed on the basis of matching at least two types of cues (e.g., 'I think he is lying because he said "no", while very briefly nodding his head').

In several of the chapters, the potential value of simultaneously matching verbal content and non-verbal behaviour is underlined. First, in their investigation of international deception Bond and Rao (Chapter 6) show that verbal/non-verbal inconsistency is one of the pan-cultural beliefs about deception. Second, as one of his guidelines to detect deceit, Vrij (Chapter 13) recommends searching for mismatches between speech content and non-verbal behaviour, but he also warns that such mismatches must be interpreted with care. Third, O'Sullivan and Ekman (Chapter 12) note that one common strategy among their wizards of deception detection is that they often match a suspect's verbal and non-verbal behaviour, and pay attention to both consistencies and inconsistencies. Fourth, and importantly, the latest (and to this date most comprehensive) meta-analytic research on actual cues to deception, presented by DePaulo and Morris (Chapter 2), shows that liars appear as significantly more discrepant than do truth-tellers. That is, information from different sources (e.g., face and voice) seems more contradictory for liars than for truth-tellers. For a discussion on why liars' attempts to control their behaviour may result in verbal/non-verbal inconsistencies, see Zuckerman, DePaulo, and Rosenthal (1981), and for a more detailed view on how to interpret discrepancies between a person's emotional cues and his or her story line, see Ekman (1985/2001).

In sum, experts in the field recommend that attention should be paid to verbal/non-verbal inconsistencies; however, this strategy does not seem to be commonly used by, for example, police officers when trying to detect deceit (Mann, Vrij, and Bull, 2004; Hartwig, Granhag, Strömwall, and Vrij, in press). The combined evidence in the current volume suggests that it might pay to take notice of verbal/non-verbal inconsistencies, not as perfect cues to deception (also truth-tellers can appear inconsistent), but as markers motivating further investigation.

Obviously, much more empirical research must be conducted in order to decide the diagnostic values of different verbal/non-verbal inconsistencies. In relation to this, it should be noted that in the paradigmatic deception detection study lie-catchers are shown videotapes, and can thus assess veracity on the basis of either verbal or non-verbal cues, or by combining the two. The self-reported cues to deception are, however, often presented in tables separating verbal and non-verbal cues – if presented at all. An analysis based on such a traditional 'balkanisation' tells us very little about how frequent and diagnostic it is to trust verbal/non-verbal inconsistencies/consistencies.

Implicit lie detection

DePaulo, Lindsay, Malone, Muhlenbruck, Charlton, and Cooper (2003) and Vrij (2000) have reviewed hundreds of lie-detection studies. Most of these have involved participants who were *explicitly* asked to assess the veracity of others. The hit rate, or overall accuracy, has been found to be just above the level of chance (Vrij, 2000). Perhaps as a consequence of this largely discouraging result, during the last years a growing interest in *implicit lie detection* can be noted. (Although the idea is not new – DePaulo and Rosenthal examined implicit lie detection in 1979.)

Examples of attempts to examine implicit (or indirect) lie detection have been to ask the observer to assess the interviewee's honesty, if the interviewee had to think hard, and was immediate in responding (i.e., personal and/or direct). Other examples have included if the observer generally liked the interviewee or felt comfortable while watching the interviewee (see DePaulo and Morris, Chapter 2, for a review).

In the current volume, DePaulo and Morris (Chapter 2) and Vrij (Chapter 13) suggest implicit methods as a promising approach for future research. Vrij speculates that the reason that participants perform better on implicit lie-detection tasks is that they do not rely on the stereotypical beliefs about deception (cf. Bond and Rao, Chapter 16; Strömwall, Granhag and Hartwig, Chapter 10). He recounts a study of Vrij, Edward, and Bull (2001) where police officers' deception detection ability was tested both implicitly and explicitly. The implicit measure was if the persons on the videotape 'had to think hard'. The results showed that only those using the implicit measure could separate the truthful from the deceptive. This result has also been found in non-forensic settings. In fact, Vrij (2001) summarises the research by stating that *all* studies on implicit lie detection have found higher accuracy compared with explicit ones. In a manner of speaking, it seems that people are better at detecting deceit than they know themselves. In much the same vein, Strömwall et al. (Chapter 10) discuss if and how human intuition can be enhanced via experience.

It has also been found that participants watching a truth-teller made higher ratings on comfortableness, confidence, level of information, and lower ratings on suspiciousness than did those watching someone lying. However, when explicitly asked to classify the statements as truths or lies, the participants performed at the level of chance (Anderson, DePaulo, Ausfield, Tickle, and Green, 1999). Hurd and Noller (1988) found that participants who were thinking aloud while assessing a deceptive statement were more prone to make utterances indicating that the message was a lie, than when they were assessing a truthful statement. That is, they were on their way towards the correct judgement. But, when committing to an explicit veracity judgement, they did not always take heed of their own intuitions; intuitions that were more correct than their explicit assessments of veracity. A different example of indirect lie detection is found in a recent study by Granhag, Landström, and Hartwig (2004), where law students placed in a mock-trial setting had great difficulty distinguishing between liars and truth-tellers (their accuracy was not distanced from chance level). However, the results of a subsequent memory test showed that the law students who had watched truthful witnesses showed a significantly better memory performance, than those who had watched lying witnesses. Taken together, these findings indicate that people have some ability to separate truthful from deceptive accounts, an ability that may surface when people are asked to assess the statements in terms of characteristics other than deceptiveness.

Viewing this from an applied perspective: how can these intriguing and promising findings be used in forensic contexts (which often demand explicit assessments)? It would be interesting to find out what would happen if people were told that, for example, their own level of comfort while watching (and listening to) someone is a useful indicator of judging that person's veracity. Would the knowing lead to an overuse, and perhaps even to a construction of a simplistic belief, which in turn would nullify the positive effect of that cue? It is for future research to find out the extent to which implicit lie detection can be used explicitly.

The importance of motivation, practice and feedback

There are several 'pop psychology' books offering simple tricks in order to become better at detecting deceit. Many of these tricks are pure nonsense, and such popular books can be entertaining, at best. None of the chapters in the current volume suggests that there exists any simple and easy to use trick for detecting deceit. The experts simply know that there is no quick fix.

Interestingly, quite a few of the chapters intersect on what it takes to improve one's skill in detecting deception. Several of the authors stress that becoming an expert at detecting deceit is a slow and complex process; a process that contains several components. First, the future expert lie-catcher needs to be highly motivated (recall the chapters by O'Sullivan and Ekman, and Strömwall et al.). Second, the road to excellence demands extensive practice (recall the chapters by O'Sullivan and Ekman, Köhnken, and Sporer). Third, in order to learn the right lesson from experience, the 'learning structures' need to be kind; importantly they should provide the lie-catcher with clear and regular feedback (recall the chapters by Strömwall et al., and O'Sullivan and Ekman). Finally, one does not become an expert lie-catcher by taking part in simple-minded training programmes (recall the chapters by Bull, Strömwall et al., and Vrij).

Future challenges

Deception detection is a field that expands quickly, and the body of research literature is growing fast. This development is mirrored in the current volume, but also in the many recent meta-analyses and overviews; for example on the validity of non-verbal cues (DePaulo et al., 2003), Criteria-Based Content Analysis (Vrij, in press), psychophysiological measures (Ben-Shakhar and Elaad, 2003), and the effectiveness of different types of training (Frank and Feeley, 2003). In spite of these efforts, significant work has yet to be conducted, and below we would like to say a few words about where we might go next.

Specifically, we will acknowledge three different types of future challenges. The first type of challenge emanates from the traditional problems found within forensic contexts. The second challenge deals with the new problems and dilemmas facing law-enforcement personnel; new problems that demand new lines of research. The third challenge stems from the fact that research on deception – conducted with the field of psychology and law – to such a low extent is driven by theory.

Challenge 1

In the new wave of deception research – where the main goal is to find ways to enhance people's detection performance, instead of just examining their ability – we would like to see more research on the following three issues.

Liars' and truth-tellers' strategies   In contrast to topics like non-verbal cues to deception and people's deception detection ability – to which much effort has been channelled – liars' and truth-tellers' strategies have been investigated to a very limited extent (DePaulo et al., 2003). We believe that this is unfortunate since reflecting on strategies and their consequences might help us understand the differences and similarities that exist between liars' and truth-tellers' non-verbal and verbal behaviour.

For example, it would be valuable to gain more knowledge about the strategies of both liars and truth-tellers as the stakes rise and their motivation to appear credible increases. In one of our studies (Strömwall, Hartwig, and Granhag, 2004), we found that liars and truth-tellers – who had been interrogated by police officers – reported having used the same principal non-verbal strategy (avoiding excess movements), but rather different verbal strategies (liars decided to tell a simple and less detailed story, whereas the truth-tellers decided to keep things real and tell it like it happened). It is noteworthy that quite a few of these truth-tellers were judged as liars (Hartwig et al., in press). In addition, in another recent study we showed that liars – when asked to give a free recall about the event under investigation – to a much larger extent than truth-tellers, avoided mentioning self-incriminating information (Hartwig, Granhag, Strömwall, and Vrij, 2004). This finding leads up to our next suggestion for future research.

Strategic disclosure of evidence   Most real-life forensic investigations generate facts (Wagenaar, van Koppen, and Crombag, 1993), and these facts can – if used properly – be of crucial importance in the process of assessing the veracity of a suspect (see Chapter 10). In the light of this, it is surprising that research on deception detection has so little to offer when it comes to guidelines on how to use facts and evidence strategically during an interrogation. What we do know so far is that (a) there are manuals that recommend that an interrogation should be started by confronting the suspect with the existing evidence (e.g., Yeschke, 1997), and (b) that archival analysis of real-life police interrogations shows that this advice is often followed (Leo, 1996; 2001).

In sharp contrast to such recommendations and practices, we recently conducted a study showing that observers who were shown videotapes where the case-specific evidence was disclosed late in the interrogation achieved a significantly higher deception detection accuracy, compared to observers who were shown videotapes where the exact same evidence was disclosed early in the interrogation (Hartwig et al., 2004). This rather crude manipulation in terms of disclosure of evidence (early vs. late) had a significant effect, indicating that it is meaningful to study how more sophisticated ways of disclosing evidence (e.g., different drip-feeding procedures) may moderate deception detection performance. We believe it will prove fruitful to pay more attention to how different interrogation strategies affect deception detection performance, and hopefully such research efforts will contribute to the cultivation of effective and ethical interrogation techniques.

Individual characteristics of expert lie-catchers   One of the more interesting future challenges is to find out more about the psychology of the expert lie-catcher, specifically to map the individual differences between good and poor lie-catchers. Preliminary analyses suggest that some personality dimensions might be related to lie-catching expertise (see Chapter 12). Below, we list three such dimensions; dimensions that we believe have particular relevance for lie-catching expertise, but need to be empirically investigated. To some extent, these personality dimensions are supported by the preliminary findings and hypothesis presented by O'Sullivan and Ekman (Chapter 12), but the initiative to tie the personality dimensions to already established conceptualisations is ours. For a more thorough discussion on how these measures may relate to deception detection tasks, as well as a preliminary empirical test, see Ask and Granhag (2003).

First, *open-mindedness* and *need for closure*. Need for closure can be seen as a stable personality dimension (Kruglanski, 1989), and a person with strong need for closure will leap to an early judgement on the basis of inconclusive evidence ('every judgement is better than no judgement'), whereas a person with low need for closure will try to suspend judgement, and instead come up with competing alternatives to the interpretations offered (Kruglanski, 1996). It could be speculated that lie-catching expertise might be positively related to a low need for closure (see also Ekman, 2001).

Second, O'Sullivan and Ekman (Chapter 12) characterise their experts as being able to 'observe and describe people in a more complex fashion', and to have a 'nuanced understanding of social, racial and individual differences'. It would be interesting to know whether this manifests itself in higher scores on measures of *attributional complexity*. Fletcher et al. (1986) developed the so-called Attributional Complexity Scale (ACS) in order to detect individual differences in the propensity to generate complex explanations of the behaviours of others. We believe it is reasonable to predict that people high on the ACS would be better lie detectors than people with more simple attribution schemata. In the same vein, it might be that expert lie-catchers are more interested in both mental and real-life role playing (O'Sullivan and Ekman, Chapter 12) and have better skills of imagination (Hogarth, 2001).

Third, it could be speculated that lie-catching experts have the ability to keep focused on the suspect throughout the entire interrogation. Provided that this ability is not specific to deception tasks – but instead manifested in a stable disposition for openness to attentionally involving experiences – skilled lie-catchers may be characterised as possessing high levels of *absorption*. In brief, absorption has been defined as 'a characteristic of the individual that involves an openness to experience emotional and cognitive alterations across a variety of situations' (Roche and McConkey, 1990, p. 92). It might very well be that high levels of absorption are positively related to deception detection success.

Challenge 2

In an ever-changing world, new challenges appear constantly. Thus, applied research always has new problems and questions to answer. Deception research will need to provide new knowledge to respond to a number of tricky issues in time to come. Professionals in forensic settings will face more and more questions of cross-cultural aspects of deception. In a world characterised by global mobility and migration, it will be crucial to have at least basic knowledge of what are cultural display rules and what is universal human behaviour (Bond and Rao, Chapter 6; Granhag, Strömwall, and Hartwig, in press). Furthermore, and in relation, the threats of terrorism challenge our deception detection ability and our beliefs about deceptive behaviour (Silke, 2003). Deception researchers will need to step out of the laboratory and into real-life forensic contexts to find these most wanted answers.

Another challenge for future research is the emergence of electronic communication. When will psychological research (cf. George, Marett, and Tilley, 2004) be published on the subject of detecting deceit in, for example, email communication or on the Internet? Here, the deception paradigms used so far will be of limited value, since neither physiological responses, non-verbal behaviour or the verbal content of long written statements resulting from structured interviews will be possible to analyse.

Changes in the judicial area will further stimulate new research. Issues such as the effects of witnesses appearing on closed-circuit television (CCTV) on observers' credibility assessments are only one such change (Orcutt et al., 2001). Children appearing on CCTV instead of live in court are one instance of the many sensitive and important issues to do with children as victims, witnesses, and sometimes suspected offenders, that need more research (Davies, Chapter 7).

Challenge 3

In their meta-analysis on cues to deception, DePaulo et al. (2003) describe the last thirty-five years' development on theoretical statements made about deceptive behaviour. Below, we will present a brief summary of this development as outlined by DePaulo and her colleagues. Ekman and Friesen (1969) are credited for having published the first influential theoretical notion on cues to deception, when they described leakage and deception cues. *Leakage cues* reveal what the liar tries to hide, for example, his true feeling of anger might show via a very micro-display of anger. *Deception cues* indicate deceit but do not signal the nature of the information that the liar tries to conceal, for example a person says she is happy, but shows a brief sign of disgust (see also Ekman, 1985/2001).

Zuckerman, DePaulo, and Rosenthal (1981) suggested four factors which could be used to predict cues to deception: *arousal* (liars might be more aroused and therefore show increased blinking, higher pitch, etc.), *feelings when lying* (liars might feel more guilt, fear, and anxiety, and therefore fidget and show gaze aversion, etc.), *cognitive aspects* (lying is seen as more cognitively complex, therefore longer response latencies, speech hesitations, etc.), and *attempted control* (liars will attempt to control their behaviour and therefore appear as less spontaneous and more rigid).

In order to be able to predict which behaviours separate liars from truth-tellers, we must, according to Ekman (1985/2001), study and understand the emotions that liars experience. Hence, Ekman presented a conceptualisation of the role of emotions during deception and argued that there exist *fear (of apprehension) cues* (e.g., higher pitch, pauses, speech errors, etc.), *guilt cues* (e.g., slower speech and downward gazing), and *duping delight cues* (excitement about lying that shows by a higher pitch, faster speech, etc.).

In the area of human communication research, Buller and Burgoon (1996) presented an interpersonal model of deception. They stressed the importance of the *interaction* between the sender and receiver, and their model predicts that liars (in interactive contexts) will display increased immediacy, involvement, pleasantness, fluency, and so on. Buller and Burgoon also highlight the role of liars' *motivation* and list three different motivations (instrumental, relational, and identity), all predicting different cues to deception.

In 1992, DePaulo outlined the self-presentational perspective on deception; a perspective which she and her colleagues recently made more precise (DePaulo et al., 2003). This theoretical framework originates from research on the nature of lying in everyday life, and its core notion is that all communication – both deceptive and truthful – involves self-presentation (i.e., both liars and truth tellers will attempt to control the impressions that are formed of them). The framework predicts that cues to deception that takes place in everyday life will be quite weak, but that there are conditions which moderate the strength of the deception cues. The self-presentational perspective predicts no less than five categories of cues to deception; namely that liars will be (a) *less forthcoming*, (b) *less positive and pleasant*, (c) *more tense*, and that liars' stories will (d) *be less compelling* and (e) *include fewer imperfections and unusual elements*. Furthermore, the self-presentational framework predicts that the strength of the cues to deception will be moderated by factors such as whether the lies are about transgressions, and by liars' and truth-tellers' planning and motivation.

The results from the so far most comprehensive meta-analysis on cues to deception (DePaulo et al., 2003) first and foremost support the predictions derived from the self-presentational perspective (and especially so when the lies were about transgressions). The same meta-analysis lends some support to the four-factor model presented by Zuckerman et al. (1981), and particularly to the 'attempted control' factor (and especially when the liars were highly motivated). The predictions derived from Buller and Burgoon's (1996) interpersonal model of deception received very meagre support. The meta-analysis did not contain enough relevant studies to test the predictions following from Ekman's theoretical notions (1985/2001).

Returning to forensic contexts, Yuille, when summing up the conference in Italy, concluded that one of the major goals with that meeting, namely to develop 'a unified theoretical approach to credibility assessment' (Yuille, 1989, p. x), had not been realised. Most scholars within the field would probably agree that we still await such a unified theory. Furthermore, we think it is defensible to argue that the research on deception conducted within the frames of psychology and law is very much dominated by practical perspectives, and to a rather low extent driven by theory.

To gain scientific knowledge with bearing on forensic contexts, it is demanded that researchers conduct studies high in ecological validity. But even if steps towards more ecologically valid research are taken, and some already have been, such initiatives must be accompanied by theoretical awareness. Despite the fact that the review above shows that the field is not without theoretical approaches and perspectives, and that progress has been made, it is for future research to show the extent to which these approaches and perspectives hold for forensic contexts. Perhaps future research will show that the above perspectives fall short in forensic settings, where many lies are consequential, often about transgressions, and told in interactive contexts by highly motivated suspects. In line with hints offered by DePaulo et al. (2003), we believe it is useful to entertain the possibility that there might exist a set of cues with particular relevance in forensic contexts. It is an important future challenge to try to develop theories that are applicable to forensic contexts, and that concern both the behaviour of liars and truth-tellers, and lie-catchers' veracity judgements.

Final words

In this final section we would like to say a few words about how to view and use the knowledge presented in the volume. There is need for caution, but also reason for optimism.

First, the combined evidence suggests that the differences between liars and truth-tellers are small and often hard to detect, no matter if we examine non-verbal behaviour, verbal content, psychophysiological measures, claimed amnesia, or confessions. Second, it is important to underscore that all so-called 'cues to deception' mentioned in this book, are cues that are probabilistically related to deception, irrespective of whether the cue is non-verbal, verbal, or a cue to simulated amnesia and so on. What this means is that these cues to deception describe ways in which liars and truth-tellers act differently. For example, the statement 'thinking hard is a cue to deception' (and some studies show it is) does not mean that only liars think hard when being questioned. It means that liars, on the average, are perceived as having to think harder than truth-tellers. Hence, cues to deception should never be used as stop-rules in the veracity assessment process. Similarly, the statement that 'facial fidgeting is not a cue to deception' does not mean that liars do not touch their faces (some certainly do). It means that liars, on the average, do no more facial fidgeting than truth-tellers. Third, we do not want to mislead anyone by the frequent use of the word *lie-catcher*. Working in forensic contexts is certainly not only about unmasking liars, it is often equally (or more) important to correctly recognise those who truthfully deny an accusation.

When giving seminars on deception to judges and police officers, we have often heard 'This is all very fascinating, but I will be back in court tomorrow and can you please tell me how I can use this knowledge.' Such a question – and sometimes ill-concealed frustration – is not hard to understand. Learning more about deception detection, by, for example, carefully reading this volume, will not guarantee that the veracity assessment made the next day will be correct. However, professionals who need to assess veracity on a regular basis will, *in the long run*, make more correct veracity assessments and fewer mistakes if armed with scientifically based knowledge.

REFERENCES

Anderson, D. E., DePaulo, B. M., Ansfield, M. E., Tickle, J. J., and Green, E. (1999). Beliefs about cues to deception: Mindless stereotypes or untapped wisdom? *Journal of Nonverbal Behavior*, *23*, 67–89.

Ask, K., and Granhag, P. A. (2003). Individual determinants of deception detection performance: Need for closure, attribution complexity and absorption. *Göteborg Psychological Reports*, *33*, 1, 1–13.

Ben-Shakhar, G., and Elaad, E. (2003). The validity of psychophysiological detection of information with the guilty knowledge test: A meta-analytic review. *Journal of Applied Psychology*, *88*, 131–51.

Buller, D. B., and Burgoon, J. K. (1996). Interpersonal deception theory. *Communication Theory*, *6*, 203–42.

DePaulo, B. M. (1992). Nonverbal behavior and self-presentation. *Psychological Bulletin*, 111, 203–43.

DePaulo, B. M., Lindsay, J. L., Malone, B. E., Muhlenbruck, L., Charlton, K., and Cooper, H. (2003). Cues to deception. *Psychological Bulletin*, *129*, 74–118.

DePaulo, B. M., and Rosenthal, R. (1979). Telling lies. *Journal of Personality and Social Psychology*, *37*, 1713–22.

Ekman, P., and Friesen, W. V. (1969). Nonverbal leakage and clues to deception. *Psychiatry*, 32, 88–105.

Ekman, P. (1985/2001). *Telling lies. Clues to deceit in the marketplace, politics, and marriage*. New York: Norton.

Fletcher, G. J., Danilovics, P., Fernandez, G., Peterson, D., and Reeder, G. D. (1986). Attributional complexity: An individual differences measure. *Journal of Personality and Social Psychology*, *51*, 875–84.

Frank, M. G., and Feeley, T. H. (2003). To catch a liar: Challenges for research in lie detection training. *Journal of Applied Communication Research*, *31*, 58–75.

George, J. F., Marett, K., and Tilley, P. (2004, January). *Deception detection under varying electronic media and warning conditions*. Proceedings of the 37th Hawaii International Conference on System Sciences, Big Island, Hawaii, USA.

Granhag, P. A., and Vrij, A. (in press). Detecting deception. In N. Brewer and K. Williams (eds.), *Psychology & Law: An empirical perspective*. New York: Guilford Publications.

Granhag, P. A., Landström, S., and Hartwig, M. (2004). Witnesses appearing live vs. on video: How presentation format affect observers' perception, assessment and memory. Manuscript submitted for publication.

Granhag, P. A., Strömwall, L. A., and Hartwig, M. (in press). Granting asylum or not? Migration Board personnel's beliefs about deception. *Journal of Ethnic and Migration Studies*.

Hartwig, M., Granhag, P. A., Strömwall, L. A., and Vrij, A. (2004). Detecting deception via strategic disclosure of evidence. Manuscript submitted for publication.

(in press). Police officers' lie detection accuracy: Interrogating freely versus observing video. *Police Quarterly*.

Hogarth, R. M. (2001). *Educating intuition*. Chicago: University of Chicago Press.

Hurd, K., and Noller, P. (1988). Decoding deception: A look at the process. *Journal of Nonverbal Behavior*, 12, 217–33.

Kruglanski, A. W. (1989). *Lay epistemics and human knowledge: Cognitive and motivational bases*. New York: Plenum Press.

(1996). A motivated gatekeeper of our minds: Need-for-closure effects on interpersonal and group processes. In R. M. Sorrentino and E. T. Higgins (eds.), *Handbook of motivation and cognition: The interpersonal context*, Vol. III (pp. 456–96). New York: Guilford Publications.

Leo, R. A. (1996). Inside the interrogation room. *Journal of Criminal Law and Criminology*, 86, 266–303.

(2001). False confessions: causes, consequences, and solutions. In S. D. Wetservelt and J. A. Humphrey (eds.), *Wrongly convicted: Perspectives on failed justice*. New Brunswick: Rutgers University Press.

Mann, S., Vrij, A., and Bull, R. (2004). Detecting true lies: Police officers' ability to detect suspects' lies. *Journal of Applied Psychology*, 89, 137–49.

Orcutt, H. K., Goodman, G. S., Tobey, A. E., Batterman-Faunce, J. M., and Thomas, S. (2001). Detecting deception in children's testimony: Factfinders' abilities to reach the truth in open court and closed-circuit trials. *Law and Human Behavior*, 25, 339–72.

Roche, S. M. and McConkey, K. M. (1990). Absorption: Nature, assessment, and correlates. *Journal of Personality and Social Psychology*, 59, 91–101.

Silke, A. (2003). *Terrorists, victims and society. Psychological perspectives on terrorism and its consequences*. Chichester: John Wiley.

Strömwall, L. A., Hartwig, M., and Granhag, P. A. (2004). To act truthfully: Nonverbal behavior during a police interview. Manuscript submitted for publication.

Vrij, A. (2000). *Detecting lies and deceit*. Chichester: John Wiley.

(2001). Detecting the liars. *Psychologist*, 14, 596–8.

(in press). Criteria-Based Content Analysis: The first 37 studies. *Psychology, Public Policy and Law*.

Vrij, A., Edward, K., and Bull, R. (2001). People's insight into their own behaviour and speech content while lying. *British Journal of Psychology*, *92*, 373–89.

Wagenaar, W. A., van Koppen, P. J., and Crombag, H. F. M. (1993). *Anchored Narratives: The psychology of criminal evidence*. New York: Harvester Wheatsheaf.

Yeschke, C. L. (1997). *The art of investigative interviewing: A human approach to testimonial evidence*. Boston: Butterworth-Heinemann.

Yuille, J. C. (1989). *Credibility Assessment*. Dordrecht: Kluwer Academic.

Zuckerman, M., DePaulo, B. M., and Rosenthal, R. (1981). Verbal and nonverbal communication of deception. In L. Berkowitz (ed.), *Advances in experimental social psychology*, Vol. XIV (pp. 1–57). New York, NJ: Academic Press.

Index